CW01497563

Maintenance Management Auditing

In search of Maintenance Management Excellence

Maintenance Management Auditing

In search of Maintenance
Management Excellence

Anthony Kelly

Industrial Press

Library of Congress Cataloging-in-Publication Data

Kelly, Anthony, 1957-
Maintenance management: its auditing and benchmarking /Anthony Kelly.
p. cm.
ISBN 0-8311-3267-1
1. Plant maintenance–Management. 2. Plant maintenance–Management–
Auditing. 3. Benchmarking (Management) I. Title.

TS192.K425 2005
658.2'02–dc22
2005054507

Industrial Press Inc.
200 Madison Avenue
New York, NY 10016-4078

Copyright © 2006. Printed in the United States of America.

Published under license from Conference Communication, Monks Hill, Tilford,
Farnham, Surrey, GU10 2AJ, England.

1 2 3 4 5 6 7 8 9 10

For my grandson David Alexander Kelly

Contents

Preface

Business Centered Maintenance (BCM) is a structured approach to the overall task of managing the maintenance of physical assets, especially those of an industrial organization. It takes as its starting point the clear identification of the business aims. These are then translated, via a framework of guidelines (a methodology), into maintenance objectives, thus underpinning the formulation of maintenance strategy. The BCM approach is covered in detail in two of my previous books.

In writing this book my main aim has been to show how the BCM methodology can be used to audit and improve the management systems of industrial maintenance departments. Auditing maintenance management involves inspecting and checking the processes involved—the strategy setting, the organization, the systems—and the essential linkages between maintenance and other company functions such as production or stores organization. The aim of the audit is to map and describe the existing maintenance management processes in order to ensure their effective operation.

I first used the idea of maintenance auditing in 1984, when I was teaching an in-plant course in maintenance management for the senior staff of a large power station. In order to ensure that the course content would be relevant I had been asked to go on site for a couple of days and model the organization of the maintenance systems. At the end of the course the opinion of the participants was that its content was fine but they gained most from the insights the models gave them regarding the operation of their maintenance systems and the problems involved

Since 1984 my colleagues in IMMS and I have carried out more than sixty audits world-wide, developing and refining our procedures in the light of experience with a wide variety of industries, ranging from gold mining to petroleum refining to building.

The book is divided into three sections.

Section 1 describes the theory of auditing and benchmarking.
Chapter 1 describes the BCM methodology and its generic models, developed to facilitate the mapping of maintenance departments. Chapter 2 emphasises the importance of the human factors involved to cost effective maintenance, identifying the most important of these factors and showing how they can be audited. Chapter 3 is the key section of the book, describing the auditing

procedure from specification to report writing. Chapter 4 describes the process of benchmarking and how auditing can facilitate it.

Section 2 gives examples of the full, snapshot, and fingerprint audits.

Chapter 5 describes a *full* audit of a large and complex chemical plant, Chapter 6 a *snapshot* audit and re-audit, three years later, of an underground coal mine (a study which also illustrates how as little as four days on-site provides enough time to map the essential characteristics and problems of any particular installation. Chapter 7 refers to two industrial examples (a bottling plant and a rolling mill) to show how, within the space of just a single day on-site, the audit methodology can capture enough data to provide an understanding—a *fingerprint* audit—of the key characteristics of strategy and organization.

Section 3 provides case studies of the application of the audit in very different technologies and with various aims in mind.

Chapter 8 describes how an audit informed the organizational restructuring of an aluminium refinery, Chapter 9 how it helped in the formation of a company–contractor alliance, Chapter 10 how it aided a review of maintenance strategy and Chapters 11 and 12 how it threw light on the maintenance firstly of an open-cast mining fleet and secondly of the various installations of an electricity generation, transmission and distribution system.

Tony Kelly
a.Kelly99@ntlworld.com

Note from the Publisher: *The author is contributing his royalties from sales of this book to cancer research.*

Acknowledgements

Firstly, I must acknowledge a special gratitude to Dr H. S. Riddell, who started auditing with me in 1984 and over the intervening years has helped me to develop its procedures and *aide-memoire*. He was also my co-auditor during the exercises described in Chapters 5 and 9.

I am deeply indebted to John Harris who has edited the complete text and also contributed valuable suggestions and ideas.

I must also thank the people in industry—John Sullivan, Richard Hoggard, Bill Sugden, Ray Parkin, Peter White, Brian Gilroy, Mark Zammit, Richard Grey, Nigel Beard, Alan Seawright, and many others—who provided access to their plants and without whose help this book could not have been written.

Maintenance Management Auditing

Part I

Business Centered Maintenance and its Application to Maintenance Auditing

The greatest thing a human soul ever does in this world is to see something and tell what it saw in a plain way.
Hundreds of people can talk for one who can think, but thousands can think for one who can see.
To see clearly is poetry, prophesy and religion—all in one.

—John Ruskin

CHAPTER 1

Business Centered Maintenance Auditing Methodology*

Introduction

The term *audit* has come to mean the process of financially inspecting and checking a company's business accounts. Most industrial companies also need to audit other parts of their management operation, e.g., those concerned with production, sales, maintenance etc., each of which involves complex strategies and systems that require periodic checking to ensure their cost-effective operation. Maintenance management auditing is inspecting and checking firstly the managerial processes involved—strategy setting, organization, systems—and then the essential linkages between maintenance and the other company functions, e.g., production, stores. The purpose of this audit is to map and describe the existing maintenance management processes, in order to ensure their cost-effective operation.

To begin with, however, I will outline a methodology for analysing and understanding the maintenance management problem *in general*: a methodology based on the concept of *Business Centered Maintenance* (*BCM*) and encapsulating those ideas that I have found to best inform and guide the auditing of industrial maintenance departments.

Maintenance in an Industrial Company

Figure 1–1 shows a model of an industrial plant, in this case a Food Processing Plant (FPP), viewed as an 'open system' converting raw materials (cereals, meat etc.) into finished products (cans of pet food) of a higher value. The management system can be considered to be made up of a number of interacting sub-systems, e.g., Corporate Management, Production, Sales, Capital Asset Acquisition, Maintenance etc., each carrying out distinct management functions viz.:

Corporate Management: sets the corporate objective and strategy and directs, co-ordinates and controls the other sub-systems to achieve the set objective;

---

* Maintenance terminology is given in Appendix 3, page 295.

3

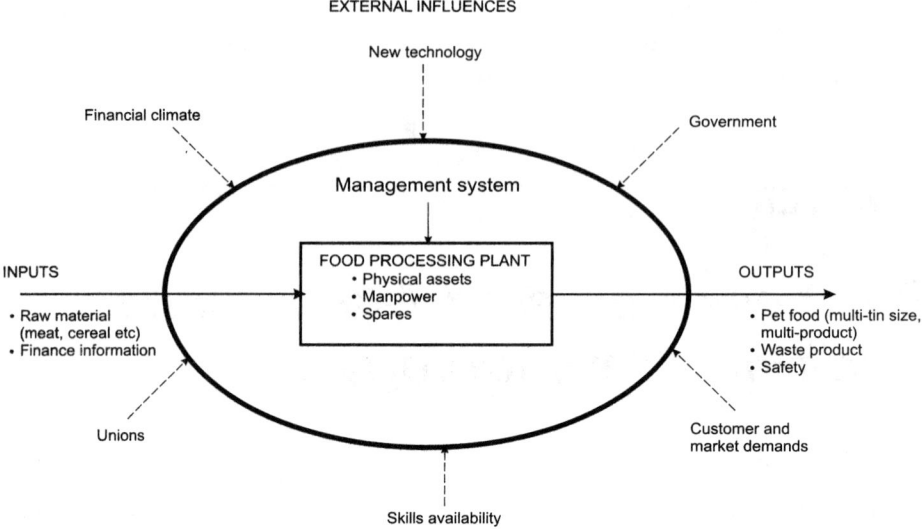

EXTERNAL INFLUENCES

FIGURE 1–1 An Organization Producing Pet Food, Viewed as an Open System

Capital Asset Acquisition: selects, buys, installs and commissions physical assets, a function which is carried out through the combined efforts of a number of other sub-systems, e.g., Projects, Engineering, Finance;

Maintenance: sustains the integrity of physical assets by repairing, modifying or replacing them as necessary.

The maintenance management sub-system is modelled in Figure 1–2. To carry out its function it needs inputs of resources (finance, spares, contract labour) and information (production requirements, safety regulations) from one or more of the other sub-systems and/or the external environment. The output from one sub-system (corporate objectives) can be the input to another sub-system (e.g., to the maintenance sub-system to enable the setting of the maintenance objective). The maintenance sub-system influences—and is influenced by—many of the other sub-systems.

This systems view of an industrial company serves to show that an audit of the maintenance department must include the following:

— an audit of the maintenance department, covering its objectives, strategy, organization and information system;
— an understanding of the linkages, inter-relationships and interfaces between the maintenance function and corporate management, production, safety, engineering and stores management

Business Centered Maintenance

The structure of a methodology for developing a maintenance strategy—which I call the Business Centered Maintenance (BCM) approach—is outlined in

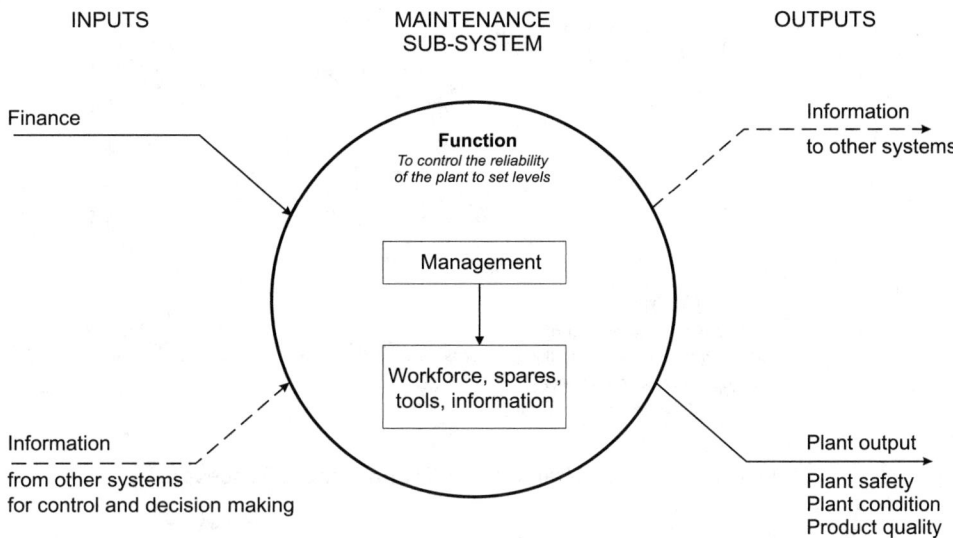

FIGURE 1–2 The Function of the Maintenance System

Figure 1–3. It is based on well-established administrative management principles (see Figure 1–4) and provides a framework for identifying, mapping and then auditing the elements of any maintenance management system.

One way of describing the **function** of maintenance was defined in the previous section, viz.

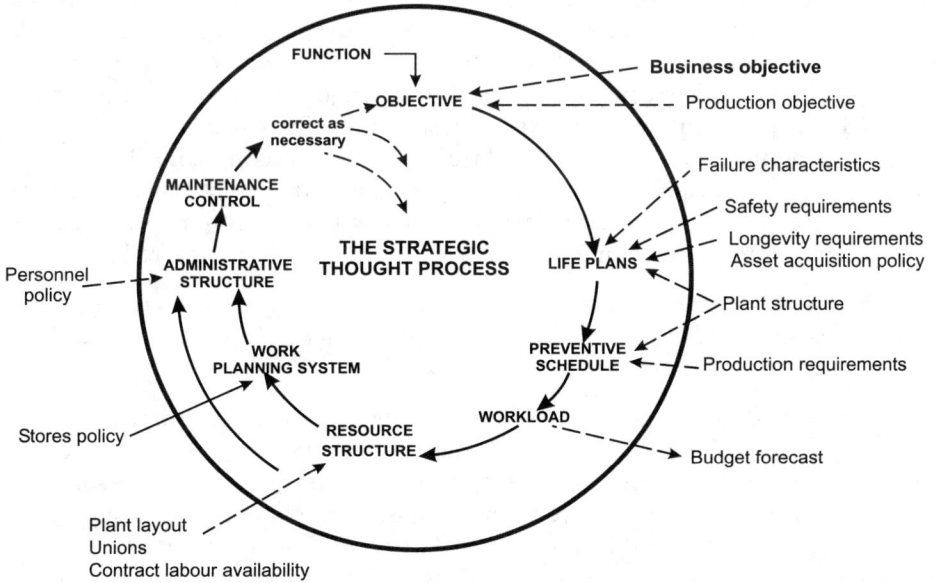

FIGURE 1–3 A Business Centered Maintenance Methodology

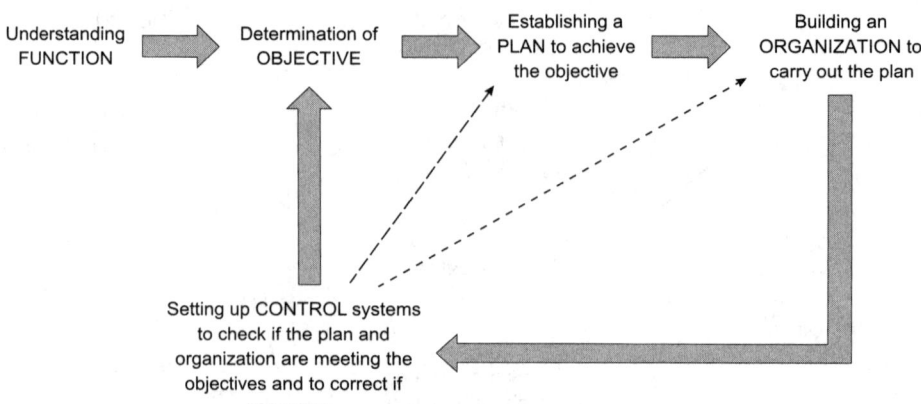

FIGURE 1–4 Basic Steps of the Management Process

'*to sustain the integrity of the physical assets by repairing, modifying or replacing them as necessary.*'

This can also be expressed as

'*to provide and control the reliability of the plant.*'

The ways in which this function might be affected by its dynamic relationship with the production system need to be clearly understood. Once this has been achieved the **maintenance objective** must be established. This can only be carried out in conjunction with the production department because the maintenance and production objectives are inseparable and both need to be compatible with the corporate objectives—associated with '*maximisation of profitability in the long term*' (which recognises company survival as an objective in itself). It is for this reason I call the approach *business centered,* the maintenance decision making process stemming from the business objectives. Any decision about 'how best to maintain a plant equipment' or 'how best to organize the maintenance resources' must be based on how that decision affects the company's bottom line. A generic expression for the maintenance objective for a plant might therefore be:

'*to achieve the agreed plant operating pattern, availability and product quality within the accepted plant condition (for longevity) and safety standards, and at minimum resource cost.*'

Figure 1–5 shows that this last overall objective can be analysed into a hierarchy of sub-objectives. One sort—those shown in the left hand leg of the diagram and brought down to the unit level (a mixer or compressor)—are concerned with *effectiveness* (Are we maintaining the equipment well enough to achieve the required availability, output, safety etc.?). The other sort (see the right hand leg of the diagram) are concerned with *organizational efficiency* (Are we using the resources in the most efficient way, e.g., maximising labour utilisation, flexibility etc.)?

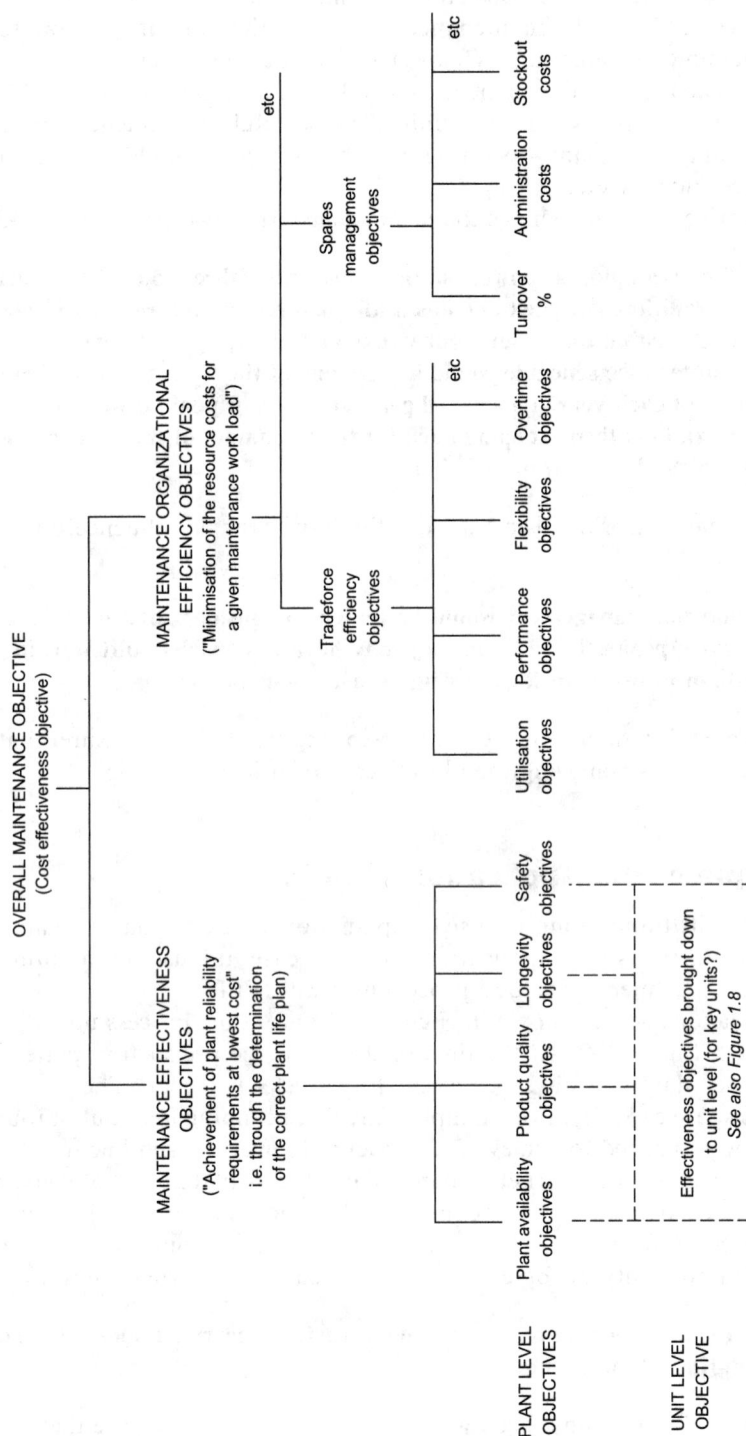

FIGURE 1–5 Hierarchy of Maintenance Objectives

By setting the effectiveness objectives at unit level we are now in a better position to establish each maintenance *life plan* (the way it is proposed to maintain the unit throughout its expected life) at this level. The *preventive maintenance schedule* for the plant as a whole is then made up from the jobs identified in the life plans for each unit. This schedule is influenced by many factors, including the plant operating pattern, statutory safety requirements, equipment redundancy etc.

The preventive schedule defines the *maintenance workload* (see Figure 1–3).

Consider, for example, a power station operating three 500 MW turbo-generators. Traditionally, each one has a life plan based on three-yearly major overhauls, each lasting for about eight weeks and requiring up to one thousand men. The maintenance schedule would involve one of the three units coming out in the summer of each year. This would generate a major peak of work for eight weeks, the work load then dropping back for the remainder of the year to a level appropriate to the base staffing of about 100 men.

The maintenance workload in turn has the largest single influence on *organizational design*.

At the station the management would be forced to consider contract labour to handle the work peaks. In addition they may have to consider shift working to handle the high priority work occurring on a 24 hour basis.

Finally, *control systems* are required (see Figure 1–3) to ensure that the maintenance effort is achieving the objectives shown in Figure 1–5.

An Example of the Application of BCM

A more detailed and comprehensive explanation of BCM may be gained by referring to an industrial application, in this case its use in auditing the maintenance department of a food processing plant (FPP).

The plant layout was as shown in Figure 1–6, an outline process flow diagram being shown in Figure 1–7. At the time of the audit the production pattern was three shifts per day, five days per week, fifty weeks per year. There was also considerable spare capacity. For example, only three canning lines out of four (see Figure 1–7) were needed to achieve full capacity. However, each line had its own product mix to satisfy the market demand. Thus, the availability of any given line for maintenance depended on the market demand and the level of finished product stored. Off-line maintenance could be carried out in the weekend windows of opportunity or, by exploiting spare capacity, during the week.

In general, the maintenance manager found it easier to carry out most of the off-line work during the weekend.

The problem the company faced was that they wanted to increase their output by using the weekends for production and by operating each canning line for as

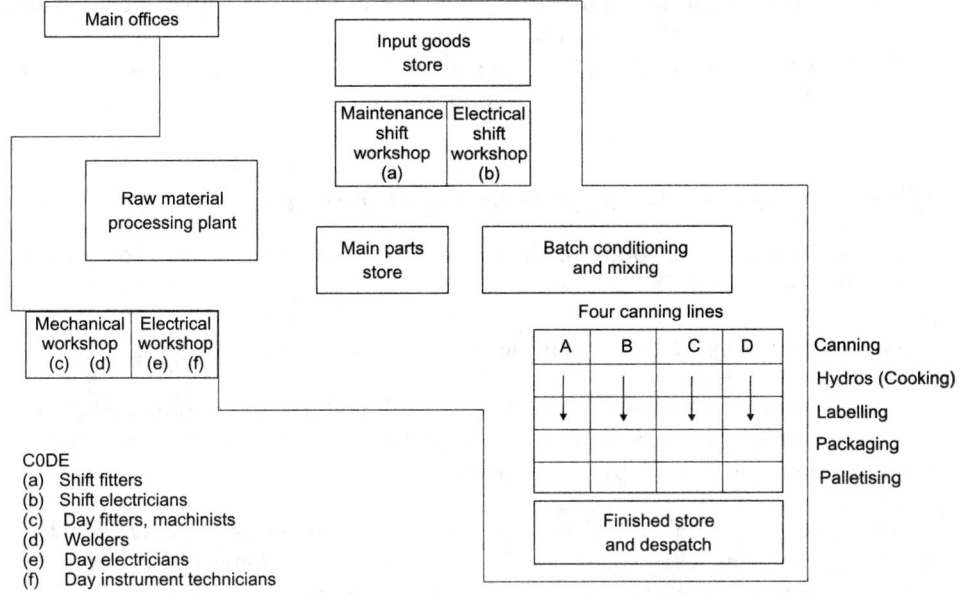

FIGURE 1–6 Layout of Food Processing Plant

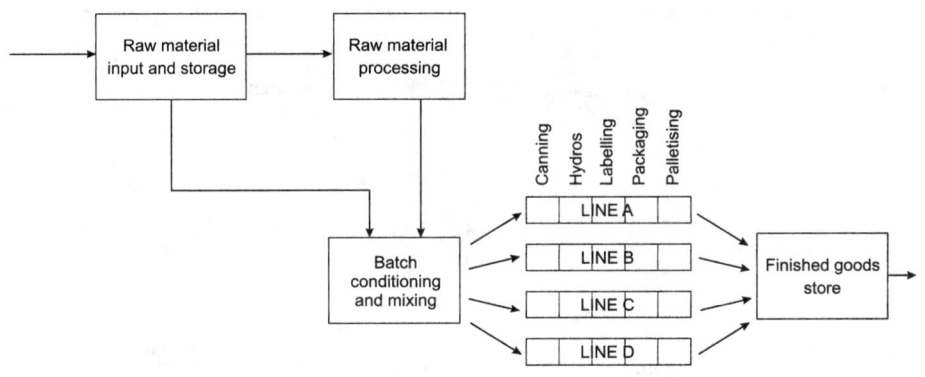

Pattern of operation 50 weeks x 5 days x 3 shifts, Monday/Friday

FIGURE 1–7 Process Flow Diagram for Food Processing Plant

long as possible. Experience had led to the feeling that each canning line could operate continuously for about four weeks before coming out, for two shifts, for maintenance. The company wanted to know how this was going to affect their maintenance strategy and the following tasks were requested:

(A) To audit their existing maintenance department in order to compare it to international best practice.

(B) To propose an alternative maintenance strategy that would facilitate the new mode of continuous operation.

(C) To provide an organizational vision (via models) of where the company should be heading in the succeeding five years.

(A) Audit of the FPP Maintenance Department

The audit procedure followed the main elements of the methodology model shown in Figure 1–3.

Maintenance Objectives: At plant level this could be stated as being:

'to achieve the 15-shift operating pattern, product mix and output (cans per week) within the accepted plant condition for longevity and safety requirements, and at minimum resource cost.'

It was the responsibility of the production, safety, and engineering departments to specify the plant requirements, and of the maintenance department to develop the strategy to achieve these requirements at minimum cost.

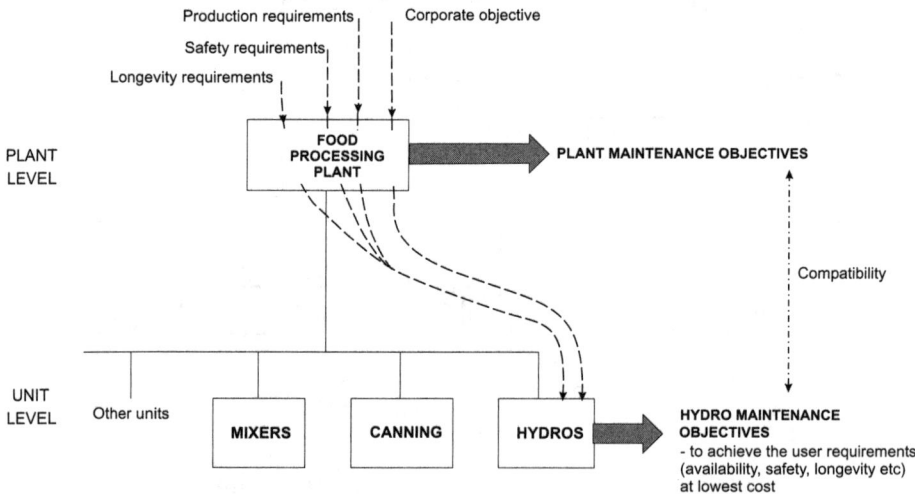

FIGURE 1–8 Expressing Plant Maintenance Objectives at Unit Level

If the maintenance department were to develop the 'best way of maintaining the plant' the maintenance objectives needed to be interpreted in a form that was meaningful at a lower level of equipment, the plant unit—a hydro, say, or the cooker (see Figure 1–8). This allowed the maintenance *life plans* for the various units of plant to be established.

The audit established that the FPP was using a management-by-objectives (MBO) procedure. Business objectives were set, and translated into main-

tenance objectives by the Chief Engineer. These in turn were translated into Key Result Areas (KRAs) which, rather than being objectives, were a series of future actions to achieve the maintenance objectives. The auditors considered the procedure to be excellent but the KRAs were not well enough directed towards maintenance objectives and were not expressed sufficiently numerically.

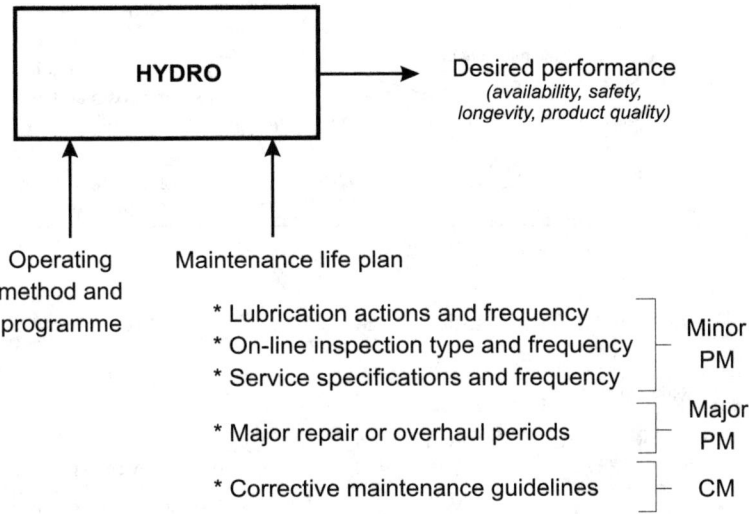

FIGURE 1–9 Outline of a Life Plan for a Unit of Plant

Life Plans and Preventive Schedule: A generic model of a life plan for a unit of plant (a hydro, say) is shown in Figure 1–9. Such a plan can be considered as a programme of maintenance jobs (lubrication, inspection, repair, replace, and carried out at set frequencies) spanning the expected life of the unit. The main decision regarding the life plan is the determination of the preventive policy (replace or repair at fixed time or fixed operating periods, or via some form of inspection), which, in its turn, determines the resulting level of corrective work. The life plans should be established, using the well documented principles of preventive maintenance[1] (see Figure 1–10) and should be reviewed periodically to ensure their effectiveness (see Figure 1–11).

The preventive maintenance schedule for the FPP was assembled from the preventive jobs identified in the life plans, see Figure 1–12. Such a schedule is only one part of the maintenance workload and has to be carried out in conjunction with the corrective work which has a shorter scheduling horizon—and often higher priority (sometimes restricting the maintenance department's ability to carry out preventive work—an aspect which will be discussed in more detail when we come to work planning).

---

[1] A Kelly, *Maintenance strategy,* Butterworth-Heinemann, 1997.

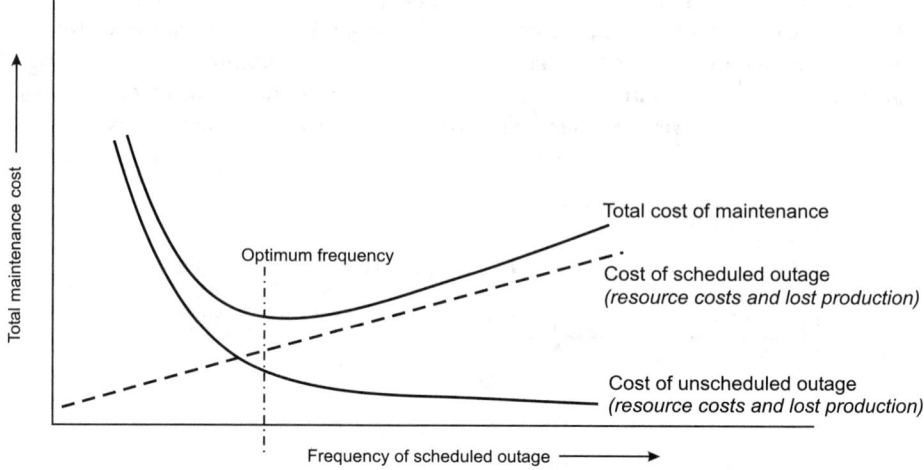

Total maintenance cost →

Optimum frequency

Total cost of maintenance

Cost of scheduled outage
(resource costs and lost production)

Cost of unscheduled outage
(resource costs and lost production)

Frequency of scheduled outage →

FIGURE 1-10 Optimisation of Scheduled Outage Frequency

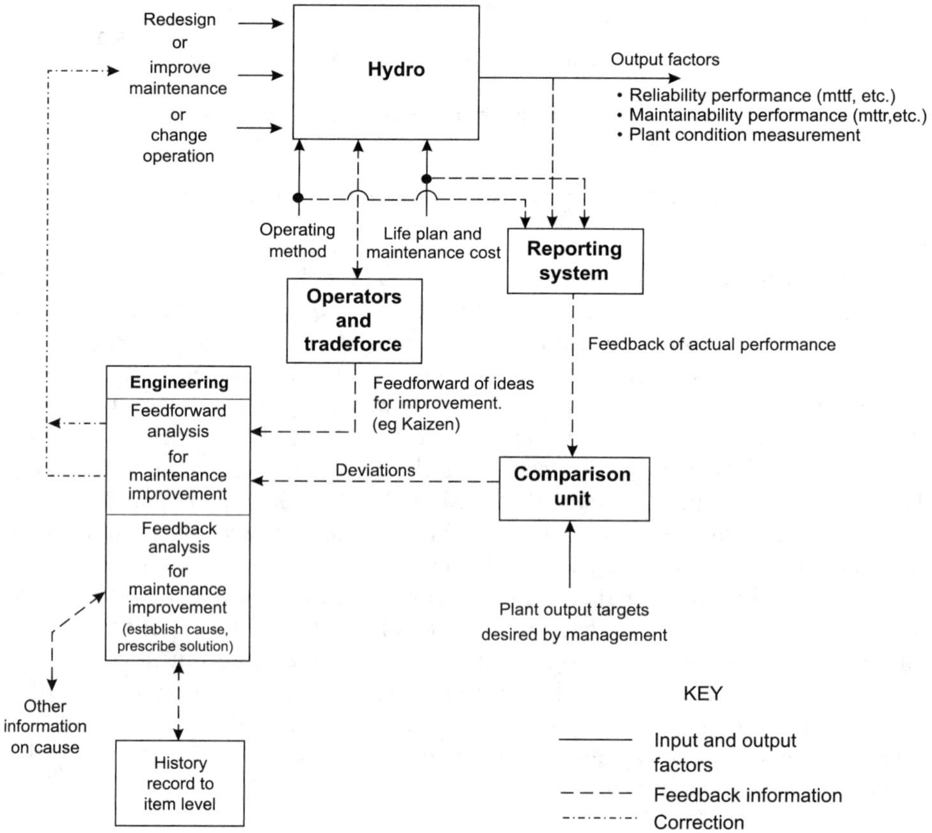

Redesign
or
improve
maintenance
or
change
operation

Hydro

Output factors

• Reliability performance (mttf, etc.)
• Maintainability performance (mttr, etc.)
• Plant condition measurement

Operating
method

Life plan and
maintenance cost

**Reporting
system**

**Operators
and
tradeforce**

Feedback of actual performance

Engineering

Feedforward
analysis
for
maintenance
improvement

Feedforward of ideas
for improvement.
(eg Kaizen)

Deviations

**Comparison
unit**

Feedback
analysis
for
maintenance
improvement
(establish cause,
prescribe solution)

Plant output targets
desired by management

Other
information
on cause

History
record to
item level

KEY

———— Input and output
factors

– – – – Feedback information

–·–·–·– Correction

FIGURE 1-11 Controlling the Reliability of a Unit of Plant

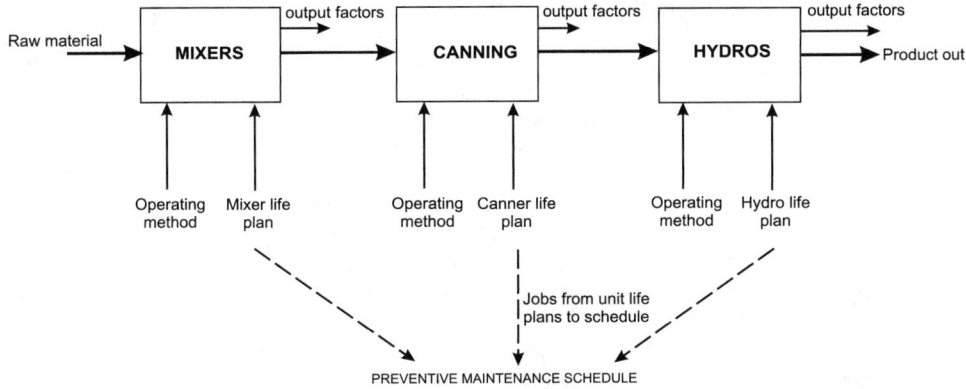

FIGURE 1–12 Build Up of Plant Preventive Schedule from Unit Life Plans

The schedule is influenced by the production plan—which itself is a function of the market demand (multi-product fluctuating demand requiring a flexible production plan), operating pattern, plant redundancy, inter-stage and final stage storage etc.. In the FPP case the important factor was the operating pattern which gave six-shift weekend windows and a two-week annual window that provided enough time to carry out the necessary preventive (and corrective) work without affecting the production plan.

In spite of the criticism of the objectives the unit life plans investigated were good e.g., see Table 1–1 for the life plan for the hydro. The hydro overhauls (the major maintenance) were based on the monitoring and inspection of condition, and their frequency, once every eight years, was determined only via an experience-based, and approximate, judgement. Nevertheless it did give an indication of the future major workload and its resource scheduling and budgeting. The preventive schedule was based on the scheduling guidelines outlined in Table 1–2. This meant that most of the second-line work was carried out at weekends. Little attempt had been made to schedule this latter work into the week, by exploiting spare capacity.

Workload: The maintenance schedule generates the maintenance workload, see Figure 1–3. The mechanical workload for the FPP is mapped in Figure 1–13 by its scheduling characteristics (the electrical workload can be mapped in the same way). *First line work* is made up from emergency jobs (which can be defined as work needing to be carried out in the shift of its occurrence) and jobs (corrective or preventive) that are small and do not require detailed planning—they can be 'fitted in'. *Second line work* involves the larger preventive jobs (services, small overhauls etc.) and corrective jobs that require planning and, via a priority system can be scheduled to be carried out at weekend (or in some other available window). *Third line work* involves major plant (or parts of the plant) overhauls. It requires the plant to be off line for considerable periods and is carried out at

TABLE 1–1 Outline of Life Plan for Hydro

Weekly	Cleaning; check operation of critical parts; lubrication	4 hours
Fortnightly/Monthly	Lubrication routine	4 hours
Quarterly	Inspection of main drive, including oil analysis	8 hours
Half-yearly	Inspection of all flights and conveyor drives. Clean hydro internally. Oil analysis of conveyor drives	3 shifts
Annually	Fixed time replacement of sprocket bearings. Overhaul drive unit and re-wind motors	1 week
Two-yearly	Replace vari-speed drive belts	1 week
Eight-yearly	Major rebuild (Exact frequency dependent on condition)	3 weeks

TABLE 1–2 Scheduling Guidelines for the FPP

	Maintenance philosophy	Work type
Monday to Friday	*Keep the plant going and keep an eye on its condition*	Reactive maintenance Operator monitoring routines Tradeforce line-patrolling routines
Weekends	*Inspect the plant carefully and repair as necessary in order to keep it going until next weekend*	Condition-based routines Schedule corrective jobs by priority Inspect and repair schedule. Fixed-time minor job schedule (services etc.)
Summer shutdown	*Schedule out the major jobs to see us through another year*	Schedule corrective jobs. Fixed-time major jobs schedule

medium or long term intervals—in the FPP case in the annual two-week windows. The planning lead time for such work can be many months. A more detailed explanation of workload characteristics is listed in Table 1–3.

The audit revealed a 50% over-manning on the midweek shifts, caused by lack of clear definition of emergency work—much of which could have been carried out at the weekends.

Maintenance Organization: The workload is the biggest single influence on the size and shape of the maintenance organization. At the FPP the first line emergency work required shift cover and the yearly shutdown peak required contract labour. Designing the organization requires many inter-related decisions

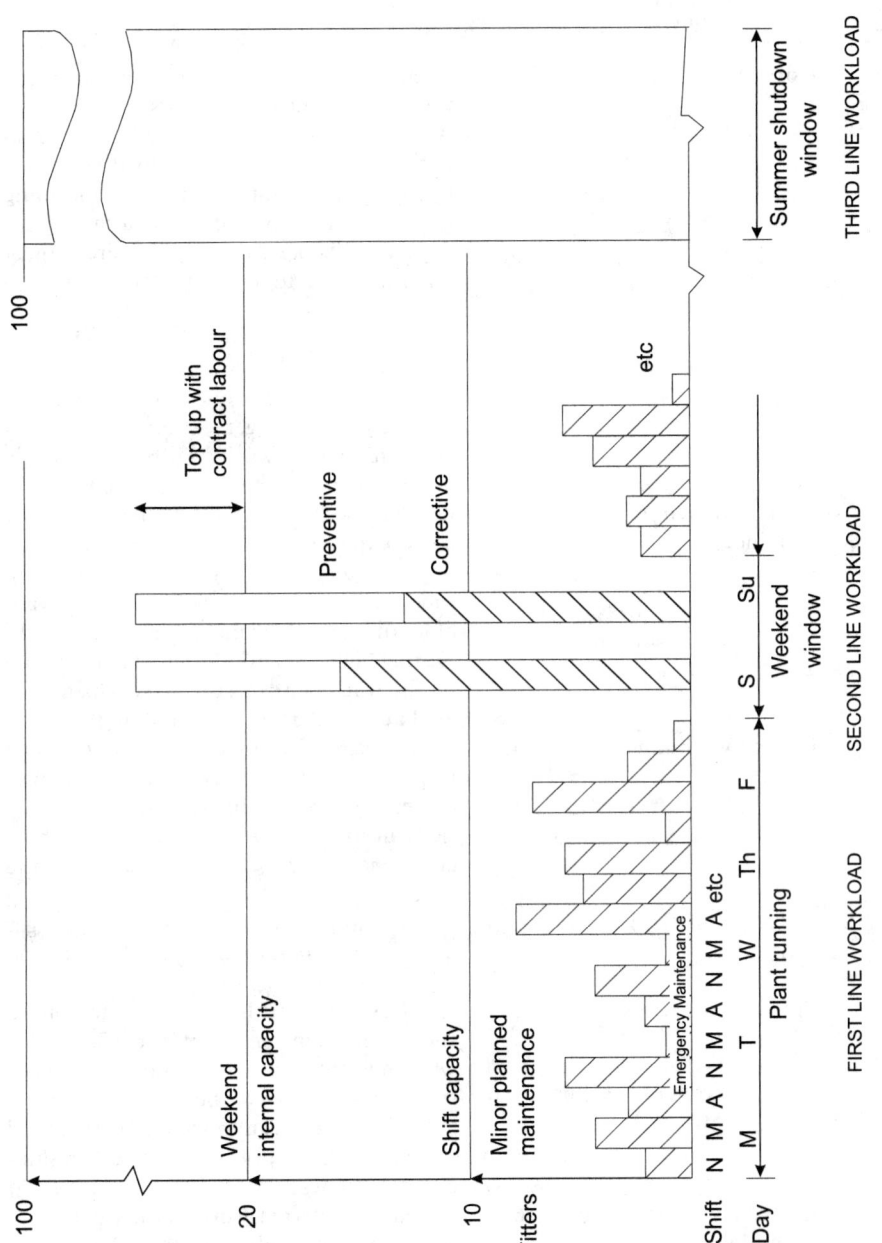

FIGURE 1–13 Work Load Profile for Fitters

TABLE 1–3 Detailed Categorisation of Maintenance Workload by Organizational Characteristics

Main Category	Sub-category number	Category	Comments
FIRST LINE	Corrective-emergency	(1)	Occurs with random incidence and little warning and the job times also vary greatly. A typical emergency workload is shown in Figure 1–13. This is a workload generated by operating plant, the pattern following the production operating pattern (e.g., 5 days, 3 shifts per day etc.). Requires urgent attention due to economic or safety imperatives. Planning limited to resource cover and some job instructions or decision guidelines. Can be off-line or on-line (in-situ corrective techniques). In some industries (e.g., power generation) failures can generate major work. These are usually infrequent but cause large work peaks
	Corrective-deferred (minor)	(2)	Occurs in the same way as emergency corrective work but does not required urgent attention; it can be deferred until time and maintenance resources are available (it can be planned and scheduled). During plant operation some small jobs can be fitted into an emergency workload such as that of Figure 1–13 (smoothing)
	Preventive-routines	(3)	Short periodicity work, normally involving inspections and/or lubrication and/or minor replacements. Usually on-line and carried out by specialists or used to smooth an emergency workload such as that of Figure 1–13
SECOND LINE	Corrective-deferred (major)	(4)	Same characteristics as (2) but of longer duration and requiring major planning and scheduling
	Preventive-services	(5)	Involves minor off-line work carried out at short or medium length intervals. Scheduled with time tolerances for slotting and work smoothing purposes. Some work can be carried out on-line although most is carried out on-line during weekend or other shutdown windows
	Corrective-reconditioning and fabrication	(6)	Similar to deferred work but is carried out away from the plant (second line maintenance) and usually by a separate tradeforce

| THIRD LINE | Preventive-major work (overhauls etc.) | (7) | Involves overhauls of plant, plant sections or major units. Work is off-line and carried out at medium or long term intervals. Such a workload varies in the long term as shown in Figure 1–13. The shutdown schedule for large multi-plant companies can be designed to smooth the company shutdown workload |
| | Modifications | (8) | Can be planned and scheduled some time ahead. The modification workload (often 'capital work') tends to rise to a peak at the end of the company financial year. This work can also be used to smooth the shutdown workload |

to be made (Where to locate manpower. How to extend inter-trade flexibility. Who should be responsible for spare parts? How to decide the responsibilities for plant operation and maintenance), each influenced by various conflicting factors. Thinking in terms of the methodology of Figure 1–3 reduces the complexity of this problem, by categorising the decisions according to the main elements of the organization, viz. its resource and administrative structures, its systems, and then considering each one in the order indicated—the procedure is iterative.

Resource Structure: The resource structure is the geographical location of workforce, spares, tools and information, their function, composition, size and logistics. Figure 1–14, for example, shows the Monday-to-Friday structure that had evolved at the FPP, to best suit the characteristics of a 24-hour first-line emergency workload. The emphasis is on rapid response, plant knowledge via specialisation, shift working, and team-working with production. In theory, the shift groups had been sized to match the reactive workload, the lower priority jobs being used to smooth the workload. Figure 1–15 shows the structure that matched the second-line weekend workload. The shift roster was arranged to ensure that two of the four shift groups were available on Saturdays and Sundays (including some overtime). Contract labour was used to top-up, as necessary, the internal labour force. A similar approach was used for the annual shutdown, but in that case the contracted workforce exceeded the internally available labour. The spare parts store and tool store was an integral part of the resource structure and in this case both were centralised, serving the whole site.

The aim of any resource structure design (or modification) is to achieve the best resource utilisation for a desired speed of response and quality of work. This, in part, involves the best match of the resources to the workload. Decisions in a number of other areas—e.g., in shift rostering, the use of contract labour, inter-plant flexibility, inter-trade flexibility and production-maintenance flexibility—can influence this matching process. Flexibility is clearly the key

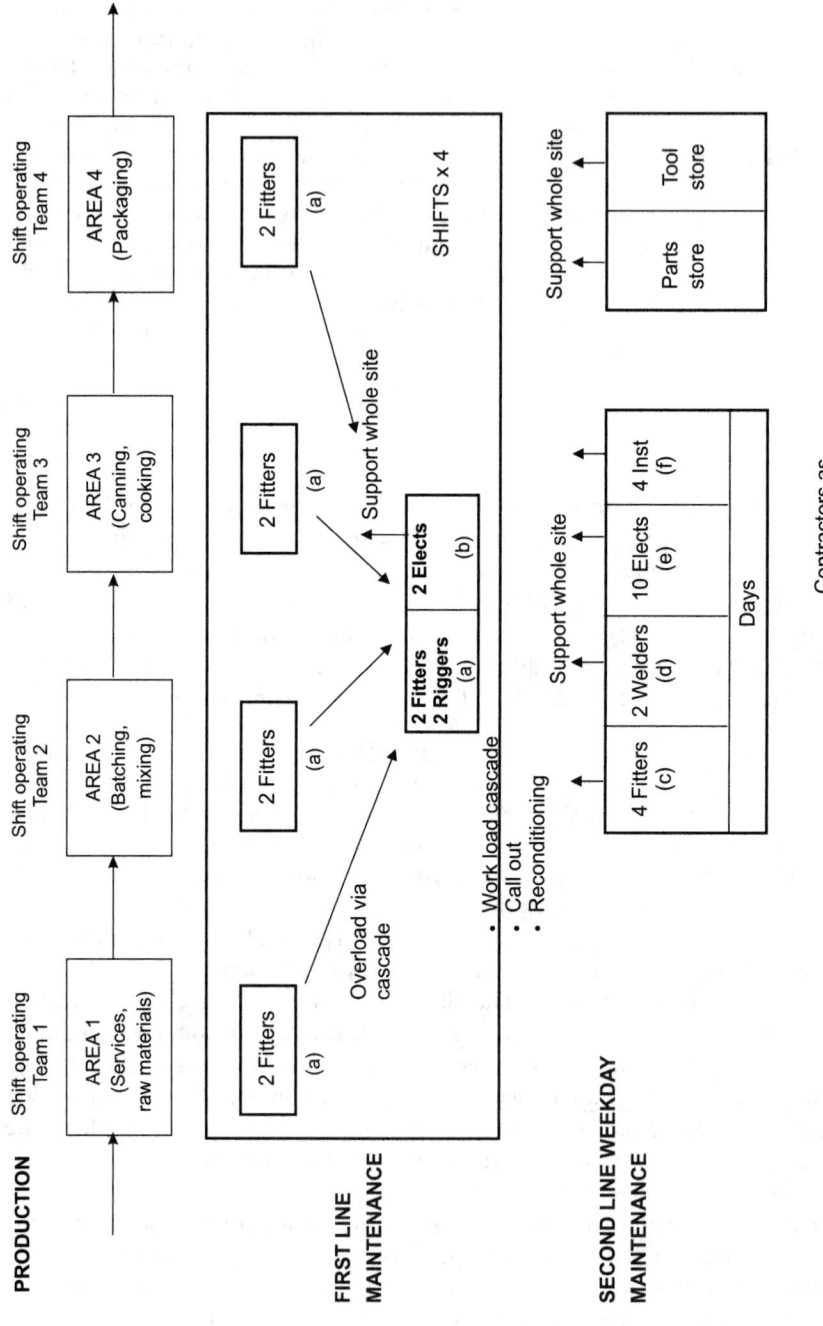

FIGURE 1–14 Weekly Resource Structure

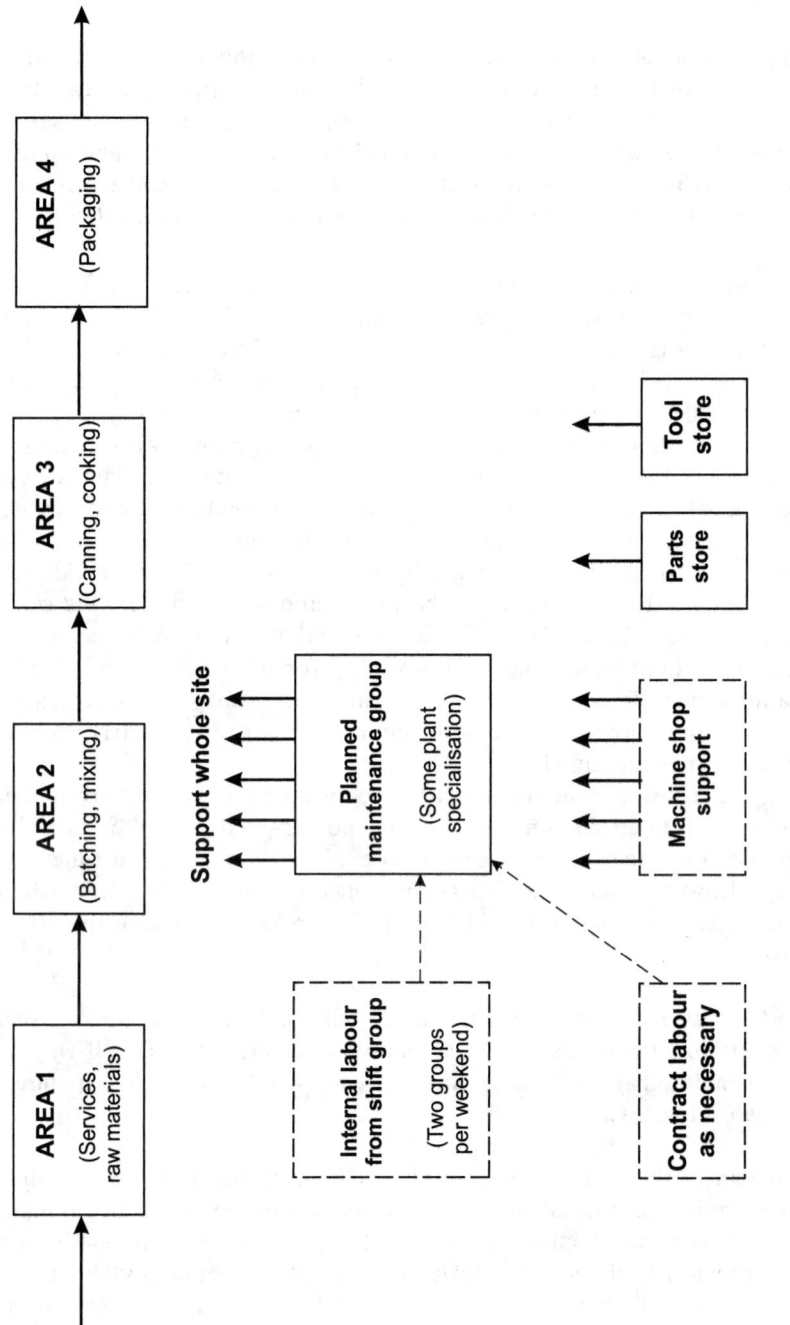

FIGURE 1-15 Weekend Resource Structure

factor here. The structure is also influenced by the availability of tradeforce skills and by various human factors (which will be discussed in more detail in Chapter 2).

The FPP audit revealed a number of deficiencies in the resource structure. The most important was the over-manning of the midweek shifts (see the workload comments). The audit was carried out thirteen years ago and it is not surprising that inter-trade flexibility, production-maintenance flexibility and contractor alliances were not being exploited. Human factors such as morale, motivation and a sense of equipment ownership were good. (*See review questions 1–1 and 1–2.*)

Administrative Structure: This can be considered as a hierarchy of work roles, ranked by their authority and responsibility for deciding what, when and how maintenance work should be carried out. The FPP structure is shown in Figure 1–16 (which uses the so-called organogram as the modelling vehicle). Many of the rules and guidelines of classical administrative theory[2] can be used in the design of such structures. The model shows the maintenance administration in the context of the full administration—simplified in this case. The key decisions in the design of the maintenance administration can be divided between its upper and lower structures. Regarding the former the audit must identify how the responsibilities for plant have been allocated. In the FPP case, Production had responsibility for the operation of the plant, and in a sense for its ownership, since they dictated how it was to be used and when it could be released for maintenance. Maintenance had responsibility for establishing and carrying out the maintenance strategy, and Engineering for plant acquisition and plant condition standards. These responsibilities have to be clearly defined and overlapping areas identified.

Initially, the lower structure has to be considered separately from the upper because it is influenced—indeed, almost constrained—by the nature of the maintenance resource structure which, as explained, is in turn a function of the workload. Lower structure decisions are concerned with establishing the duties, responsibilities and work roles of the shop floor personnel and of the first level of supervision.

The FPP was using the traditional supervisor—planner—tradeforce structure. This needs to be compared with the more recent structures of self-empowered operator-maintainer shift teams and self-empowered second line maintenance teams (see Figure 1.25).

Maintenance Work Planning: The third element in the design of a maintenance organization is the formation of the work planning and scheduling system. Figure 1–17 outlines such a system for the FPP resource and administrative structure previously shown. The design of this should aim to get the right balance between the cost of planning the resources and the savings in direct and indirect maintenance costs that result from use of such resources. It can be seen that the

---

[2]A Kelly, *Maintenance organization and systems,* Butterworth-Heinemann, 1997.

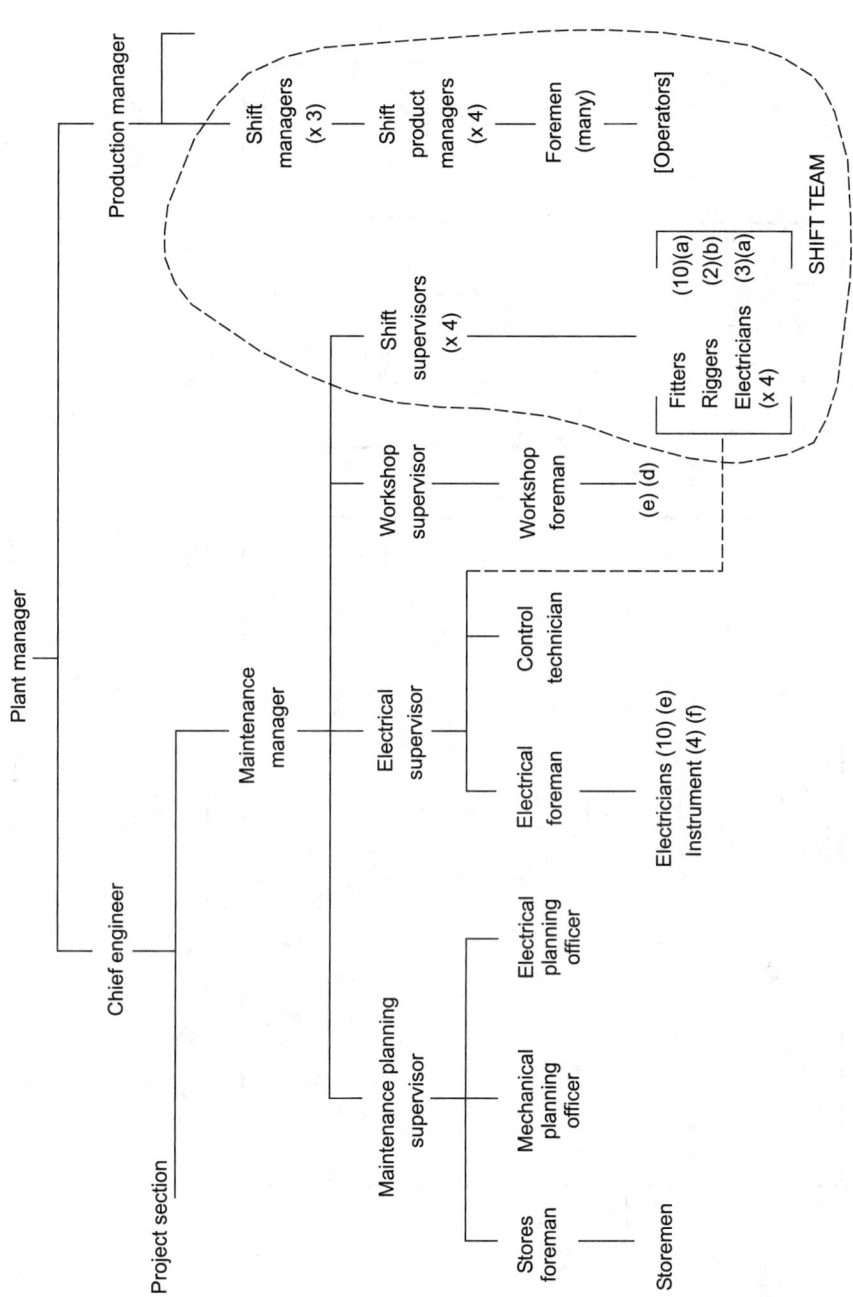

FIGURE 1–16 Administrative Structure

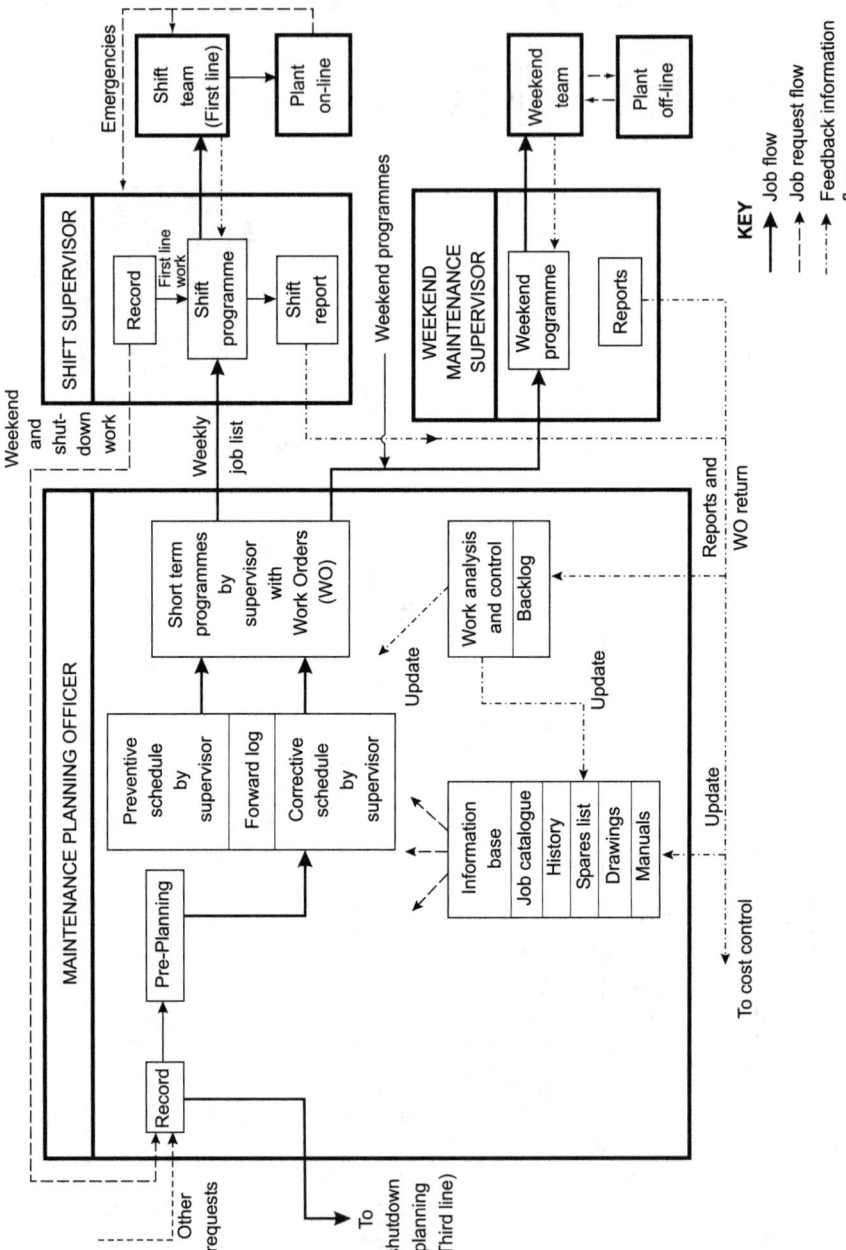

FIGURE 1–17 Work Planning System

planning system is designed around the resource structure —it has a shift planning system (first line), a weekend planning system (second line) and an annual shutdown planning system (third line). The audit must identify how well each level of planning is being carried out. At each level there are key procedures to verify, e.g., at the FPP's second level:

How good is the information base in terms of standard job procedures, spare part list, history?
Who identifies the job method?
Are job times estimated before they are put into the forward log?
How are multi-trade jobs handled?
How good is the return of information in terms of quantity and quality?

Figure 1–18 shows the work control system, which is complementary to the work planning system, its main function being to control the flow of work (preventive and corrective) via a job priority procedure and via the feed-forward of information about future resource availability. At the FPP a number of performance indices were being used to assist this process, viz.

Total man-days in the forward log.
Man-days in the forward log by priority.
Man-days in the backlog.
Percent of planned work completed per period.
Percent of preventive work completed per period.

The audit revealed that the FPP's work planning system was satisfactory for what was essentially a weekly planning system, the work being planned during the week for the weekend. It was my opinion that it, and the software, would have to be up-rated if major jobs were to be planned at short notice during the week (see Section B). (*See review question 1–3.*)

Maintenance Control System: This is needed to ensure that the maintenance organization is achieving its objectives (see Figures 1–3 and 1–5) and to initiate corrective action (e.g., change the life plan, if it is not). My own opinion is that the best practical mechanism for controlling the *overall maintenance effort* would be a properly designed maintenance costing system. This, see Figure 1–19, could be designed to provide a variety of outputs, including 'Top Tens,' or Pareto plots indicating areas of low reliability, high maintenance cost, poor output performance etc.

The FPP audit identified that the plant had a costing system similar to that outlined in Figure 1–19 but used cost centers that were accountancy-oriented rather than equipment-oriented. In addition, the maintenance expenditure was not linked in any way to the output parameters.

Even if properly designed, a maintenance costing system has to be a high level, longer term system, providing a means of controlling the overall maintenance effort. This needs to be complemented by control systems operating at a lower

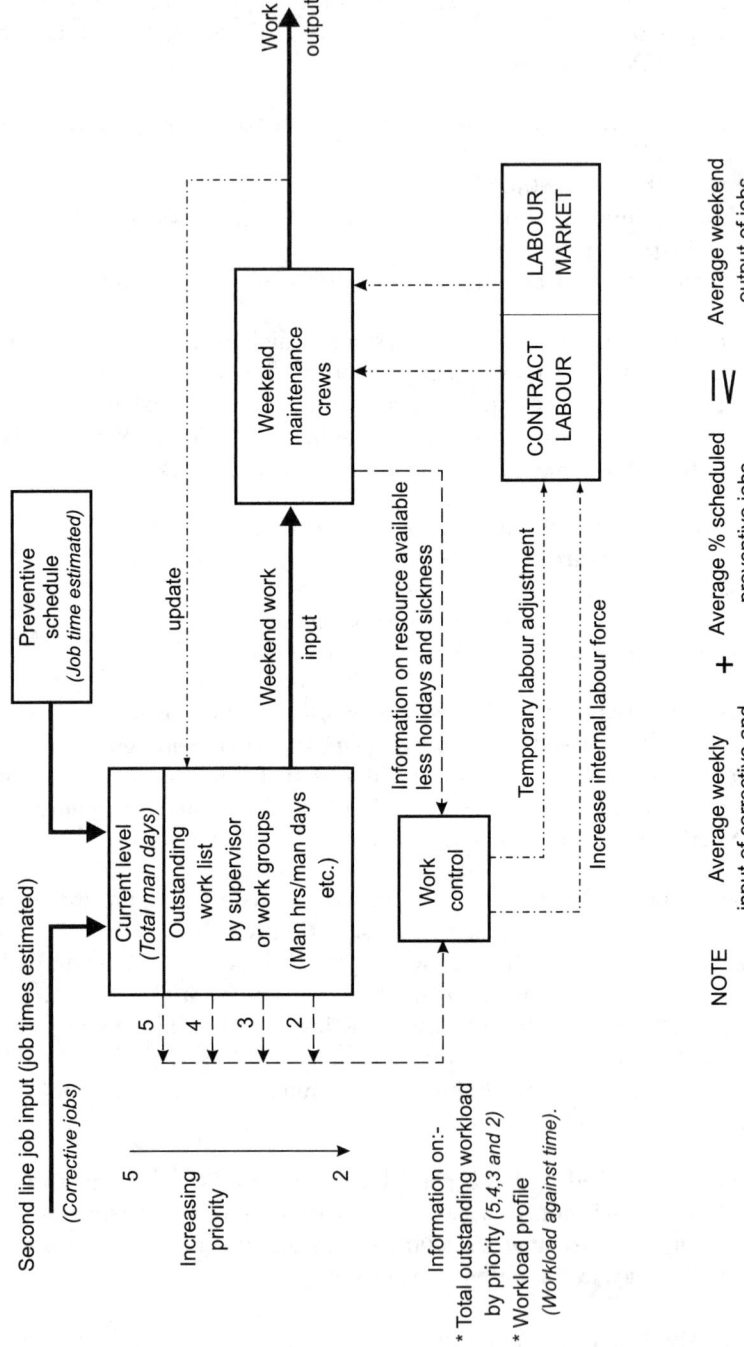

FIGURE 1–18 Principles of Work Control

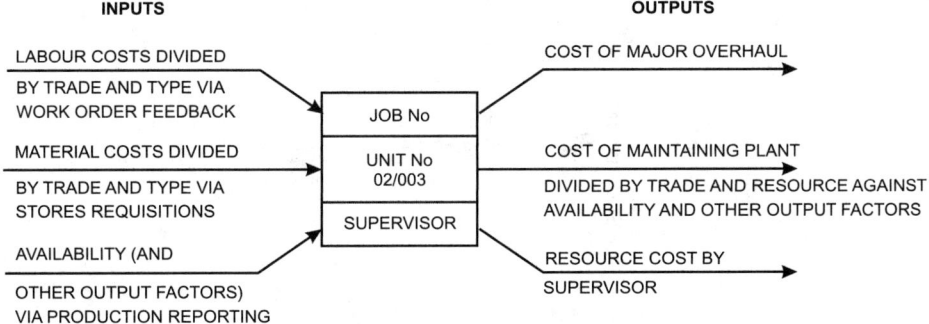

Job No.	Plant code		Trade and supervisor		Work type
	Plant	Unit	Electrician	Night shift	Preventive
521	02	003	2	NS	2

FIGURE 1–19 Outline of a Maintenance Costing System

level (and on a shorter time scale). Indeed, it could be argued that a control system is needed for each sub-objective that is set, (see Figure 1–5). For example, if an overtime limit is set then the actual overtime needs to be monitored and reported for corrective action. The two principle lower levels of maintenance control are best understood with reference to the objective hierarchy shown in Figure 1–5.

Maintenance Effectiveness: The basic model for controlling the effectiveness of maintenance is shown in Figure 1–11. It illustrates the classic ideas of reactive control—using the feedback of operational and maintenance data—and also highlights pro-active control via the feed-forward of ideas for reliability and maintenance improvement. Such mechanisms are required for each major unit of plant. Figure 1–20 shows these ideas incorporated into the FPP maintenance administration.

The FPP audit showed that the first level system was not working well. In the 1980s few companies had incorporated the ideas of continuous improvement and equipment ownership at the tradeforce-operator level of an organization. Considerable design-out-maintenance effort was in evidence at the second level—via the project engineers, although they were not helped by the poor history and data recording.

Maintenance Organizational Efficiency: The prime organizational objective is outlined in Figure 1–5 and can be defined in more detail as:

'to deal with a given plant maintenance workload (governed by the life plans) at minimum cost, by using maintenance resources (man, spares, tools) in the most efficient way.'

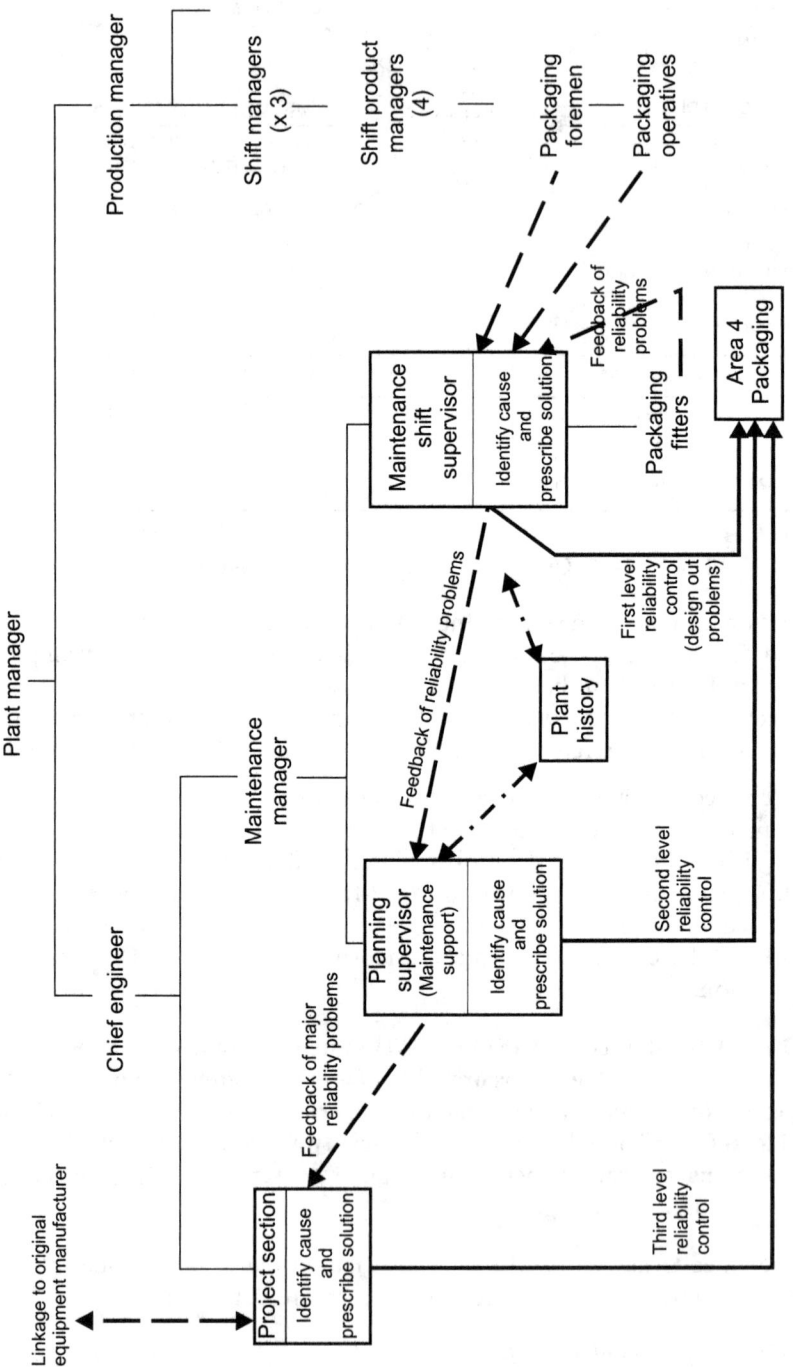

FIGURE 1–20 A Model of Plant Reliability Control in the FPP Organization

However, the idea of a single objective for organizational efficiency is a somewhat notional one. The best approach is through a series of sub-objectives (or performance indices), as shown in Figure 1–5.

The auditors could find no such objectives or indices in use at the FPP. (*See review question 1–4.*)

Maintenance Documentation: Figure 1–3 indicated that some form of formal documentation system—for the collection, storage, interrogation, analysis, and reporting of information (schedules, manuals, drawings or computer files)—is needed to facilitate the operation of all the elements of maintenance management.

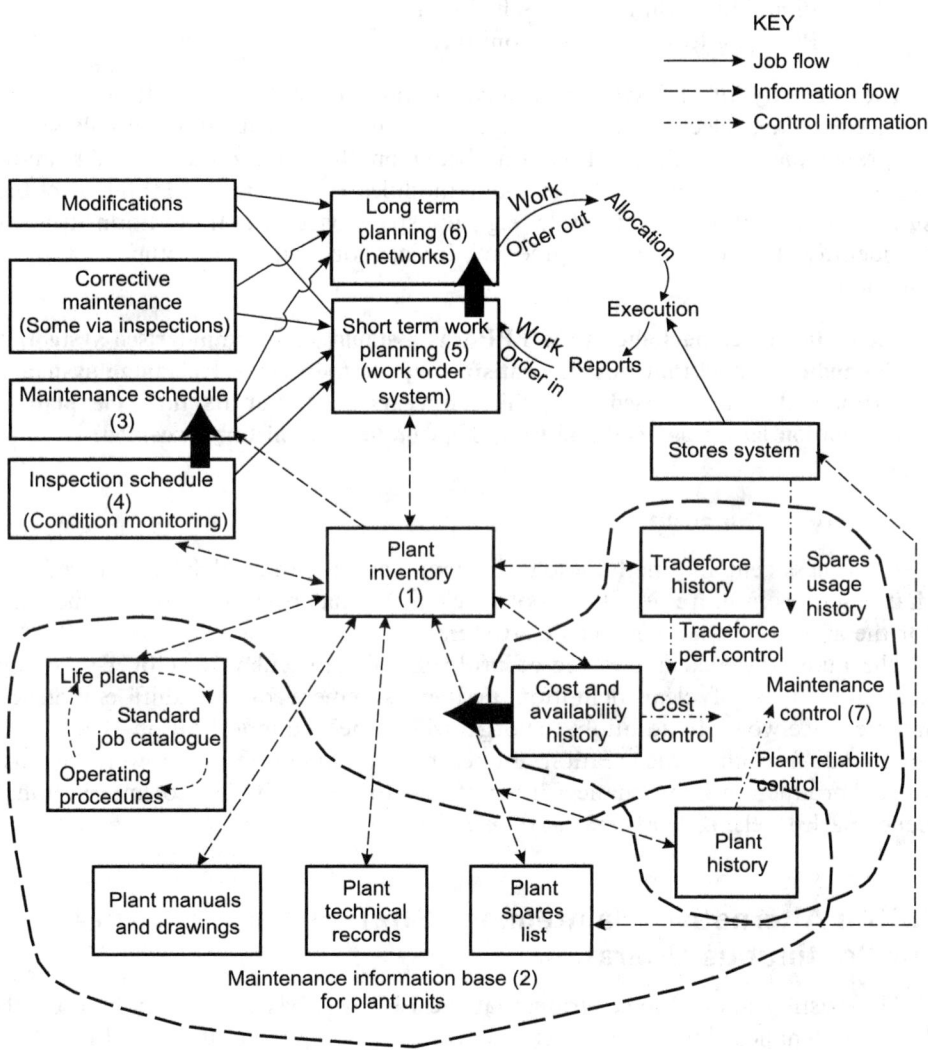

FIGURE 1–21 A Functional Model of a Maintenance Documentation System

Figure 1–21, a general functional model of such a system (whether manual or computerised), indicates that it can be seen as comprising seven principal inter-related modules (performing different documentation functions). Considerable clerical and engineering effort is needed to establish and maintain certain of these functions (e.g., the plant maintenance information base). The control module, in particular, relies on an effective data collection system. Almost all of the companies that I now audit have computerised maintenance documentation systems. The large arrows on Figure 1–21 indicate the possible linkages between the maintenance documentation system and other company information systems, viz.:

Maintenance Costing to Financial Management;
Spare Parts List to Stores Management;
Work Planning to Shut-down Scheduling;
Work Planning to Condition Monitoring.

The majority of the systems I have audited have these functions directly connected, i.e., electronically—in fact, the most recent audit involved an integrated package—all the functions being on the same data base. An audit needs to investigate each of the main modules of Figure 1–21 and also the sub-functions within each module, e.g., the spare parts list. In addition it needs to identify the level and degree of integration with the other company functions.

The maintenance package at the FPP was a stand-alone computerised system. The audit revealed that this was satisfactory for the weekend planning system that was then being used (i.e., thirteen years ago). For its time the plant information base was good and being kept up to date (history excepted).

Summary of the audit

A business centered methodology, in conjunction with models and procedures that describes in more detail each of its elements, has been used as a framework for the audit of a maintenance department.

The audit revealed a number of problems, in particular shift over-manning caused by lack of clear definition and measurement of the shift emergency maintenance work. In addition, the organization needed modification—improved inter-trade flexibility, the creation of operator–maintainer self-empowered teams, closer production-maintenance integration—to bring it up to international benchmark levels. (*See review question 1–5.*)

(B) An Alternative Maintenance Strategy for Continuous Operation

The existing maintenance strategy at the FPP was based on carrying out off-line maintenance during the weekend windows of opportunity and during the once-per-year holiday window. Little attempt had been made to exploit the excess capacity of the plant, or spare plant, to schedule off-line work while the plant was

T<small>ABLE</small> 1–4 Changes in Maintenance Strategy to Accommodate Continuous Operation

---

* A movement towards shutdowns of complete sections of plant based on the longest running time of critical units (e.g. the hydros – about 4 weeks). The frequency of these shutdowns will be based, as far as possible, on running hours or cumulative output. However, for critical items, inspection and condition monitoring routines may be used to indicate the need for shutdowns, which will provide more flexibility about shutdown dates.
* All plant designated as non-critical, e.g. as a result of spare capacity, will continue to be scheduled at unit level (e.g., the smaller mixers).
* A much greater dependence on formalised inspections and condition monitoring routines, for reasons given in (a) and also to detect faults while they are still minor and before they become critical.
* A concerted effort either to design-out critical items (short life or poor reliability) or to extend their effective running time.

---

operating. The new, continuous, operating pattern meant that off-line maintenance would have to be carried out in this way. Indeed, the life plans and schedule would have to move in the direction indicated in Table 1–4. This, in turn, would change the work load pattern, i.e.:

— The first-line work would extend to 21 shifts per week. However, investigation of the mechanical emergency workload had revealed considerable over-manning. When the first-line work was defined as '*the work that must be carried out during the shift of its occurrence*' and subsequently activity sampled, it was shown that it could be carried out by five fitters.

— *The second-line work* (line shutdowns, unit shutdown, preparation for shutdown, services, inspection) was more difficult to forecast in terms of pattern and size. The main peaks would come during line shutdowns at a frequency of about once per week. The size of the workload was unlikely to decrease (even with better preventive maintenance) because the plant was going to be more heavily utilised.

— *The third-line major work* could still be carried out during the holiday window.

To cover this workload the maintenance organization would also have to change. The most likely resource structure (see Figure 1–22) would be based on a first-line, 21-shift, group (the mechanical manning per shift being reduced to five fitters) and a second-line day-group of fifteen fitters operating five days per week. This, in turn, would influence the administrative structure as shown in Figure 1–23. Because of the changes to the way the work would be scheduled (the mid-week work peaks would occur at relatively short notice via the condition monitoring of the lines) it was also necessary to advise management that their work planning system would need to be improved, in order to be far more flexible and dynamic.

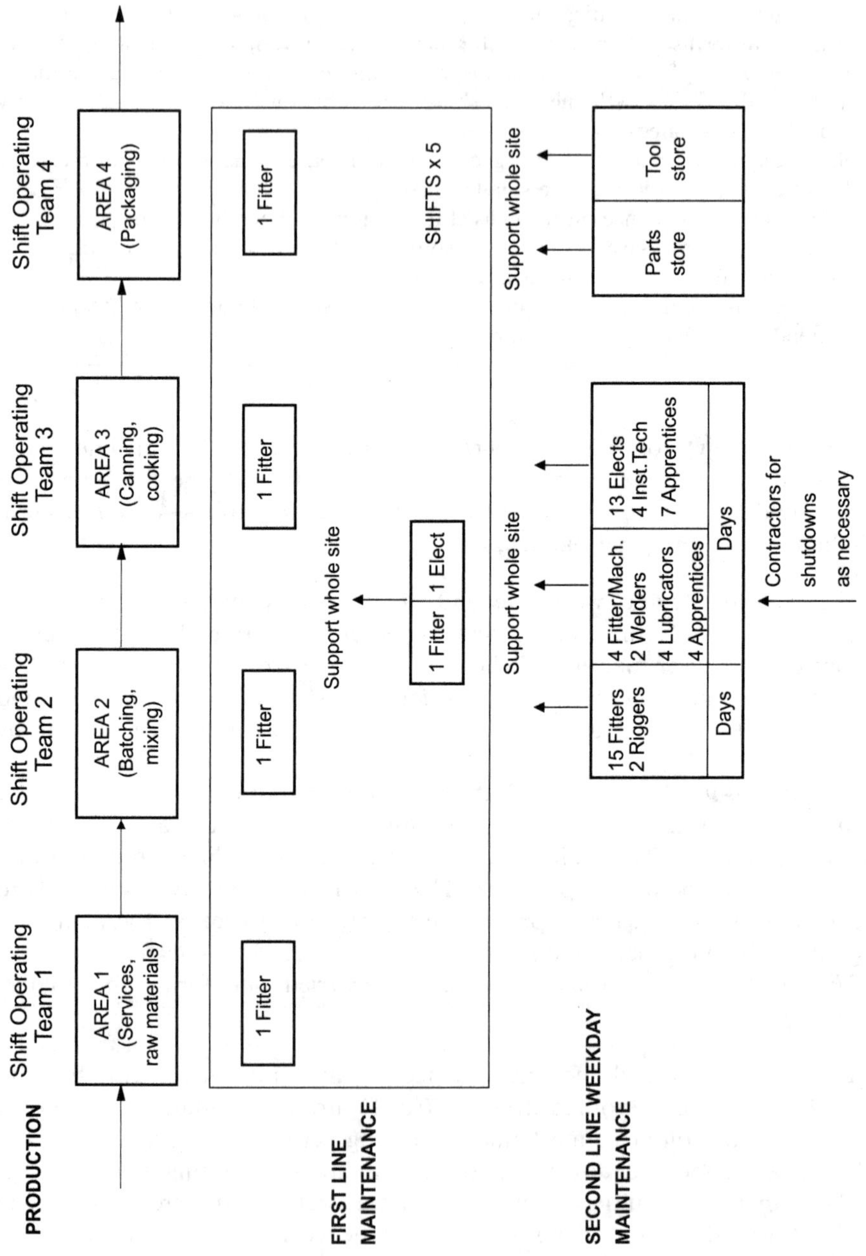

FIGURE 1–22 Maintenance Resource Structure for Continuous Operation

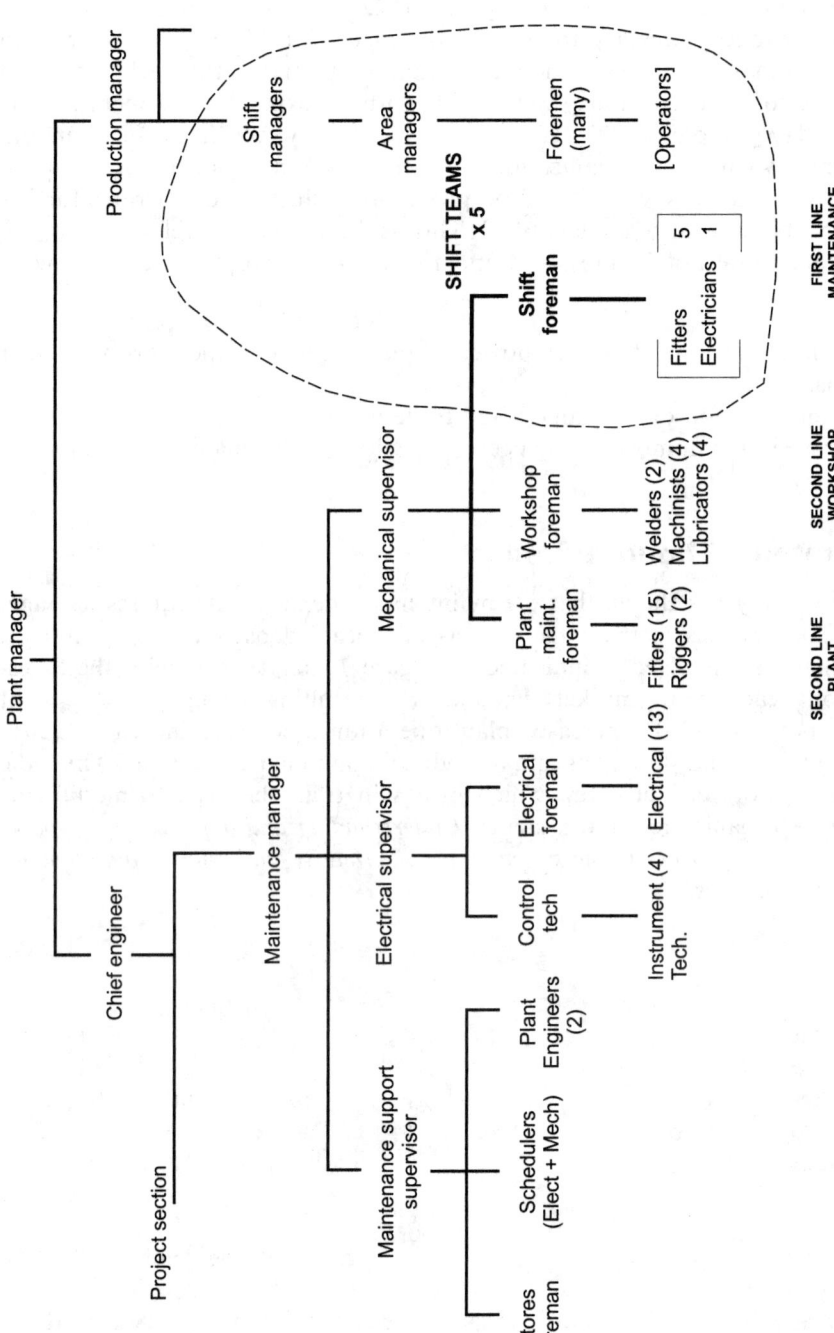

FIGURE 1–23 Maintenance Administrative Structure for Continuous Operation

(C) A Longer Term View of Organizational Change

The organization outlined in Figures 1–22 and 1–23 incorporated the immediate changes necessary for continuous operation. Their purpose was to allow the company to increase the plant availability (and output) while holding the resource costs steady. It may well be that with the experience of operation the size of the day group of tradesmen will be reduced. However, in the medium and long term, when this organization is benchmarked against the best of international standards within the food processing industry, considerable further improvements may also be identified This is best seen by reference to the organization models of Figures 1–24 and 1–25, which incorporate the following actions:

- The introduction of self-empowered plant-oriented operator-maintainer teams.
- The introduction of self-empowered trade teams.
- Increase in the number of engineers, plant located for maintenance support.

The Strategic Thought Process

The case study has shown that the maintenance department requires managerial strategic analysis in the same way as any other department. The thought process that was involved is indicated in Figure 1–26. It starts with the Sales-Production reaction to market demand, the resulting change in the plant operating pattern and the increased plant operation time. This, in turn, requires amended maintenance life plans and a modified maintenance schedule. Thus, the maintenance workload changes, which brings in train the need to modify the maintenance organization and systems. *Understanding and applying this type of strategic through process is the cornerstone of effective and fruitful maintenance management analysis.*

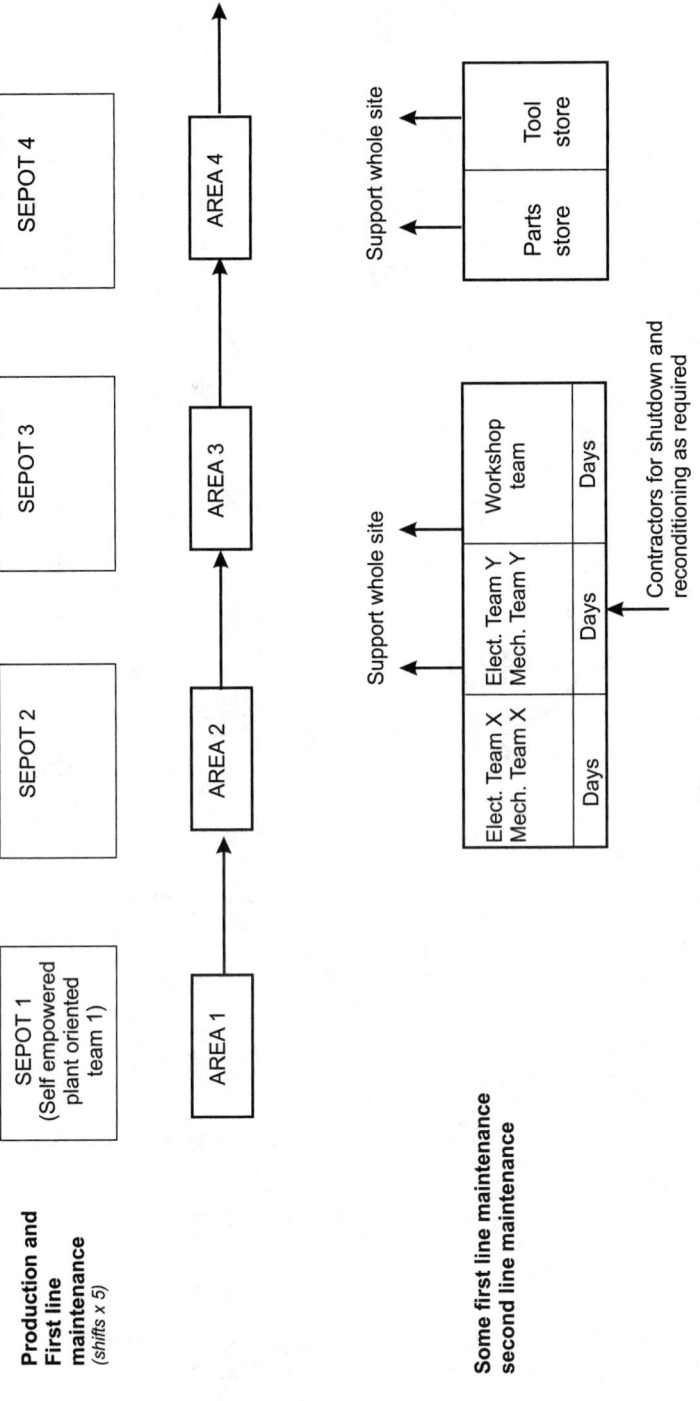

Production and First line maintenance
(shifts x 5)

SEPOT 1 (Self empowered plant oriented team 1)

SEPOT 2

SEPOT 3

SEPOT 4

AREA 1

AREA 2

AREA 3

AREA 4

Some first line maintenance second line maintenance

Elect. Team X Mech. Team X — Days

Elect. Team Y Mech. Team Y — Days

Workshop team — Days

Support whole site

Contractors for shutdown and reconditioning as required

Support whole site

Parts store

Tool store

FIGURE 1–24 Organizational Vision: Resource Structure

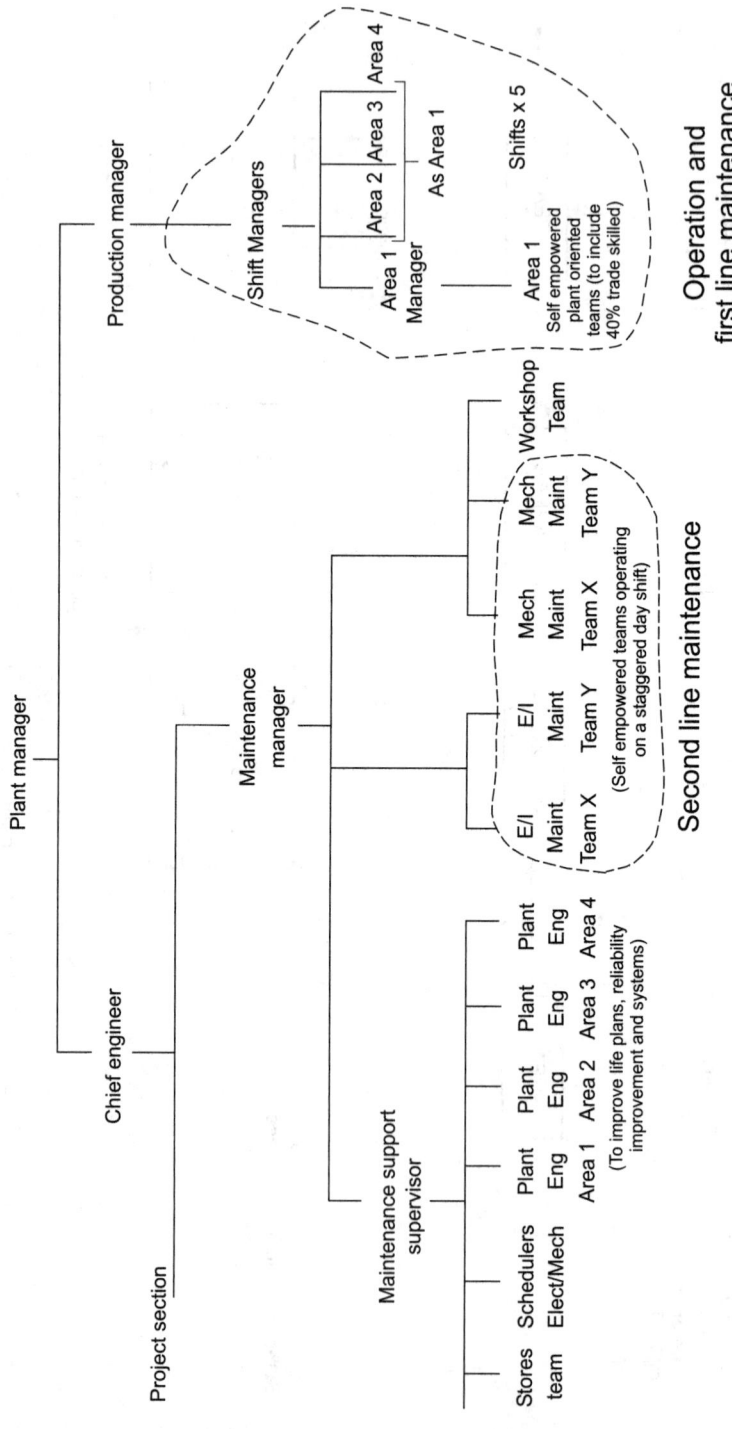

FIGURE 1–25 Organizational Vision: Administrative Structure

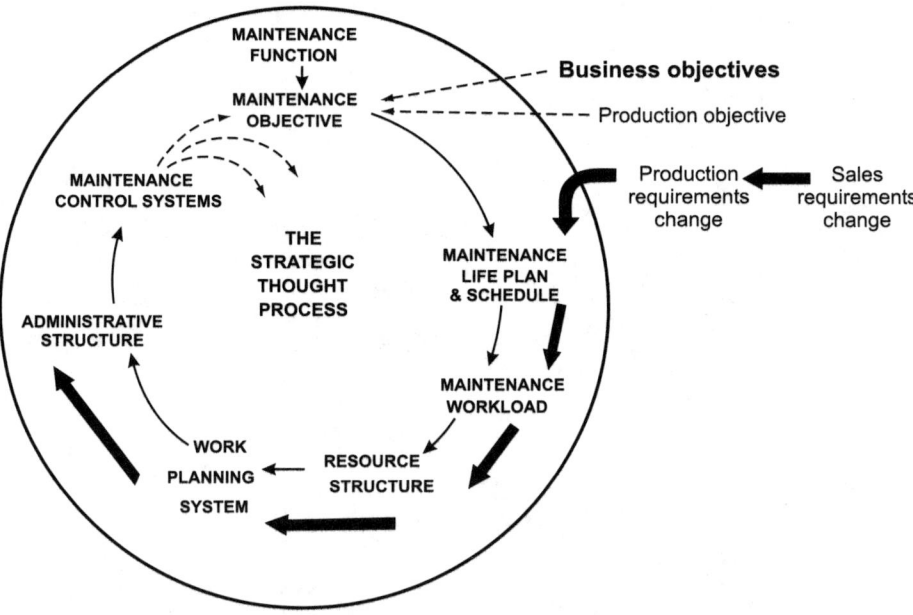

FIGURE 1–26 The Influence of the Market Demand on Maintenance Strategy

Please see review questions and model answers starting at page 295.

CHAPTER 2

Auditing Human Factors in Maintenance Management

Introduction

In the first chapter I have drawn on an audit of a food processing plant to discuss maintenance strategy, organizational structure and systems. The models on which that analysis was based were derived from the work of the administrative and systems theorists (see Table 2–1), rather than from the school of managerial theory which is centered on studies of *human relations*. We will now look at how human factors can influence the way in which maintenance work is carried out and how they can be audited.

What are 'Human Factors' in Organizations?

An organization is a system of interdependent human beings, and their characteristics affect both its structure and its functioning. Human relations management studies the characteristics and inter-relationships of individuals and groups within organizations and takes account of these factors when designing and administering those organizations.

The Human Relations Approach to Management—A Brief Review

The first major development in the human relations approach was the work of Elton Mayo at the Hawthorn Plant.[1] He established that social and psychological factors were important to worker satisfaction and productivity. Considerable advances were made during the period 1950–70, most notably by Maslow, Herzberg and McGregor, in understanding worker motivation.[2–4]

Maslow identified and ranked what he considered to be the needs of the individual, i.e.,

---

[1] E. Mayo, *The social problems of an industrial civilization*, HGS & A, Boston, 1945.

[2] A. A. Maslow, *Motivation and personality*, Harper and Brothers, New York, 1954.

[3] F. Herzberg, *One more time: how do you motivate employees?* Harvard Business Review, Jan/Feb 1968.

[4] D. McGregor, *The human side of enterprise*, McGraw Hill, New York, 1960.

TABLE 2.1 Summary of Management Theories

Mechanistic management—monitors and controls the way the job is performed at shop floor level; includes method, timing, and direction.

Administrative management—applies universal management functions and structural principles to the design of an organization and to its operation.

Human relations management—studies characteristics and relationships of individuals and groups within an organization and takes account of these factors when designing and administrating it.

Decision management—applies procedural and quantitative models to the solution of management problems. A theory for communications and decision making in organizations.

Systems management—studies organizations as dynamic systems reacting with their environment. Analyses a system into its sub-systems and takes account of behavioural, mechanistic, technological and managerial aspects.

Contingency management—takes the view that the characteristics of an organization must be matched to its internal and external environment. Since these environments can change it is important to view the organizational structure as dynamic.

Higher needs	5. Self-fulfilment
	4. Autonomy
	3. Self-esteem
Basic needs	2. Sociality
	1. Security

Herzberg also divided the needs of the individual into those that are basic (biological) and those that are higher (growth). He then identified and quantified the factors affecting these needs, see Figure 2–1. He pointed out that it is the factors bearing on the higher needs that can affect job satisfaction and that, in the industrial setting, these are to be found in the job content. Factors which influence the basic needs are those affecting job dissatisfaction and these are concerned with the job environment. He emphasised that it is the factors which bear on the job content that are the true motivators and that a motivated worker is responding to an internal stimulus—he wants to get the work done.

McGregor's work—his so-called 'Theory X' (the then traditional view that the worker needs to be controlled and directed because of his inherent dislike of work) and 'Theory Y' (the idea that the majority of workers can be self-directing if they have job satisfaction and become committed to an objective)—provided managers with an insight into the characteristics of the worker.

The behavioural scientists of this period argued that work had become over-controlled and boring. They were advocating changes of the following kind:

— 'Replacement of detailed instruction by clarification of objectives.
— 'Increase of responsibility and provision of greater chance of achievement by making the job of planning, organization, directing and controlling a joint function with employees.

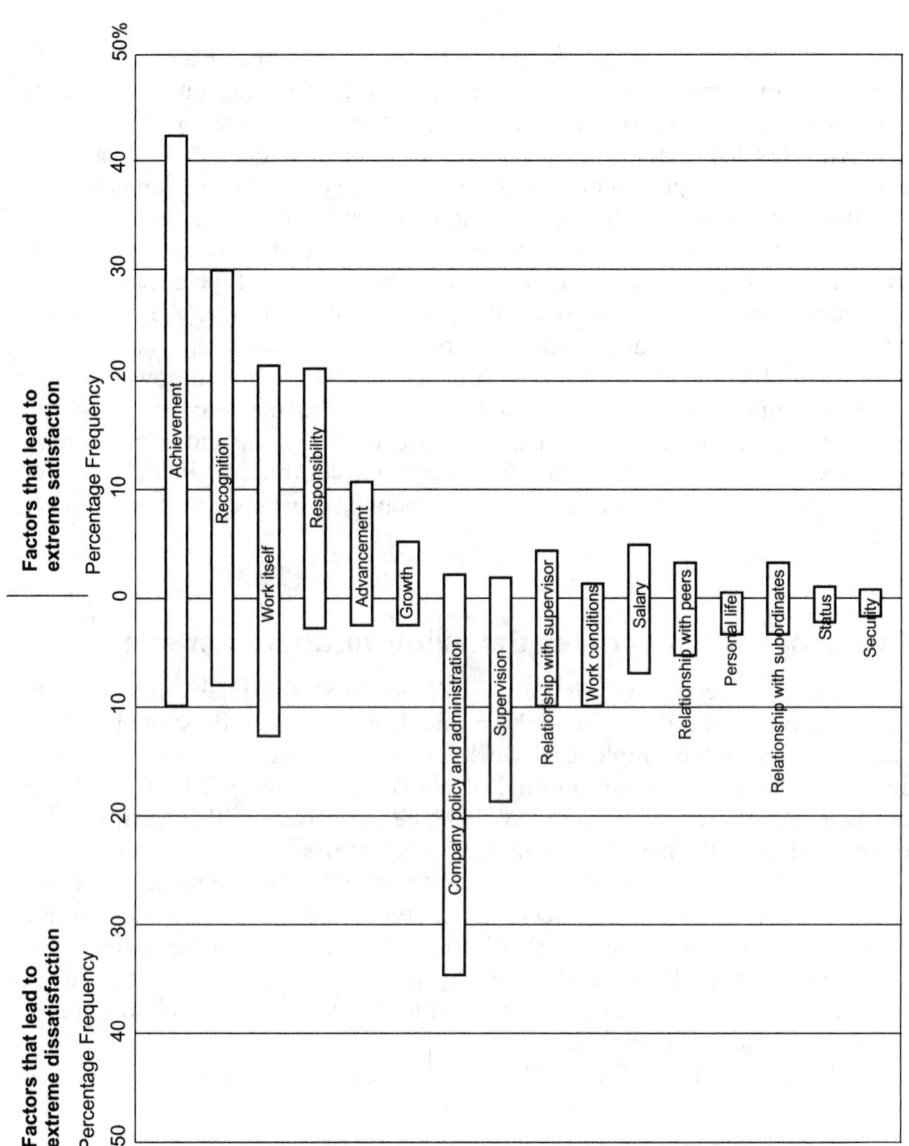

FIGURE 2–1 Factors Affecting Job Attitudes

— 'Study of the organization of jobs and trying to design them so as to give greater satisfaction of human needs.
— 'Replacement of control activities by those which seek to emphasise the manager as helper, supporter and tutor—in order to develop abilities
— 'Setting out to build effective teams within the workforce.

During the last twenty years there have been many exercises in the application of this approach. Some of the early ones, focusing on job re-design with emphasis on autonomous small work groups, were undertaken in Scandinavia. Swedish management and unions, working together, implemented (and modified via experience) many of the ideas of job enrichment and participative management.[5] In the UK, however, similar early exercises, in the 1970s, in participative management met with limited success, principally because the industrial environment was very different from that in Scandinavia and was not conducive to this style of management.[6] The UK's political and industrial environment changed in the subsequent two decades and with this came the introduction of participative management and self-empowered shop floor teams (many of the latter reflecting the Japanese concept of the autonomous operator–maintainer team). More recently, the industrial climate has changed again and brought in downsizing and contract alliances, changing yet further the style of human factors management—in a sense it has moved backwards.

Maintenance Management Behavioural Characteristics

In the previous section it has been explained that the main efforts of the human factors school have focused on identifying and understanding those elements that make an employee's work more satisfying and therefore more effective in terms of the organizational objectives. Here, we will look at human factors from a different viewpoint. We will be concerned with identifying the main ones that influence the organization's efforts towards achieving its maintenance objectives. Some (e.g., a sense of ownership of equipment, affecting reliability performance) will affect the maintenance objective via output considerations, and some (e.g., motivation) via the efficiency of resource usage. It is important to understand that management can take actions to change human factors; the creation of plant-oriented teams, for example, might improve the sense of equipment ownership.

When identifying human factors the following points are helpful:

— 'It is important to differentiate between human factors and the actions that influence them (see above).

---

[5] Swedish Employers' Confederation (Tech. Dept.), *Job reform in Sweden*, 1975.
[6] A. V. Johnson, *Motivation of labour, staff and management*, Organization of Maintenance, Proc. Conf. ISI, 1968.

— 'Human factors can interact, e.g., morale affects motivation.
— 'Some researchers consider that some human factors, such as goodwill towards the company, can be considered as dominant.
— 'Some performance indicators provide a measure of certain human factors, e.g., the level of absenteeism is an indicator of morale.

I am not trying to be 'academic' about this. When auditing maintenance departments I try to get a feel for how good or bad the human factors are. There is little point in confirming that the strategy, structure and systems are good without providing corresponding information about human factors.

When seeking the key human factors in maintenance management I have found the following definition useful:

Characteristics which define the way in which an individual or group behaves or acts in an industrial setting can be called human factors. Those that influence the way the maintenance department operates are termed maintenance management human factors.

The more important of these may be divided into those that can affect individual behaviour and those that can affect the behaviour of industrial groupings of people—complete companies, manufacturing units, teams. As far as possible, industrial examples will be used to show how important these are to maintenance management.

Individual Behavioural Characteristics

Equipment Ownership: a factor which involves the degree to which a tradeforce and/or operators and/or the team feel *a sense of personal ownership for an equipment or an area of plant.* This is probably the most important single factor in achieving a high level of equipment reliability. Where ownership exists the equipment tends to be operated and maintained correctly.

This first became evident to me in the result of a major study of maintenance costs of fork lift trucks in the UK. Those operated and maintained by a single operator (operator–maintenance) incurred one third of the maintenance cost of pool-operated trucks in the same industry.

One of the key organizational characteristics of Total Productive Maintenance (the Japanese-developed strategic approach to maintenance management) is the move towards small, self-empowered, *plant oriented operator-maintenance teams*—of up to seven operator-maintainers with the responsibility for operating a definable sub-process or area of plant and carrying out simple maintenance tasks on it, such as lubrication, adjustment and minor servicing. The teams comprise operators (trained in superficial maintenance) and tradesmen (given operator training). The teams are also given considerable training in the way the plant operates and the relationship between the way it is maintained and operated and its failure or its inability to produce at its design level of quality. They are encouraged, with the help of engineers, to carry out modifications to improve operation and reliability (the so called continuous improvement or *Kaizen*). All of these actions engender a considerable level of plant ownership in the individuals and in the team—they care about the equipment in the same way as if it were literally their personal property

Some of the necessary ingredients for fostering ownership were present in the FPP organization of Chapter 1 (see Figures 1–14 and 1–15). The operators and fitters were plant oriented. However, the separation of operators and maintainers and the shift system worked against ownership. To compensate for this, individual tradesmen were made responsible for carrying out the preventive work on designated equipment—both on shifts and when they were in the weekend group.

Goodwill: 'the state of wishing well to a person, a cause or an enterprise' (a dictionary definition). This involves the tradesmen or operators feeling a sense of belonging with the company and wanting it to prosper. It is closely allied to 'loyalty' but is something more than this. The author considers it to be in many ways a key factor. When goodwill is evident at the shop floor level other problems seem to be more amenable to solution. It takes a long time to build up—perhaps many years of good relationships and trust in the management and the company. It is a function of the company treating the workforce fairly and with respect.

I recently audited an Australian underground coal mine. On a scale of 1 (= no goodwill) to 10 (= excellent relationship and trust) I would have rated goodwill as of Level 1!

Motivation: much researched and much written about, because of its importance to all industrial personnel. I consider the *behaviourist* theories (see Table 2–1) to be too general and insufficiently dynamic to describe the motivational characteristics of the shop floor. To quote from one of my earlier books:

'*In general the industrial worker sees his job as a means of obtaining money, a lower order need, in order to satisfy elsewhere his other, higher order, needs. This view is based on the observation that people are only truly motivated when they are doing something (work, hobby, sport, home repairs) that they really want to do. Most often the worker does not experience this at work. The nature of the work is such that it is normally difficult to institute changes sufficiently to arouse true motivation*'.[7]

Applying these ideas to the maintenance tradesman is not without difficulty. To a certain extent, maintenance work has many of the ingredients needed to provide Herzberg's idea of worker satisfaction and motivation. It has autonomy, craftsman status, pride in the quality of the work, varied and interesting job content etc.—all of this reinforced with the movement in many

---

[7] A. Kelly, *Maintenance planning and control*, Butterworth-Heinemann, Oxford 1984.

companies to self empowerment. These work ingredients also emphasise how important tradeforce motivation is to maintenance management. Maintenance workers are among the few on the shop floor who still have considerable autonomy as regards their day-to-day actions. Thus it is difficult to check how well a preventive maintenance inspection routine has been carried out. It is also difficult to judge how well a repair has been carried out and, in some cases, whether the spares used have been the best from the company's point of view. Maintenance workers know that if they carry out inferior work the consequences of their actions take time to surface and often will be difficult to attribute to them.

In the case of the maintenance tradesman, the most realistic indicators of his level of motivation are (a) *the extent to which he knows what is wanted from him* and (b) *the level of his effort to provide it with a minimum of external control.*

When trying to influence, understand or audit motivation within a maintenance department the following aspects must be taken into consideration:

— The shop floor's industrial relations history, its present position and its deficiencies.
— The factors that influence job content and job environment.
— The external social and political environment and its influence (because this governs the extent to which internal change is possible).
— The tradeforce's identification with the maintenance objectives (the most important factor in their motivation).

Morale: defined in the Oxford Dictionary as—'*the mental state of an individual with regard to confidence and discipline.*' Finding a definition in a management text proved difficult; the best was '*an individual's satisfaction and confidence with membership of an organization*'.[8] The same work pointed out that production is not a function of morale and therefore morale is not a very meaningful concept in management thought! My own auditing experience, however, has convinced me that poor morale, whether of individuals or trade groups, most certainly affects both the quantity and the quality of maintenance work.

Morale within the maintenance department may be defined as:

an individual's perception, which may be positive or negative, of his future work prospects, and which may be induced by the success or failure of the company employing him and the ability (leadership, organizational and engineering performance) of its management.

As this implies, the negative factors affecting morale may be those that appear to threaten the individual's or group's future work security, e.g.,

---

[8] H. G. Hicks and C. R. Gullett, *Management*, McGraw Hill, Singapore, 1985.

— 'a company's poor economic performance;
— 'poor company organization and systems, inducing problems with product quality, for example;
— 'recent workforce redundancies and the threat of more to come.

Resentment: defined in the dictionary as '*a strong feeling of ill will against the perpetrator of a wrong or affront.*' The following example, drawn from one of my own auditing exercises, explains this in the context of the maintenance tradesman:

'Hell hath no fury like a fitter scorned.' A small power station, supplying a chemical plant, consisted of a number of large diesel generators. It was maintained by five fitters, one of them a leading hand. One of the younger (very bright) fitters had been promised promotion to supervisor level but this had not materialised—and did not 'look like doing so. He had become resentful and obstructive (the bad apple) and this feeling had spread to two of the other, younger, fitters. They were using every IR trick in the book (bad backs, bad arms etc.) to avoid work and undermine the rest of the trade group. Weak management had allowed this situation to fester for about a year. The condition of the diesel units was deteriorating and this was likely to have a considerable effect on the overall operation of the plant.

Protectionism: can be defined in the maintenance context as '*resistance to sharing knowledge and information;*' it can be affected by other human factors such as insecurity and low morale.

A typical example is provided by the technician who has built up considerable knowledge over many years about specific equipment but is reluctant to document his knowledge or convey it to other employees.

Parochialism: the dictionary definition is '*local narrowness of view and attitude.*' I have encountered this in many organizations. It can occur, for example, within the manufacturing units of a decentralised organization.

A power station, which I was auditing, provided electricity to an alumina refinery. It was set up as a semi-autonomous manufacturing unit. There was considerable narrowness of view exhibited by its manager. He was an ex-marine engineer and ran the station as if it were a ship. On each visit I felt that the gangway had to be lowered before I could go on board. The attitude of the staff was that they were set apart and different. The refinery senior management seemed to know little about the way the power station was being operated and maintained. I established that two out of the three generating units were needed at all times for full refinery operation. However they were all in poor condition and in need of major overhaul. It was difficult to take a unit out because of the unreliability of the two left in service. Before leaving the site I insisted that the refinery general manager discuss this problem with the power station manager.

Organizational design creates the boundaries between departments and it is management's job to minimise parochialism and its effects. It generates other human factor problems, e.g., polarisation (see later).

Other human factors: which I do not audit directly but are covered indirectly during the one-to-one interviews which make up the bulk of the audit programme. Some of these are as follows:

Jealousy	— of those on shifts exhibited by those on days, or vice versa.
Attitude	— a positive tradeforce attitude towards data collection.
Envy	— of those promoted.
Resistance to change	— to the introduction of new working methods, team working, or computer systems.
Pride	— in an individual's trade and in the quality of work carried out.
Prejudice	— a pre-conceived, biased, opinion or position on a subject, e.g., the maintenance view of production—'*They break it, we mend it;*' the production view of maintenance—'*They don't understand our objectives we give them a line for four hours they keep it for twelve.*'

Group Behavioural Characteristics

Culture: has been defined as '*the collective mental programming of people in an environment*'.[9] It is not a characteristic of individuals, it encompasses a number of people who are conditioned by the same education and life experience. Thus, when auditing it is important to recognise and understand the culture of the country. For example, that of Saudi Arabia is very different from that of Australia and this can influence the organization—most of the tradesmen in Saudi Arabia are expatriates.

A company can have its own culture.

A food processing plant which I audited was part of a USA multi-national that had been operating in Australia and the UK for many years. It had developed a company culture that I had observed in both of these countries, one that put a very high premium on success, hard work, fairness, tight scheduling and efficiency of thought—it could almost be 'felt.'

Further down the organization a culture can also develop within departments.

A petrochemical complex used a functional organizational structure in which the maintenance department was large and carried out all the maintenance, even the

---

[9] F. E. Kast and J. E. Rosenzweig, *Organization and management*, McGraw Hill, Singapore, 1985.

major shutdowns. **Over many years the culture within this department had developed a mix of norms, standards and behaviour weighted much more towards maintaining equipment for engineering excellence rather than achieving organizational efficiency. The department was considerably over-manned.**

Esprit de corps: defined as '*a spirit of regard for the company or group honour and interest, and for those of each member belonging to it.*' Clearly a concept of military origin and one which I observed in the major Japanese companies during visits to that country in the late 1970s. During my auditing of some fifty companies world-wide I have not come across any other companies, departments or manufacturing units which have had an *esprit* of the kind defined above. It has been suggested that one of the reasons for breaking down large functional organizations into semi-autonomous manufacturing units is to generate *esprit de corps* in each of those units (although I have not, as yet, observed this actually occurring to any extent).

Horizontal polarization: has been defined as '*having opposite views and attitudes across departmental boundaries.*' This can best be explained via the simple model of a functional organization shown in Figure 2–2. Conflict builds up across the boundaries of the main departments—viz. Production, Maintenance, Engineering, Stores—and to a lesser extent across the sub-departments, e.g., Electrical Maintenance and Mechanical Maintenance.

The Production–Maintenance conflict has been well documented. The maintenance view is that '*Production built it and we mend it.*' In other words '*they mal-operate and never let us have the equipment for proper maintenance.*' The production view is that '*we make the money and maintenance do not understand our objectives—we give them the plant for a shift and they keep it for a day.*'

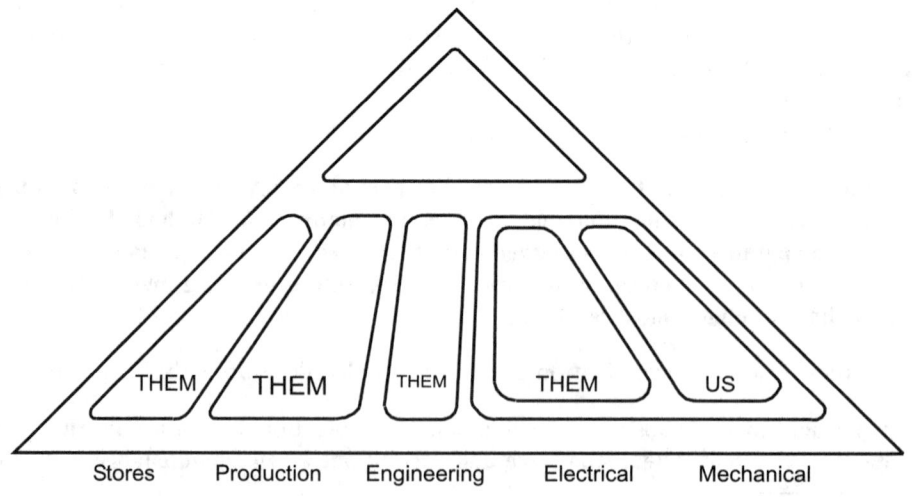

FIGURE 2–2 Horizontal Polarisation in an Administrative Structure

I was consulting on the maintenance of a paper-making machine. A production supervisor pointed out that a machine came down every three to four weeks for the replacement of a wire belt (a task of eight hours duration which the production operators carried out). When asked if this provided a window for maintenance work the supervisor replied 'we don't tell them when the machine is coming down otherwise we lose it for more than eight hours—we keep this information to ourselves.'

I often observe polarisation across the Maintenance-Stores interface when these functions are the responsibility of different departments. From the company point of view the spares holding objective would be to minimise the sum of the holding and stockout costs. Maintenance try to keep the inventory high, Stores Management try to keep it low—hence conflict and polarisation.

Figure 2–2 shows that the organization can develop the '*us and them*' syndrome across the horizontal boundaries. '*We*' are mechanical maintenance and everybody else (including electrical maintenance) is a '*them*'—the larger the number of 'thems' the greater the polarisation. Once severe polarisation develops, information might flow but communication and understanding is lost.

Vertical Polarization: considerable antipathy can build up between the various *levels* of an organization, especially if these are many and the organization is large (see Figure 2–3).

The greatest degree of antipathy is often between the shop floor and the higher levels of management—a conflict in objectives and attitudes. Not only does such conflict affect communication but it also negatively affects some of the more important individual behavioural characteristics, e.g., goodwill and motivation.

The other important vertical maintenance interface is that which lies between the maintenance supervisors and their professional engineering managers. Supervisors mostly come from the trades, do not have professional engineering

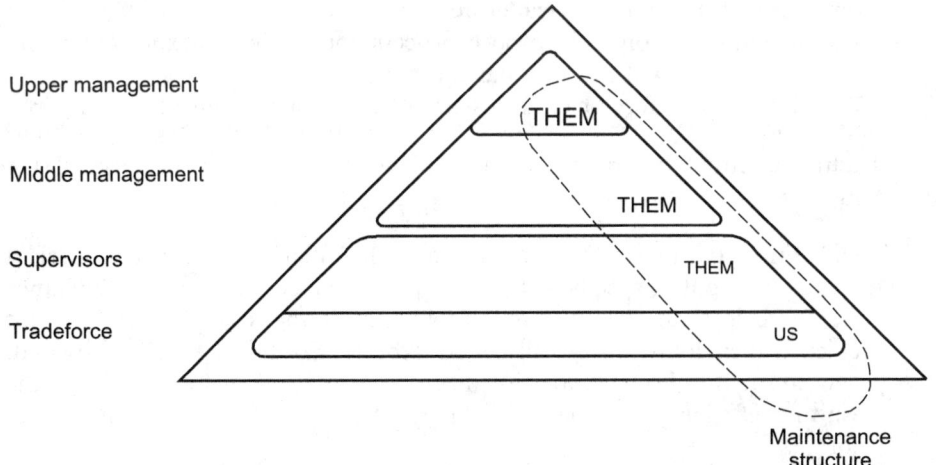

Figure 2–3 Vertical Polarisation in an Administrative Structure

qualifications and only rarely move into the upper reaches of management. They are, however, unique in that they constitute the only level of management that looks downwards to non-management personnel. In addition, they tend to be less mobile within the organization than professional engineers and are the main source of trade and plant-oriented knowledge. More recently, their direct man-management role has been threatened by the introduction of self-empowered teams. In many industries their role has changed to that of technical advisor, planner and team leader. They have become uncertain and defensive. This has led to conflict and polarisation.

The 'us and them' syndrome (of both the vertical and horizontal varieties) is most evident in large organizations which are highly functionalised at the top, with long chains of command down to operators and maintainers. Severe polarisation in such organizations can cause complete lack of communication, organizational contraction and eventual failure.

The Effect of Outsourcing Alliances on Human Factors

So far, the discussion has been confined to a review of human factors within *traditional* organizations, those in which all the maintenance work is carried out by company-employed personnel (other than during periods of peak loading). The most recent trend in maintenance organization, however, has been towards company-contractor *alliances* where, for example, the second-line and third-line work (and perhaps the operation of the stores) are transferred to the alliance, whose workforce combines personnel transferred from the company with new personnel brought in by the contractor. My own experience indicates that this introduces some largely negative human factors, viz.

— 'The transferred personnel suffer low morale—resenting and resisting the change, they find their position less secure. They feel that they have little in common with the contract tradeforce.
— 'The incoming personnel lack both process and equipment knowledge and any form of goodwill towards the company.
— 'The alliance workforce has little sense of plant or equipment ownership.

A leading contract company, when challenged with this view, argued the following case:

— 'The contract between the company and the alliance to deliver a 'level of service' is tightly specified by key performance indices. The alliance tradeforce is aware of this and know that if the service levels are not achieved their job-security will be jeopardised. So they are well-motivated.
— 'The contractor brings expertise in engineering and in job planning, the resulting efficiency enhancing the perception of job security and hence morale.
— 'A sense of equipment ownership is more important within the production-oriented first line teams than within the alliance workforce.

My experience of auditing human factors within alliance arrangements of this kind is, however, somewhat limited, so I present these views only for discussion. *(A fuller treatment of this topic is given in the Chapter 9 case study)*

Auditing Maintenance Management Human Factors

Human behaviour can have a profound effect on the performance of organizations. In this chapter we have been concerned with identifying and discussing those human factors that can have an influence on maintenance performance. But although they can be identified it is much more difficult to audit them objectively. Table 2–2 shows an extract from one of the several questionnaires which are used in my own maintenance audit programme, this one during one-to-one interviews with members of the maintenance tradeforce. It is only one relatively small part of the interviewing process. For tradesmen, questions on equipment ownership, motivation, morale and goodwill would be included in the interview plan, different sets of human factor questions being posed to the operators, supervisors, and managers. The auditor explains the question, explaining what he means by 'ownership' and the scale adopted for its measurement. During such interviews he also records some of the individual comments about human factors, e.g.,

'We are a centralised group—we do not have a sense of equipment ownership'
'Rotation works against ownership and plant specific knowledge'
'There is no sense of ownership in the process teams, they don't even clean'

TABLE 2.2 Extract from a Human Factor Profiling Questionnaire

Maintenance Audit—Company
Human Factor Profiling Questionnaire
(Maintenance Tradesmen)
Answer the following questions in terms of the scale below

0	1	2	3	4	5	6	7
Do Not Know	Not At All	Very Little	A Small Amount	A Fair Amount	Quite A Lot	A Great Deal	Completely

To what extent do you feel/believe:
1. You have a 'sense of ownership' for the equipment you maintain? ☐
2. The operators have a 'sense of ownership' for the equipment they operate? ☐
3. You have a 'feeling of goodwill' towards the company and its senior management? ☐
4. You have a high morale? ☐
5. You are motivated to work hard in the interests of the company? ☐
6. Your relationship with the production operators and supervisors is good? ☐
7. You have a good relationship with first line management? ☐
8. You have an effective service from the stores ☐

Continued

A representative selection of such comments may be included in the audit report.

Auditing group behavioural characteristics requires a different approach, which is also illustrated in Table 2–2 in the case of horizontal polarisation. Question 6 is directed at determining the maintenance view of the attitudes, co-operation and communication between Production and Maintenance. Other questions (not shown) attempt to determine Production's view of the service they get from Maintenance.

When auditing large organizations I carry out surveys of opinion which include questions on human factors. Questionnaires in such cases are sent out ahead of the audit and returned during the audit period. The main aim of the human factors audit is to identify those factors which are affecting maintenance performance, either positively or negatively. When positive, advice is given on how they can be re-inforced and maintained; when negative, how they might be eliminated or their influence mitigated. For example, if, in a traditionally functioning organization, the sense of equipment ownership is found to be poor at tradeforce and operator level it may be improved by the creation of *self-empowered plant oriented operator-maintainer teams*. If such a structural modification is not possible or desirable then alternative courses of action must be sought within the traditional structure, e.g., individual tradesmen made responsible for specific equipment for preventive routines. While such a structural change may improve ownership it may well affect other factors in a negative way, e.g., plant oriented teams may well increase parochialism. The point here is that organizational change requires a complex mix of structural, strategic, systems and human factors decisions. Before such decisions are taken it is essential to have as clear a picture as possible of the existing situation—an audit provides such a picture.

CHAPTER 3

Auditing Maintenance Departments

Introduction

Maintenance auditing is a structured process of 'inspection and checking' the strategy, organizational structure and systems of the maintenance management department. Its purpose is to:

(i) map and describe the operation of the existing management procedures;
(ii) assess the procedures in the light of general managerial principles and concepts, and against internationally established best practice;
(iii) identify the strengths and weaknesses of the department;
(iv) formulate proposals for reinforcing the strengths and eliminating or reducing the weaknesses of the department.

I have been invited to undertake industrial audits for a variety of reasons:

The General Manager of an **aluminium smelting operation** wanted to know how well, in terms of equipment performance and maintenance costs, his maintenance department was operating compared to those of other smelting works. He wanted strengths and weaknesses identified. This is the standard reason for an audit.

In addition to wanting the above, the management of Chapter 1's **food processing plant** also required advice on a revised maintenance strategy which would cater for the plant moving from 15-shift to continuous operation.

The management of a **pharmaceutical plant** had decided to acquire a new computerised maintenance documentation system and needed to clearly identify the 'user requirements.'

A large company, operating many **cement plants**, wanted to make meaningful comparisons of one with another and also with the plants of other companies. To this end, the most productive plant was to be audited to set up appropriate benchmarks.

51

The Audit Aide-Memoir

The BCM approach of Chapter 1, adopted in conjunction with the human factors approach of Chapter 2, facilitates the assembly of a comprehensive list of checkpoints and questions ordered according to the methodology model of Figure 1–3. This *audit aide-memoir* (see Appendix 1) lists the information required when mapping, modelling and auditing the maintenance department and its linkages with other company functions, such as Production, and its logic informs the construction of the audit programme (see next section). It also acts as a check list during the audit to ensure that all the information needed has been collected. It is not used during the interviews.

The main sections of the aide-memoir are ordered as follows:

Assets
Objectives
Strategy
{
1. Characteristics of plant operation.
2. Business, production and maintenance objectives.
3. Maintenance life plans for process plant.
4. Maintenance life plans for electrical and instrumentation equipment.
5. Condition based maintenance.
6. Corrective maintenance and plant condition review.
7. Preventive maintenance schedule.

Organization
{
8. Maintenance workload.
9. Maintenance resource structure.
10. Maintenance administrative structure.

Systems
{
11. Work planning and work control.
12. Maintenance control.
13. Stores management.
14. Maintenance documentation.

The above information can be divided into *hard data*—that which is written down, e.g., job descriptions, or is recorded in some other way, e.g., on an organization chart—and *soft data*—that which derives from expressed opinions, e.g., concerning human factors, or *is* recorded but is not directly or easily accessible, or needs to be modelled.

Data Collection Methods

It will be appreciated from the aide-memoir that the main effort of an audit is data gathering. In order to do this efficiently, a well thought out programme for this (see next section) is needed and the most appropriate collection methods—viz., interviews, questionnaires, surveys, models—must be employed. Such methods can be used on their own, e.g., interviews only, or in combination, e.g., interviews plus models. Much of the hard data can be collected by company personnel either before or during the site visit.

Appendix 2 shows the pre-site-visit information list. Such information is usually collected by the audit facilitator (whose main responsibility is to arrange the audit interviews). Figure 3–1 shows a schematic of an air compressor, with rotable

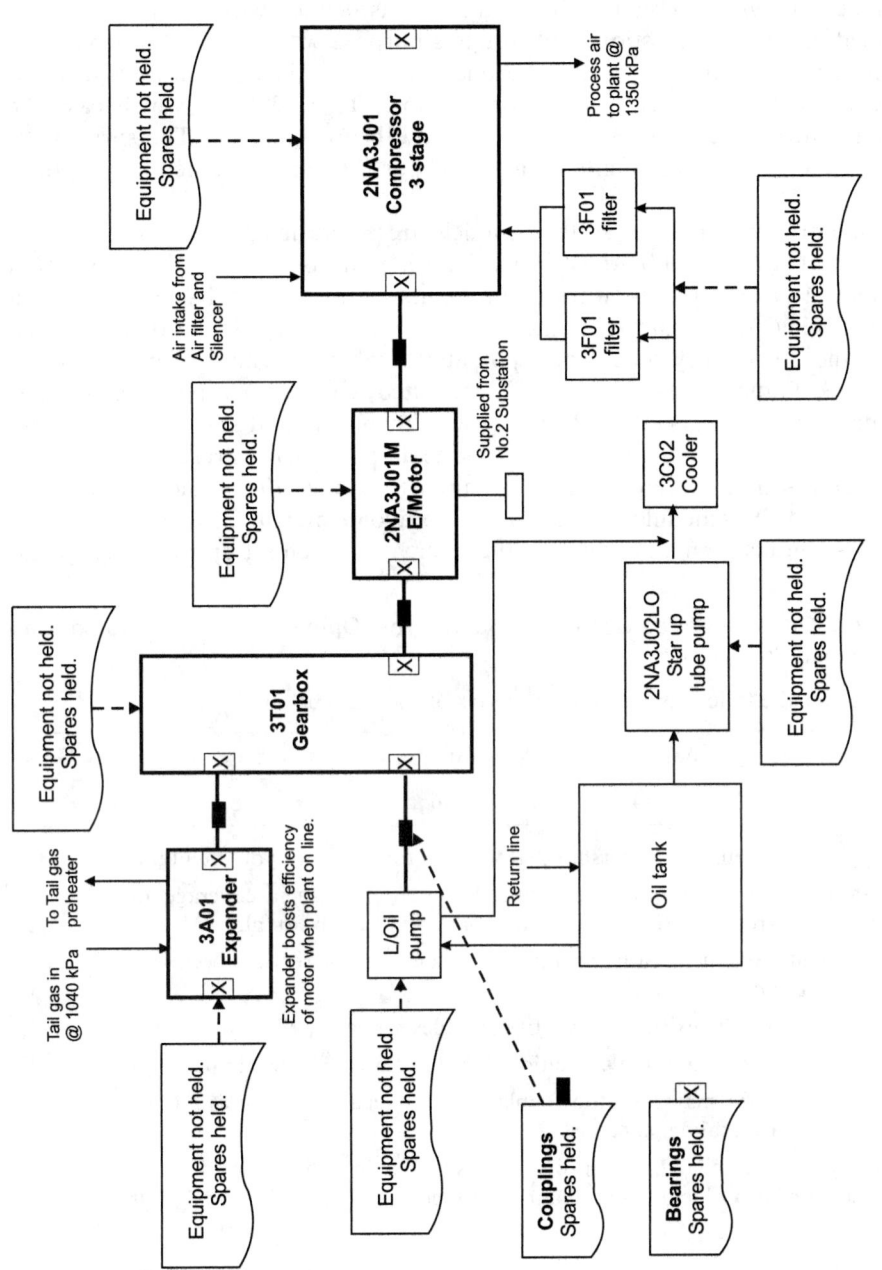

FIGURE 3–1 Schematic of Air Compressor

spares information. This was drawn up (after explanation of what was required) by an area technician during the site-visit phase of a chemical plant audit.

The questionnaires are used in two ways. Firstly, in interviews during which the questions (and where necessary the rating scale associated with the questions) are explained; the use of questionnaires for this purpose was discussed in Chapter 2 and an example given in Table 2–2. Secondly, to survey the opinions of a group of people on a particular issue (see, for example, Table 3–1) in which case the questionnaires are completed directly by those being surveyed. The surveys are conducted during the site visit and, as far as possible, are explained to the group concerned.

Outline organization and systems models are constructed and agreed early in the site visit and are subsequently used during the one-to-one data collection interviews. For example the work planning model (see Figure 1–17), is used as a reference when discussing with the planners (and others) the way the system works, and to identify actual and potential problems. The resource structure model, (see Figures 1–14 and 1–15) is consulted when discussing issues such as skills profiling and inter-plant flexibility with managers and supervisors.

The main information gathering technique, in particular as regards 'soft data,' is the one-to-one interview, which is limited to a one-hour session. Additional interviews can be scheduled if necessary. To avoid interruptions, interviews are normally conducted in an auditors' office which has been set up within the plant.

TABLE 3–1 Questionnaire Used for Survey of Opinions of Tradeforce and Maintenance Supervisors

Please answer the following questions in terms of the scale below

Very Poor		Poor		Adequate		Good		Very Good	
1	2	3	4	5	6	7	8	9	10

How strong is the sense of ownership that you feel for the plant you maintain? ☐

How effective are the lubrication routines in terms of their coverage of equipment, correct selection of oils and reliability of their completion? ☐

To what extent have the existing preventive routines and/or services been well thought out and documented? ☐

To what extent are the existing preventive routines/services well carried out? ☐

How effective do you think the Condition Based Maintenance techniques are? ☐

How effective is the major shutdown planning as regards carrying out the major preventive maintenance tasks? ☐

How do you rate reliability improvement systems in your plant i.e. the identification of problems (high maintenance cost; low reliability) and their solution? ☐

Comments _____

_____

_____

_____

_____

Interviewing technique varies from one auditor to another, but as a minimum the following requirements should be met:

- The auditor should try to put the interviewee at ease, explaining who he is and what the audit is about, and asking the interviewee to discuss his own background and role.
- The auditor should explain the way in which the interview will be conducted and what is required from it. He should point out that he will take notes and, where necessary, should seek permission to use a tape recorder.
- The interviewee must be assured that all sensitive information will be regarded as confidential, e.g., that any information gained will not be attributed to its interviewee source.
- At some point the interviewee should always be invited to identify any other problems or issues to which he thinks attention should be drawn.

Some difficulties that can be encountered during the interview are:

Resistance to giving information: Some of the personnel may jointly decide not to co-operate and provide little information. It is usually obvious when such collusion has occurred and it can mostly be overcome by identifying the leading 'malcontent'—someone who is aggrieved about the way he has been treated, and who will provide the necessary information about departmental problems. Armed with this it will be much easier to break down the barriers to co-operation.

Lack of credibility: The interviewees often feel that outsiders suffer from a lack of knowledge about the company (which is true). So they do not believe providing information will do much good—they are cynical. The auditors can often overcome this by using their models to demonstrate their depth of understanding of the subject.

Prejudiced views: Maintenance personnel may give biased views about Production or Stores, and vice versa. It is important to interview enough people to get a balanced view.

The interviewee wants to push his own views and/or is too talkative: The auditor must bring the discussion back to his structured approach.

The other way to collect data is via an office or site visit: the former to examine systems (e.g., the drawings and manuals library), the latter in order to acquire a familiarity with the plant or to review the plant's condition or level of housekeeping. These visits must be conducted with a member of the company familiar with the plant.

A Generic Auditing Procedure

The six main steps (A to F) of the audit procedure are shown in Figure 3–2. Figure 3–3 shows the constraints on on-site data collection, e.g., collection of work planning information needs to come after mapping of the resource

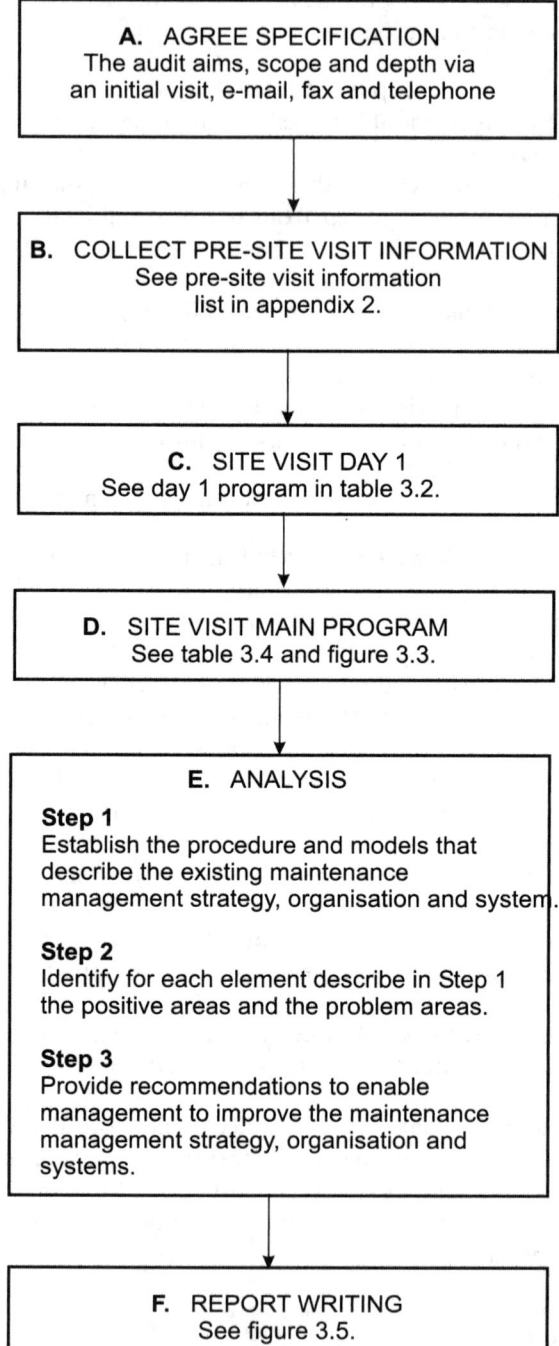

FIGURE 3–2 Overall Audit Procedure

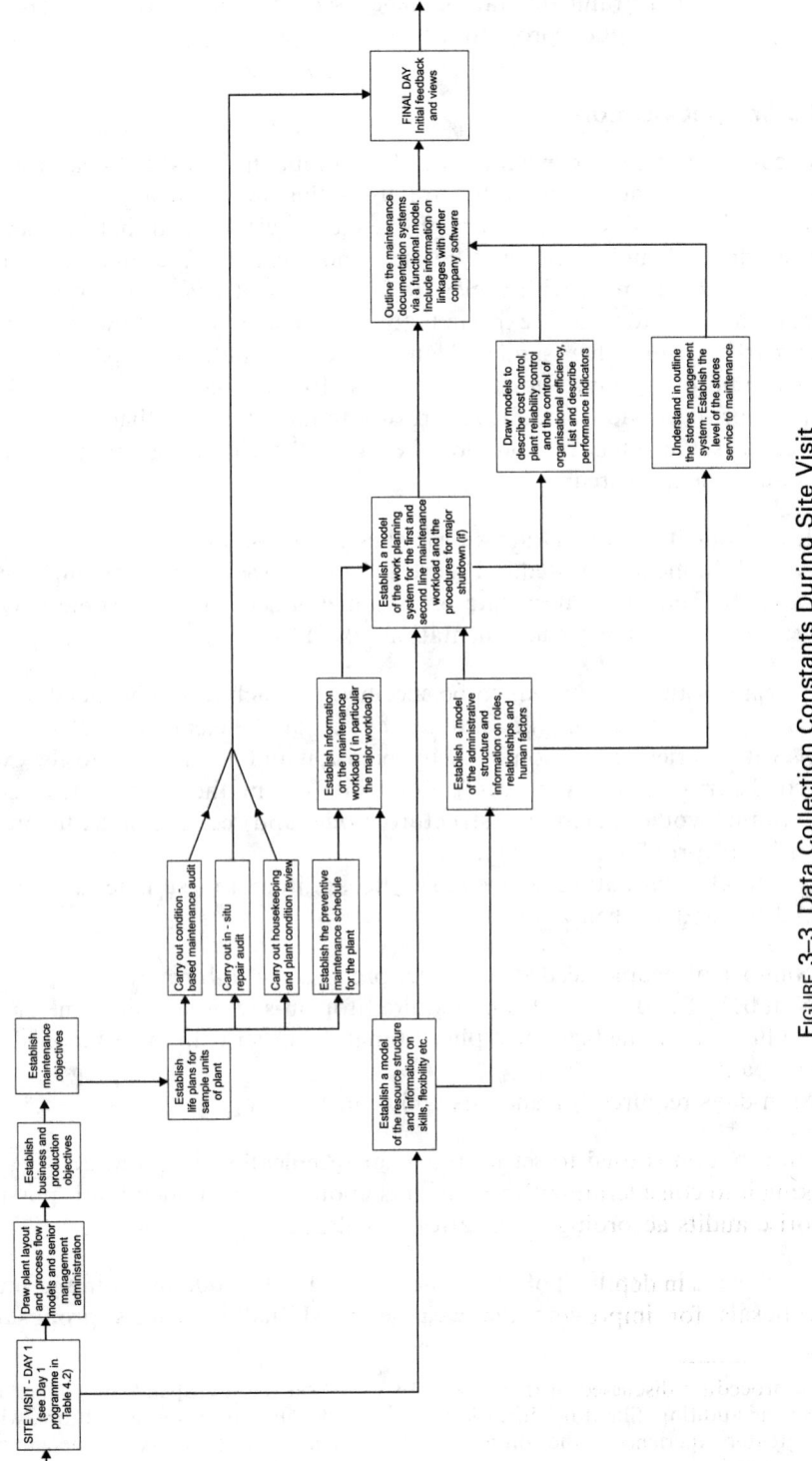

FIGURE 3-3 Data Collection Constants During Site Visit

structure. This constraint diagram can be used to assist in the construction of the on-site data collection programme.

(A) Audit Specification

The company management must be clear about the aims, scope and depth of the audit. If outside consultants* are used this must be agreed as a major condition of the audit contract. It might be clearly established that the **aim** of the audit is, for example, to map, model and describe the operation of the maintenance department with a view to identifying strengths and weaknesses— or that the auditors are expected to go further and show comparisons (benchmarks) with other similar plants. Are the auditors expected to make strategic and/or organizational proposals for overcoming the weaknesses identified, or to provide an audit report or a report plus a feedback presentation?

As regards the intended **scope** of the audit the following questions, among others, must be answered:

– If a multi-site company are all the sites to be included?
– Are all the elements listed in Figure 1–3 *to be covered*? (Some companies may want the audit to concentrate on organization or systems, some may want certain elements, e.g., documentation, excluded)

The **depth** of the study needs to be specified for each of the included elements. Do management want only an outline of each of the elements, i.e., mainly the models with a brief description of their operation and linkage. Or do they want a detailed description in every case? For example, in the case of the resource structure this would include the structure model and sections on skills profiling, human factor profiling, flexibility, etc.

This initial information will enable the auditors to estimate the resources required to conduct their audit, viz.:

– Number of people needed to collect pre-site visit information.
– Number of auditors and time required for on-site data collection.
– Audit programme facilitator plus estimate of other help to be supplied by the company.
– Man-days required for analysis and report writing.

This information is used to set up the **audit specification** and contract.

Taking into consideration the comments about scope and depth it is possible to categorise audits according to the effort involved, viz.:

Full: Covers in depth all of the elements listed in the aide-memoir and includes proposals for improving the weaknesses. Usually includes proposals for

---

*The procedure discussed in this chapter is based on the use of outside consultants to conduct the auditing. Slight modification would be required if in-house auditors, who will have a greater experience of the company and its systems but not the same independence of view, were used.

re-organization. For a large single-site company this can involve two auditors plus data collectors on site for up to three weeks.

Snapshot: Covers most elements in outline but some in depth. Always includes organizational models and highlights organizational weaknesses. For a medium-sized company employing, say, thirty maintenance personnel, this involves one auditor for up to five days on site.

Fingerprint: Covers the main elements (strategy and organization) superficially. It always includes the organization models in outline. It attempts to describe the essential characteristics of maintenance operation and to identify any main weakness. It can take as little as one day on-site.

Examples of each audit type are given in Part 2.

(B) Collection of Pre-Site-Visit Information

A list of typical pre-site-visit information is given in Appendix 2. It is required at least a fortnight before the start of the site visit. The following are the main reasons for acquiring it:

(i) To enable the auditors to use the organization chart to set up a preliminary interview program—taking into consideration the information that needs to be collected (see the aide-memoir, the constraints outlined in Figure 3–3 and the availability of personnel). At this stage only the first day is scheduled (see Table 3–2). In addition, the auditors pencil into the longer term program those interviewees with limited availability.

(ii) To enable the auditors to construct in outline some key models, e.g., of the resource structure, which help them put together an 'audit overview' on the first day of the site visit.

(iii) To save time on site, since collection of some of the pre-audit information is time consuming.

The auditors also request that the designated Facilitator (supplied by the company to assist during the on-site visit) is also responsible for collecting the pre-site-visit information.

(C) Site Visit: Day 1

The program for this is shown in Table 3–2, the audit beginning with the initial meeting with the senior plant manager (see Table 3–3). The main purpose of this meeting is to ensure that the objectives and scope of the audit have been clearly understood by the plant managers and the auditors.

The General Manager Maintenance, of an Aluminium Smelter in the Middle East had agreed that the scope of the audit should not include the maintenance administration. At the initial meeting the Managing Director insisted that, on the contrary, this be included, a clearly important revision which changed the audit specification.

Table 3-2 The Day 1 Programme

9.00–10.00	Initial meeting with senior manager(s) responsible for initiating the audit, see Table 3.3 for the agenda.
10.00–10.30	AK and HSR to obtain and discuss site layout and process flow diagrams (see Question 1 of the preliminary information questionnaire in Appendix 2).
10.30–12.30	Brief site tour to highlight critical units, areas of high maintenance costs, maintenance workshops and stores.
12.30–14.00	Working lunch (sandwiches)—AK and HSR to decide on itinerary for Days 2 and 3.
14.00–17.00	AK and HSR to obtain department overview from one (or at most two) senior managers, including the following elements of the audit-process flow diagrams; production and maintenance objectives; critical path units; maintenance life plans and preventive schedule; maintenance organization; maintenance work planning and documentation.
Evening	*AK and HSR to review information gathered. *Check whether Day 2 and 3 itinerary is still the best.
Note 1	In general AK and HSR will prepare their schedule at least two days ahead. However please indicate the availability of key people as soon as possible.
Note 2	DH will be on site to assist AK with the condition-based-audit. These dates are to be arranged.
Note 3	TL will be on site over 16th and 17th August and will set up a separate schedule.

The other purpose of the meeting is for the auditors to explain how the exercise will be conducted and to clarify outstanding administrative matters. In particular, they will want confirmation that all of those to be interviewed are aware of what the audit is about and have agreed to co-operate.

I was conducting a preliminary visit to the integral Power Station of an Alumina Refinery when I was instructed to leave by the Station Manager, who pointed out that he had not been aware that his area was to be included in the Refinery audit. The Power Station had, however, been included in the audit specification and this misunderstanding cost considerable time.

The remainder of Day 1 is devoted to obtaining an overview of the maintenance department—almost a fingerprint audit. The pre-audit information is an essential part of this task, e.g., the site layout and process flow diagrams are used during the plant visit, which is conducted in the morning and involves the first stage of the housekeeping and plant condition review—follow-up visits to each individual plant will be held as the audit progresses.

Over lunch the itinerary for Day 2 is confirmed and an outline for Day 3 drawn up, see Table 3-4. The Facilitator is responsible for arranging the interview schedule at least two days in advance. This scheduling process continues throughout the audit, taking into consideration the aide-memoir, the constraints

TABLE 3–3 Agenda for Day 1 Meeting with Senior Management

1. Introduce ourselves.
2. Confirm the audit specification (aims, scope and depth of audit).
3. Give 20-minute presentation of the structured approach to a maintenance audit.
4. Explain our method of working:
   We have a comprehensive and structured questionnaire, which I use as a guide through the audit.
   Our questions are probing and to the point; we hope staff will not misinterpret this as criticism or challenge.
   We interview on a 'one-to-one' basis. Most interviews last about one hour.
   We review our progress at regular intervals, e.g., lunch time, evenings and weekends.
   We decide on interviewees and topics on the basis of these review sessions. We may therefore wish to go back to some people for more detail or clarification.
5. Ask for support in the following areas:
   Response to the pre-site visit questionnaire.
   Opportunity to talk freely with any manager, supervisor, tradesmen, operator.
   Full co-operation of staff in providing access to information data, documents, etc.
   Availability of one manager (name, location, internal and home telephone number) as the Audit Facilitator when we need help or support, particularly in arranging interviews.
   Availability of an office as the base for work and private discussions.
   Access to a typist, copying machine, stationery, telephone, telex, etc.
6. Site rules
   Are there any site safety rules or other regulations or procedures that we need to be aware of as we move around site?
7. Arrange for daily transport to, from and across the site.
8. Agree on objectives and content of final round-up discussions at end of last day.

of Figure 3–3 and the availability of interviewees. The auditors update their programme every lunchtime and evening and, in practice, need to exercise considerable flexibility.

A maintenance department overview is put together during the afternoon with the assistance of a 'key' manager—one who has enough experience of the operation to enable the auditor, with the help of the pre-audit information, to assemble (at least in outline) the 'key models,' viz., of the resource structure, administrative structure, and of the work planning system. The key manager and Facilitator also help in clarifying the pre-audit information with regard to the equipment life plans and control systems.

This Day 1 overview is important because it gives the auditor(s) a 'maintenance *department* perspective' when they are auditing the individual elements.

(D) Site Visit Data Collection Programme

The remaining time on site is devoted to a data gathering exercise, the purpose of which is to collect, in the most efficient way, the information listed in the aide-memoir and the associated questionnaires.

TABLE 3–4 Day 2 and Day 3 of Audit On-Site Programme

	Auditor 1 (AK)		Auditor 2 (HSR)	
	Element	Interviewee	Element	Interviewee
Day 2				
9.00–12.00	Life Plans and P.M. schedule	R.M. Staff Eng. A.B. Ammonia Eng.	Objectives	R.H. Works Manager S.W. Ammonia Manager
		R.M. Staff Eng.		S.C. Technology Manager
12.00–13.00	Lunch			
	Review and share information and confirm Day 3 programme			
13.00–17.00	Life Plans and P.M. schedule	B.D. Tech Officer K.J. Tech Officer D.K. Rel. Manager K.J. Tech Officer	Maintenance resource structure	R.M. Staff Eng. K.G. W'shop Supt. R.M. Staff Eng. R.M. Staff Eng.
	Evening Session Review and share information and outline Day 4 programme Put together the interview agendas for Day 3 programme			
Day 3				
9.00–12.00	Life Plans and P.M. schedule	F.M. Tech Officer R.D. Urea Manager S.W. Amm. Manager	Maintenance resource structure	R.D. Urea Manager S.W. Amm. Manager F.P. Gran. Manager
12.00–13.00	Lunch			
	Review and share information and confirm Day 4 programme			
13.00–17.00	Life Plans Electrical	B.K. I/E Eng. B.K. I/E Eng. A.Y. E. Tech	Workload	B.S. Services Manager R.M. Staff Eng. B.S. Services Manager
	Plant review (2 hrs)	R.M. Staff Eng.		R.M. Staff Eng.
	Evening Session Review and share information and outline Day 5 programme Put together interview agendas for Day 4			

Table 3–4 shows the preliminary programme for the second and third days. It has been put together by reference to the aide-memoir and taking into consideration the constraints of Figure 3–3 and the audit scope. This provides the ideal data collection sequence. The Facilitator and the auditors identify the company personnel who can best provide the information needed. The interview list (see Table 3–4) is put together at least two days in advance. Plant and office visits are fitted into the schedule. Considerable flexibility has to be built into the programme.

When, as in the case illustrated, more than one auditor is involved, effort is made to communicate key data as quickly as possible, i.e., over lunchtime or evening sessions. Efforts are made to minimise overlaps of data collected and backtracking to data collected earlier. These sessions are also used to put together agendas for each of the subsequent days' interviews.

During recent audits I have found that in specialist areas considerable assistance can be provided by company personnel.

At an Ammonium Nitrate plant I involved, with the agreement of the management, the maintenance technicians in assembling the life plans and rotable spares holding for critical plant units (see Figure 3–1). From the point of view of the company this resulted in a considerable saving in audit time.

It is important to use some time in the evenings to re-inforce and tidy up the notes taken during the day.

This was not done in one of my early audits (of a Power Station), with the consequence that at the analysis and review stage the notes were difficult to understand and it was impossible to recall any of the discussions.

The evenings are also used by the auditors to discuss and record problems that have been identified during the day.

It is usual to arrange a final day meeting with the management to discuss the findings of the audit, it being emphasised that these can only be preliminary at that stage and may well change on further analysis. The meeting is useful for the auditors because it gives management an opportunity to respond to some of these findings.

(E) Analysis

The procedure here is best explained using the three sub-steps listed in Figure 3–2.

In Step 1 the information collected is used to establish a comprehensive picture of the existing maintenance management procedures. Each element of the methodology model of Figure 1–3 is analysed separately. The order of the analysis of the elements is guided by the constraints model (see Figure 3–3). This allows information to flow in the right direction, e.g., the completion of the resource structure is an essential precursor to analysis and modelling of the work planning arrangements. The description of each of the elements is aided by a combination of: conceptual models; schematic models; hard copy of actual data, forms and diagrams used as exhibits; performance indices.

In Step 2 it is identified where, for each of the elements, the company is doing well or where it is not. In the case of the problem areas the auditors outline possible causes for the difficulties. This analysis is aided by comparing each of the elements against management principles and guidelines, standard models and international benchmarks. At this stage the auditors also stand back and examine how the complete maintenance management system operates, i.e., how the elements fit together to allow the whole department to operate. They try to identify and rank the identified problems by their degree of importance.

Step 3 is concerned with developing improved strategy, organizational structure and maintenance systems. Where necessary, guidance is given on how to introduce the recommended changes in a phased manner.

TABLE 3–5 Audit Report Contents List

Section	Sub-section		Page	Models and Surveys
Executive Summary			(i) to (xxi)	
Introduction			1	
Overview			2	Site layout model. Plant process flow model. Senior management admin struct.
Objectives	Business		7	
	Maintenance		9	
	Comments and recommendations		12	
Maintenance strategy	Ammonia plant	Operating characteristics	18	
		Strategy outline	18	Ammonia processes flow model
		Syn-Gas life plan	18	Syn-Gas life plan
		Pressure vess. life plan	21	
		Ancillary equip. life plan	22	
		E/I life plan	23	
		Plant condition audit	25	
	Urea plant	Similar contents list to the ammonia plant	29	Urea plant process flow model. Amm. charge pump life plan. CO2 comp. life plan
	Granulation plant		34	Granulation plant process flow model
	Condition-based-maintenance		42	
		Vibration analysis	42	
		Oil monitoring	45	
		H.D.T.	47	
		Thermography	49	
		Perform. monitoring	50	
	Comments and recommendations		51	
Workload	Outline		55	Major workload profile
	Discussion		55	
Maintenance organization			59	
	Resource structure		59	Resource structure
	Comments and recommendations		68	Resource inventory. Survey of production views. Survey of tradesmens' comments. Proposed modified resource structure

TABLE 3–5 (*Continued*)

Section	Sub-section	Page	Models and Surveys
	Administrative structure	75	Ammonia admin. structure Urea admin. structure Granulation admin. structure Site services admin. structure Engineering admin. structure Matrix at Eng. level Senior staff matrix Staff inventory
	Comments and recommendations	85	Supervisor duties survey Team facilitator notes survey First line span of management Modified structure—proposal A Modified structure—proposal B
Maintenance systems		100	
	Short term work planning	100	Work planning model
	Comments and recommendations	104	
	Plant reliability control	107	Plant reliability control model
	Comments and recommendations	108	
	Turnaround planning	113	
	Comments	118	
	Spare part management	119	
	Comments and recommendations	121	
	Rotables	122	Rotable flow model
	Comments and recommendations	123	Rotable procedures model
	Maintenance control	127	
	Comments and recommendations	128	
	Maintenance documentation	129	
	Comments and recommendations	134	
13 Appendices		135	

(F) Reporting

The aim is to produce a report that covers all of the points raised in the specification. The best way of understanding this procedure is via the contents list of a full audit report (see Table 3–5).

The report follows the sequence shown in the methodology model, Figure 1–3. Each element is written up separately. For example, maintenance strategy has a section for each plant audited and includes a description of unit life plans, the preventive schedule and a plant condition review. The descriptions are supplemented by numerous models (see the right hand column). Each element concludes with a 'comments and recommendations' section.

The executive summary, in the illustrative case, see Table 3–5, is 22 pages long and welds together the models, comments and recommendations of each section into a cohesive report. Experience of numerous audits has taught me that the most valuable aspect of the exercise is that it provides senior management teams with an independent view of how the maintenance-production system works, and identifies the problems on which their focus needs to fall in deciding the way forward.

CHAPTER 4

Benchmarking, Benchmarks and Performance Indices

Introduction

I indicated in the previous chapter that, at the analysis stage of an audit, 'benchmarking' to compare the company's performance with industry best practice may be usefully employed. Before moving on to the case studies section of the book we will therefore describe this activity, especially as it is applied to maintenance, in more detail.

Benchmarks and Benchmarking

The dictionary definition of the *benchmark* is:

A surveyor's mark, cut in a rock, to indicate a reference point in a line of levels for the determination of altitudes over the face of the country.

This is the original, land surveying, definition of the benchmark—a reference point for subsequent measurements. In the 1970s this idea was interpreted in the world of industrial management as follows:

'Benchmarking is the search for industry best practices that lead to superior performance.'[1]

The benchmarking procedure involves the following main steps:

1. Identify that division of your own organization (e.g., the maintenance department) the management and/or performance of which is to be benchmarked.
2. Identify a best-performing counterpart, elsewhere but in the same industrial sector, that can be used as a 'standard of comparison.'
3. Identify the practices, structures and systems that best describe the operation of the division under study.

---

[1]C. E. Bogan and J. M. English, *Benchmarking for Best Practice,* McGraw Hill, 1994.

4. Identify the benchmarks that can be used to quantify and measure the management and/or performance of the division under study.
5. Identify the practices, structures and systems that best describe the operation of the 'standard of comparison.'
6. Use the identified benchmarks to compare the management and/or performance of the division under study with that of the 'standard of comparison' and identify the reasons for any observed shortfalls or performance gaps.
7. In the light of the findings from Step 6, propose an action plan for improving the practices in the division of your own which is under study.

A generic model of a benchmarking process proposed by Camp[2] is shown in Figure 4–1.

One of the most publicized applications of benchmarking in maintenance was carried out by DuPont Chemicals who, in 1986, benchmarked sixteen of its chemical plants against an equivalent number of industry leaders.[3] It showed that the company's maintenance cost was up to 30% higher than that of the best comparative companies. In addition, DuPont employed 20% more tradeforce, 50% less planning personnel and 15% less maintenance support staff. The company accepted that there was a performance gap and set in place an improved, cost-reducing, maintenance strategy (see Figure 4–2).

Using the Audit Procedure for Benchmarking

The auditing procedure outlined in Chapter 3 provides a means not only of modelling and mapping a given maintenance department but also of identifying the appropriate benchmarks for comparing that department against the best of its kind in industry, i.e., for 'benchmarking' it (see, for example, the Key Performance Indicators (KPIs) identified in the audit *aide-memoire*, Appendix 1). The following are brief descriptions of applications of the latter kind.

1. Benchmarking the Maintenance Departments of Coal Fired Power Stations

A postgraduate project was aimed at benchmarking the maintenance departments of base-load coal-fired power stations operating steam-driven 300 MWe turbo-alternators.[4] Fourteen stations were benchmarked world-wide, using the fingerprint audit technique (see page 155) Key benchmarks were used to compare performance (see Figure 4–3 and Table 4–1). In addition, information was obtained on the key maintenance practices, structures and systems in use at each station. Figure 4–4 shows an extract from the tables of overhaul cycles

---

[2]R. C. Camp, *Benchmarking*, American Society for Quality, 1989.

[3]B. Holmes, *Benchmarking Best Practice in Maintenance*, EIT Maintenance Conference, Australia, 1997.

[4]K. Gallagher, *MSc Thesis*, University of Manchester, 1991.

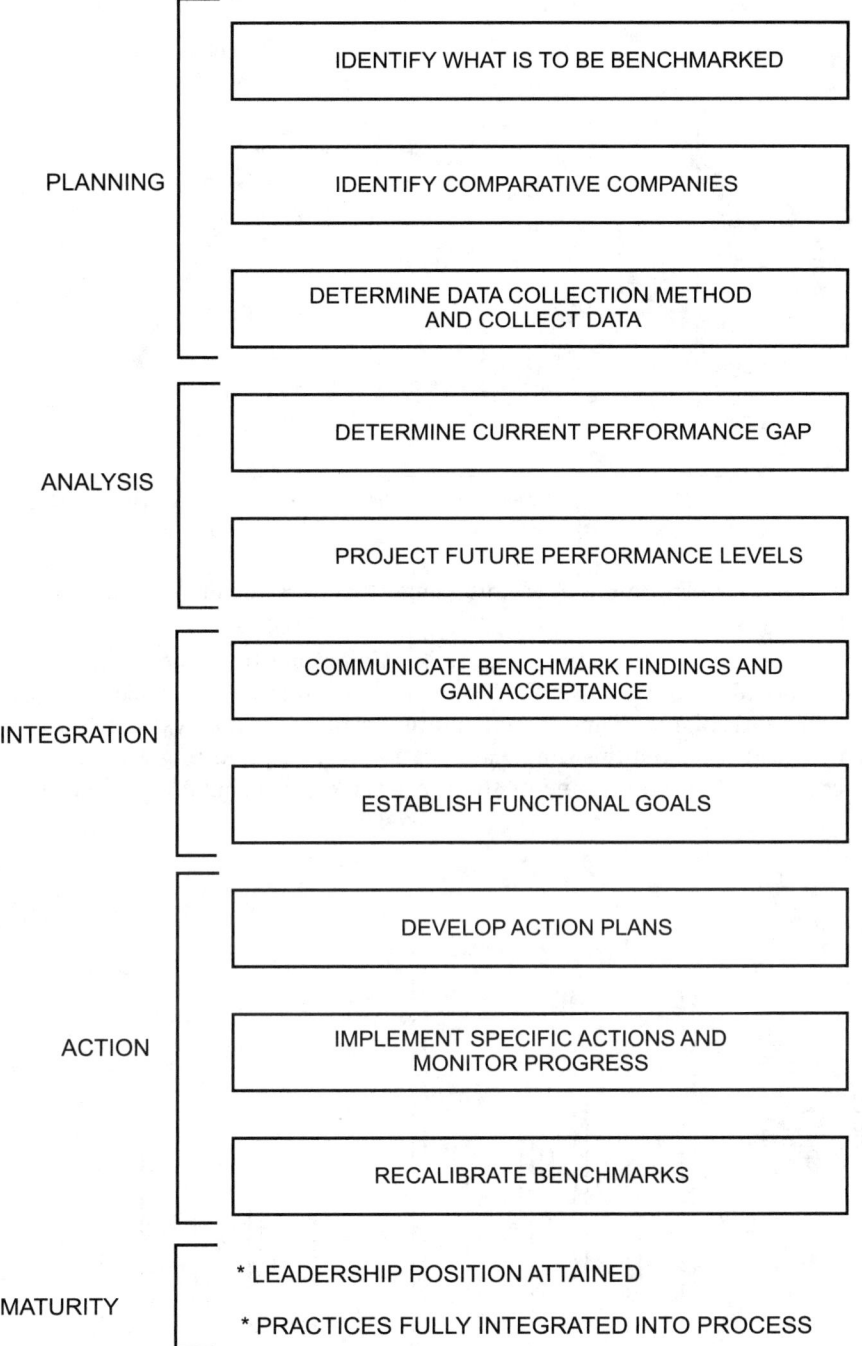

FIGURE 4–1 Steps in Generic Benchmarking Process

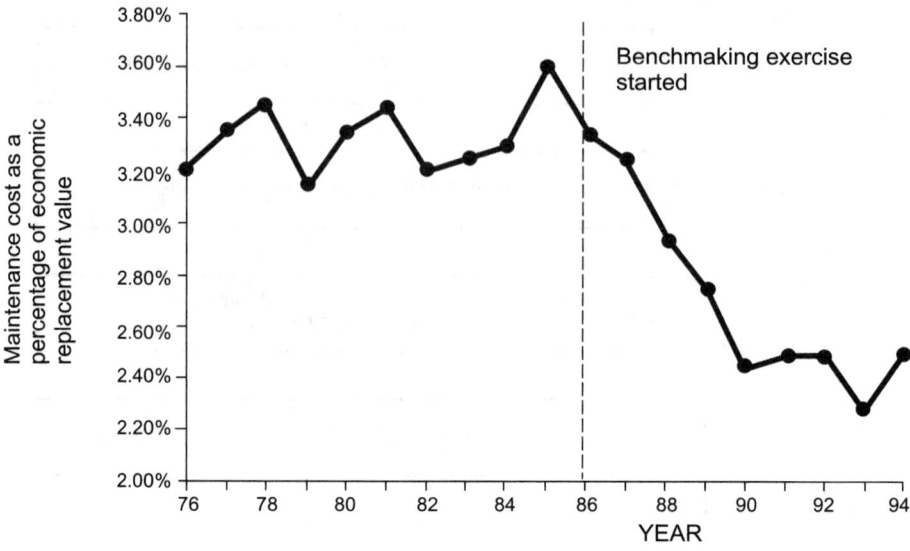

FIGURE 4-2 Improvement in Maintenance Cost as a Result of Benchmarking

(maintenance strategy practice), Figure 4-5 an extract from the modelling of the organizational structures. Similar comparative models were assembled for the resource, work planning and documentation structures and systems.

The conclusion from this simple application of benchmarking was that caution is needed in interpreting some of the top level key benchmarks as indicators of

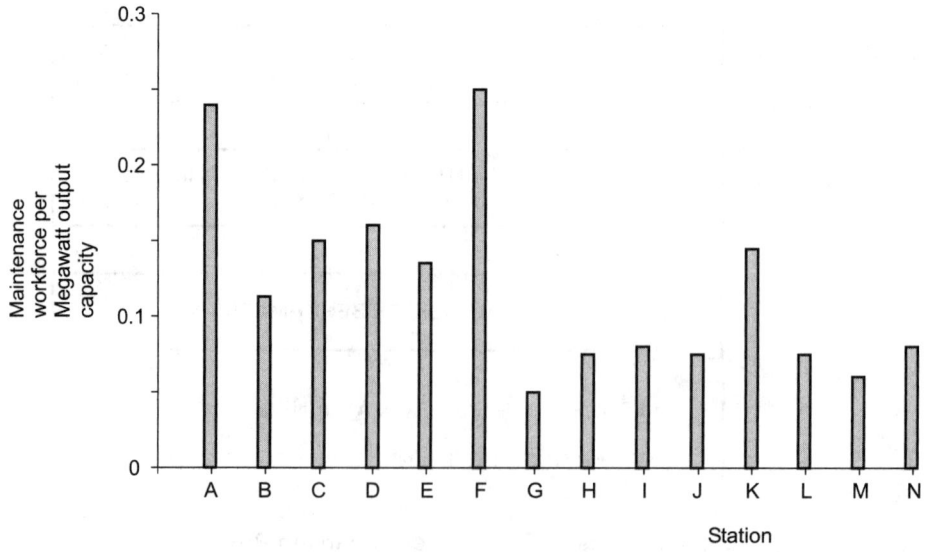

FIGURE 4-3 International Comparison of Power Station Maintenance Benchmarks

TABLE 4–1 Extract from an International Comparison of Power Station Benchmarks

Station	Units	Availability	Thermal Efficiency	Annual Budget £M	Tradeforce Total	Tradeforce Fitters	Engineering and Technical Staff in Maint.	First Line Supervisors	Planning Staff
A	3 × 300	82	38	4	165	51	3	17	9
D	4 × 300	84	34	3.25	187	54	20	20	14
G	4 × 300	86	35	2.5	50	24	3	20	2
M	4 × 350	94	35	3.75	83	23	22	12	3

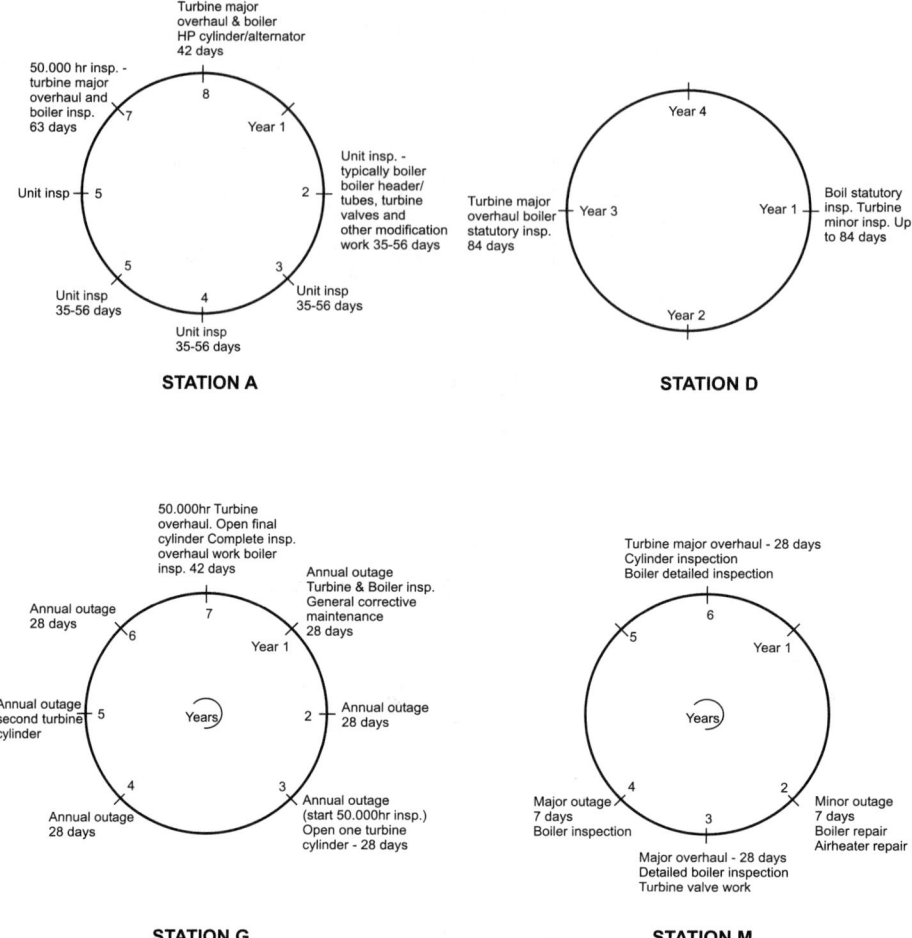

FIGURE 4–4 Extract from an International Comparison of Power Station Overhauls

maintenance performance. For example, a possible interpretation of the data displayed in Figure 4–3 was that Station M scored highest in terms of maintenance productivity. On closer investigation, however, it was found that the main reason for this apparent superiority was that the designers of this station had selected the most reliable and maintainable plant. That is not to say that the benchmarking information was not important; it could be used to influence decisions regarding future plant acquisition, for example. The maintenance practices at Station M were by no means the 'best of the best', however.

This result is not untypical of my experience in trying to use performance indices to benchmark best practice. Even when comparing the maintenance of power stations of roughly the same size there are many differences—in detailed design, technology, manufacture, age—that exercise greater influence on the indices than do such aspects as the maintenance life plan or work planning

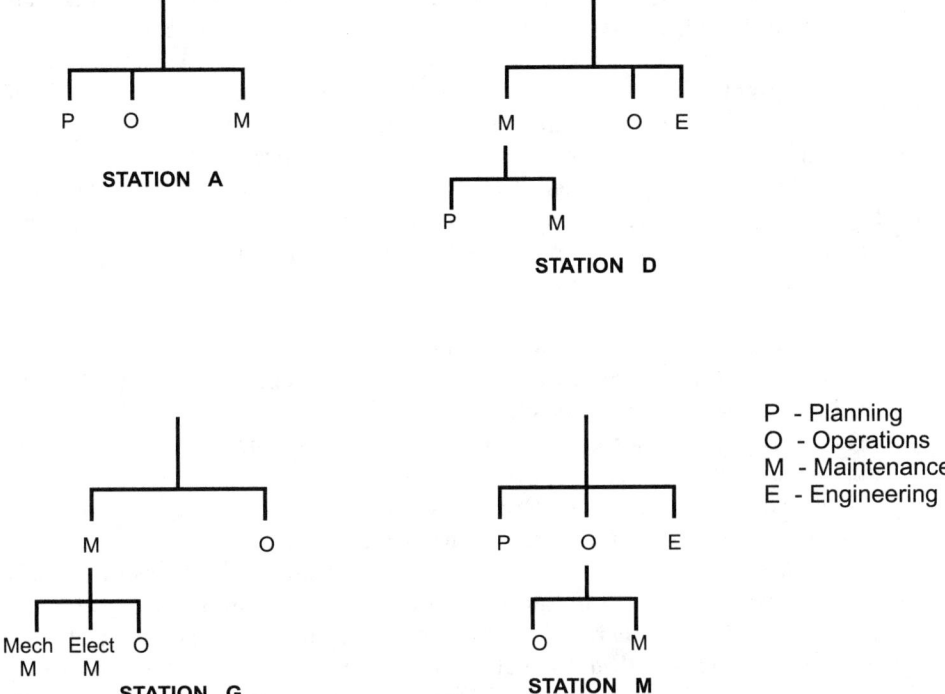

FIGURE 4–5 Extract from an International Comparison of Power Station Administrative Structures

systems. Normalisation techniques can be used to compensate for some of these differences, but care must still be exercised when evaluating the results.

Nevertheless, much information that was useful for the sponsoring company came out of this exercise. They were able to see clearly that they were overmanned and would need to improve inter-trade and operator-maintenance flexibility, and reduce the number of first line supervisors on site (via empowerment). In addition they could see that the organizational trend (in particular in the USA) was towards contractor alliances.

2. Benchmarking Operator–Maintainer Teams

I recently carried out a full audit of maintenance at a chemical plant (Fertec B Ltd), see page 89. For several years the company had been using operator–maintainer teams. Self-empowered and plant-oriented, they were expected to both operate and carry out simple first line maintenance tasks for their own area of plant.

The audit revealed that the teams were not working well. However, a sister plant (Cario Ltd) within the same organization, was reported to be using such teams successfully. I decided to carry out a simple benchmarking exercise, to compare the practices of the teams of Fertec with those of the teams at Cario.

Fertec B Ltd—was an integrated chemical complex made up of six plants. The administrative structure was de-centralised and each plant was considered as a distinct manufacturing unit. Figure 4–6 shows the administrative structure for one of the main plants, Figure 4–7 the corresponding resource structure. The self-empowered teams had been introduced some five years earlier using the conventional wisdom of the time (see, for example, Figure 4–8 for the guidelines for moving from traditional supervision to self-empowerment). A Team Manager (see Figure 4–6) was brought in, mainly to help to resurrect the training process in the operator teams. The following were some of my principal observations regarding the team operations:

— '25% of the process teams were incorporated ex-tradesmen.
— 'The process teams undertook no first-line maintenance tasks despite this being a part of their responsibilities.
— 'The process teams seemed to be a law unto themselves, with a wholly negative human factors impact.
— 'The ratio of managers, planners and facilitators to 'on-the-tools' technicians in the maintenance teams was 2.8 to 1.
— 'The planner was introduced when a new computer system was installed; it was regarded as user unfriendly and the associated training was poor.
— 'The maintenance teams did not operate as self-empowered. They had reverted to the traditional structure (where the facilitator is the supervisor).
— 'The facilitator and planner positions were permanencies.
— 'There was a genuine confusion over the roles of the planner, facilitator and some of the technicians. In addition, there was no clear understanding of the roles of the plant engineer and process engineer and their relationships to the teams. Job descriptions were not used or were not available.
— 'The teams didn't monitor themselves nor did they get involved in continuous improvement activities.
— 'Flexibility between mechanical trades, and between instrument and electrical trades, was good. Demarcation remained strong, however, between the two technological cultures (mechanical and electro-instrumentational).
— 'The maintenance technicians were rotated, on a two-yearly basis, around the teams of the different plants.
— 'There was no rotation between maintenance and process technicians.
— 'Maintenance technicians were on an annualised-hours scheme; the process technicians were not (which didn't help co-ordination when work was required out of hours).
— 'The plant was some thirty years old and gave rise to a great deal of first line high-priority maintenance. Because of their involvement with this, the maintenance teams (on days) only carried out 50% of the planned work per 'period—and it was often the preventive routines that, as a result, were omitted.
— 'Out of hours emergency work was covered by a call-out system that was regularly used.

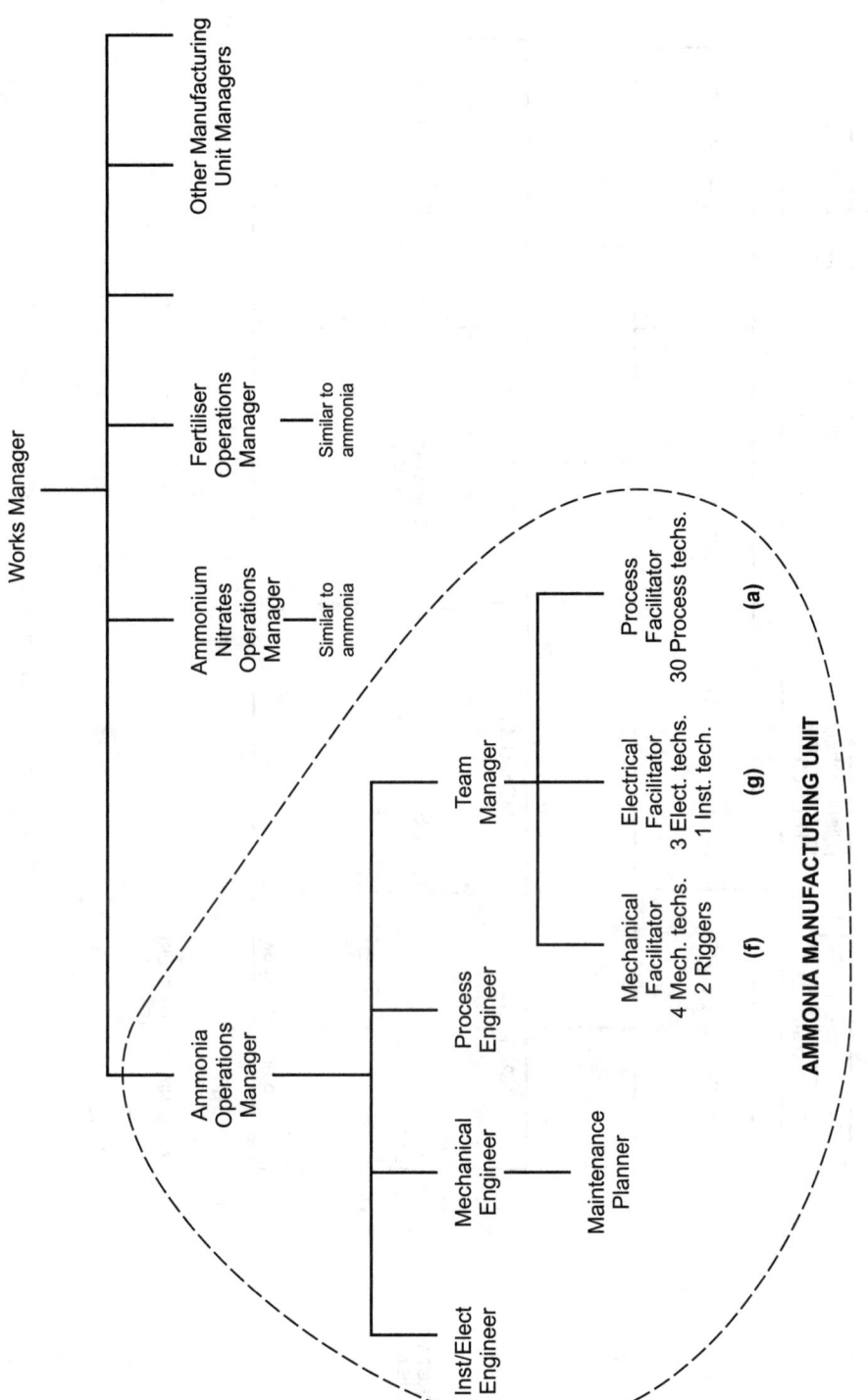

FIGURE 4–6 Administrative Structure, Ammonia Manufacturing Unit

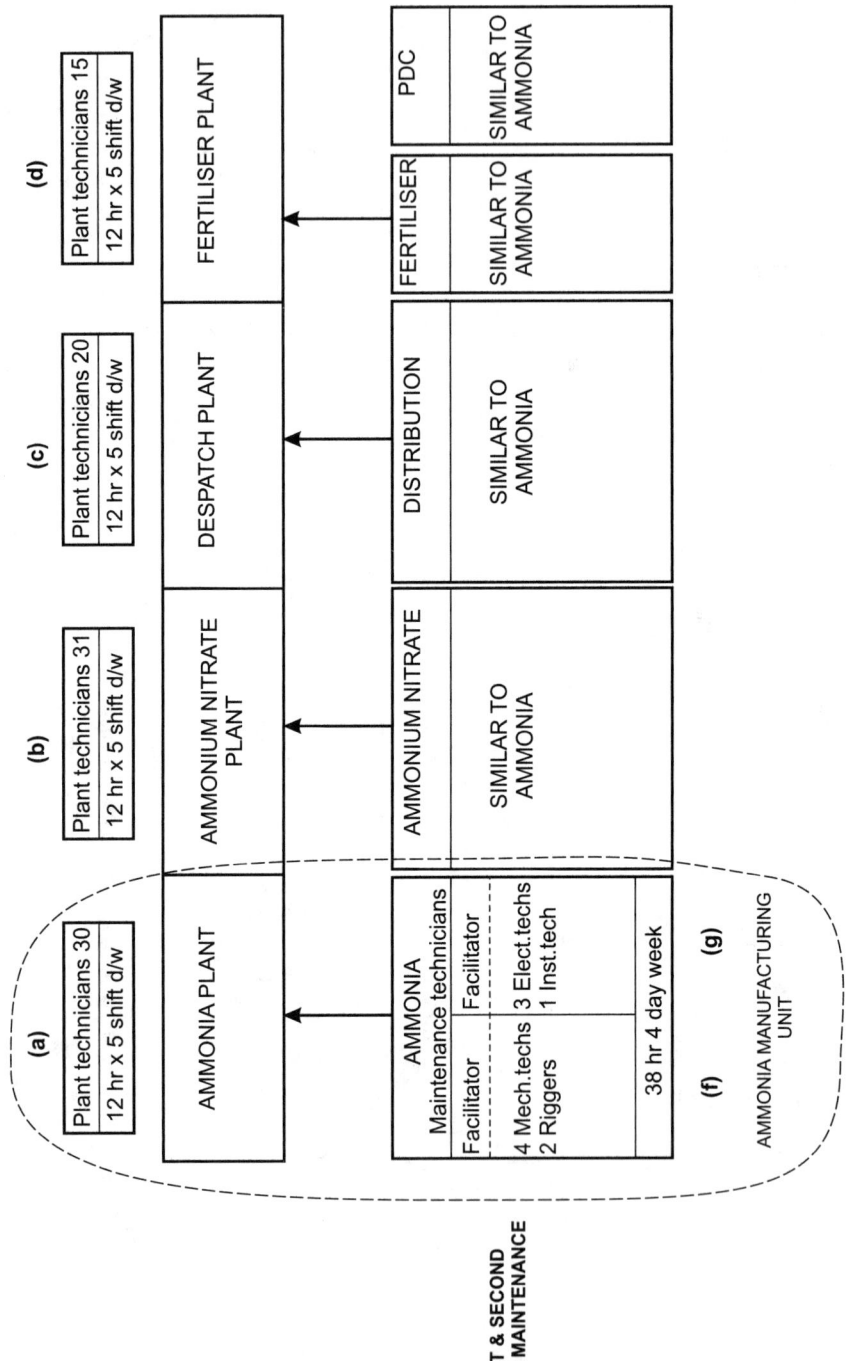

FIGURE 4–7 Resource Structure, Fertec B Ltd

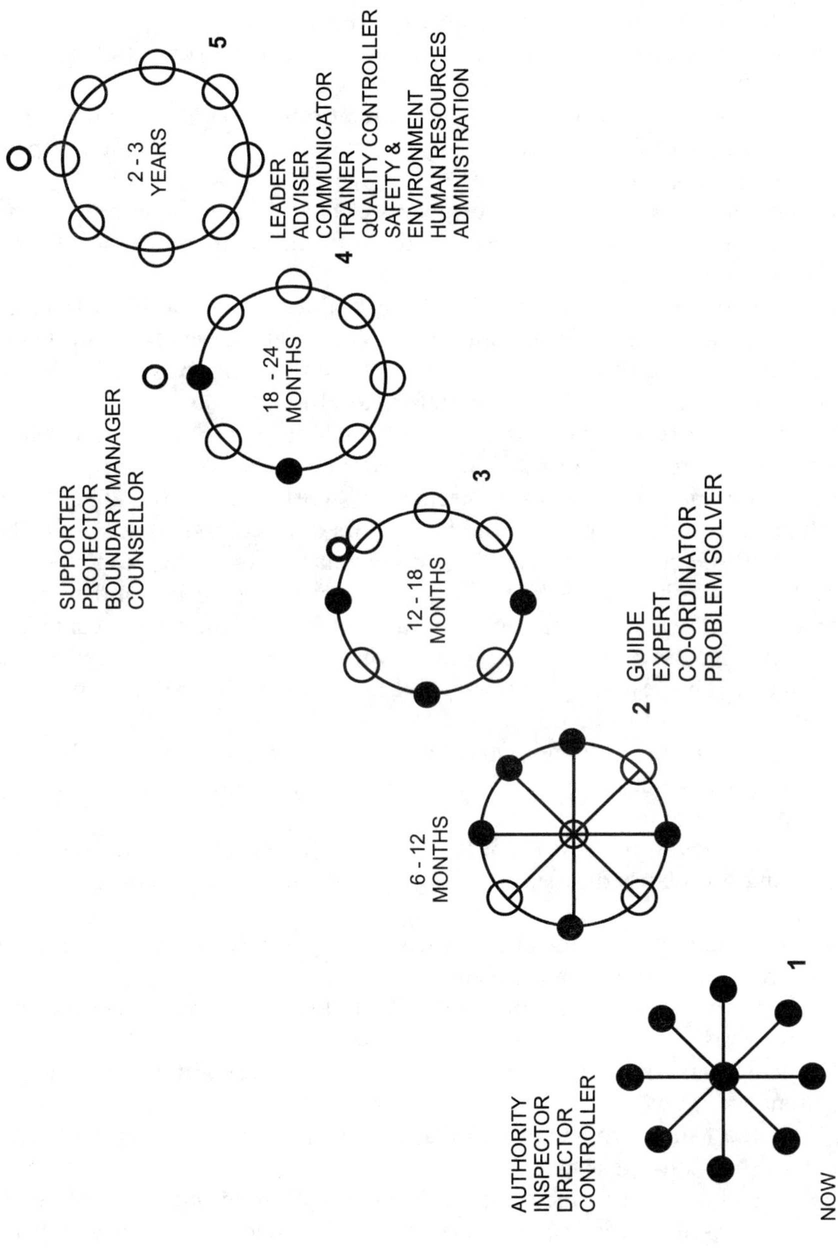

FIGURE 4-8 The Five Steps from Traditional Supervisor to Self-Empowered Team with Facilitator

— 'Team-working had been introduced into a 'brown field' site where there was a considerable history of industrial relations problems. There was no human factor profiling in the selection of team members. Considerable training was used at first but rapidly fell away.

Cario Ltd—was a similar company to Fertec B but only six years old. The administration is shown in Figure 4–9 and the resource structure in Figure 4–10. As regards its team operations:

— 'Some 40% of the process teams were ex-tradesmen.
— 'The process teams carried out minor preventive work (lubrication, inspection) and small emergency corrective jobs.
— 'The process teams (on shifts) had a good relationship with the maintenance teams and human factors were mainly positive. They were the highest paid of the shop floor workers.
— 'In each team there was a planner, team-selected every three-months, who spent little time on the tools. Overall, the ratio of planners to on-the-tools tradesmen was 1 to 5.
— 'The planners and tradesmen had been trained up to a high level of competence in the use of the computer system—which was far from being the most advanced of its kind and was not installed enterprise-wide (it *was* user friendly, however, and *was* therefore used).
— 'The maintenance and process teams were self-empowered, accountability for duties and responsibilities being shared across each team
— 'The two planners (electrical and mechanical) worked out of the same office. In effect, the planners became the facilitators and worked closely with the day-shift Production Planner (PP) to co-ordinate plant outages etc.
— 'The PP was volunteered from shifts, for a one-year period and without losing shift allowance, being replaced on shifts by a maintenance technician (with the necessary experience), and who in turn was replaced by a contractor. This exchange helped to break down the barriers between Maintenance and Production.
— 'The roles of the team, Planner and Engineer had been clearly identified and written up as job descriptions. The Engineer considered himself to be very much part of the team.
— 'The teams spent a proportion of their time on design-out maintenance and improving life plans, these tasks being carried out in conjunction with the Engineer.
— 'The electrical and mechanical teams worked separately but gave each other considerable assistance when needed.
— 'The payment scheme was the same for both the maintenance and the process teams.
— 'The plant was six years old and gave rise to very little high-priority maintenance.
— '95% of the teams' workload was planned. In fact, one of their objectives was have 'no call-outs—ever!'.
— 'The teams had been formed during the commissioning phase of the plant. Profiling of skills and human factors was used to select the team members.

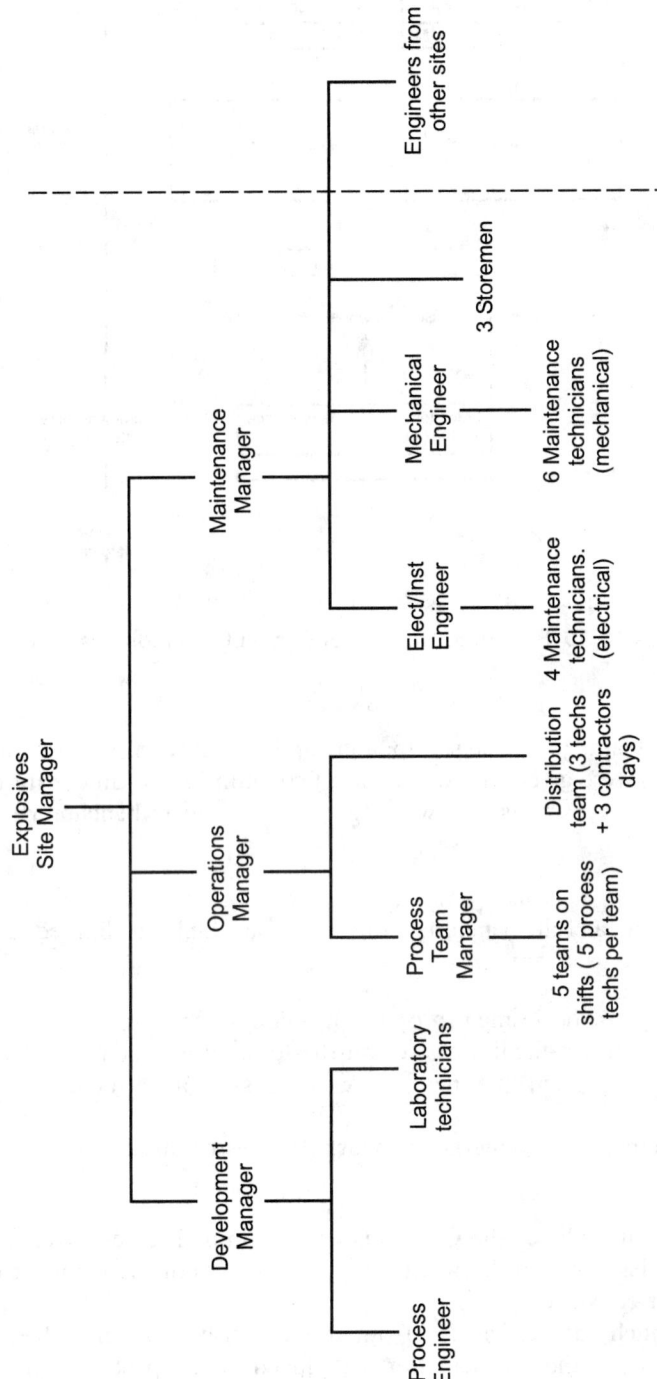

FIGURE 4–9 Administrative Structure, Cario Ltd Explosives Plant

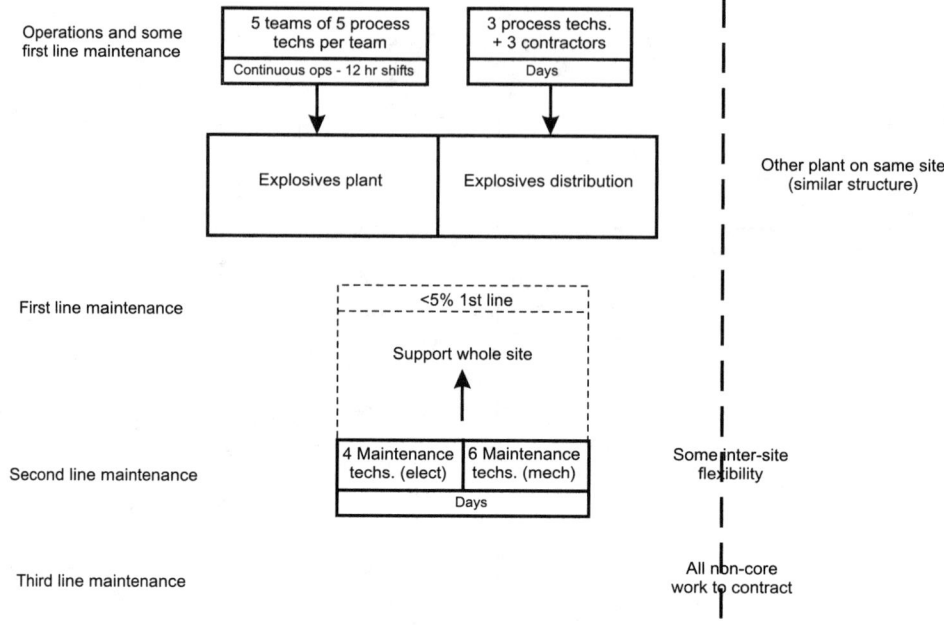

FIGURE 4–10 Resource Structure, Cario Ltd Explosives Plant

Once the teams had been set up, a group from the company (including team members) were given the equivalent of six months full-time team-training at a similar site overseas that was regarded as a world benchmark.

Comment

This was not a full benchmarking exercise. Only a limited number of benchmarks were used, viz.:

— 'percentage of tradesmen in operator–maintainer teams,
— 'ratio of planner–facilitators to 'on-the-tools' tradesmen,
— 'maintenance team planned work (expressed as a percentage of each period),
— 'maintenance team emergency work (expressed as a percentage of each period).

The fingerprint audit of the Cario teams was limited to just over half a day's work, nevertheless, the gap between the performances of the teams at Cario and of those at Fertec was clear.

Although much can be learned from this exercise about how best to set up teams, this was not the problem Fertec B faced. Their process teams were not working well and were refusing to carry out *first line* work. Consequently, the day-maintenance teams were carrying out all such work, which was disrupting their *planned* work. The preventive work was being neglected, causing more corrective work and a downward spiral in plant condition. We recommended that a key action would be to *insist* that the process teams carried out first line work. This would need a careful study of the process teams' work profiles and a resurrection of the skills training. It might also be necessary to re-structure the teams, perhaps removing the 'bad apples'—all of which might have worsened industrial relations, which was the reason these actions had not been taken sooner. An additional recommendation was that the duties, responsibilities and accountability of the teams, and their relationships with other members of the administration, should be clearly defined.

In the longer term other improvements could have been made, e.g., bringing Operations and Maintenance into the same payment system; improving computer training so that the facilitator does the planning; etc.

The Uses and Limitations of 'Universal Maintenance Performance Indices' in Maintenance Auditing

In general, the conventional audit procedure does not involve comparing the audited plant directly with a 'best practice' plant. Instead, at the analysis stage of the audit the practices of the plant under study are compared against management principles and guidelines, standard models, the auditors' own experience of best practice and published or unpublished *'maintenance management performance indices'*—benchmarks by any other name. I call these *'universal benchmarks.'* It will be instructive to examine them in more detail.

Several index-based approaches to measuring maintenance performance have been developed.[5,6] These *published* methods were developed for use in controlling the maintenance effort (setting objectives, measuring performance and correcting as necessary—see page 23) rather than for inter-firm comparison. Industrial examples of the use of these methods for either control or inter-firm comparison are hard to find.

I have come across a number of *unpublished* methods for inter-firm comparisons. Table 4–2, for example, has been extracted from Eastman Ectona's indices for measuring organizational efficiency.[7] The indices have been developed for a specific type of chemical plant and process. Table 4–3 is an extract from the Fluor Daniel 'best-of-the-best' maintenance benchmarks.[8] There are 24 benchmarks in total, some of which, e.g., *Availability,* have been measured for different types of processes. Fluor Daniel emphasised that they can identify the best practices that go along with the top quartile benchmarks. Tables 4–4(a) and (b)

---

[5]A. K. S. Jardine, *Operation Research in Maintenance*, Manchester University Press, 1970.

[6]C. C. Rostad and P. Schjoberg, *Key Performance Indicators*, Euromaintenance Conference, Gothenburg, 2000.

[7]I. Bendall, *Maintenance Control*. Paper given on a short course at Manchester School of Engineering, 1999.

[8]Fluor Daniel, *Best of Best Maintenance Benchmarks*. Internal paper, 1998.

TABLE 4–2 Organizational Efficiency KPIs—Eastman Ectona

Measures/Indices	Description and Comments
Number of different trades employed	Measure the amount of flexibility Range 2–4
Plant investment/maintenance tradesman	Measure of organizational effectiveness
Total number hours on maintenance	Includes onsite contractors and work sent off site
Absenteeism	Can be indicative of morale of workforce Less than 2%
Overtime	Can be used to look at effectiveness of planning/support systems
Ratio of maintenance tradesmen/first line supervision	Indicative of span of control, and level of autonomy Range 15–25
Ratio of maintenance tradesmen/direct support personnel	Support includes: planners, engineers, stores and first line supervision Range 2–3.5
Ratio of maintenance tradesmen/Maintenance planners	Indicative of the amount of planning support given Range 10–25
Ratio of maintenance tradesmen/Total plant employees	Useful for comparison of manning levels

have been extracted from the results of a world-wide benchmark study of ammonia plants of a similar size.[9] A UK consultancy company has carried out 'self assessment' audits of maintenance managements for many years and has built up a considerable benchmark data base—although this has not been published.

In general, benchmarks such as these are not sufficiently well-defined for general use. The ammonia plant benchmarks, however, are sufficiently specific to industry, process and plant size to be of use if it were possible to get hold of a full set (with the qualifying assumptions). The Fluor Daniel benchmarks are only usable if that consultancy company itself carries out the benchmarking exercise. In addition, they need clearer definition and greater orientation to the type of industry being audited.

Some Thoughts on Developing Maintenance Benchmarks

Not enough thought has gone into identifying and ranking benchmarks that adequately measure the performance of the maintenance department. They should be based on the maintenance objective and on the derived hierarchy of

---

[9]PSI, *International Benchmarking Study of Ammonia Plant Performance*, 1997.

TABLE 4–3 Table of Quartiles for 'Best of Best' Benchmarks by Fluor Daniel

Benchmark	Quartile			
	Lowest	Third	Second	Top
OSHA injuries per 200,000 hours	> 5.5	5.5–3.1	3.0–1.0	< 1.0
Mechanic wrench time	< 31	31–41	42–52	> 52
Percentage of work that is planned	< 65	66–78	79–94	> 95
Request compliance percentage	< 68	68–77	78–90	> 90
Schedule compliance percentage	< 15	15–35	36–70	> 70
Work order discipline percentage	< 54	55–83	84–95	> 95
PM, percentage undertaken by operators	0	0–9	10–24	> 25
Stores/Replacement value (percentage)	> 1.3	1.3–8	0.7–0.3	< 0.3
Replacement value ($MM) per mechanic	< 3.2	3.2–5.0	5.0–7.5	> 7.5
Suggestions per mechanic per year	not measurable	< 0.5	0.5–4	> 4
Stores turnover	< 0.5	0.5–0.7	0.7–1.2	> 1.2
Stores service level	< 93	93–96	97–99	> 99
Percentage of costs incurred via contractors	< 8	8–19	20–40	> 40
Maintenance cost/Total sales (percentage)	> 8	8–7	6–3	< 3
Stores issues/Total material (percentage)	> 82	82–68	67–20	< 19
Maintenance cost/Replacement cost (percentage)				
Discrete	> 5.0	5.0–3.2	3.2–2.0	< 2.0
Batch process	> 3.5	3.5–3.2	3.2–2.4	< 2.4
Chemical, refining, power	> 4.8	4.8–3.0	3.0–2.5	< 2.5
Paper	> 9.0	9.0–5.5	5.5–3.2	< 3.2
Availability (percentage)				
Discrete	< 78	78–84	85–91	> 91
Batch process	< 72	72–80	81–90	> 90
Chemical, refining, power	< 85	85–90	91–95	> 95
Paper	< 83	83–86	87–94	> 94
Total equipment effectiveness	Not measurable	< 48	48–70	> 70
Training and staffing ratios				
Span of control	< 9	9–17	18–40	> 40
Mechanics per effective planner	< 25	25–59	60–80	> 80
Mechanics per plant worker (percentage)	> 32	32–21	20–10	< 10
Total craft designations	> 7	7–6	5–3	2
Training hours per mechanic	< 40	41–69	70–80	> 80
Training cost per mechanic	< 500	501–1800	1801–3000	> 3000

TABLE 4–4(a) International Benchmarking Study of 1000 tpd Ammonia Plants — Output Factors (extract)

	North America	Europe	Rest of World	Total
Plant outages (days/year)	10.4	15.8	16.7	14.1
Plant shutdowns (days/year)	9	14.7	17	13.5
Plant related (days/year)	19.4	30.5	33.7	27.6
Service factor	94.7%	91.6%	90.7%	92.4%
Time between shutdowns	—	—	—	
Av. shutdown time	—	—	—	—
Energy efficiency Gj/t	—	—	—	—
Downtime				—
Total downtime (days/year)	21	32.3	36.2	29.5
Onstream factor	94.2%	91.2%	90.1%	91.9%

TABLE 4–4(b) International Benchmarking Study of 1000 tpd Ammonia Plants—Cost of Production Factors (extract)

Gas usage per day	—
Gas conversion eff. Gj/t	—
Gas cost $/ton	(112)
Elect cost $/ton	—
Water $/ton	—
Operation labour $/ton	(6.0)
Maint. labour $/ton	(2.3)
Contract labour $/ton	—
Total production cost $/ton	

objectives shown in Figure 1–5. Figure 4–11 shows this model extended and developed into a hierarchy of performance indices. The indices indicated at the lowest level in Figure 4–11 could be developed further via consideration of each of the sections of the Appendix 1 *aide-memoire*. When developing indices for comparing one firm with another it should also be borne in mind that:

- the indices may well need further separate definition for different types of industry or process,
- the indices shown in Figure 4–11 have been developed for the purposes of maintenance control ('*Are we getting better/worse, and, if so, why?*') and may need modification.

The highest level indices are the KPIs, but these are much more difficult to define than those at lower level. In the power generation industries I have seen a *maintenance productivity index (MPI)* defined as:

$$\text{MPI} = \frac{\text{Output in Megawatt-hours per period}}{\text{Total maintenance cost per period}},$$

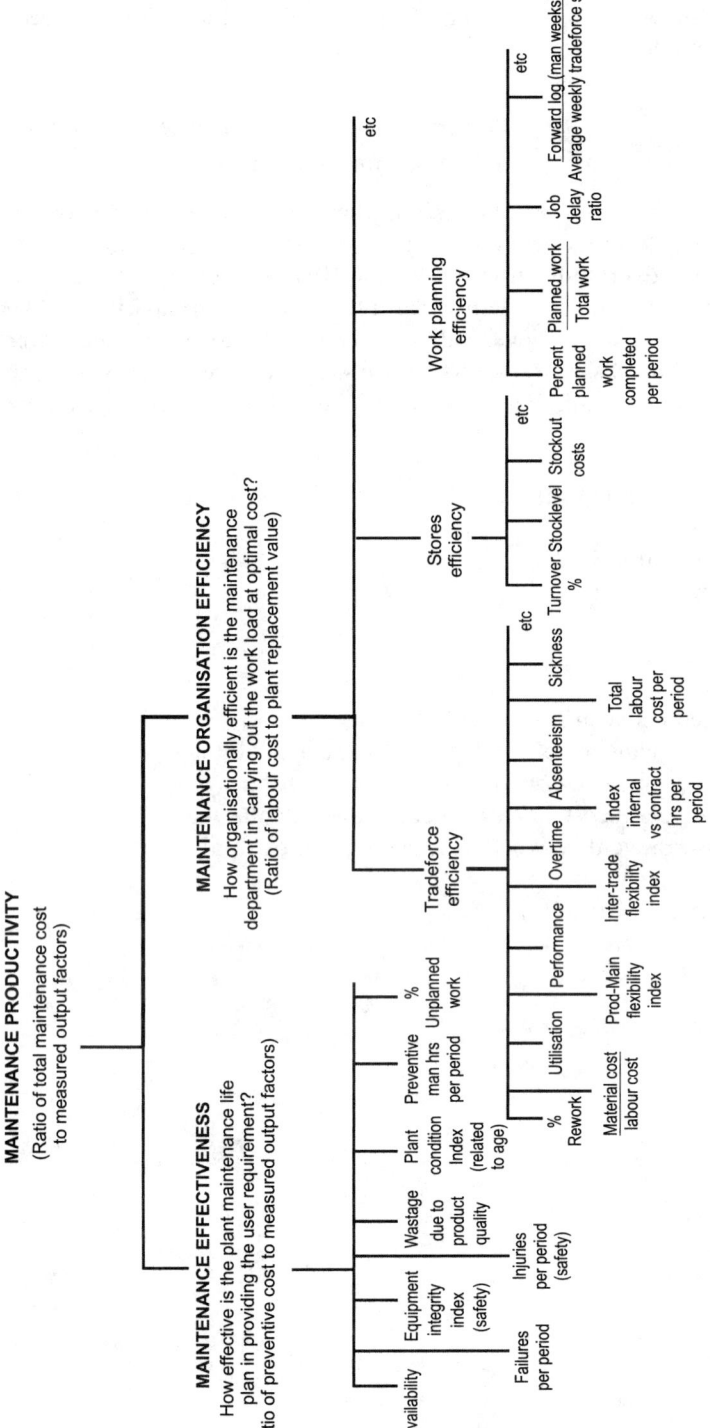

MAINTENANCE PRODUCTIVITY
(Ratio of total maintenance cost
to measured output factors)

MAINTENANCE EFFECTIVENESS
How effective is the plant maintenance life
plan in providing the user requirement?
(Ratio of preventive cost to measured output factors)

MAINTENANCE ORGANISATION EFFICIENCY
How organisationally efficient is the maintenance
department in carrying out the work load at optimal cost?
(Ratio of labour cost to plant replacement value)

Availability
Failures per period
Equipment integrity index (safety)
Injuries per period (safety)
Wastage due to product quality
Plant condition Index (related to age)
Preventive man hrs per period
Unplanned work %

Tradeforce efficiency
Rework %
Material cost / labour cost
Utilisation
Prod-Main flexibility index
Performance
Inter-trade flexibility index
Overtime
Index internal vs contract hrs per period
Absenteeism
Total labour cost per period
Sickness
etc

Stores efficiency
Turnover %
Stocklevel
Stockout costs
etc

Work planning efficiency
Percent planned work completed per period
Planned work / Total work
Job delay ratio
Forward log (man weeks) / Average weekly tradeforce size
etc

FIGURE 4–11 Hierarchy of Maintenance Performance Indices

the period extending at least from one major overhaul to the next. In the food processing industry, however, an equipment replacement value (ERV) features strongly in its performance indices, i.e.:

$$\text{Organizational efficiency} = \frac{\text{Total maintenance cost per period}}{\text{Equipment replacement value}}$$

Indices of both kinds present problems. In the former case the period of comparison has to be at least six years if it is to allow adequately for the various lengths of time between overhauls; in the latter the ERV is extremely difficult to define in a way that can be used consistently for inter-company comparisons. The best way of measuring the higher level indices may well be to profile the lower level ones. The benchmarks suitable for profiling the effectiveness of the maintenance of a production-limited ammonia plant, for example, could be those in the following list—

Time between major planned shutdowns.
Shutdown duration.
Downtime between shutdowns.
Shutdown duration overrun.
Overall availability.
Shutdown budgeted cost.
Shutdown overcost.
Cost of maintenance between shutdowns.
Wastage cost due to incidence of inadequate product quality.
During shutdowns, planned work as a percentage of total work.
Between shutdowns, planned work as a percentage of total work.
Between shutdowns, preventive work as a percentage of total work.
List of CBM techniques in use.
Equipment integrity index (safety).

Part 2

Examples of Full, Snapshot and Fingerprint Audits

We trained hard . . . but it seemed that every time we were beginning to form up into teams we would be reorganized. I was to learn later in life that we tend to meet any new situation by reorganizing; and a wonderful method it can be for creating the illusion of progress while producing confusion, inefficiency and demoralization.

—Petronius Arbiter, 210 B.C.
(disputed authorship but very relevant to the next section).

CHAPTER 5

The Full Audit

Introduction

My aim in this chapter will be to show, via a real-life case study[1] drawn from my own consultancy practice, how the methodology that I have been describing can provide the basis of a comprehensive and detailed maintenance audit of any large, complex, plant—mapping and modelling it in order to identify problems and prescribe possible solutions. The case study will also highlight the following three important features:

* How the reliability section of the company concerned developed excellent procedures for developing life plans for pressure vessels.
* How having an organizational structure set up to international benchmark standards does not necessarily promote positive shop floor attitudes.
* How the maintenance management module of an expensive software package, applied enterprise-wide, does not necessarily provide a suitable data base for the maintenance of the major units of plant.

The particular audit was a full one carried out at Fertec Ltd, a manufacturer of agricultural fertilisers. The company ran two plants, A and B, located in different cities, and this exercise was carried out at Plant A (Plant B being audited later). Fertec was owned by a parent company, Cario Ltd.

The contents list of the audit was outlined in Table 3–5 and the resulting report, of which this chapter is essentially a summary, amounted to some 156 pages of text, figures and tables—a book in itself, the format of which can also be followed in Figure 3–3.

Fertec A

The plant layout was as in Figure 5–1 which indicates the location of the main process areas and the maintenance resources, i.e., labour and parts store. (The labour resources are identified by a letter code that will be carried through into the organizational models.)

---

[1]*Work carried out jointly by A. Kelly and H.S. Riddell.*

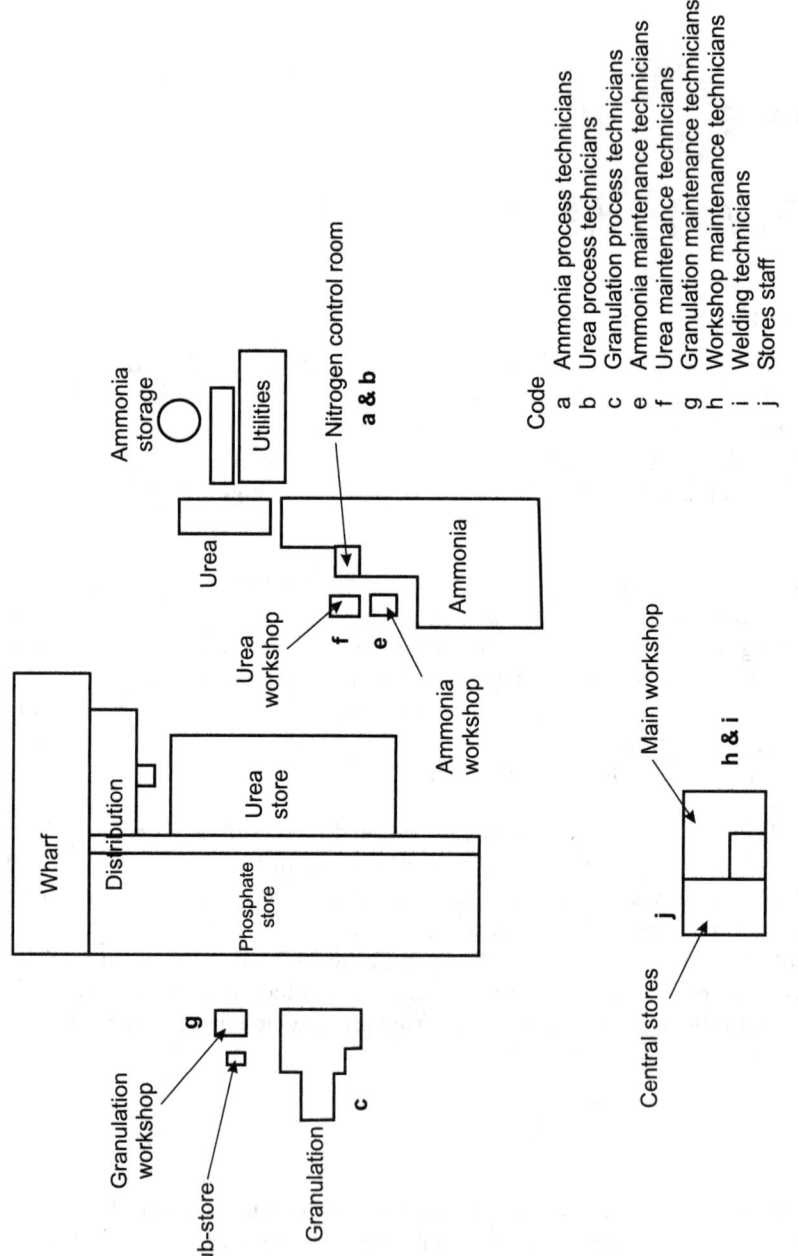

FIGURE 5-1 Plant Layout Showing Locations of Technician Resource

Figure 5–2 outlines the process flow. The Ammonia Plant was production critical, because it supplied the other plants with the necessary ammonia and carbon dioxide, although there was some interstage ammonia storage. At much greater expense ammonia could also be imported.

The complex was some thirty years old but much of it had been up-rated (the Urea Plant was undergoing such change at the time of the audit), especially as regards the instrumentation and control systems. The cost of energy (generated by burning natural gas) formed a very high percentage of the Ammonia Plant's operating bills. The energy efficiency of this last plant was low compared to the world's best because it was based on old technology. Plant reliability (which has a major influence on energy efficiency) needed to be improved.

Fertec was one of several companies that belonged to the parent group, Cario Ltd. The senior management structure of Fertec A and its relationship with that of the B plant and with its parent group is shown in Figure 5–3. It should be noted that the Reliability Manager had responsibilities that covered both the A and B plants.

A number of the senior positions in Fertec A had just changed and had been filled with a young, forward-looking, team, who commissioned the audit because they felt that in order to remain competitive they needed to improve plant reliability and at the same time reduce maintenance costs. In addition, they considered that there were attitudinal issues that needed resolving, with respect to both tradeforce performance and to maintenance management standards. They wanted answers to the following fundamental questions:

* Taking into consideration the ageing nature of the plant, how effective was the maintenance strategy (the life plans, preventive schedule etc.) in giving Fertec what was wanted in terms of reliability and output?
* How organizationally efficient was the maintenance department in providing its service at optimal cost?
* How good were the maintenance systems?

(*See review questions 5–1 and 5–2.*)

Objectives

An outline of the process of setting objectives and business plans is shown in Figure 5–4. This is a form of management by objectives (MBO)—to which my own Business-Centered Maintenance approach is closely allied.

The Fertec A senior management group (which included the group reliability manager) produced a statement of the works objectives and required performance. At this level the objectives were concerned with manufacturing performance. Maintenance objectives had been set for those areas that directly affected manufacturing. For example, one objective was to improve the availability of the Ammonia Plant from the existing level of 88% to match the world's best at 96%. Objectives had also been set for improved energy efficiency.

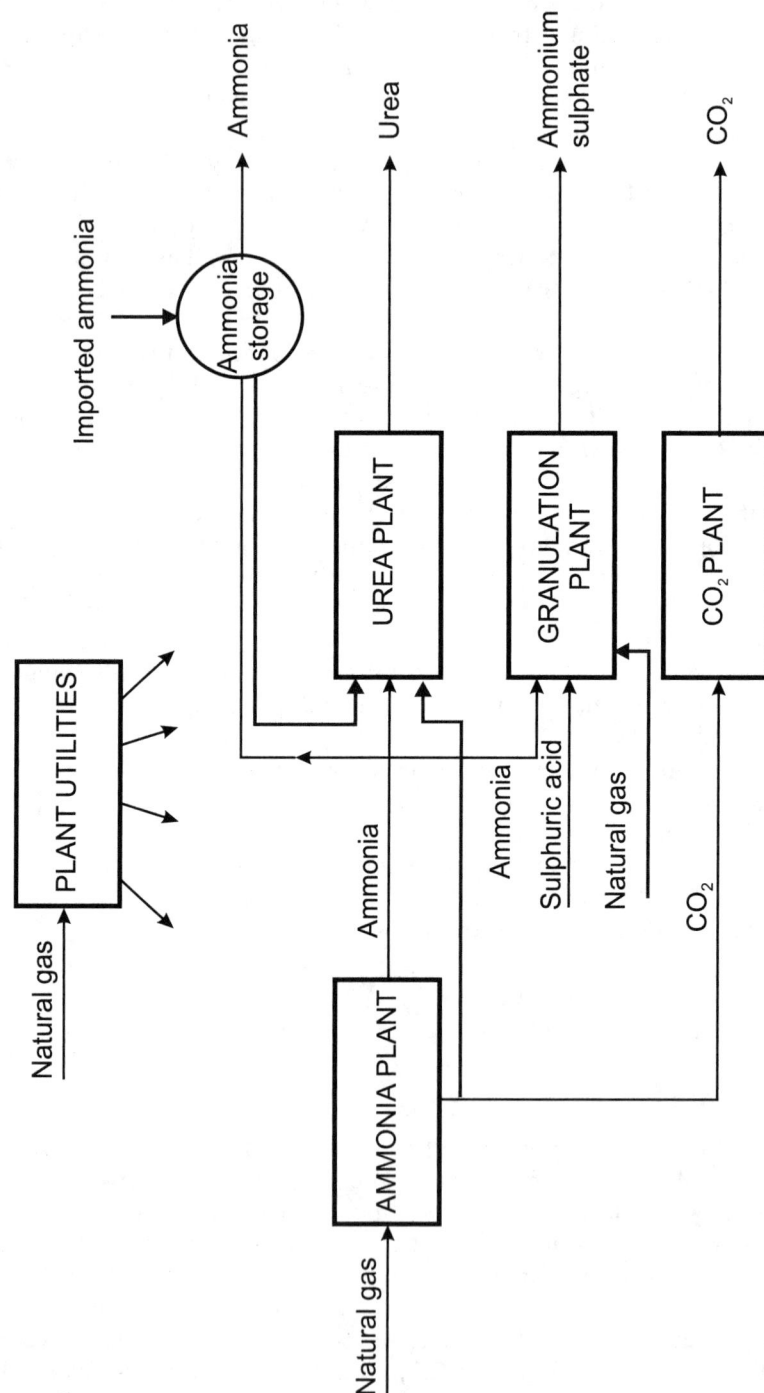

FIGURE 5–2 Outline Process Flow Diagram

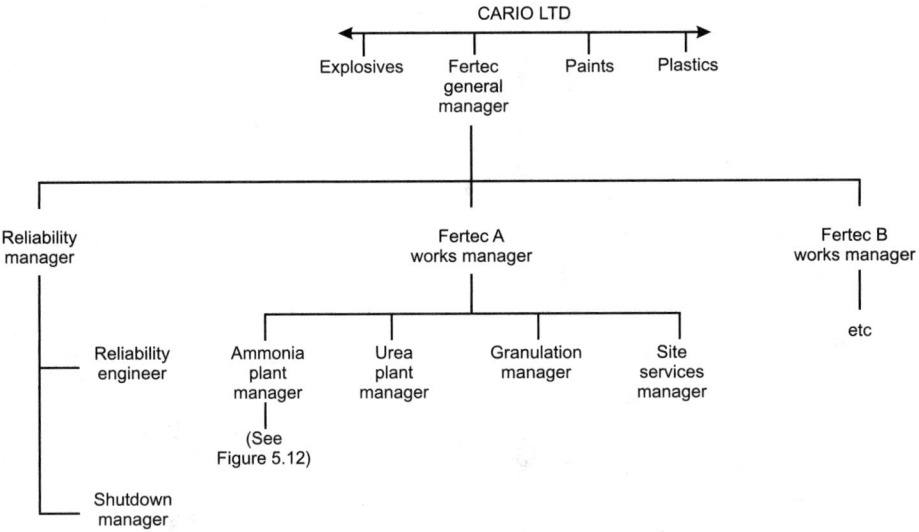

FIGURE 5-3 Senior Management Structure

At plant manager level the works objectives had been translated into local plant objectives through three separate but linked 'objective and action' statements, viz.:

the people plan (for achieving organizational efficiency),
the performance plan (for achieving effectiveness),
the safety plans.

For example, in the case of the performance plan objectives for reliability improvement had been set for critical units of the Ammonia Plant, such as the Syn-Gas compressor. In addition, a series of tasks—e.g., introducing the application of Reliability Centered Maintenance (RCM)—had been identified to achieve these improvements. These actions had been allocated to specific engineers and supervisors and were reviewed by the plant manager at three-monthly intervals. Similarly, the works objectives and actions were reviewed by the senior management group at three-monthly intervals. In addition to this, each of the managers, engineers and supervisors had been set annual objectives which encompassed many of the objectives and actions indicated in Figure 5-4.

Observations

We were impressed with the objectives and the procedure for setting them. It had only recently been set up and required time to bed in. Our main criticism was that the procedure had not been translated down to the 'self-empowered team' level. We were told that this would have to wait until process-team human factors became less negative (see Page 74). (*See review questions 5–3 and 5–4.*)

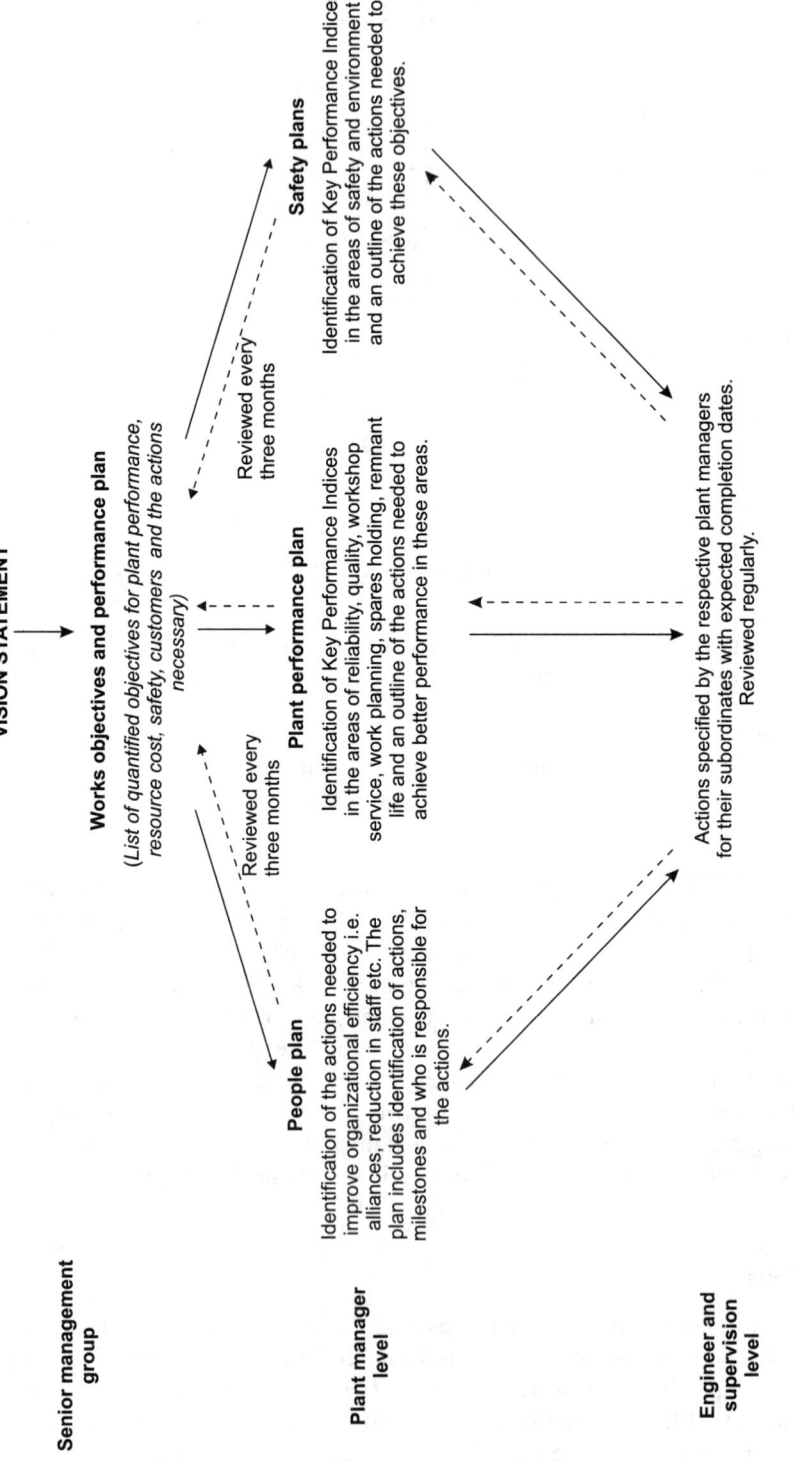

Figure 5–4 Management by Objectives at Fertec

Maintenance Strategy

Plant Operating Characteristics

The outline process flow diagram for the Fertec A complex was shown in Figure 5–2. The Ammonia Plant was the rate-determining process, it was production limited. Ammonia Plant failures could only be made up by importing ammonia, which was costly. We were told that a one percent loss of annual availability translated into a loss of many hundreds of thousands of pounds. The ammonia storage tank gave a degree of protection (some days' worth of feed) to the Ammonia Plant in the event of an Urea Plant outage. Failure of the Ammonia Plant also brought the Urea and CO2 plants to a halt, although the Granulation Plant was largely independent of the rest of the complex. As a rule of thumb, the Ammonia Plant downtime costs were very much greater than those of the Urea Plant, which themselves were much greater than those of the Granulation Plant.

Ammonia Plant Strategy

The complete audit actually covered the maintenance strategy for the full complex. The overall approach will be adequately illustrated, however, by a review of its application to just one section, viz the Ammonia Plant, for which an outline process flow diagram is shown in Figure 5–5. It can be seen that at unit level this plant was a series process with limited redundancy. There were many units whose failure could affect its output and those (e.g., the Syn-Gas compressor) that presented the highest risk of failure were regarded *critical*.

The existing strategy was to operate the Ammonia-Urea-CO2 complex for a four-year period before a four-week shutdown. This period was determined by a statutory requirement to inspect the pressure vessels (which has since come under a self-regulating regime) and the need to inspect-repair-replace other plant units whose reliability diminishes after four years. The shutdown was timed to coincide with low annual urea demand. The four year operating period had been determined by the company's Reliability Group from an empirical study of the susceptibility of the risk of failure to the length of the period of operation of a pressure vessel before inspection. They established that the critical 20% of the units accounted for 80% of such risk.

Continuous vibration monitoring was used on the large machines—mainly for operational safety but also for maintenance prediction. To aid condition based maintenance several other on-line monitoring techniques were employed, both on the large machines and on the pressure vessels. In fact, the Ammonia Plant maintenance strategy was dominated by Condition-Based Maintenance (CBM), the scope of the four-yearly shutdown work being mainly based on the observations from:

on-line inspections,
off-line inspections from previous shutdowns,
history from previous shutdowns.

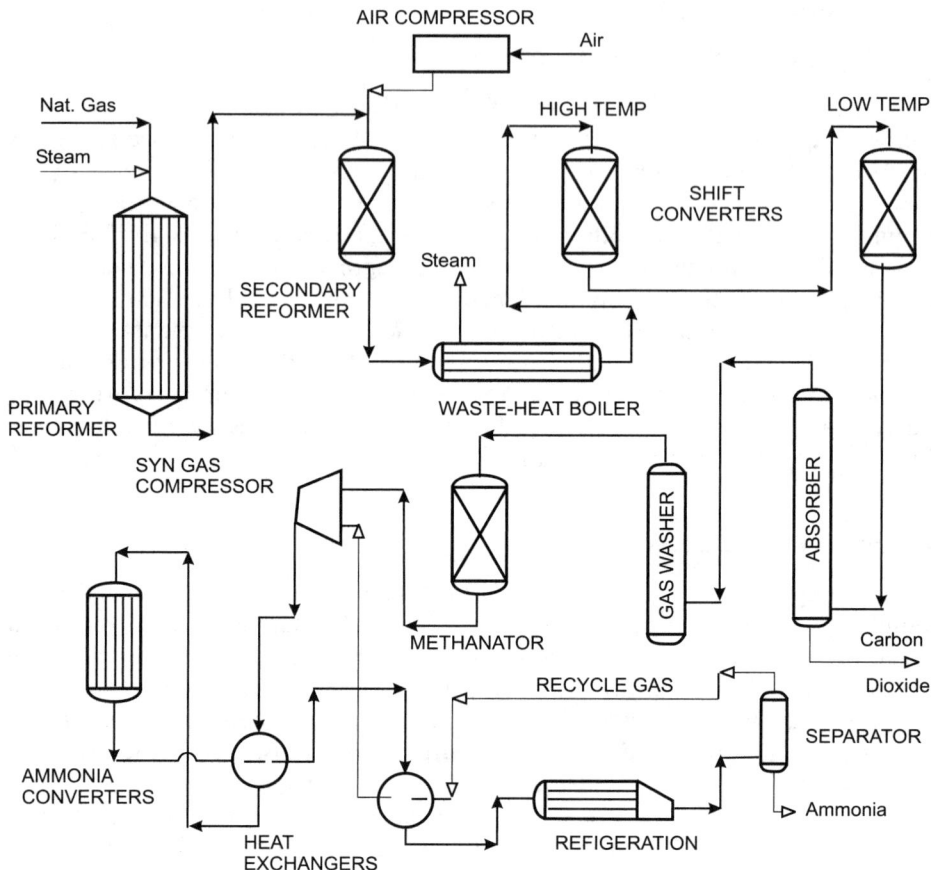

FIGURE 5–5 Outline of Process Flow, Ammonia Plant

The duration of the shutdown was normally four weeks, which included a 'dead week' needed for shutdown and start-up. The critical path during the shutdown encompassed the reformer pressure-vessel inspection and the work on the Syn-Gas compressor.

As regards maintenance characteristics the plant could be categorised into large machines, pressure vessels, ancillary equipment (e.g., duplicate pumps) and electrical and instrumentation equipment.

Life Plan for the Syn-Gas Compressor (SGC): A schematic of the SGC is shown in Figure 5–6, which includes details on spare parts holding. The CBM carried out on the machine is shown in Table 5–1. The machine was expected to operate continuously for four years. The shutdown workscope was established from previous shutdown history, the schedule of deferred corrective maintenance, and information from on-line monitoring. Additional (i.e., unplanned) work was identified from off-line inspection during the shutdown itself.

Standard job procedures (e.g., for inspection-overhauls of the high pressure case) were comprehensive and detailed. The machine history records had not been

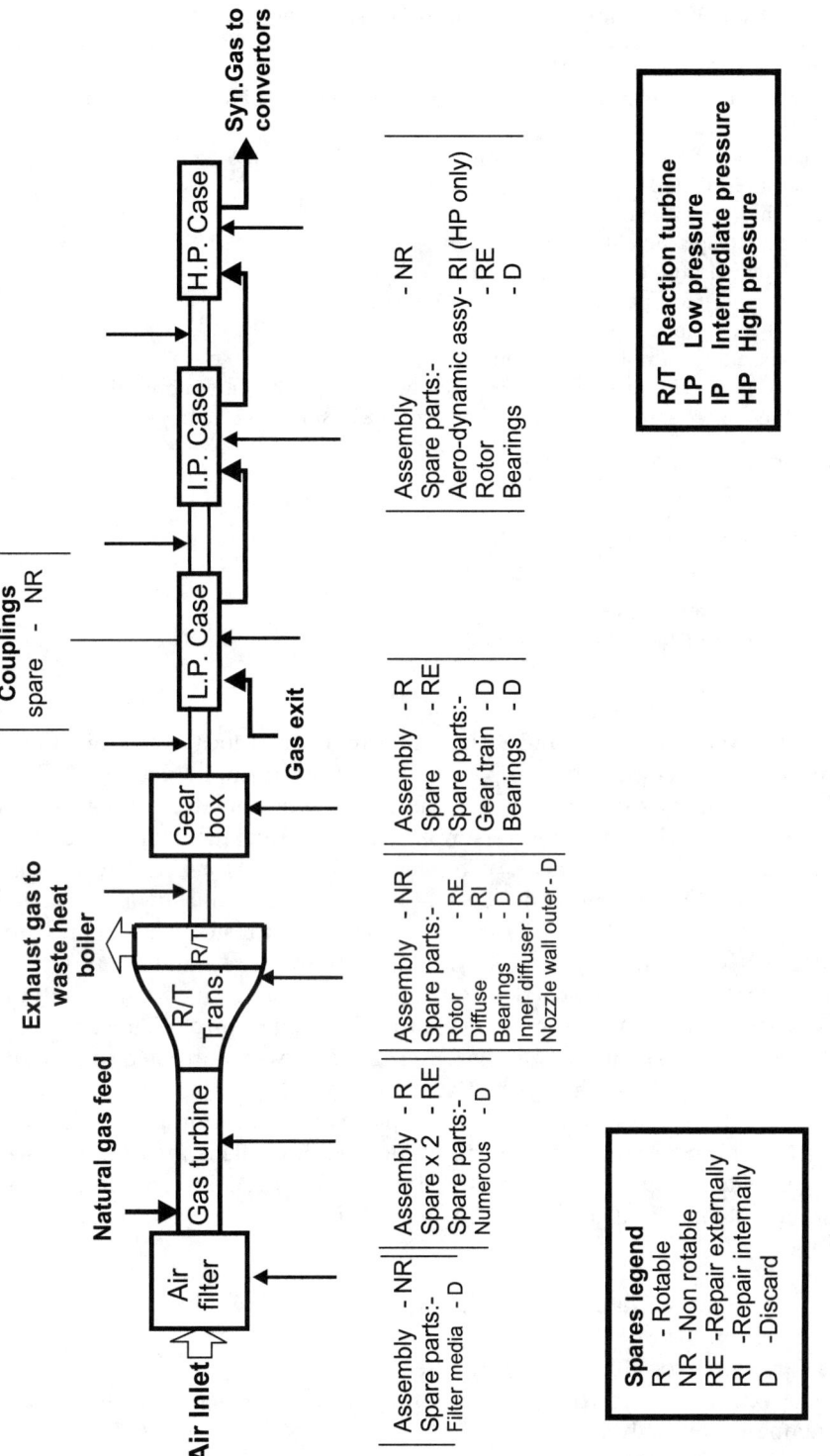

FIGURE 5–6 Schematic of Syn-Gas Compressor

TABLE 5–1 Syn-Gas Compressor Condition Based Maintenance

Bently Nevada System

This sophisticated system records various data and has the ability to combine inputs to produce multi dimensional displays.

Produces data in real time plus long and short trend patterns.

Items measured include:

Radial shaft displacement

Axial shaft displacement

Bearing temperatures—radial and thrust

Accelerometer readings (gearbox and gas turbine only)

Shaft orbit readings (multi dimensional)

Shaft phase angle (multi dimensional)

In addition to the above approximately 200 process variables are monitored.

All the above have alarm points and key items have shutdown settings.

Oil Analysis

Routine oil analysis.

Seal by-pass test (compressor only)

Routine seal accumulator drop test.

Oil debris analysis (gas turbine only)

On-line continuous monitoring.

---

formalised, were hard copy and resided in a number of locations looked after by several different people. The life plan had not been formally documented.

Although not shown in Figure 5–6 there was an automatic lubrication system for the SGC, for which there were simple computer-documented service routines.

Life Plan for Pressure Vessels: The generic life plan for pressure vessels was based on CBM. The maintenance carried out during the shutdowns was based on condition prediction in the light of previous shutdown history and on any on-line non-destructive testing performed between shutdowns. Additional work was identified from inspections carried out (open and closed) during the shutdown.

There were variations of the life plans to suit specific vessels. Those vessels that rated high on the risk factor analysis (see Table 5–2) were subjected to an in-depth analysis for uprating the life plan. Every pipe, weld and hot support that might give rise to failure was examined to develop the most appropriate non-destructive testing (NDT) technique and inspection methodology. This inspection-based life plan was backed up by a comprehensive computerised information base—the pressure systems data base, which included for each vessel the following information:

* Process and mechanical data sheets.
* Inspection history.
* Inspection procedures and plans (see Table 5–3).
* The vessel life plan (the formulation of which involved risk assessment and remnant life analysis).
* Hard copy reports of previous shutdown case studies.

TABLE 5–2 Assessment of Criticality Ranking for a Pressure Vessel

Likelihood of Failure

Is there a known active metallurgical damage mechanism?	No known damage mechanism	0
Is there a known active mechanical damage mechanism?	Vibration fatigue	2
Have the inspections been effective?	Ineffective—no confidence	5
What is the frequency of inspections?	More than 30 years	4
How reliable are the control systems & operating parameters?	Poor	1
Are the vessel limits exceeded in plant upsets?	Yes	1
Are the vessel limits exceeded in normal operation?	No	0
Have process conditions changed, (but still within design)?	Yes	1
Are the vessel limits exceeded in plant start-ups or shutdowns?	Yes	1
Are the vessel protective systems effective?	No	1
Has detection of damage previously warranted further investigation?	Yes	1
Have repairs been required in the past?	Yes	1
How old is the vessel?	Over 30 years	3
Is the vessel original design to current standards?	No	1
Is the vessel material specification to currently acceptable standards?	No	1
Total		23

Consequence of Failure

Are the vessel contents ...?	A lethal gas?	7
What is the temp of the vessel contents?	Above 500°C	3
Are the contents flammable if they leak?	Auto ignites	3
Would a failure promote consequential damage elsewhere in plant?	Yes	5
Would emergency services help be required to contain a situation?	Yes	3
What is the vessel pressure?	Above 10 Mpa	3
What is the volume of worst rating contents in the vessel?	Over 1000 cubic metres	8
Will a leak cause secondary damage to other equipment?	Yes	1
What is the distance to internal personnel?	Less than 10 metres	2
What is the distance to the general public?	Less than 1000 metres	4
What is the business impact of a vessel failure?	Over £10,000,000	11
Total		50

Likelihood total 23   Consequences total 50   Risk = 23 × 50 = 1,150.

Table 5–3 Inspection Plan for Exchanger

Equipment item	Visual	Ultrasonic	Radiography	Mag/Part	Dye/Pen	Thermovision	Vibration	AE	Attenuation	Metallographic	Other
2RK65 to tray ring weld	Yes				x						
Alignment	Yes										
Associated piping	Yes		O/Head line only								
Davits/Lifting devices	Yes	Prior to S/D		Prior to S/D							
Earth connection	Yes										
Heads	Yes	Bottom									
Instrumentation	Yes	Evidence of bulging									
Insulation	Yes										
Internal Liner	Yes	4 per petal			To bot tray						
Manway & bolting	Yes	Manway plant									
Nozzles	Yes	Manway liners			Internal						
Platforms/Handrails	Yes										
Pressure relief devices	Yes										
Protective coating	Yes										
Shell	Yes	Lower 1.5/m			Liner welds						
Supports & bolting	Yes										
Thermowells & sockets	Yes				x						
Vessel bolting	Yes										
Vibration	Yes										
Welded joints	Yes										

This computerised data base was independent of a just-purchased company-wide computerised enterprise system.

Ancillary Equipment: The life plans of various pumps, pressure relief valves, control valves and the like—equipment that could be maintained at times other than during the main shutdowns—were based on service routines which were embedded in the main computerised maintenance system (linked to other company systems). A typical routine would be as follows:

Pump preventive routine: Three-monthly
* Oil change.
* General inspection—Check coupling
  Lift bearing cap etc.

These routines were established some twenty years previously and were in need of review. Many of them had been loaded into the new computer system without review. Vibration monitoring – mainly via portable instruments but also using some permanently wired systems (see page 105). In general, the monitoring procedures had not been tied into the routines. In addition to these routines a contract lubrication system, operated by one of the large oil companies, had been introduced.

We noted that the operating procedure for units with duplicated drives was as follows:

Electric motors—Change over weekly.
Electric motors and steam turbine—Use the electric motor and
  proof test the turbine weekly.

Electrical and Instrumentation Equipment: The life plans were based on '*Clean, inspect and calibrate where necessary*' preventive routines. These had been set up many years ago and needed review. It was noted that much of the more recent equipment (e.g., PLC's) was not included in these routines and had not been reviewed. The large electrical machines had no documented life plans. More importantly, neither had any of the electrical and instrumentation equipment been reviewed with a view to identifying critical spares. The information base data (job specifications, modifications, plant histories etc.) were either held on hard copy (in a number of different locations) or in people's memory.

Observations and Recommendations

(i) When auditing maintenance strategy we asked interviewees for their opinion of the preventive maintenance in use in their plant. The following are some of their replies:

'The main shutdowns are carried out well—this is where most of our preventive work is carried out'
'We must tie up the preventive routines with vibration monitoring'
'Routines are used as fill-in work—they are not regarded as important'

'The electrical routines are in people's heads—they must be documented'

'The refrigeration units in the plant services are in poor condition and are operation-critical—we must sort out our spares'

'We should re-think our operating period—the USA plants do it differently and at lower cost'

'Our condition monitoring is heading towards international benchmark levels'

'We should be replacing old equipment—mono pumps out and granfor pumps in'

'Our life plans for large machines are not right yet—we should seek help from the original equipment manufacturer'

(ii) We observed that the operating period of the plant had been extended from two to four years and would shortly extend to four and a half years. This was due to the considerable efforts of the Reliability Group in the area of pressure vessel maintenance. (Involving NDT techniques, good computerised information base, criticality and remnant life analysis, metallurgical knowledge). However it appeared, from Ammonia Plant failure data, that the main production losses occurred as a result of problems with the large machines. The data showed that these failed more often, and more randomly, than did the pressure vessels, with a mean time to failure of less than four years. This was not surprising, because they were up to thirty years old and were complex arrangements of many rapidly moving parts. As a result of many overhauls, often carried out without standard job procedures, their condition appeared to have fallen, over the years, below the original equipment manufacturer's (OEM's) standard specification. This led us to the following observations:

(a) If the company was to get the best out of a four-and-a-half year operating period they would have to bring the condition of the large machines back to an 'as new' standard—perhaps with the assistance of the OEM. Because the machines were old this was almost equivalent to a life-extension decision, involving assessment of the probable remaining life (remnant life) of the plant.

(b) The company should use the Top-Down—Bottom-Up (TDBU)* approach to review the life plans of the large machines and this should include an identification of the critical spares that should be held. In addition, the plant information base for its large machines should be brought up to the same standard as for its pressure vessels.

(iii) We had been made aware, by the plant's engineers, that companies in the USA operated a different maintenance strategy from that outlined above—some, for example, adopting an operating time of two years and a shutdown of two weeks—and decisions in this area could be influenced by many factors, including:

---

*A procedure developed by the author for establishing life plans and preventive schedules for complex plants and shown in the following reference:-

A. Kelly, *Maintenance Strategy*, Butterworth-Heinemann, 1997.

* the shortest expected running time of other critical units, e.g., the large machines, before they needed maintenance;

* the remnant life of the plant—at the time, the gas contract was for seven years and the position after that was uncertain;

* the market demand (assuming the plant was production limited).

* the duration of a shutdown if the workscope was to be completed—this had to take into consideration a one-week dead period for shutdown and start-up, so a two year cycle of operations encompassing a two week shutdown would require a proportion of time devoted to maintenance that was a third less than for a four year cycle with a four week shutdown (see Figure 5–7).

Clearly, when making such decisions the objective should have been to minimise the sum of the planned and the anticipated unplanned downtime costs. This was a complex problem involving information that was not available to us, e.g.,

Why was the dead period apparently shorter in the USA?
Could the duration of the shutdown, four weeks, have been reduced by shortening the Reformer critical path? If so, how much would this have cost?
Did the large machines need realignment or off-line inspection at two years?

In spite of this (and without statistical cost modelling) we concluded that if the company were to comply with the points listed in ii(a) and ii(b) they would be moving towards an optimum maintenance strategy.

(iv) We recommended that 'opportunity scheduling' should complement the existing strategy, i.e., when a failure of a unit occurred unexpectedly all other outstanding work should be looked at with a view to carrying it out

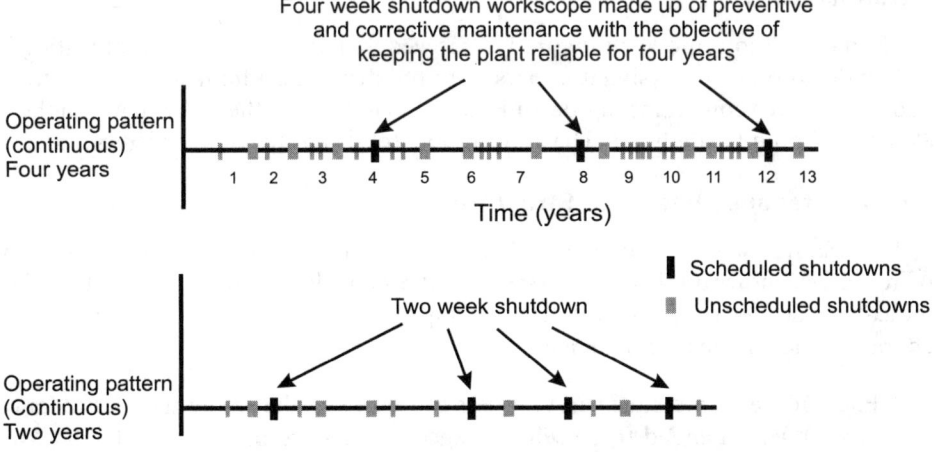

FIGURE 5–7 Illustration of Strategy Based on Four-Year and Two-Year Operation Periods

in the window of opportunity provided. We accepted that the planning system would also have to improve if this plan were to be adopted.

(v) Both the mechanical and the electrical-instrumentation routines were in need of review and update, using the TDBU approach to focus the routines on necessary and worthwhile tasks and to modify as necessary the type and frequency of routines, e.g., to change the replacement or repair of pumps and motors from a fixed time to a condition-based activity. (*See review questions 5–5 and 5–6.*)

Condition Monitoring

In the previous section the extent was shown to which the company relied on CBM as the driver of its maintenance strategy. The use of inspection techniques was also audited to identify the techniques being used and to establish how well they were being used. The techniques that were being applied are summarised in Table 5–4. In general, it was felt that the condition monitoring programme was comprehensive and well executed. Minor recommendations were made for each of the techniques listed. For example, in the case of oil monitoring the following improvements were proposed:

* Samples were not to be taken from the oil drain point. 'Minimess' sampling points were to be installed in an area where the oil was actively circulating.
* Receiving results by fax and re-typing them into a computer was an obvious source of error—they should be transferred electronically. It was also recommended that software be purchased for trending the results and displaying them graphically.

Maintenance Organization

Introduction

The methodology model of Figure 1–3 showed that a maintenance organization is best understood by analysing it into its resource structure, administrative structure and systems, the constraints model of Figure 3–3 indicating the order in which these elements should be analysed. The audit report followed the same order.

The Maintenance Resource Structure

The resource structure for Fertec A is modelled in Figure 5–8 and the inventory of resources shown in Table 5–5 (see also the plant layout of Figure 5–1, which indicates the location of the tradegroups). The following were the main characteristics of this arrangement:

* Each of the maintenance and process groups (e.g., the ammonia maintenance group) was intended to be self-managed and co-ordinated by its facilitator.
* Tradesmen accounted for 25% of each process group and they were expected to carryout some first-line maintenance. In fact these groups carried out little or no maintenance.

TABLE 5–4 Summary of Company Condition Monitoring Techniques

Technique	Equipment Monitored	Comments
Bentley Nevada continuous on-line vibration monitoring	The ten large machines including the Syn-Gas compressor.	Uses displacement sensors.
Bentley Nevada Trendmaster. A periodic on-line vibration monitoring system	Used for about 300 of the less critical machines, e.g., duplicate pumps.	Monitors about 20 points per unit. Each point is monitored every 2 hours.
SKF Microlog Prism— hand held vibration monitoring	Used for all machines, pumps etc. not covered by the Bentley Nevada.	Item monitored at 2 week, 4 week and 12 week intervals. Can be used to detect changes in the spectrum at higher frequencies.
Oil monitoring	Applied to about 34 of the most important units, including all of the large machines.	Spectroscopy analysis by contract. Also viscosity tests and water contamination. Results faxed back and transferred to computer spreadsheets.
Thermography	Insulated vessels, reformers, boilers, etc. Electrical switchgear.	Vessel inspection monthly. Electrical switchgear annually. History held on video tape.
Performance monitoring	The five critical compressors and gas turbines.	Take TDC and local instrument readings every two weeks to carry out a mass and energy balance and machine efficiency (useful check for mechanical condition of seals).
Non destructive testing. Mainly ultrasound and radiography (some dye penetrant and magnetic flux)	Some 2800 pressure vessels plus piping.	Mostly off-line external and internal inspections at main shutdown. Inspections directed at known vessel problem areas. Limited external on-line inspection for problem vessels.
Acoustic emission	Ammonia storage tanks.	Impractical to enter this vessel. Vessel inspection period greater than ten years, cost about £800,000 per inspection.

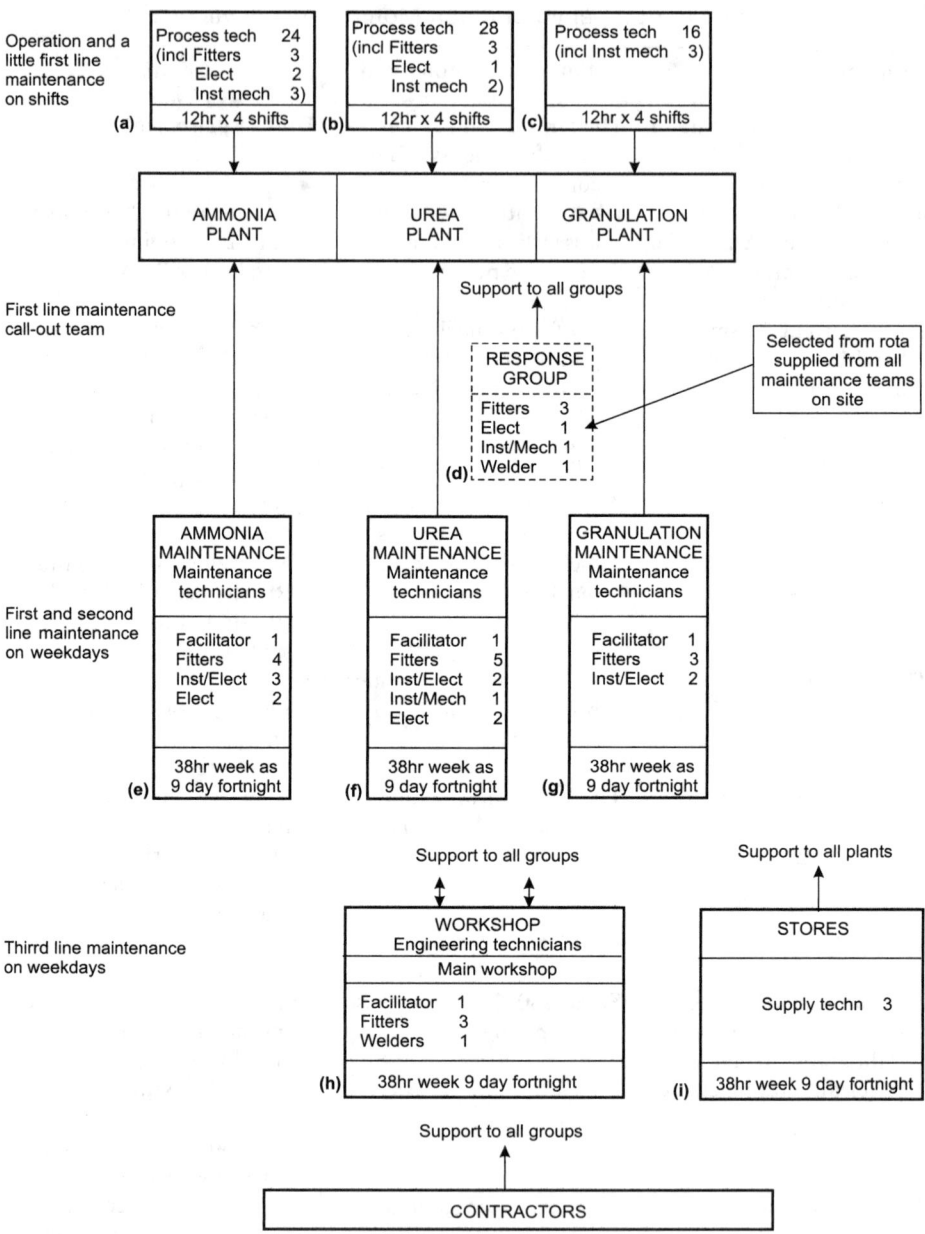

FIGURE 5–8 Resource Structure

TABLE 5–5 Maintenance Resource Inventory

Resource Categories	Total
Technicians:	
Maintenance facilitator	4
Fitter	15
Inst/Elect	7
Inst. Mech	1
Electrician	4
Welder	2
Semi-skilled:	
Stores technicians	3
Sub-Totals:	
Total maintenance facilitators	4
Total technicians (less facilitators)	29
Total semi-skilled resources	3
Total skilled & semi-skilled resources	32
Total maintenance resources	36
Total process technicians	68
Ratios:	
Operators per maintenance employee	1.85
Percent semi-skilled of maintenance resource	8%
Total skilled & semi-skilled resource facilitators	6.5
Total skilled techns/facilitators	5.8

* The out-of-hours priority maintenance was carried out by the response group (d) supplied on a rota from all the engineering technicians on site, who were on an annualised hours agreement and did not get paid for call outs. On average, overtime ran at a level equal to about 5% of normal hours. To enable all maintenance technicians to support the response group they were rotated across the plants on a two yearly cycle.
* The plant-located day-groups (e.g., the ammonia maintenance group) carried out most of the first and second line maintenance work in their own areas. To ensure completion of the higher priority second line work, they were supplemented, to a further 25%, by contract labour. In spite of this the lower priority corrective work, and the preventive routines, were neglected.
* To cover the smaller overhauls, inter-plant flexibility was encouraged by the management. In general, such sideways movement was resisted by the technicians.
* The area maintenance groups were supported—as regards fabrication, machining, reconditioning and spares—by the workshop facilities, stores and external contract workshops (see Figure 5–9 for the reconditioning cycle). The workshop technicians also provide a maintenance service to non-manufacturing facilities.

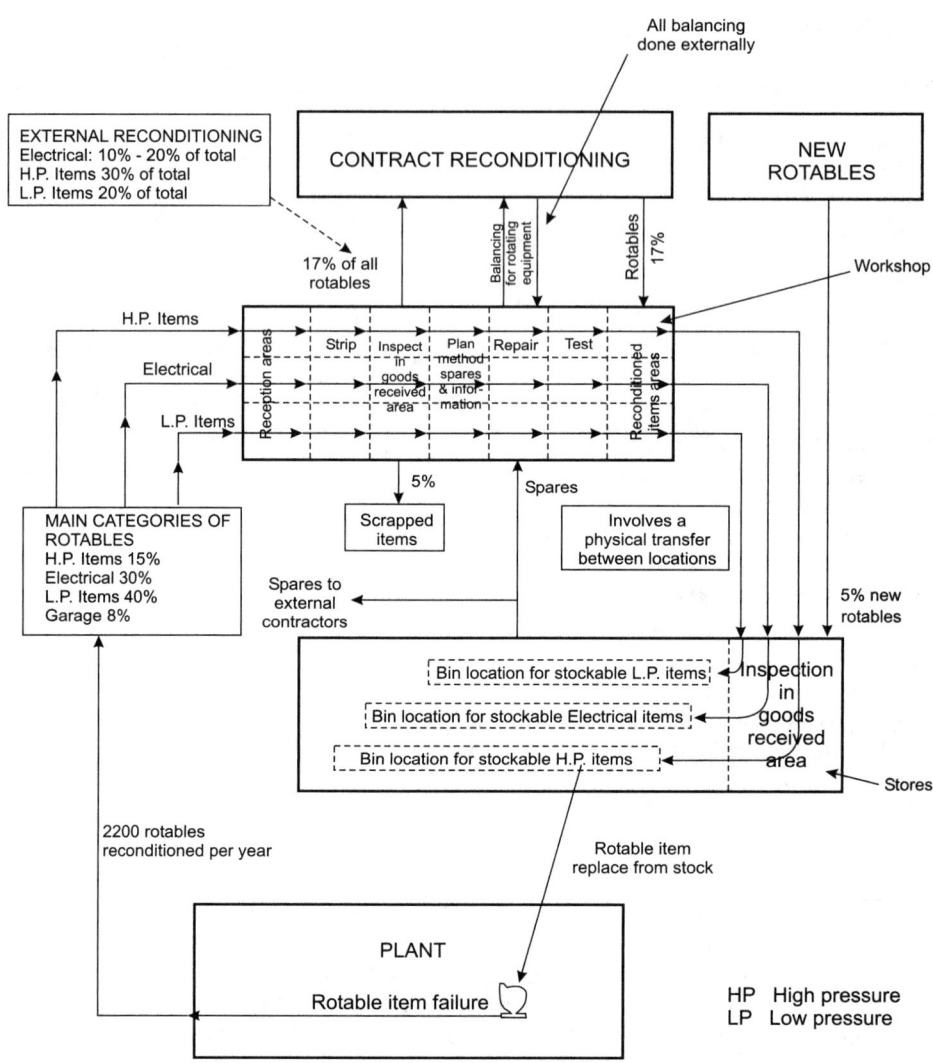

All balancing
done externally

EXTERNAL RECONDITIONING
Electrical: 10% - 20% of total
H.P. Items 30% of total
L.P. Items 20% of total

CONTRACT RECONDITIONING

NEW
ROTABLES

17% of all
rotables

Balancing
for rotating
equipment

Rotables
17%

Workshop

H.P. Items

Electrical

L.P. Items

Reception areas

Strip | Inspect | Plan | Repair | Test
       | in | method |
       | goods | spares |
       | received| & infor-|
       | area | mation |

Reconditioned
items areas

5%

Spares

Scrapped
items

Involves a
physical transfer
between locations

MAIN CATEGORIES OF
ROTABLES
H.P. Items 15%
Electrical 30%
L.P. Items 40%
Garage 8%

Spares to
external
contractors

5% new
rotables

Bin location for stockable L.P. items

Bin location for stockable Electrical items

Bin location for stockable H.P. items

Inspection
in
goods
received
area

Stores

2200 rotables
reconditioned per year

Rotable item
replace from stock

PLANT

Rotable item failure

HP High pressure
LP Low pressure

N.B. All percentages have been estimated by the
site service planner

FIGURE 5–9 Logistics of Rotable Maintenance

* To supplement the internal labour, the four-yearly shutdown (third line work) demanded an influx of many hundreds of tradesmen for a four-week period The normal resource structure was changed for this period.
* The management had just recognised the need for engineering skills training and had introduced a comprehensive range of goal-oriented learning units.
* A number of surveys had been carried out, i.e., of:
  — Production's perception of the maintenance service—in general it was regarded as just satisfactory.
  — Maintenance technicians' 'human factors', such as morale and goodwill towards management—in general these were poor, and equipment ownership was less than satisfactory; there was a feeling of strong vertical polarisation.
* An alliance between the company and an internationally known contractor, to carry out all non-core maintenance activities had been proposed. This would have included all workshop services, spare parts management and other non-maintenance activities.
* There was little or no skills flexibility between the mechanical trades and the electrical and instrumentation trades, despite the two groups having a common facilitator and planner.

Recommendations

The following alternative proposals for modifying the resource structure were suggested.

Proposal A

The existing structure could be retained, with a transfer of as much of the first line work as possible to the process technician teams. This would involve a study of the workload of both the maintenance and process teams. The existing plant-based maintenance teams would handle the residual first line work and the second line work. In addition, improvements were needed in

* skills flexibility between the mechanical and electrical and instrumentation trades,
* the exploitation, via improved work scheduling, of transferability of skills between the Ammonia, Urea and Granulation plants,
* the development of maintenance team facilitators as facilitator-planners—a good benchmark for improved team operation being provided by Cario Ltd (see Chapter 4, page 78)

Finally, the workshop-based maintenance and other non-core activities could be undertaken by a contractor alliance.

Proposal B

The existing structure could be changed to that shown in Figure 5–10. The first-line work for the Ammonia and Urea plants would be carried out by a combination of the process technician teams and a skeleton plant-based first-line

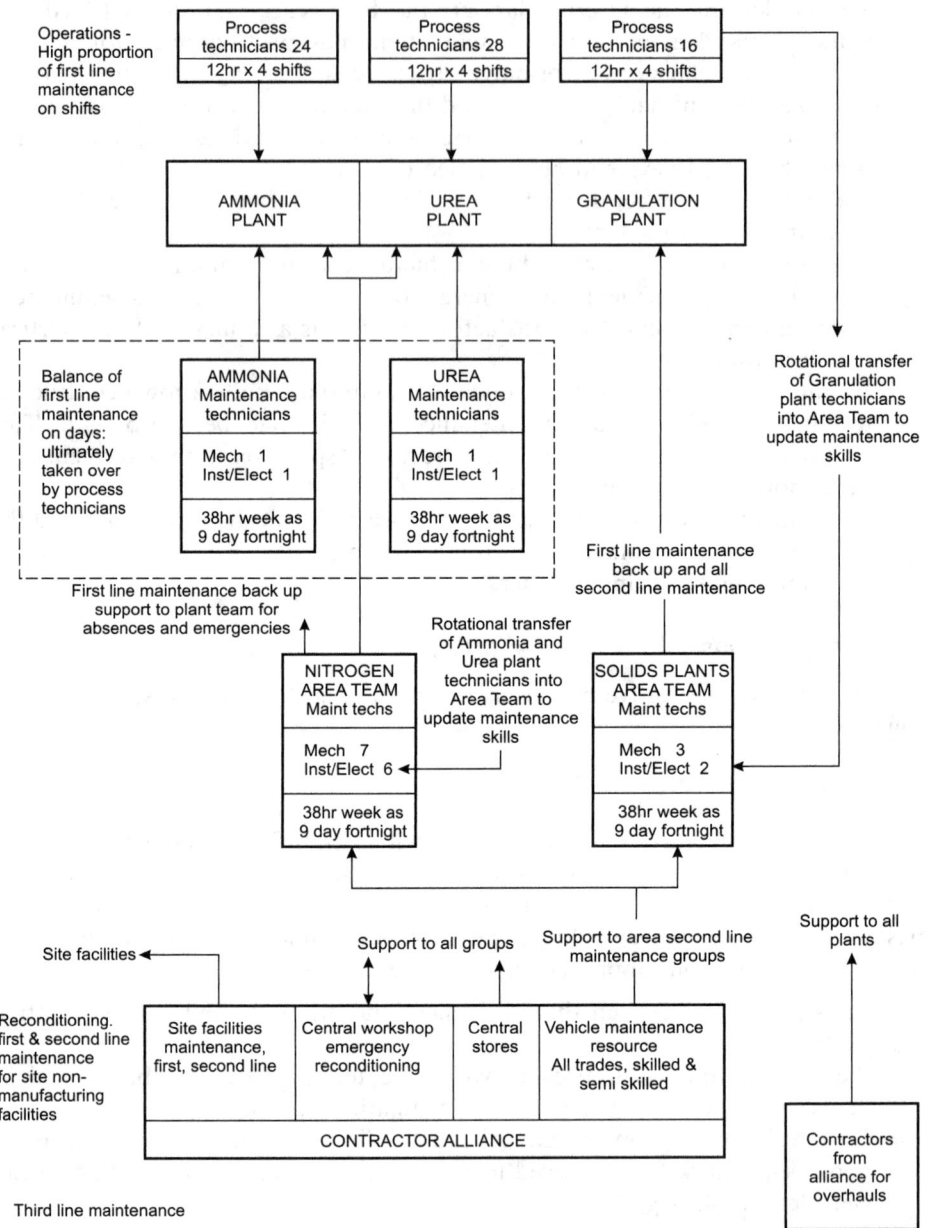

FIGURE 5–10 Proposals for Modified Resource Structure

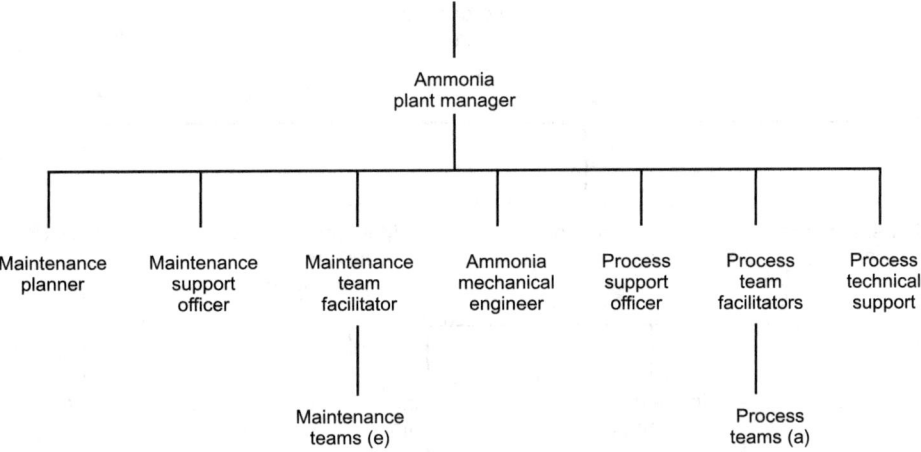

FIGURE 5–11 Ammonia Plant Administrative Structure

day-maintenance cover, the second line work by a Nitrogen Area group (Ammonia plus Urea) backed by the workshop contractor alliance—these modifications to be preceded by a study of the workload of both the process technician and maintenance technician teams, clarifying the true level of the first line work, and the nature of such work that the process technicians could undertake effectively, after appropriate training. This, in turn, would allow the correct manning levels for the first line skeleton cover, and the second line maintenance teams, to be established. In the longer term, and for either Proposal A or B, the process teams would have been able to cover all of the first line work. (*The possibility of linking the second line groups into the proposed alliance was also suggested.*) (*See review question 5–7.*)

The Maintenance Administrative Structure

The senior management administrative structure for Fertec A was shown in Figure 5–3 and, at the lower level, the related structures for the Ammonia Plant (those for the Urea and Granulation plants are similar), Site Services and Reliability Group are shown in Figs. 5–11, 5–12 and 5–13. Table 5–6 is an inventory of the staff. These had to be looked at in conjunction with the resource structure and inventory (Figure 5–8 and Table 5–5) and the plant layout (Figure 5–1).

The following were the main characteristics of this structural framework:

* It was built around the idea of semi-autonomous manufacturing units (e.g., the Ammonia Manufacturing Unit of Figure 5–11) Each plant manager reported to the Works Manager, who was solely accountable for all operational activities on site.

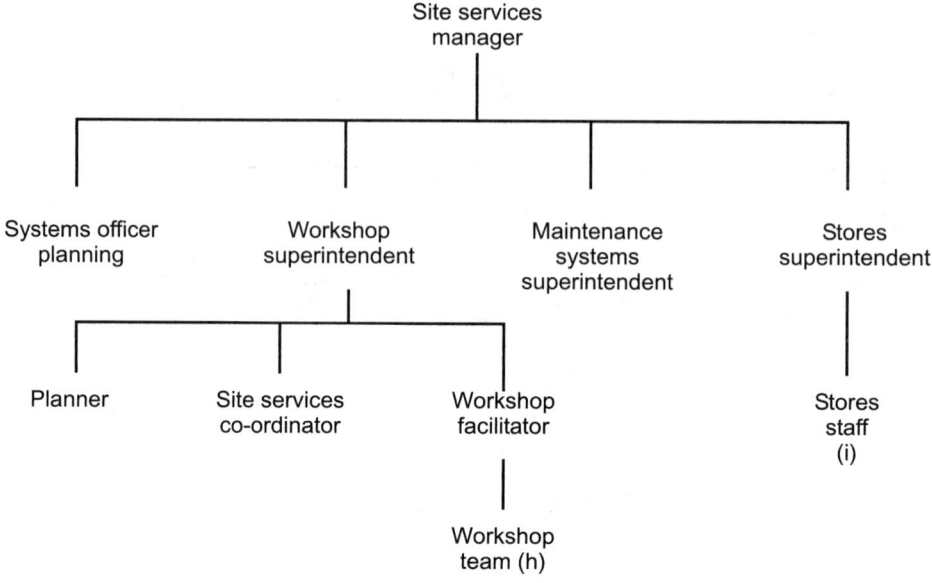

FIGURE 5–12 Site Services Administrative Structure

* Via a matrix structure, the manufacturing units were supported (on sites A and B) by the Reliability Group (see Figure 5–14). In general, we found the co-ordinating mechanisms across this matrix to be satisfactory.
* Within the units (e.g., see Figure 5–11) the process technicians (25% of whom were tradesmen) reported via their Facilitator to the Plant Manager.
* The maintenance technicians also reported, via their Facilitator, to the Plant Manager. In the case of the Ammonia Plant the team comprised ten tradesmen. The operation of the teams had reverted to the traditional structure, with the Facilitator acting as the Supervisor and the Planner carrying out the clerical duties. In addition, technical support came via the Mechanical Engineer and mechanical support officers. The electrical and instrument technicians felt vulnerable because no electrical engineer was employed within the works structure.
* The site services were only looked at in outline because a decision had already been taken to establish a contractor alliance to cover this area of activity.

Recommendations

Bearing in mind the resource structure proposals (see page 109) we offered two alternative suggestions for the administrative structures.

Proposal A

The existing resource structure could be retained, incorporating the recommendations outlined on page 109, and a modified administrative structure to tie

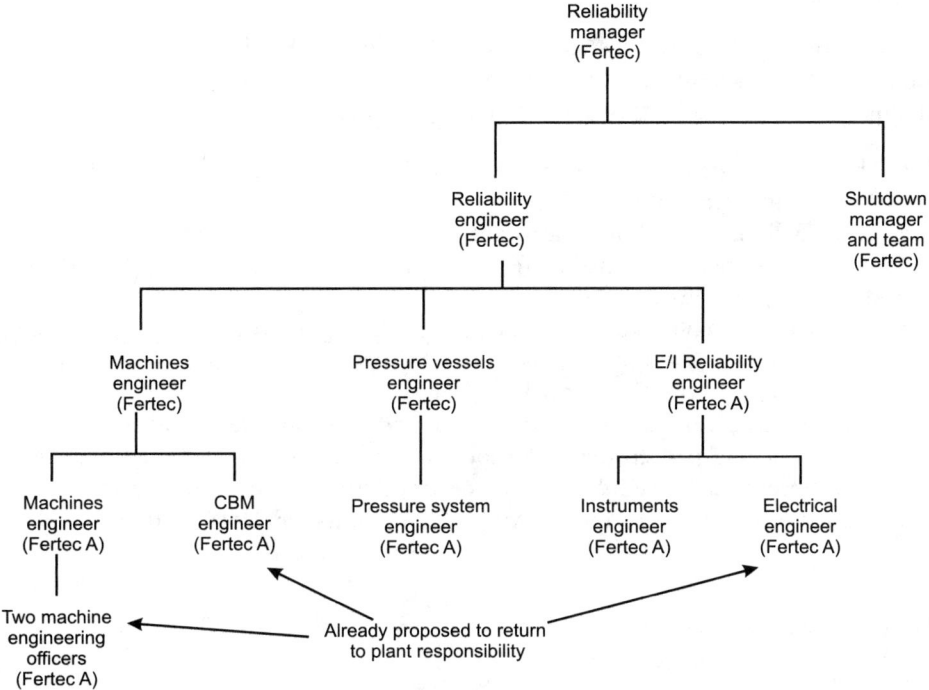

FIGURE 5–13 Reliability Group Administrative Structure

up with this could be as shown in Figure 5–15. The resulting main changes would then be as follows:

* The management of the Ammonia and Urea Plants would be combined at Plant Manager level.
* A professionally qualified electrical engineer would be appointed within the works' structure.
* The existing planners and facilitators would act as combined Planner-Facilitators. Training in the use of the existing computer system would have to improve before this could be implemented.
* The maintenance teams would report directly to the Plant Maintenance Engineer, with a link (as necessary) between the electrical and instrumentation technicians and the professional Electrical Engineer.
* All workshop and other non-core work would be undertaken by a contractor alliance.
* A benchmark, for assessing the operation of self-empowered maintenance and operation teams, should be sought, the performance gap should be evaluated, and corrective actions identified (see the case study, Chapter 4, page 73).

Proposal B

The proposal-B resource structure (see Figure 5–10) being implemented, the administrative structure could be modified as shown in Figure 5–16. The main changes incorporated in this would then be as follows:

* The management of the Ammonia and Urea Plants would be combined at Plant Management level.
* A professionally qualified Electrical Engineer would be appointed within the works structure, responsible for supporting and controlling all electrical standards, systems and safety.
* The first line maintenance technicians would report to their respective Plant Engineers, with a link (as necessary) between the electrical instrument technicians and the Electrical Engineer.
* A CBM co-ordinator would be appointed, responsible for all monitoring equipment and procedures and reporting to the Ammonia Plant Engineer.
* A Maintenance Scheduler would be appointed (from among the existing planners), reporting to the Nitrogen Plant Manager. His function would be

TABLE 5–6 Maintenance Staff Inventory

Staff Categories	Total
Plant or site services manager	4
Mech. Engineer	4
Maintenance support officer	2
Maintenance planner	4
Maintenance team facilitator (in team)	4
Workshop superintendent	1
Maintenance systems superintendent	1
Systems officer planning	1
Site services co-facilitator	1
QA officer	1
Total maint. Staff	**23**
Sub-totals	
Total managerial staff	4
Total supervisory	5
Total planning staff	5
Total engineers (non managing)	4
Total special duties	5
Ratios	
Supervisors per manager	1.5
Supervised per planner	7.4
Eng. technicians (skilled) per planner	5.8
Eng. technicians (skilled) per engineer	7.2
Eng. technicians (skilled) per maint. staff	1.3
Maint. resources per maint. staff	1.6

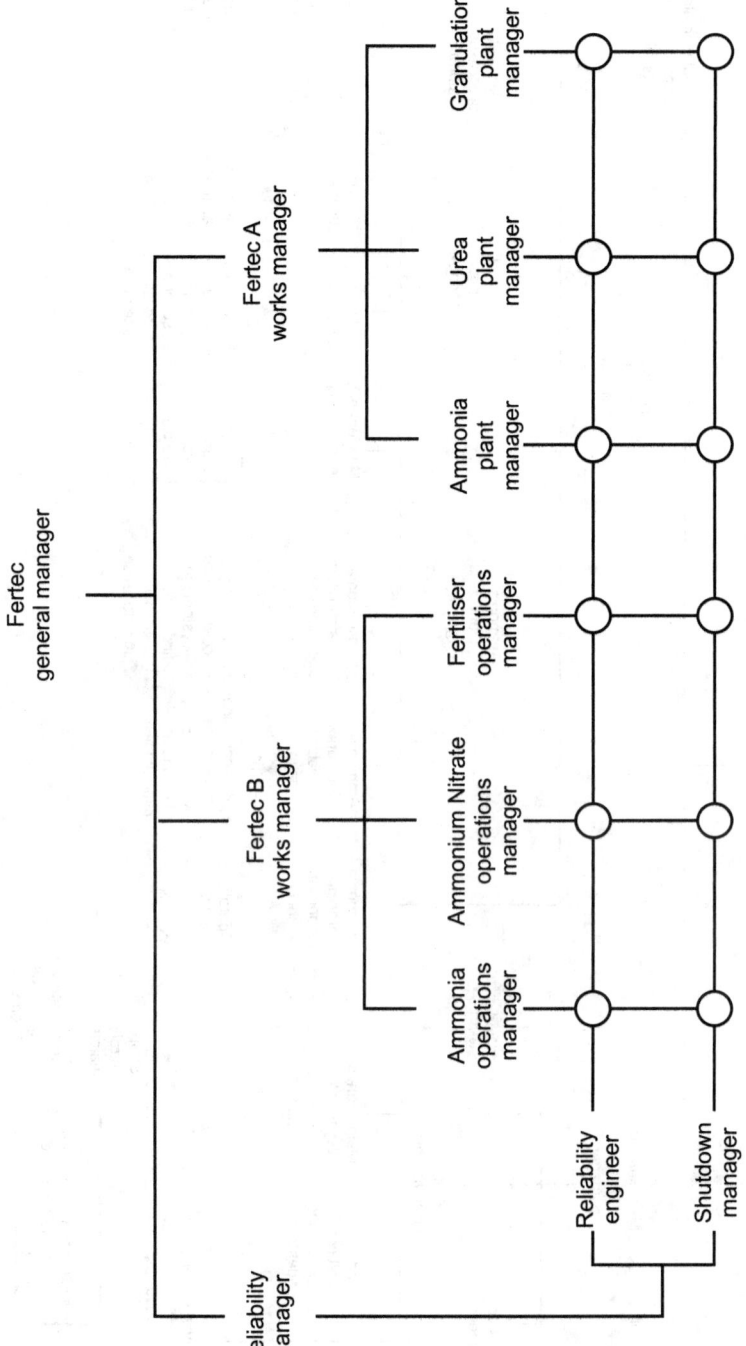

FIGURE 5–14 Senior Management Matrix Relationships

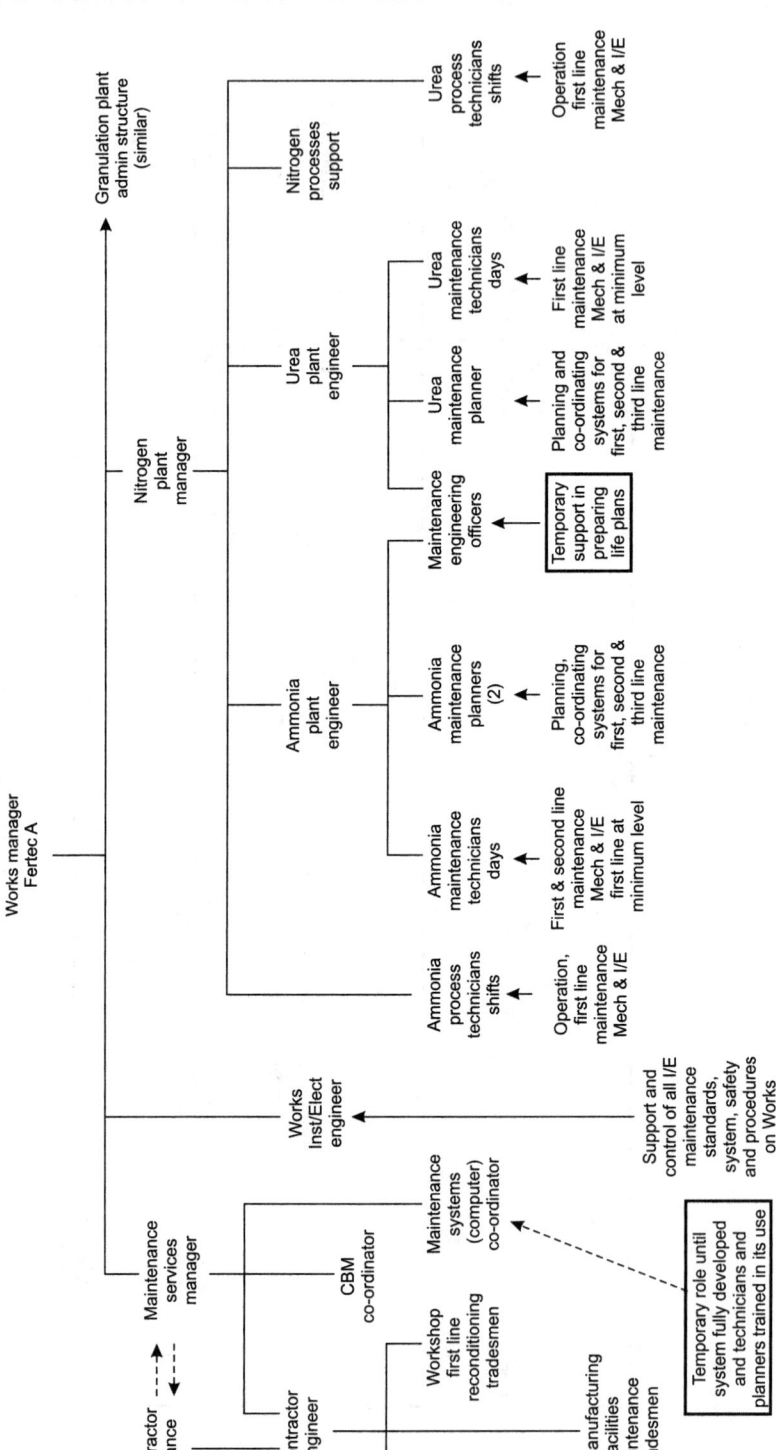

(Note - this is a discussion model - not a working model)

FIGURE 5–15 Modified Administrative Structure, Proposal A

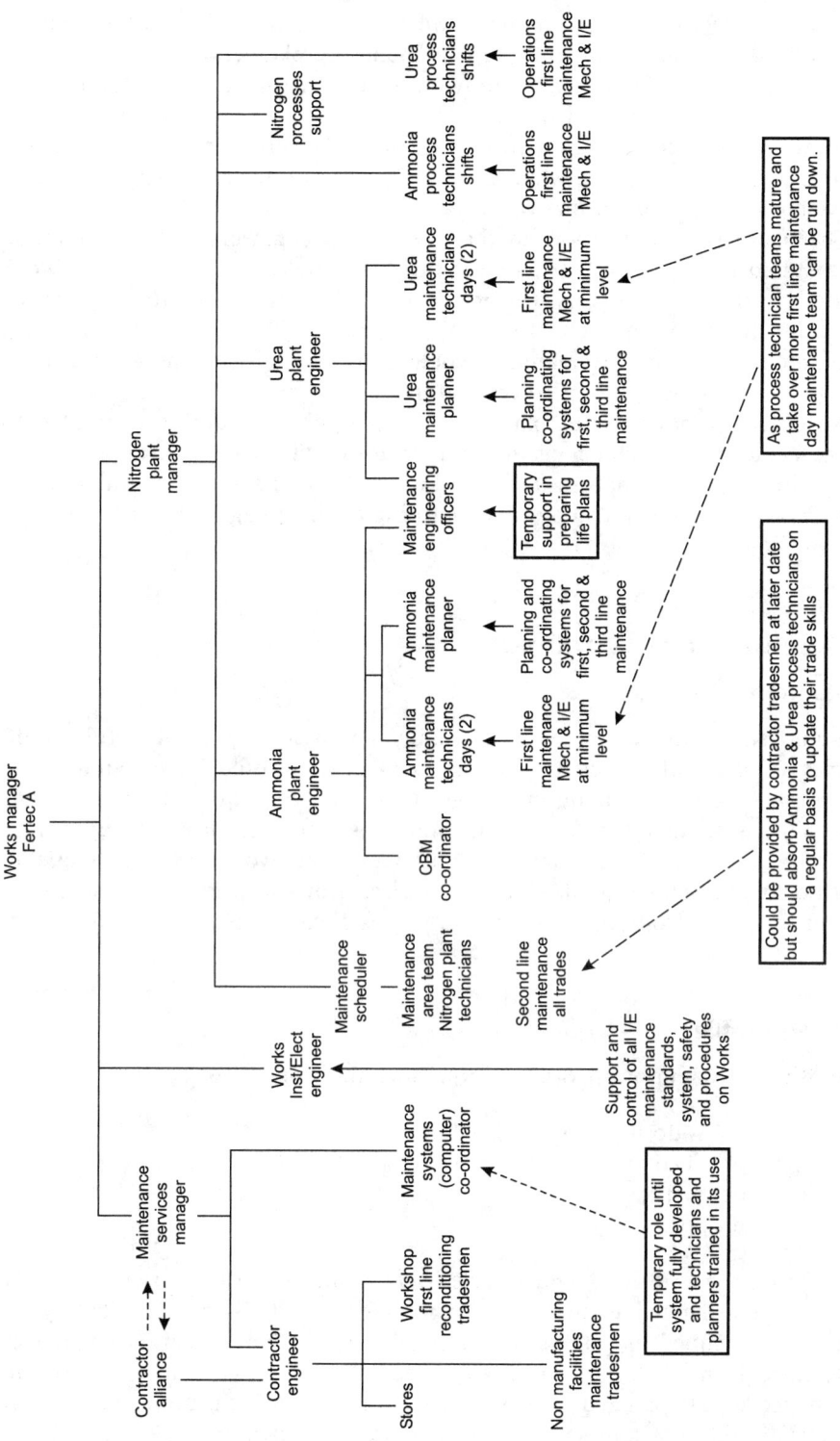

(Note - this is a discussion model - not a working model)

As process technician teams mature and take over more first line maintenance day maintenance team can be run down.

Could be provided by contractor tradesmen at later date but should absorb Ammonia & Urea process technicians on a regular basis to update their trade skills

FIGURE 5-16 Modified Administrative Structure, Proposal B

to set up the weekly programme of work on the Ammonia and Urea Plants (working in conjunction with their maintenance planners).

* The second line Nitrogen area team would report to the Maintenance Scheduler. The area team would also have an 'on the tools' facilitator.
* All workshop and other non-core work would be carried out by a contractor alliance linking with the Maintenance Services Manager. Later, this might extend to cover second line work.
* The planners would report to their respective engineers in the Ammonia, Urea and Granulation Plants. Their function would be to organize the work coming from the plants (priority checks, methods, spares, transport, specifications, etc) as well as providing administrative support for the local maintenance team. The planners would work closely with the Maintenance Scheduler and area group co-ordinator.
* An officer responsible for plant team development would be appointed to assist the plant technicians to mature into self-directing groups and to acquire and apply appropriate trade knowledge and skills for first line work. This task should be aided by benchmarking the teams against a 'best practice' team. (*See review question 5–10.*)

The Maintenance Workload

Introduction

An analysis of the workload is normally an integral part of a full audit. However, because of a lack of data in this area it would have required the application of Work Sampling and other analytical techniques and would have considerably extended the audit time and cost. It was therefore agreed at the specification stage that only an outline of the workload characteristics would be sought. This was obtained from discussions with key personnel, such as planners, and from analysis of wage costs categorised by maintenance activity.

Workload Profile

The priority system in operation throughout the works was as follows:

(1) immediate—do it today,
(2) interrupt schedule—do it this week,
(3) do it next week,
(4) do it on opportunity.

In general, the Priority 1 and 2 tasks were handled in the short term by the Facilitator (and defined as unplanned) while the 3's and 4's were handled by the Planner (and defined as planned). Priority 1's could be defined as emergency maintenance. It should be noted that, each week, the planner committed 75% of the maintenance team to planned work, which included preventive routines. On average about 70% of this was completed, giving a workload which was 50% planned.

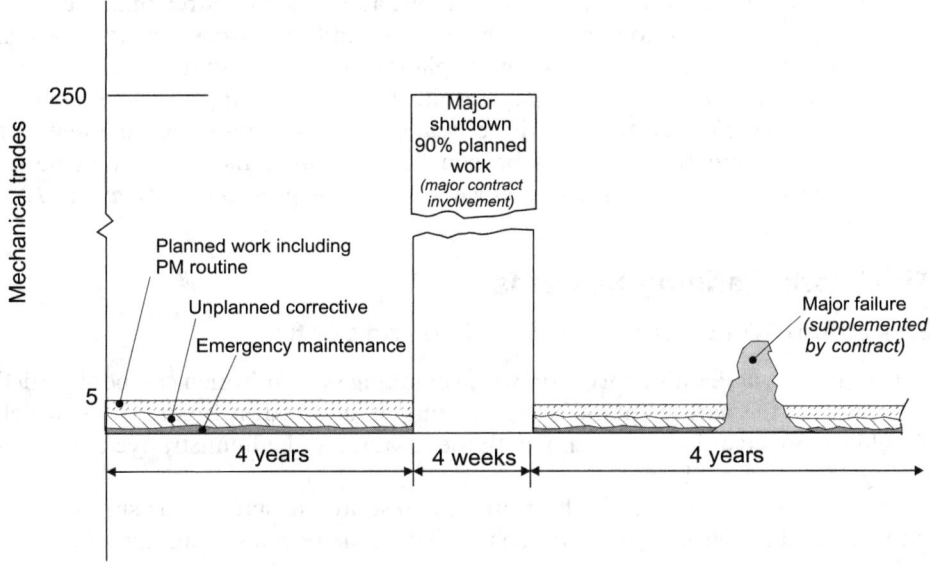

FIGURE 5–17 Estimate of Mechanical Workload Profile for Ammonia Plant

It was agreed by all those interviewed (including operations personnel) that, at most, the process team' only covered shift emergency maintenance, until the response team arrived. They did not carry out minor first line tasks.

A survey of the performance level ('How hard did they work?') of the maintenance team indicated a surprising consistency, of about 60%. The main comment was that they '*worked hard but not smart,*' which was a reflection of the high percentage of unplanned work which was carried out (and which itself was clearly symptomatic of a plant that was some thirty years old).

Using this information the workloads for the various plants could be drawn up (see, for example, Figure 5–17, the workload profile for the Ammonia Plant). The profile for the Urea Plant was similar and the shutdown work was carried out as a single project. The major workload for the Granulation Plant was much smaller and was scheduled to occur well away from the main shutdown— as far as possible this was resourced via the exploitation of inter-plant flexibilities.

Observations

(i) The workload estimates did not relate particularly well to the analysis of wage costs as a function of work category. For example, approximately 70% of the total work carried out was some form of planned preventive maintenance.

(ii) On continuous process plants of the type studied the main preventive maintenance effort is applied during the four-yearly main shutdowns.

Each of these may involve, for example, about four hundred man-weeks of fitting work, as compared with the thousand man-weeks of fitting work between shutdowns, i.e., when the plant is on line. A comparison based on costs would show a similar result. It therefore appeared to us that considerable savings could be realised in the on-going maintenance activity and that it would be beneficial to bring the area maintenance teams into the contractor alliance. (*See review questions 5–11 and 5–12.*)

The Work Planning Systems

Short Term Work Planning, Scheduling and Control

The Ammonia Plant's short-term work-planning system (which can be regarded as typical of the various plant-based systems) is outlined in Figure 5–18, which should be looked at in conjunction with the resource and administrative structures of Figs. 5–8 and 5–11.

This planning model was built around the resource structure. The shift process teams carried out little or no maintenance work, the response team handling out-of-hours emergency work, the day maintenance team the first and second line work.

The priority system was as follows:

(1) Now, or as soon as possible,
(2) This week, interrupting the schedule,
(3) Next week,
(4) Shutdown, product change, opportunity.

Preventive routines were not prioritised and were 'fitted in'. The system was computer-operated using a software package for maintenance planning which was part of an enterprise-wide management software package.

A notification (a request for work) could be raised from a number of sources. Figure 5–18 outlines the mechanism by which this could be done by the process facilitator. The notification carried most of the information that would be later transferred to the history record. In theory, resources (labour, spares etc) could not be employed until the notification had been raised to the status of a work order (WO). If, on shifts, the process team was available, and the job was within their capability, then (in theory) the WO was raised against them. In practice, however, the process team rarely carried out maintenance work. In the case of an out-of-hours emergency the response group was summoned and the appropriate WO raised.

In most cases the notification went directly into the facilitator's and planner's in-tray (their notification list). In total about ten WO's per day were received of which only one would be of Priority 1. Most WO's specified a single technician, although a few might require up to five. The facilitators and planners could re-assess the priorities. In general, i.e., across the whole site, facilitators dealt with the Priority 1 and 2 work (if necessary, with assistance from the relevant planner) and the planners the Priority 3 and 4 work.

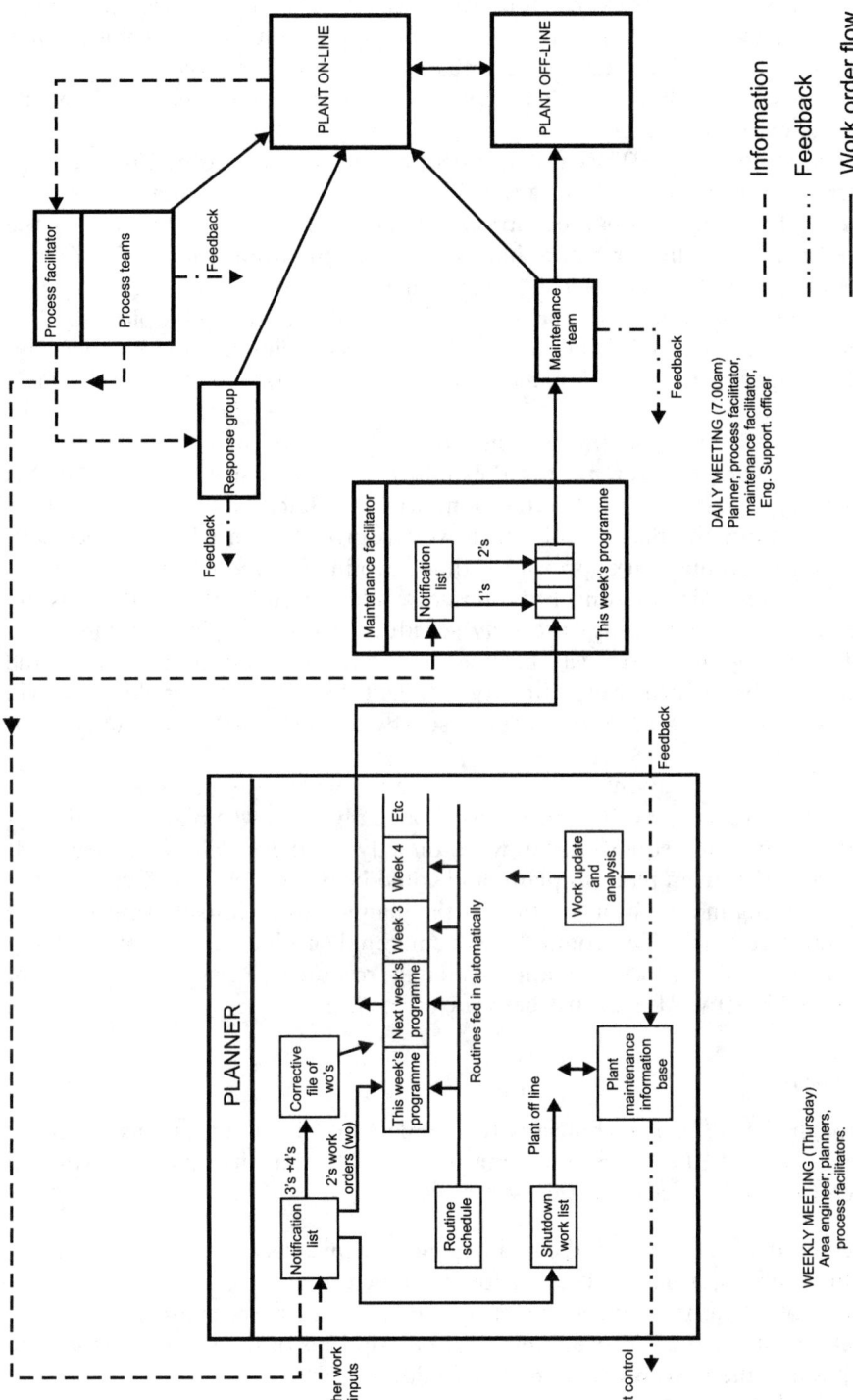

FIGURE 5-18 Ammonia Work-Planning Model

It was agreed that job instructions were issued only for the large machines. Planners and facilitators felt that windows of opportunity were exploited in a satisfactory manner. The number of actual labour-hours employed was entered into the system at a later date (sometimes at a very much later date!) by the technicians involved.

The permit to work (PTW) system operated via the facilitator. For the non-emergency jobs he took the WO's and PTW's to the Process Facilitator at the end of the day. The tagging was then carried out overnight and was checked by the daytime Process Facilitator before handing over to the Maintenance Facilitator. The Maintenance Facilitator started work at 6.30 am, in order to cover the PTW's and the jobs over-spilling from the night shift. A daily meeting took place, at 7.00 am—of the Maintenance Facilitator, the day Process Facilitator, the Planner, and technical support personnel—the main purpose of which was to draw up the day's programme.

The main function of the Planner (in all the systems audited) was to organize the work programme for the following week. He was helped in this by a meeting, every Thursday afternoon, with his Facilitator, Plant Engineer and process staff, the purpose of which was to provide him with the necessary information (ongoing work, priority ratings, production requirements, routines outstanding etc). His resulting programme would commit 75% of the existing manpower—some jobs beings precisely scheduled to match plant requirements while the timing of others was flexible. The most difficult to plan were the multi-trade jobs, which were directly handled by the Planner himself, via single WO or—as was more often the case—by a Master WO and linked Sub-WO's.

We were told that about 70% of the planned work was completed—which meant that approximately 50% of the work actually done was planned and 50% unplanned (i.e., the request for it went directly to the Facilitator). This last percentage varied from plant to plant, and could be higher than the figure quoted above—resulting in a high proportion of the planned work (mostly routines) not being addressed at all. The computer system could produce lists of outstanding work, categorised by priority and available resource. Regular reporting of backlog (deferred) work had just been introduced.

Observations

Although the ratio of technicians to Planners and Facilitators was relatively low the users of the work planning system felt that it was not working satisfactorily. Some factors in this were:

* a computer system which the maintenance technicians and Facilitators found 'unfriendly,' not having been properly trained in its use,
* an incomplete, user-unfriendly, maintenance data base, characterised by a lack of standard job procedures, poor descriptions of the spares in stores etc (although these problems were being addressed),
* a high level of reactive work (in some plants) caused by the age of the installations and by earlier poor maintenance regimes,

* a pedantic PTW and tagging system (a problem which was being addressed)

The fundamental problem here was the unsatisfactory resource structure (see page 106). The process teams were not carrying out any first line work, all the maintenance work cascading into six small trade groups. Requests for Priority 1 and 2 work were going direct to the Maintenance Facilitator, disrupting the Planner's weekly programme, which meant that in many areas up to 50% of the total workload was unplanned (for effective weekly forward planning the unplanned element would need to have been less than 15% of the total workload).

Recommendations

It was proposed that the Figure 5–10 resource structure be adopted. This would overcome the disruption related above. The Priority 1 work and a proportion of the less complex Priority 2 tasks would be carried out on shifts by the process technicians, and on days by the plant-dedicated maintenance technicians (who would work closely with the process technicians). The remainder of the work, 90% of which should be planned, would be carried out by the Nitrogen team. Also, the Facilitators should receive increased training to enable them to carry out the planning role. (*See review question 5–13.*)

Planning of the Major Shutdowns

This was not a full audit of the shutdown planning procedure—which would have required our presence during the actual shutdown. The exercise was limited to a review of that procedure by comparing it with the standard procedure outlined in Figure 5–19 and attempting to answer Questions 5.1 to 5.9 of the Aide-Memoir given in Appendix 1.

Over the years Fertec had had some poorly planned and executed shutdowns and, as a result, had set up a permanent shutdown planning team, reporting to the Reliability Manager (see Figure 5–14), including a Shutdown Manager and the Shutdown Planners located at both the A and B plants, and supplemented by key personnel immediately before and during any particular shutdown. The ongoing administrative structure of Figure 5–3 and Figures 5–11–5–13 was modified during the period of the shutdown. The resource structure of Figure 5–8 was also modified to include an influx of personnel. The scheduling and resourcing of the shutdown was carried out with the aid of a network planning package, Primavera. The tasks identified in the main network were organized via the main computerised work planning system.

Recommendations

As a result of their history of poorly executed shutdowns Fertec had made major efforts to improve the planning, organization and execution of such exercises. We considered that, as a consequence, they had developed a shutdown planning procedure approaching international best practice. The following further improvements were recommended:

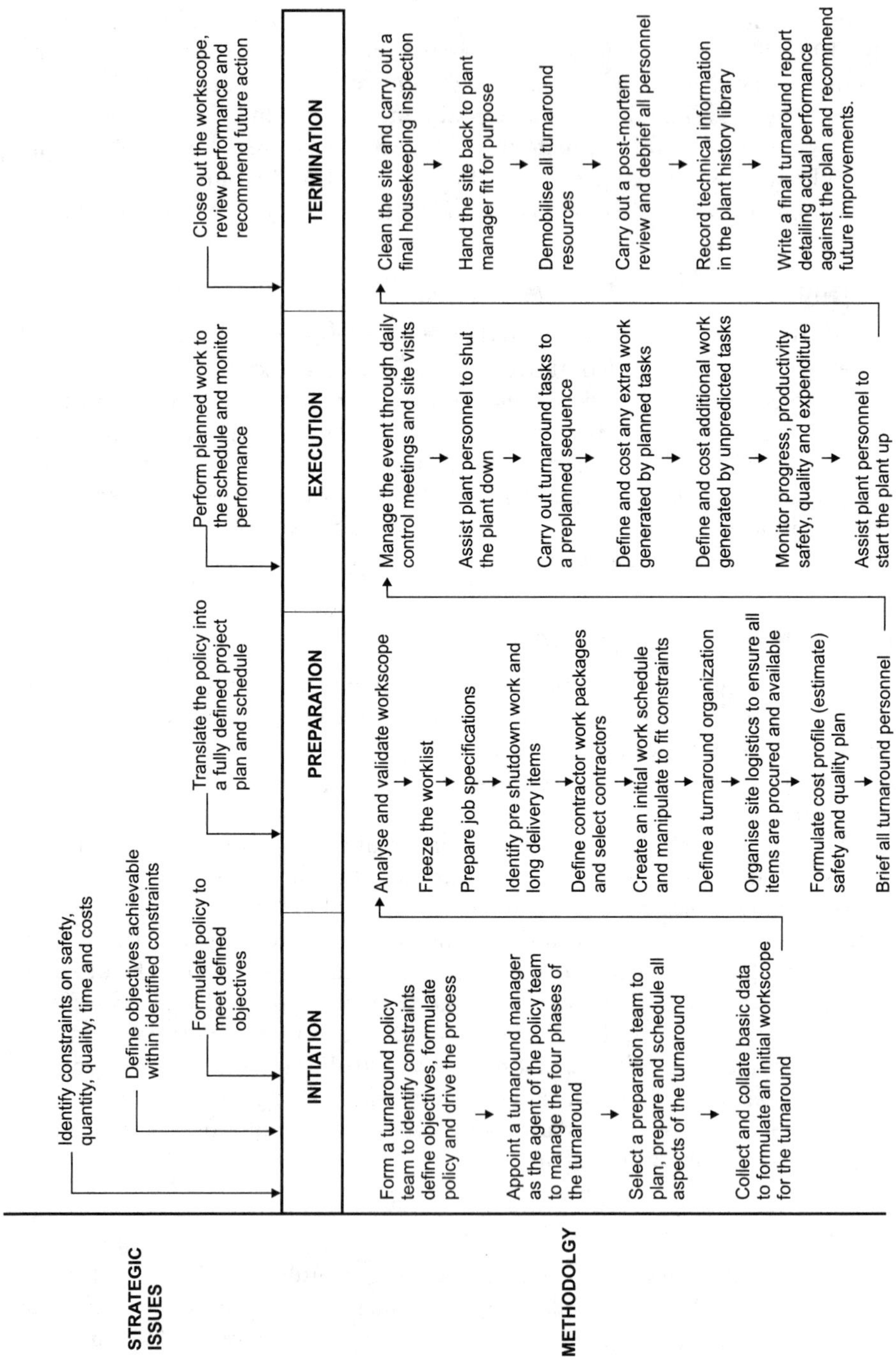

STRATEGIC ISSUES

- Identify constraints on safety, quantity, quality, time and costs
- Define objectives achievable within identified constraints
- Formulate policy to meet defined objectives
- Translate the policy into a fully defined project plan and schedule
- Perform planned work to the schedule and monitor performance
- Close out the workscope, review performance and recommend future action

METHODOLGY

INITIATION	PREPARATION	EXECUTION	TERMINATION
Form a turnaround policy team to identify constraints define objectives, formulate policy and drive the process	Analyse and validate workscope	Manage the event through daily control meetings and site visits	Clean the site and carry out a final housekeeping inspection
Appoint a turnaround manager as the agent of the policy team to manage the four phases of the turnaround	Freeze the worklist	Assist plant personnel to shut the plant down	Hand the site back to plant manager fit for purpose
Select a preparation team to plan, prepare and schedule all aspects of the turnaround	Prepare job specifications	Carry out turnaround tasks to a preplanned sequence	Demobilise all turnaround resources
Collect and collate basic data to formulate an initial workscope for the turnaround	Identify pre shutdown work and long delivery items	Define and cost any extra work generated by planned tasks	Carry out a post-mortem review and debrief all personnel
	Define contractor work packages and select contractors	Define and cost additional work generated by unpredicted tasks	Record technical information in the plant history library
	Create an initial work schedule and manipulate to fit constraints	Monitor progress, productivity safety, quality and expenditure	Write a final turnaround report detailing actual performance against the plan and recommend future improvements.
	Define a turnaround organization	Assist plant personnel to start the plant up	
	Organise site logistics to ensure all items are procured and available		
	Formulate cost profile (estimate) safety and quality plan		
	Brief all turnaround personnel		

FIGURE 5–19 Generic Major Plant Shutdown, Planning Methodology

* More thought should be given to the development of the plant shutdown and start up plans.
* A more rigorous approach to site logistics should be developed, to ensure that 'the right thing is in the right place at the right time'.
* So that a comprehensive and detailed shutdown workscope could be formulated the recording of the existing shutdown history needed to be improved (although for pressure vessels it was already satisfactory). In addition, the recording of on-line condition monitoring data needed to be improved—at the time of the audit there was no linkage between this data and the history in the plant information base.
* One of the main reasons for poor quality work during the shutdowns was the lack of standard job procedures with inspection test plans. We were aware that improvements in this area were in hand but felt it necessary to re-emphasize the considerable effort and demand on resources that this would require.
* The shutdown planning software in use needed improvement, particularly as regards its interfaces with other systems. At the time of the audit the 'Primavera' package was about to be used to produce the shutdown schedule, which then needed feeding (manually, at that time) into the computerised work planning system in order to identify, and control, costs. However, since neither of these systems produced satisfactory S curves, an Excel-based program was being employed for this.

Spare Parts Management

Introduction

In this case the actual brief did not include an audit of the stores management system—which would have been a major exercise in its own right. The purpose of this part of a maintenance audit would have been to establish how good the stores system was in giving the maintenance function the service it needed.

Outline of the Stores Organization and Systems

Figure 5–1 shows the location of the main stores, sub-stores and maintenance workshop. The main workshop carried all the catalogued parts and was operated using the enterprise-wide computer system. The total value of the spares holding was around £3M, involving some 12,500 groups of items. The annual turnover was estimated at 60% of the value of the holding. The main stores had recently introduced an open stores policy (i.e., 'Serve yourself'), the parts being located via the computer system and withdrawn after a work order had been raised.

In terms of inventory policy the items were grouped into six categories (including 'slow-moving spare parts'). The initial ordering policy for new equipment ('What and how many to hold?') was taken by the unit engineers as part of their 'life plan' analysis. A stand-alone software package (SCAS) was used in formulating policy for the 'slow-moving and expensive' category. Responsibility for the main stores was exercised, via the stores superintendent, by the site services manager (see Figure 5–12). The sub-stores held a mixture of consumables, non-stores-controlled parts, and tools—and were the responsibility of the Area Facilitators.

Reconditioned items were supplied to the stores from the workshop and also direct from outside contractors (see Figure 5–9), the workshop being the responsibility of the site services manager (but would eventually come within the ambit of the proposed contractor alliance).

Observations and Recommendations

(i) We were told that the SCAS system for deciding the number of slow moving spares to be held was not then in use, and that the general policy for parts holding had not been reviewed for upwards of twenty years, during which time the plant had undergone many major shutdowns. It was our opinion (supported by the interviewees) that there was serious over-stocking of the expensive slow moving spares. We recommended that a review be carried out of the stock held and that this should include a Pareto analysis of parts, by cost and turnover. All expensive slow moving parts should be subjected to a SCAS review.

(ii) The proportion (17%) of reconditioned items going out to contract was low for a company located in an industrial area. It was recommended that a small project team be set up to study this problem in more detail, with the object of outsourcing re-conditioning as much as possible, a policy which initially should be applied to the electric motors.

(iii) There were very few key performance indices (KPI's) used in the stores management system; ones which should be introduced as soon as possible were:

— a service factor index (the number of times per period a request for parts could not be met);

— a re-work index (for reconditioned items). (*See review question 5–14.*)

Maintenance Control

The Control of Overall Maintenance Performance

A conventional budgeting and cost control system was in operation, using a computer work order system of the kind outlined in Figure 1–18. The plant was divided into its main units of equipment and each one given a functional alpha-numeric location coding, e.g.:

Syn Gas Compressor 6   C   02

where '6' indicated that the unit was in the Ammonia Plant, 'C' that it was a compressor and '02' exactly which unit it was (of the several compressors at that location). The main assemblies or systems within each unit were then further categorised and listed, e.g., 'Reaction Turbine RT02'. The costs incurred on a unit were also divided via an alpha-numeric code according to trade, department, work type etc. Cost reports regarding specific aspects could therefore be generated, e.g.:

Total cost per period per functional location per equipment number;
'Top Ten' functional locations as regards incurred costs or man-hours of work of a given type.

A different system was in use to record plant and equipment uptimes and availabilities and a series of KPI's, based on the objective hierarchy of Figure 1–5, had just been established, including, for each main plant:

Monthly maintenance cost per ton of product.
Monthly availability.
Total cost of maintenance.

The Control of Organizational Efficiency

Until shortly before the audit, no data had been collected for this purpose. However, a newly introduced system of KPI's included the following organizational indices for each plant:

Planned-work percentage.
Unplanned-work percentage.
Preventive man-hours percentage.
Re-work man-hours percentage.
Mean time between raising of work order and completion of work.
Units with a spare parts list.
Man-hours of deferred work
Overtime man-hours as percentage of total.
Inventory value.
Stores turnover as percentage of total inventory
Costs incurred as a consequence of stockouts.

The Control of Maintenance Effectiveness, or Plant Reliability Control (PRC)

An outline of a PRC system was given in Figure 1–11, and Figure 1–20 indicated how it might be operated organizationally. With these concepts in mind we felt that at Fertec:

The PRC structure should be formalised and the roles of the people involved clearly specified, i.e.:
+ the Level 1 system should be set up to include the involvement of the process and maintenance teams in continuous improvement (which was non-existent at the time); the teams should also be involved in the improvement of the life plans and given increased training with a view to improving the quality of history feedback;

+ the roles of the Plant Engineer and Engineering Officers in plant reliability control should be clarified (Level 2); such clarification should include their own inter-relationships and those with the Reliability Group and it should be pointed out that they should spend at least 30% of their time on designing-out maintenance problems;
+ the role of the Reliability Group and their linkages to the Plant Engineers and the OEM should be clarified.

Documentation

The main computerised information system at Fertec was a fully-integrated 'enterprise wide software package (EWSP)' with several functional subsystems, among which was the maintenance management system. The EWSP was supplemented by a number of other computer systems and by hard paper documentation files.

When auditing this area we were guided by the functional documentation model of Figure 1–21 and by Section 14 of the aide memoir. The following were our main observations

Unit life plans: Except for the pressure vessels, these were not formally documented

Standard job catalogue: Some of the original preventive routines for the ancillary equipment were recorded in the EWSP, but needed updating. Several reconditioning specifications for the large machines were held in hard copy.

Equipment drawings: Many were out of date.

Manuals: There was no master library. The manuals investigated were in poor condition and held in several locations.

Spare parts lists for the various units: The electrical lists were only 50% complete.

History: Held in a number of locations as follows:

* The ancillary equipment history was held in the EWSP and was of poor quality due to poor feedback from the teams.
* The pressure vessel history, which was of excellent quality, was held in a stand-alone computerised database which included job specifications, life plans and operating procedures.
* The large machine history was held in hard copy and at several different locations.

Condition monitoring: Each monitoring system seemed have its own particular arrangement for record storing. The external consultants providing hand held vibration monitoring, for example, held their own records.

Short term work planning: Carried out via the work order system of the EWSP, which also held the preventive schedule for the ancillary equipment, but not the shutdown schedule.

Shutdown planning: The 'Primavera' package was used to create the shutdown schedule, the work order system of the EWSP to allocate the jobs and record the costs. 'Excel' was used to produce S-curves.

Observations and Recommendations

   (i) The Reliability Group felt that the EWSP was not suitable for holding and operating the kind of data that is needed for the maintenance of the large machines and pressure vessels viz life plans, job specifications, history (including that of NDT mapping), case studies of overhauls and so on. They indicated their intention to develop stand-alone databases not only for the pressure vessels (where they had already done so) but also for large machines and electrical and instrumentation equipment, and in the light of our audit we had some sympathy with this view. The EWSP had evolved in manufacturing industry where the major shutdowns are different in kind from those in the process industries. However, the development of new databases and interfacing would be an expensive business. We recommended that a small project team (helped by the EWSP experts) should examine this problem further to establish whether the EWSP could be modified to satisfy the needs of the Reliability Group. We could not see the need, for example, for a separate electrical and instrumentational equipment database. The point was that if the EWSP were to have remained limited to its then equipment coverage the company would have paid a very high price for what was essentially a simple work order and costing system.

  (ii) The EWSP was not operating as well as it should, partly because it was not user-friendly and partly because training in its use had declined. We recommended that the training be reviewed re-started, and its subsequent progress kept monitored

 (iii) We recommended that a master library of equipment manuals be set up as soon as possible.

Final Comments

The audit report included an executive summary, comprising some 22 pages of text and diagrams, which answered the three basic questions listed on page 91 by highlighting those recommendations put forward in the strategy, organization and systems sections of the full report.

Many of the criticisms regarding the condition and reliability of plant and the lack of documented life plans were already being addressed by the Reliability Group.

The main thrust of the planned maintenance effort expended on the continuously operating plants was applied during the major shutdowns. The experience and procedures of the newly formed Shutdown Management Group were impressive. This group should overcome the problems identified by the audit in the important area of preventive maintenance.

The structure of the maintenance organization conformed with best practice internationally, i.e., comprising such features as:

plant based manufacturing units;
self-empowered process teams, expected to carry out some first line
maintenance; self-empowered mechanical teams;

self-empowered electrical and instrumentation teams;
progress towards workshop-contractor alliances;
minimisation of the employment of non-trade labour.

In spite of this the audit showed that the organization was not working well, mainly as a result of human factors problems at shop floor level, in particular the refusal by the process teams to involve themselves in first-line maintenance work. A number of recommendations were made to correct this and other problems and included proposals for re-organization as detailed in pages 109 to 111 and 112 to 118. (*See review question 5–15.*)

CHAPTER 6

The Snapshot Audit and Re-Audit

In this chapter I will show how, in the space of two brief visits to an industrial installation—the first to carry out a 'snapshot' exercise, the second a short re-audit—the audit method can be employed for mapping the essential characteristics and problems of the maintenance function. The case study used to illustrate this also highlights the importance of making (as far as possible) supervisors and teams 'equipment-responsible' and also shows how difficult it is to make strategic and organizational changes in a trade-union-dominated environment.

Introduction

Over a period of five days in 1994, and working on my own, I carried out a snapshot audit of the maintenance and engineering departments at an underground coal mining company, COALCOM. Three years later, and also working alone, I carried out a three-day re-audit.

COALCOM comprised three underground collieries—operating three shifts per day, for a five day week and for fifty weeks per year—and a coal preparation plant (see Figure 6–1). The coal was taken to the preparation plant by truck, and then by rail to coal loaders some two hundred miles away on the coast. The senior management structure is shown in Figure 6–2. At this level each of the collieries and the coal preparation plant functioned as semi-autonomous production units. An Engineering Manager (with a secretary) had then just been appointed to assist in the co-ordination of the de-centralised engineering departments, which carried out capital project work and had the responsibility for the off-site overhauls of major equipment (some of which was shared between the collieries).

The management commissioned the snapshot audit because they were concerned that the availability of their underground equipment was low and their maintenance costs high. They believed that the main problem was an inadequate structure for organising maintenance and engineering. The audit was expected to answer the question:

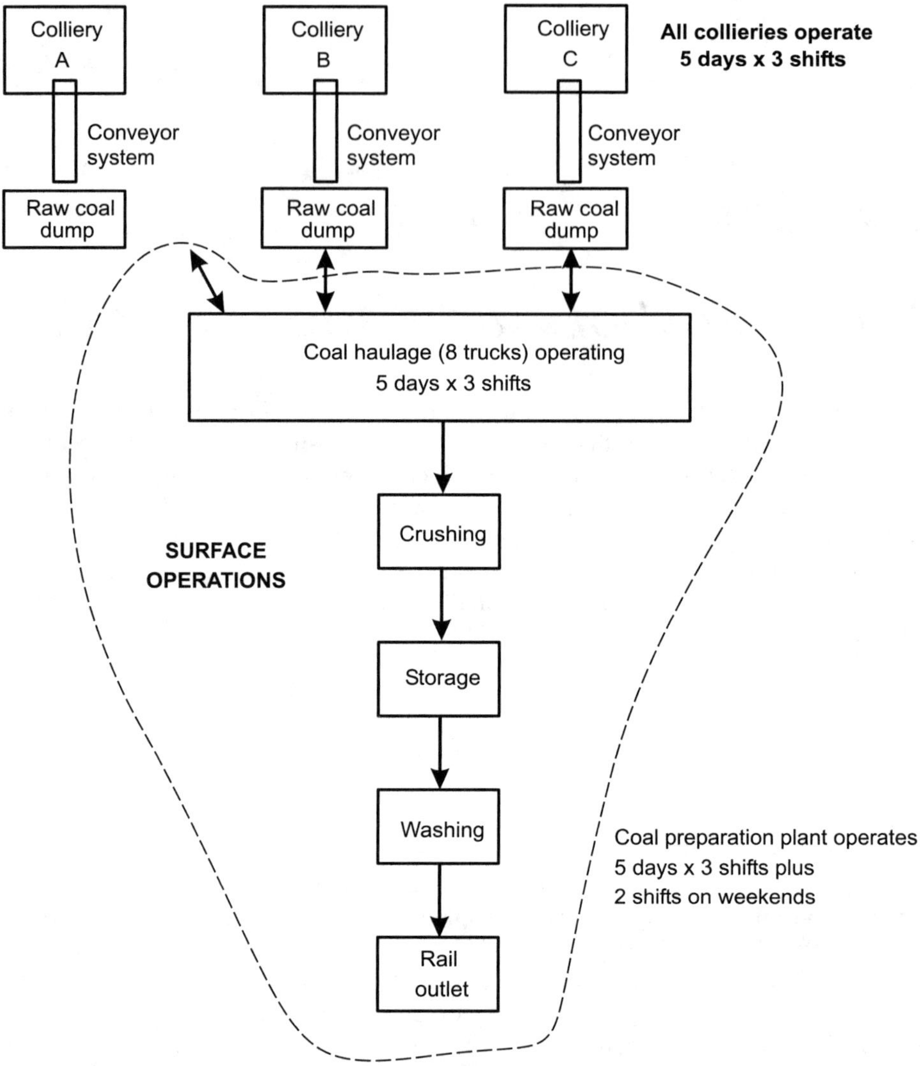

Figure 6–1 COALCOM Process Flow

'What changes in the maintenance strategy and organizational structure were needed in order to improve equipment availability and reduce maintenance costs?'

Because all three collieries operated in a similar way and had similar problems I decided to concentrate my main effort on Colliery A. In addition, I interviewed the Engineering Manager and the other colliery engineering superintendents in order to acquire an understanding of the way the engineering effort across COALCOM was co-ordinated.

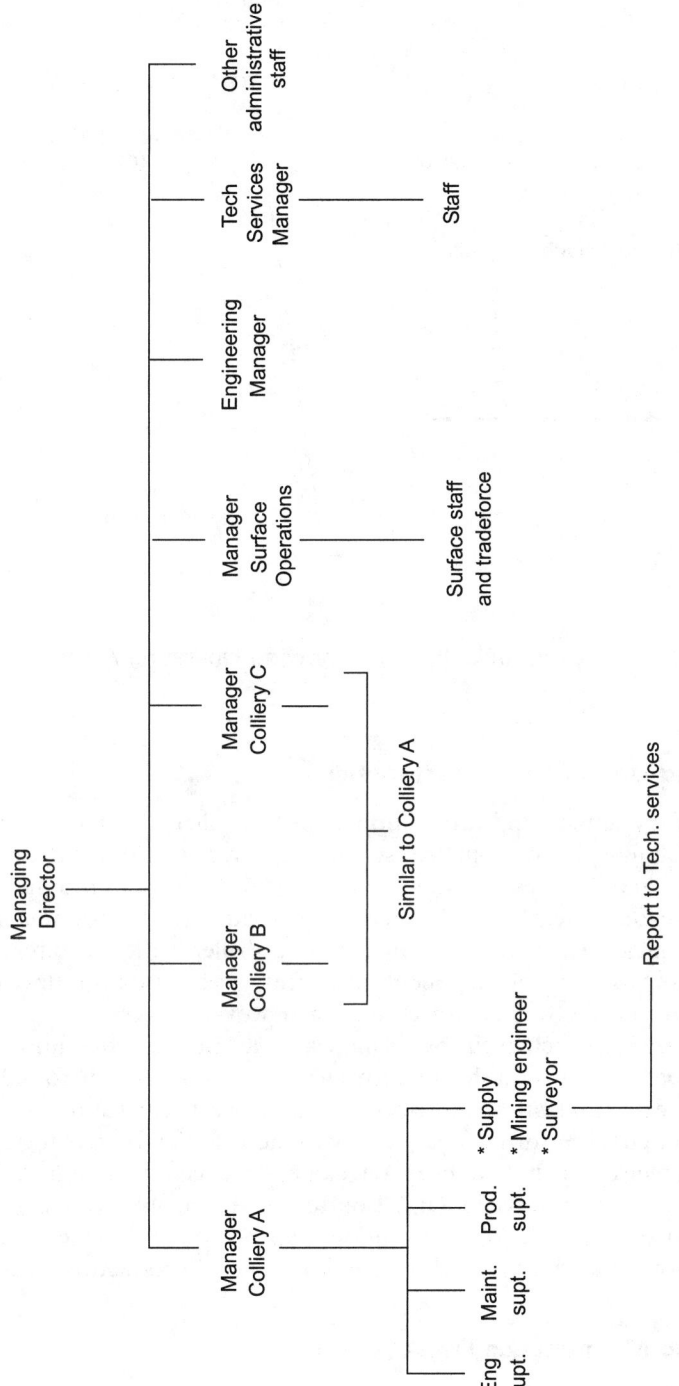

FIGURE 6–2 COALCOM Senior Management Structure

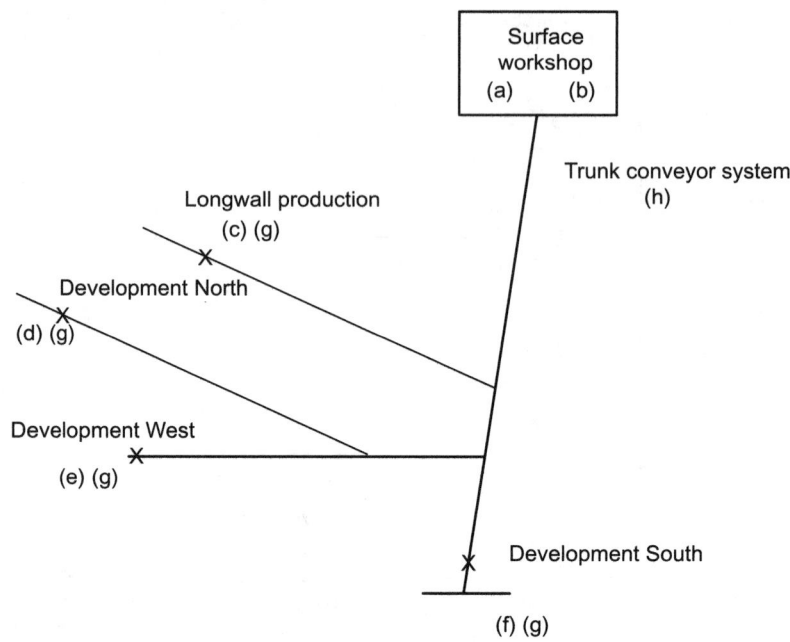

FIGURE 6–3 Layout of Colliery A, Showing Operating Areas

Colliery A

Equipment and Operating Characteristics

The layout of the tunnels and production areas of Colliery A—a drift mine, the main tunnel inclining down from the surface to three development areas and the Longwall production area—is shown in Figure 6–3. The main tunnel carried the trunk conveyor system and the personnel roadways. Continuous miners (diesel-driven vehicles, each with a front-mounted driller–cutter for creating the development tunnels through the coal measures) were used to develop the production areas and the tunnels for conveyor or worker access.

Coal extraction was achieved by 'Longwall' cutting, an operation which employed a system comprising a shearer, armoured-face conveyor (up to 100 metres long), main conveyors and various services, such as an electricity supply (see Figure 6–4). The shearer cut slices of the coal seam two metres thick by moving across a hundred-metre block which had been developed between two tunnels by the continuous miners. The removed coal fell on to the armour-plated conveyor and was then moved outwards to the conventional conveyors. A balance had to be maintained between the rate of development work and of production.

Production and Maintenance Objectives

A production plan was being used to balance development and Longwall production to meet target outputs. The mine was production limited. These target

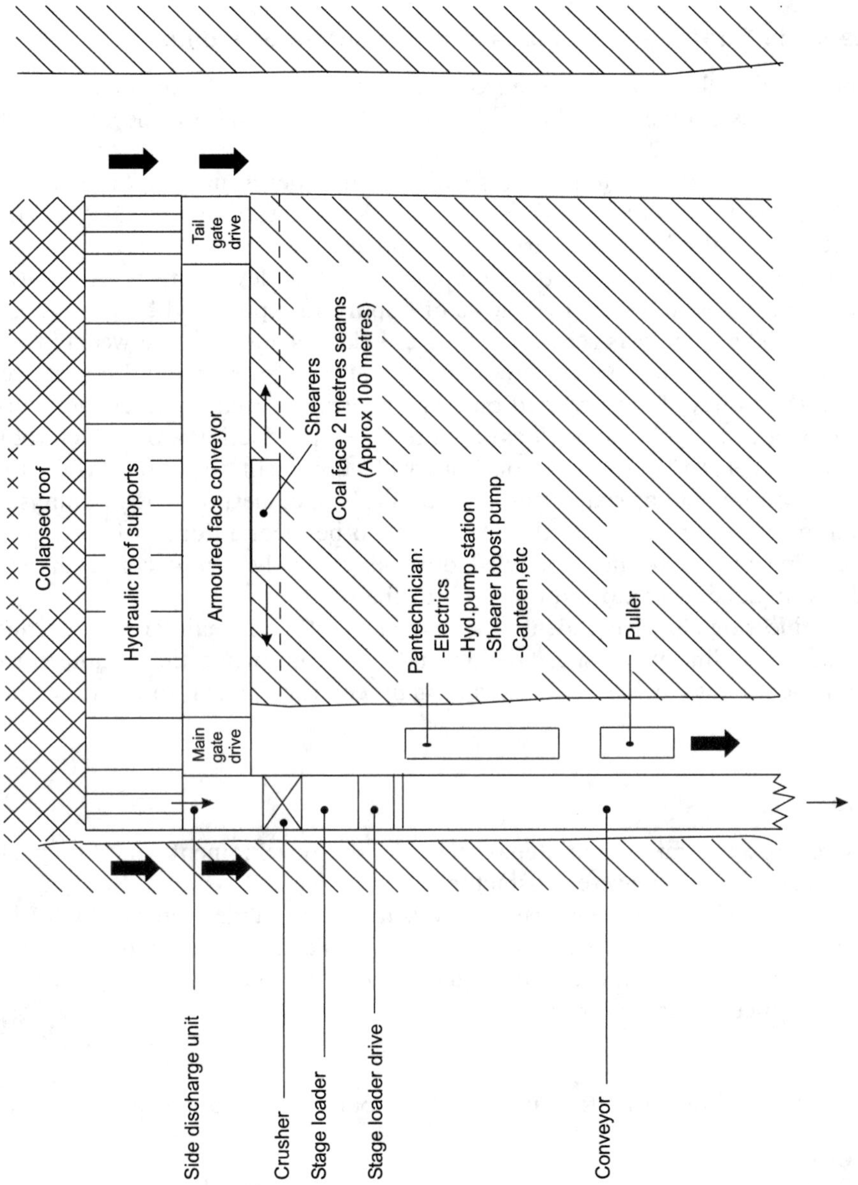

Collapsed roof

Hydraulic roof supports

Armoured face conveyor

Tail gate drive

Main gate drive

Shearers

Coal face 2 metres seams
(Approx 100 metres)

Pantechnician:
-Electrics
-Hyd.pump station
-Shearer boost pump
-Canteen,etc

Puller

Side discharge unit

Crusher

Stage loader

Stage loader drive

Conveyor

FIGURE 6–4 Longwall Process

outputs were being used to set availability targets for the Longwall. However, it was my impression that the engineering-maintenance department had not established equipment life plans to achieve these availability targets. Also, I could find no key performance indices for any area of organizational efficiency.

Maintenance Strategy—Life Plans and Preventive Schedule

An outline life plan for the armoured faced conveyor (AFC) of the Longwall cutting system is shown in Table 6–1 and Exhibit 6–1 shows one of the job specifications.

The minor work of the life plan was carried out underground while the major work (the overhaul) was undertaken off-site by contractors (or the OEM). This was typical of most of the underground equipment.

The minor maintenance of the equipment in the development areas was scheduled during the week into windows of opportunity provided by production changeovers. The work was scheduled to avoid clashes and also the weekly two-shift Longwall down-day, when minor maintenance (preventive and corrective) arising on the Longwall was carried out. The major Longwall maintenance took place during a Longwall change (locating it to a new production area, which took about three weeks). Major units of Longwall equipment (e.g., the AFC, the shearer, etc.) were held as spares common to all three collieries, which minimised Longwall overhaul and allowed the equipment to be reconditioned off-site.

There appeared to be no scheduled down-day for the trunk conveyor and limited maintenance was carried out on it at the weekends.

The Engineering Superintendent was responsible for all maintenance carried out off-site, including work specification and tendering, while the Maintenance Superintendent was responsible for all maintenance carried out within the mine.

Observations

* As regards the minor maintenance work, the development and Longwall equipment life plans were satisfactory.
* The major off-site maintenance work was not being carried out satisfactorily. This was partly due to a lack of communication and understanding, concerning its specification and quality control, among the engineering-maintenance departments.

TABLE 6–1 Outline of Life Plan for the Armoured Face Conveyor

Chain tension	1 week
Rudd link insp	1 month
Oil test	1 month
Service	3 months
Code C service (statutory electrical)	3 months
Overhaul	At Longwall change

Exhibit 6–1 Example of a Preventive Job Specification

Armoured Face Conveyor	Plant No.	Weekly Service (Fitter)

Location	Date Due	

Complete the Following and Report Condition (Repair as required)

Safety	Ensure correct isolation & tagging procedures are fulfilled before commencing. If working underneath equip. ensure it is adequately supported
Drives	Top up M/G drive box oil (p/gear heavy):
	Top up M/G slat box oil (p/gear heavy):
	Top up M/G drive sprocket (p/gear heavy):
	Inspect M/G drive sprocket for wear:
	M/G chain strippers—condition Security:
	Test operation of M/G slat box (incl. operation of interlock):
	Ensure M/G drive box mounting bolts are tight:
	Ensure M/G drive water cooling is operating correctly:
	Ensure all covers & guards are fitted & secure:
	Top up T/G drive box oil (p/gear heavy):
	Top up T/G slat box oil (p/gear heavy):
	Top up T/G drive sprocket (p/gear heavy):
	Inspect T/G drive sprocket for wear
	T/G chain strippers—condition: Security:
	Test operation of T/G slat box (incl. operation of interlock):
	Ensure T/G drive box mounting bolts are tight:
	Ensure T/G drive water cooling is operating correctly:
	Ensure all covers & guards are fitted & secure:
Chains	Check chain tension—goaf side (10 →13):
	Face side (10 →13):
	Inspect chain & joiners for damage or wear:
	Inspect flight bars for damage or wear:
	Ensure all flight bar bolts are tight:
	Inspect for missing flight bars:
Pans	Inspect for wide pan gaps or dropped pans—(this may indicate a broken dog bone):
	Rack bars – condition: Wear:
	Rack bar pins – security: Any missing?:
	Spill plates – condition: Security:
	Cable trough – condition: Guide rail cond.:
	Inspect all cables, hyd., water & air hoses for damage:
	Relay bar → AFC pan pin— condition: Security:

Work Outstanding

* The life plans for the conveyor systems were satisfactory. However the off-line preventive and corrective work arising from the inspections was not being carried out. This was partly because of the absence of a down-shift. The windows of opportunity (those provided by shift changeovers and those occurring at the weekends) were not being used for planned maintenance.
* Although the colliery was production limited the management preferred to use mid-week down-days for Longwall maintenance (a 13.5% availability loss) rather than sanction overtime or seven-day maintenance shift rostering for the weekends.

Maintenance Organization

Resource structure: Figure 6–5 shows the Monday to Friday maintenance resource structure, an inventory of the maintenance personnel being shown in Table 6–2. Only a small amount of labour was available for weekend work. The tradeforce was plant-specialised, to provide a first line maintenance shift cover (e.g., the Longwall had two fitters and an electrician—Group (c)—on each shift). A small centralised pool (g), working in conjunction with the surface resource (a) and (b), moved to supplement the first line teams during mid-weekly down-shifts.

During major underground maintenance work (mainly locating the Longwall to a new production area) the resource was centralised as a shutdown group. Little or no contract labour was employed underground.

Observations

* The first-line shift resource was poorly utilised.
* Demarcation was strong. Inter-trade and operator-maintenance flexibility were non-existent.
* Team-working, involving both the miners and the tradesmen in the development and production areas, was poor.
* Tradesmen and miners had little sense of equipment ownership.
* Plant specific training was poor.
* The resource structure required modification. In the short term, the second-line group (g) needed to be augmented by three fitters, at the expense of the under-utilised first line Longwall group (c). In the longer term, increased skills training and flexibility (which was being introduced as a national initiative) would allow the operator teams (the miners) to take on some of the first line work. This would allow the further build up of group (g), which would provide better resourcing of the down-days and, via a staggered day-shift roster would allow planned work to be carried out at weekends.

Administrative structure: The Colliery A administrative structure existing at that time is shown in Figure 6–6, which should be looked at in conjunction with Figures 6–3 and 6–5.

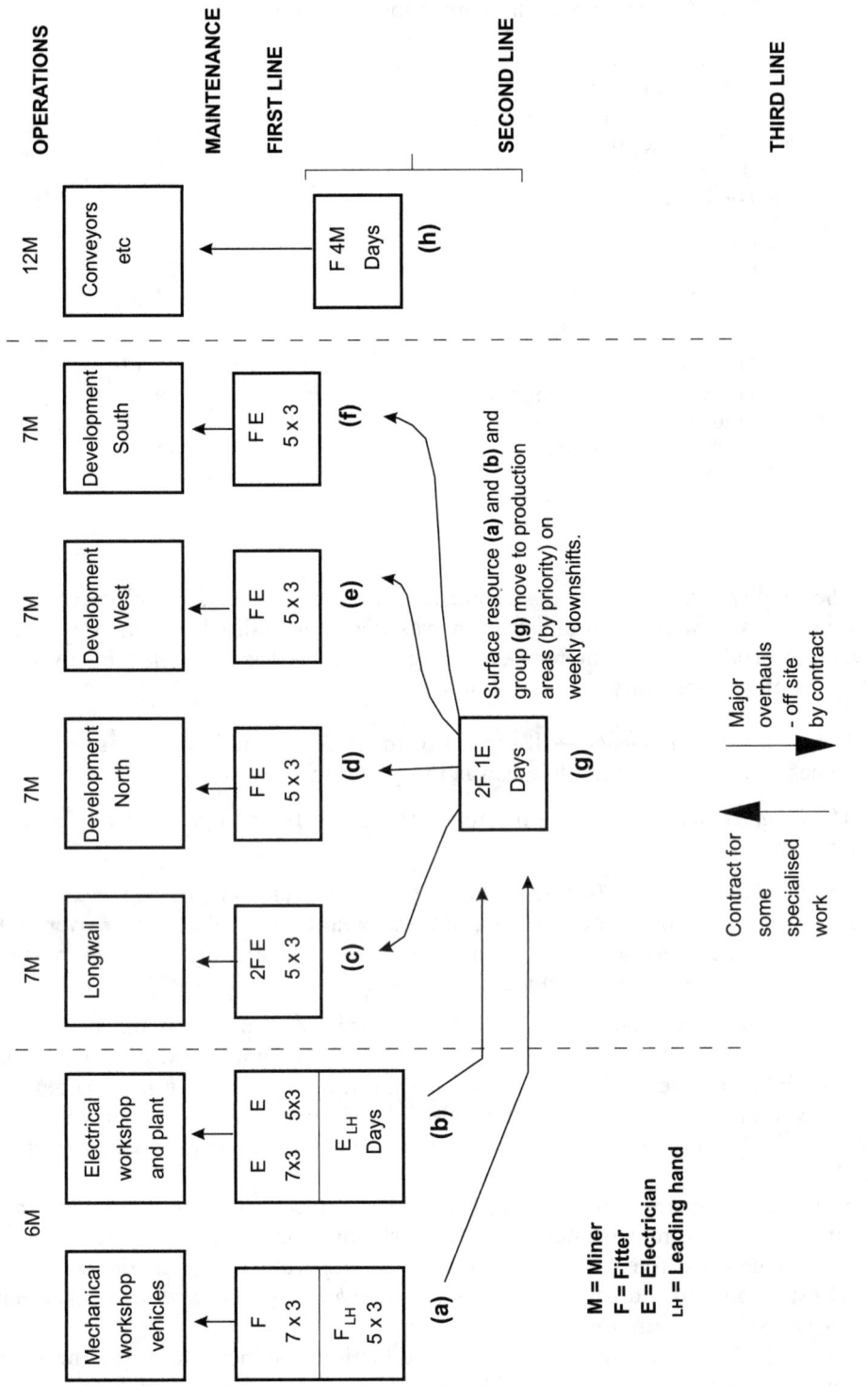

FIGURE 6–5 Colliery A Resource Structure

TABLE 6–2 Manpower Inventory for Colliery A

Maintenance manager	1
Support engineers	5.5
Maintenance supervisors	10
Maintenance planner	1
Other staff	2
Total staff	19.5
Fitters	25
Electricians	22
Non trades	4
Total	51
Tradeforce/Staff	2.6:1
Tradeforce/Support engineers	9.3:1
Tradeforce/Supervisors	5:1
Tradesmen/non-trades	11.7:1

The colliery manager was responsible for the process, equipment and manpower. Below him, administration was departmentalised at superintendent level into production, maintenance and engineering. It appeared that the division of areas of responsibility was as follows:

Production superintendent—all aspects of the process, and in that sense was the owner of the equipment while it was in operation;

Maintenance superintendent—the maintenance of the equipment while it was on-site;

Engineering superintendent—specification and procurement of new plant and major modification work; specification and quality control of major overhaul work; engineering support to the maintenance department; upkeep of the equipment drawing and documentation systems.

The maintenance and engineering superintendents were mainly managers – they only became involved in technical matters in a limited way. The main responsibility of the electrical and the mechanical supervisors was to organize the down-days and major maintenance in conjunction with the process co-ordinators. The maintenance planner was used as a maintenance documentation clerk.

The electrical and the mechanical maintenance engineers provided an additional layer of management. The former's function seemed to be to support the 'management role' of the maintenance superintendent in the area of administration and industrial relations ('*I provide direct technical assistance for about ten percent of my time*').

The main feature of the maintenance-production administration was the shift reporting structure (see Figure 6–7). At supervisor and shop floor level it had

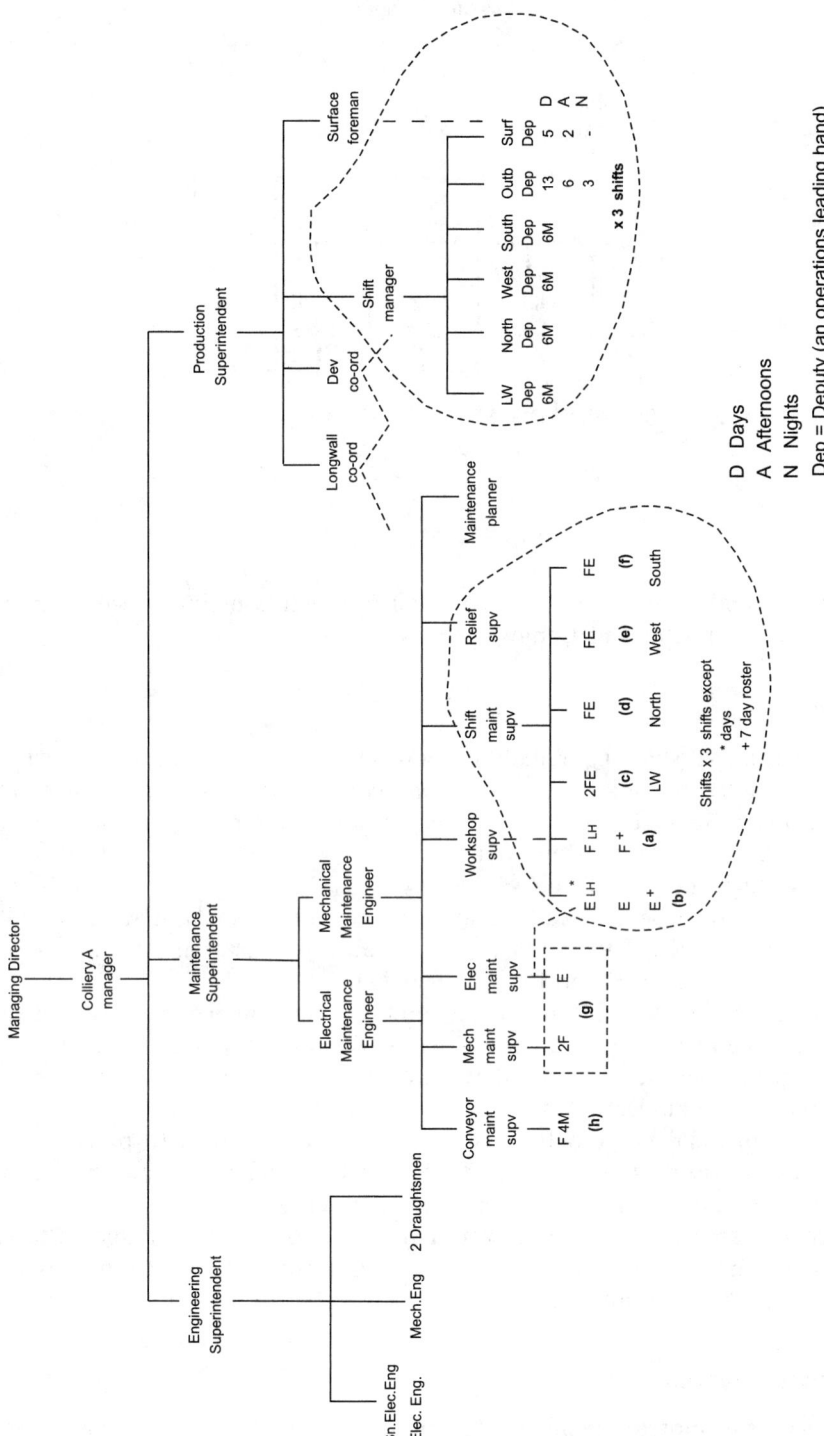

FIGURE 6–6 Colliery A Administrative Structure

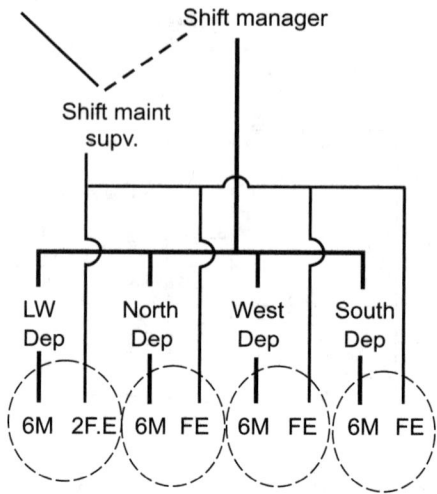

FIGURE 6–7 Colliery A Shift Reporting

resulted in a number of process-related small production-maintenance teams in each of the development and Longwall areas.

Observations

* As regards satisfactory reliability and availability the most important activities were *the selection and procurement of equipment* and *the major maintenance work*. These were the responsibility of the engineering super-intendents and were not done well.
* The first line shift tradeforce was poorly utilised.
* Relatively little progress had been made in creating operator–maintainer self-empowered teams. There was a considerable polarisation (them and us) between the tradeforce and the management.
* The responsibilities of the engineering and the maintenance sections—for the maintenance of underground equipment—were not clearly enough defined.
* At superintendent level a considerable polarisation of attitudes and percep-tion made communication difficult.
* The structure did not function as indicated in Figure 6–6. In practice, the electrical supervisors reported to the electrical maintenance engineer and the mechanical supervisor to his mechanical counterpart.
* There appeared to be an 'organizational power base' at shift-manager level. Among other problems, this was causing serious polarisation between production and maintenance.

Maintenance Systems

I had been told not to spend much time on this area. A new computerised package had been bought and would shortly be installed and commissioned.

Thus, the systems were audited superficially in order to obtain the complete picture.

The **work planning system** is modelled in Figure 6–8. Its main feature was that planning of the Longwall down-day needed to be better. One supervisor should have been responsible for the planning, scheduling and supervision of the down day.

Plant reliability control (see, for example, Figures 1–11 and 1–20) was not satisfactory. There was no Level 1 system and the dominance of reactive work meant that the maintenance engineers and project engineer had little time to spend on support for the Level 2 system.

Maintenance documentation was not satisfactory and would remain so with the new software unless considerable effort was made in improving the upkeep of spare parts lists, standard job specifications, history records, etc.

Recommendations

(a) For each of the collieries the adoption of the revised organization shown in Figure 6–9 was proposed. The main features of this were as follows:

* A centralised Engineering Project Group (EPG) should be formed with the following responsibilities:

  — to produce new equipment and perform other major engineering work;
  — to provide back-up to the colliery maintenance departments for sophisticated technical problems, which might take the form of direct assistance or linkage with an outside third party;
  — to be responsible for the drawing master library and its updating system.

  The EPG should not get involved in the direct execution of project or sophisticated engineering work that could be carried out cost effectively by contract. The size of the EPG should reflect such a policy and be set at a level which could cope with the lower limits of the work load. Contract engineers should service the work load peaks and deal with specialised tasks. Such a group could be made up of two or three engineers (transferred from the collieries) reporting to the Engineering Manager and should have a balance of expertise spanning the engineering disciplines and the main types of colliery equipment. Although there should be a degree of specialisation it would be essential that the individual engineers should work flexibly.

* Within each colliery a Maintenance Support Group (MSG) should be formed from the existing maintenance engineers—supplemented by an engineer drawn from the Engineering Department as it then was. The group should include mechanical and electrical expertise and it should be devoted to supporting the maintenance department in improving equipment reliability.

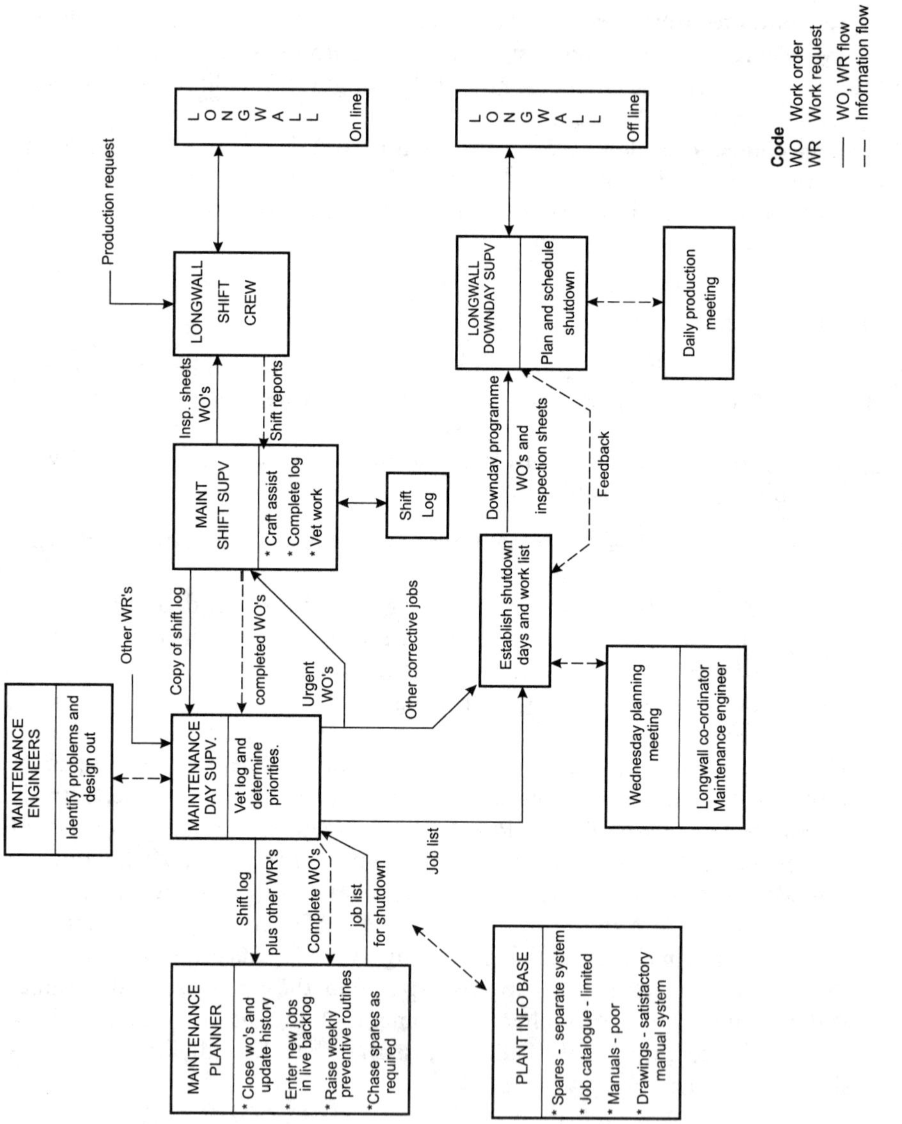

FIGURE 6-8 Colliery A Work Planning System

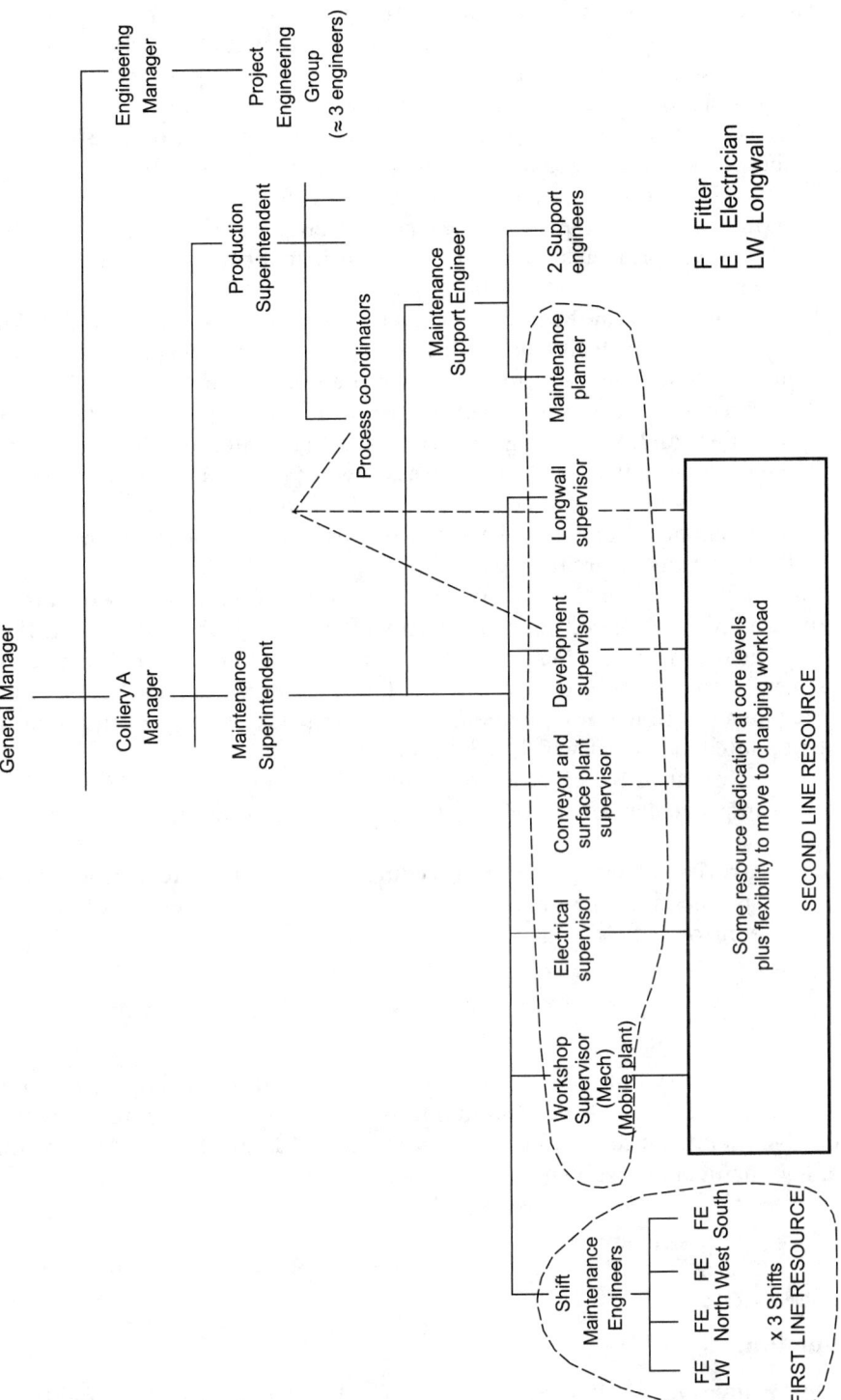

FIGURE 6-9 Proposed Administrative Structure

* It was to be firmly understood that this recommended re-organization would only work if the roles and duties of the EPG and the respective MSGs were clearly defined—regarding areas of responsibility overlap, inter-relationships, communication systems and so forth.

* The day maintenance supervisors should be made plant-responsible (one should be responsible for the Longwall, for example). The second-line day-shift resource should be increased, as discussed on page 138, and should report to the mechanical and electrical surface supervisors for day-to-day problems, and to the plant-oriented supervisors during their down days.

* In the longer term the national exercise for improving flexibility and skill training might facilitate evolution of the shift structure—via some intermediate stages— into self-empowered teams (see Figure 6–10).

* The second line resource (see Figure 6–9) required a much improved planning and scheduling system — with greater emphasis on pre-planning of individual jobs and weekly work programmes (see Figure 6–8)—if it were to be used effectively. This, in turn, would require the Maintenance Planner to be employed as his job title indicated rather than as a documentation clerk.

(b) The management of the collieries needed to develop a policy of operating the Longwall on a continuous fifteen-shift basis, which would mean that maintenance work on the Longwall equipment and on the trunk conveyor system would have to be accomplished at the weekends. The maintenance life plans for all major equipment (miners, shuttle cars, etc.) would need to be updated, a project which would include:

— an audit of the existing condition of the equipment;

— improvement of the on-line inspection procedures and the follow up work;

— a review of the overhaul procedures—of overhaul frequencies, work specifications, contractor selection, standard job procedures, quality control, etc.

Note

The ability to carry out recommendation (b) depended on the implementation of (a). For example, the collieries would not have been able to move from reactive to proactive maintenance without the creation of the kind of resource pool for second line maintenance shown in Figure 6–9.

The Re-Audit

Introduction

In 1997 (three years after the original audit) I was asked to re-audit the colliery—in order firstly to identify and appraise the changes that had taken place,

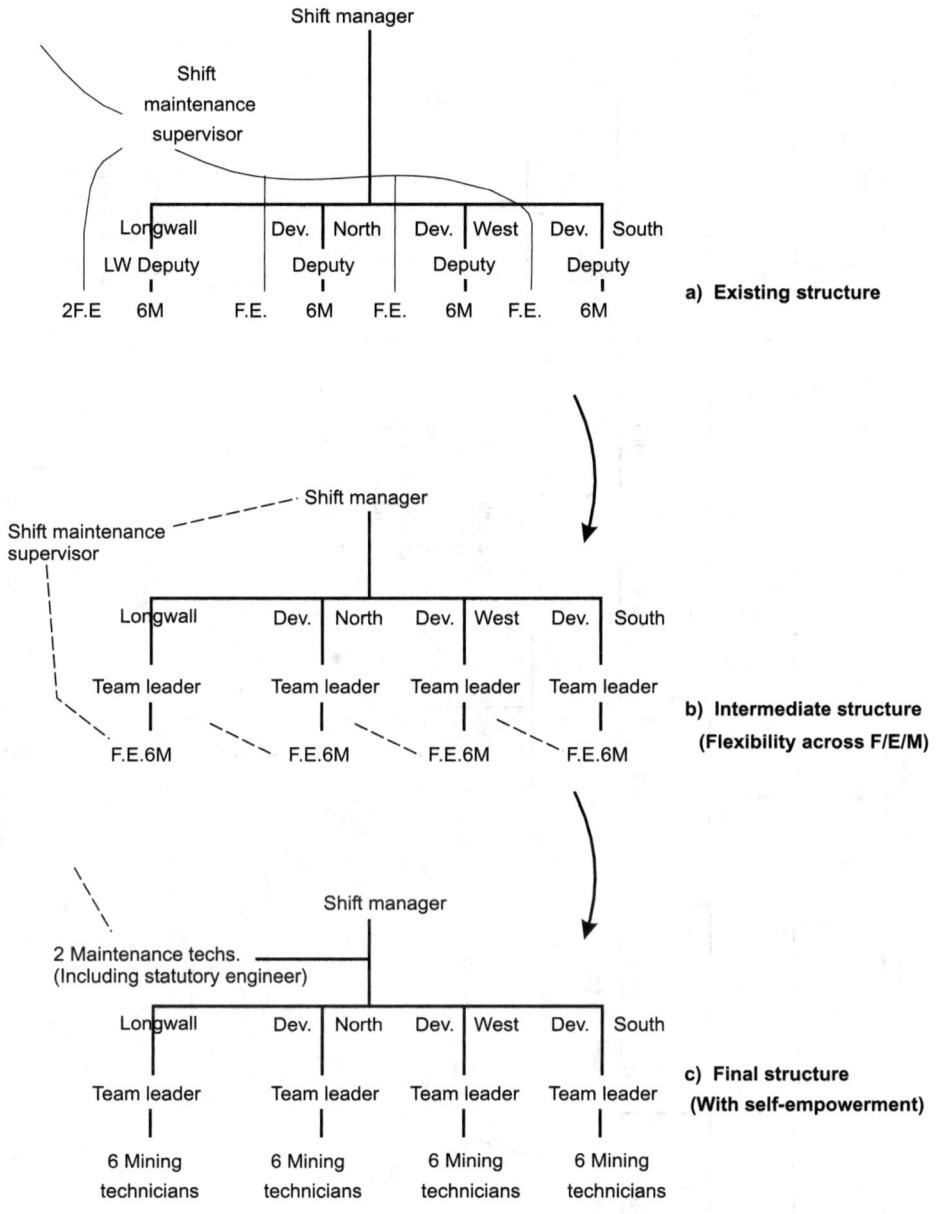

FIGURE 6–10 Moves Towards Self-Empowerment

and secondly to identify any recommendations that had not been implemented and the reasons why. The Colliery A resource and administrative structures, and its manpower inventory, at that later time are outlined and summarised in Figures 6–11 and 6–12 and Table 6–3. The following is a summary of the re-audit report's main observations.

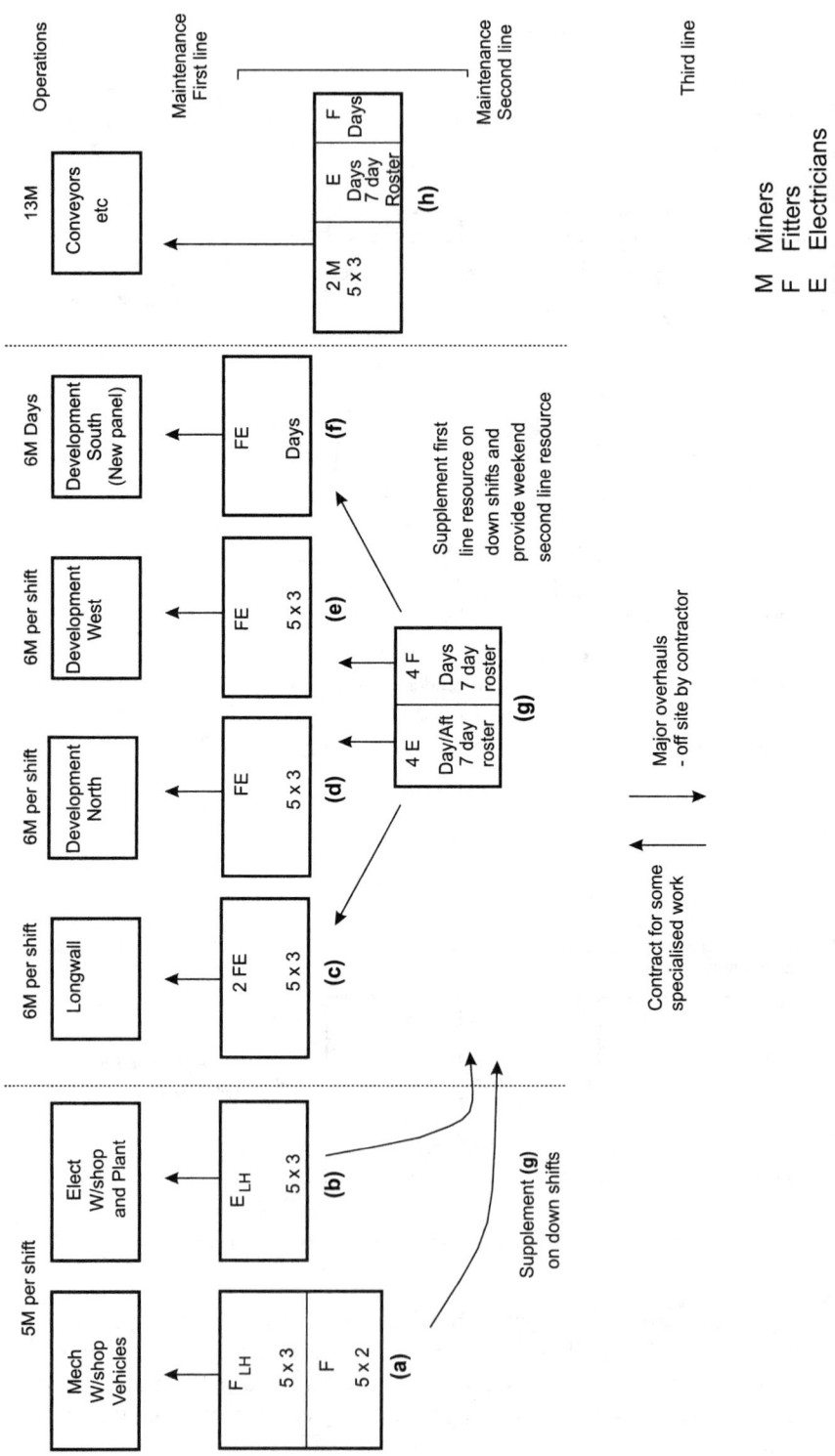

FIGURE 6–11 Resource Structure (1997 Audit)

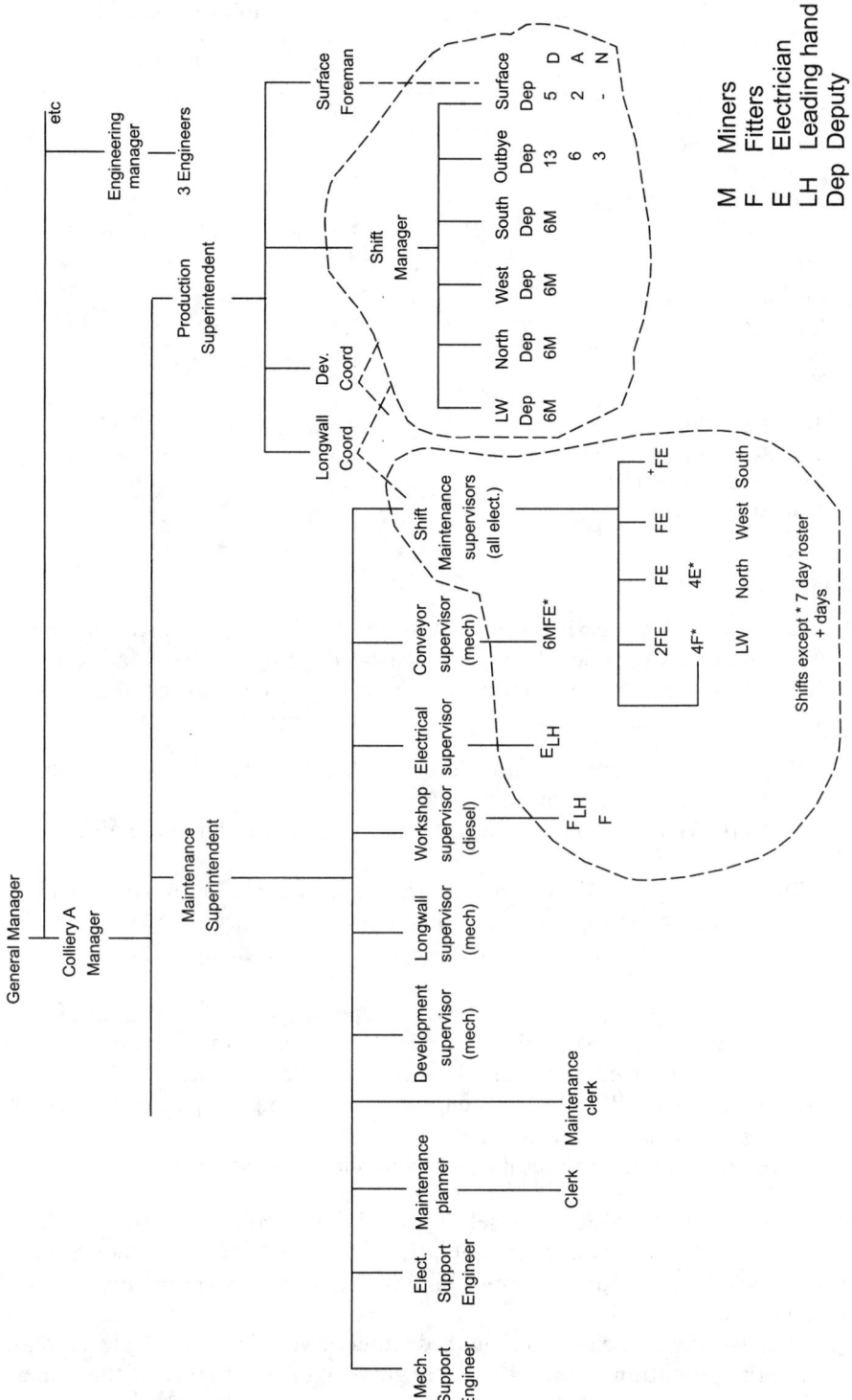

FIGURE 6–12 Administrative Structure (1997 Audit)

TABLE 6–3 Changes in Manpower Inventory from Audit to Re-audit

	Audit	Reaudit (97)
Maintenance manager	1	1
Support engineers	5.5	2
Maintenance supervisors	10	8
Maintenance planner	1	
Other staff	2	1
Total staff	19.5	13
Fitters	25	22
Electricians	22	21
Non trades (miners)	4	6
Total	51	49
Tradeforce/Staff	2.6:1	3.7:1
Tradeforce/Support Engineers	9.3:1	24.5:1
Tradeforce/Supervisors	5:1	6:1
Tradesmen/non-trades	11.7:1	7.2:1

Organization

(a) A centralised Engineering Project Group (EPG), set up shortly after the 1994 audit was completed, was headed by the Engineering Manager and three professional engineers transferred from the colliery engineering section. Its responsibilities were:

   (i) to procure new equipment and where necessary to assist in its installation and commissioning;
  (ii) to provide a project management service for capital and maintenance projects;
 (iii) to develop standards for underground equipment overhaul and to assist in standardising the equipment maintenance life plans (e.g., for the Longwall), and maintenance support agreements, throughout the collieries;
  (iv) to aid in ensuring that information (operation standards; areas of high maintenance cost; reliability problems and solutions) on common equipment is communicated throughout the collieries;
   (v) to help the colliery support engineers in solving complex or technically sophisticated problems;
  (vi) to co-ordinate the use of equipment shared between collieries.

   The size of the group was set at a level which could deal with the core workload (arising from responsibilities (iii) to (vi)) and was increased as necessary (i.e., to handle responsibilities (i) and (ii)) by employing contract engineers.

   There was a consensus among those interviewed that over the three years since the formation of the EPG the engineering performance of the colliery equipment had steadily improved, particularly regarding the specification and control of quality of off-site overhauls. Projects were under way to move from '*buy and maintain*' to '*lease, and employ the OEM to maintain.*'

(b) It appeared that the appointment of supervisors dedicated to specific equipment had been a success. For example, in the Longwall production group it was felt there had been a considerable improvement, especially in the planning of the down days and of Longwall changes.

(c) The only change to the resource structure had been an enlargement of the second line group (g) and their rostering on a staggered day shift to cover the weekend work. However, the development and production areas remained at the same levels of resource, which were under-utilised.

(d) The main difference between the 1997 administrative structure and that proposed in the original audit was that all the tradeforce reported directly to the shift supervisors (who were regarded as the resource owner). To arrange resources, the equipment supervisors had to proceed via the shift supervisors. In some cases, the equipment supervisors had become planners and had lost touch both with the tradeforce and with a knowledge of equipment condition—they spent limited time underground.

(e) There had been no movement towards the longer term improvements indicated in Figure 6–10.

Strategy

(f) The two mid-week down shifts were still used for Longwall maintenance, even though the second line resource worked at weekends via a staggered day shift. The reason given for this was that the coal shearing unit, and some others, would not operate the full fifteen shifts without maintenance (although this was done in USA mines).

(g) There had been only a marginal improvement in the underground equipment life plans and no improvement whatsoever in the identification and design-out of items exhibiting low reliability or high maintenance cost.

Recommendations – 1997

In the light of points (b) to (e) the structure should be modified, in the short term, to operate as indicated in Figure 6–13, this being essentially what was recommended in 1994 but with some clarification in order to overcome the problems identified in point (d). The first line resource should continue to report to the shift supervisors and the second line resource to the Electrical Supervisor and Workshop Supervisor (mechanical). These positions should, however, be renamed Electrical Co-ordinator and Mechanical Co-ordinator. When allocated to a downshift, both the shift resource and the second line resource should report to the equipment supervisors responsible for that downshift (e.g., Longwall downshift resources should report to the Longwall Supervisor on all matters associated with the Longwall). This would be a matrix reporting structure, and if it is to function satisfactorily the supervisors must work as a team and link closely with the process co-ordinators—a development which, for

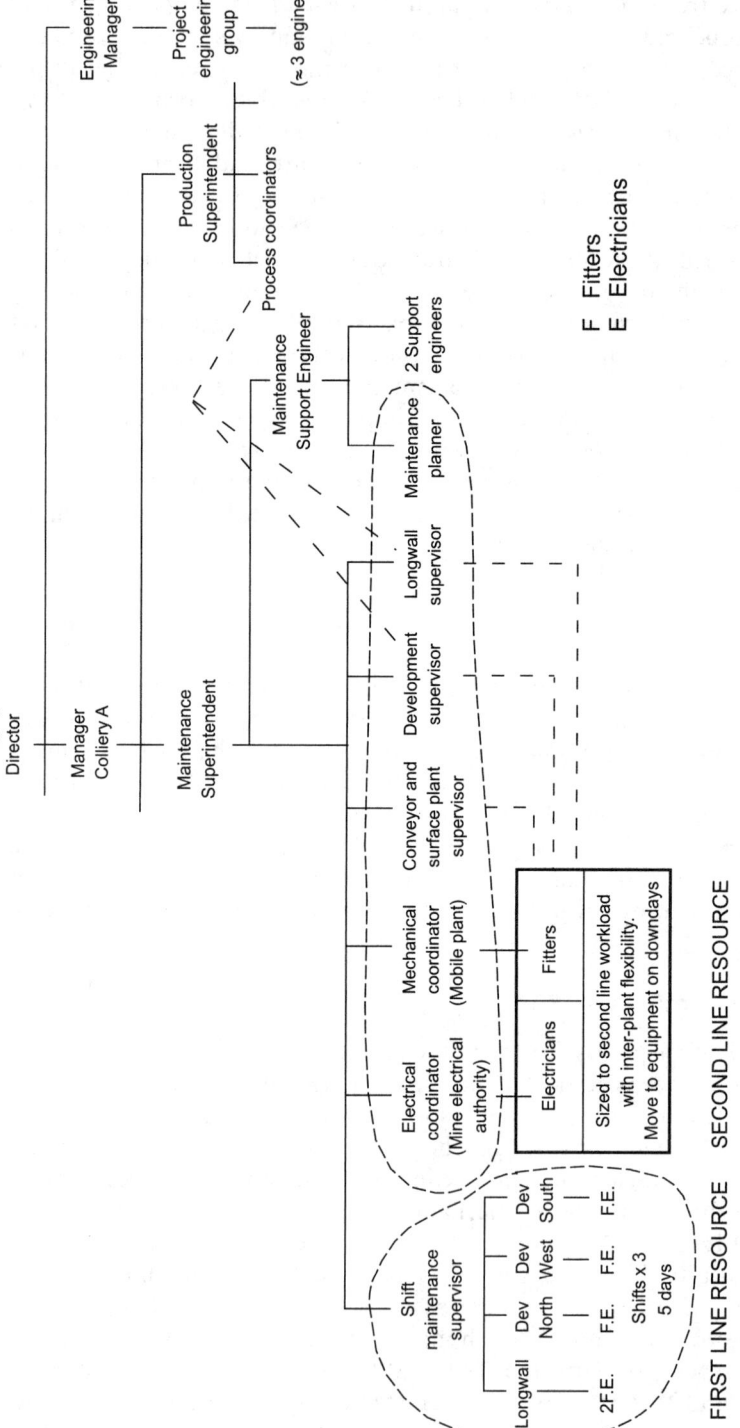

FIGURE 6-13 Proposed Administrative Structure (1997 Audit)

its success, may well call for the running of a team training exercise, off-site and also involving the shift managers. It would be essential that the equipment supervisors develop, for their own areas, improved life plans, spares lists and information systems.

Because of the importance of the Longwall, an inter-disciplinary team (a project manager plus representatives from engineering, maintenance, production, technical services and, where necessary, the operations workforce and the tradeforce) should be formed to carry out the following tasks:

— Identification of the reasons for loss of cutting time and low performance. This may well be a combination of poor maintenance, design and operation.
— Formulation of actions to overcome the listed problems.
— Formulation of a schedule for the implementation of the identified actions.

This should be a precursor to improving plant reliability control at first level (involving operators, tradesmen and equipment supervisors), at second level (involving equipment supervisors and support engineers) and third level (involving support engineers and the Central Engineering Group).

Many of the recommendations arising from the first audit had not been carried out because of shop floor industrial relations problems (see points (c), (d), (e) and (f) of the re-audit review above). The management's difficulties with problems of this kind were understandable. However, if the company wished to compete internationally then it was essential that these recommendations be pursued. At the time of the re-audit, availability and cost performance were well below international benchmark standards for underground coal mining.

CHAPTER 7

Fingerprint Audits

A streamlined adaptation of the audit methodology—a 'fingerprint' audit—can be used to capture, during just a single day's visit to a site, the salient characteristics of its maintenance department. Two case studies, drawn from my own practice, will illustrate this. They will also show that having a state-of-the-art organization does not guarantee cost effective maintenance. Being structured into manufacturing units and self-empowered plant-oriented teams is important, but must be implemented within the context of a sound maintenance strategy and appropriate systems.

Example (A): A Bottling Plant

Introduction

BOTPLANT Ltd produced an alcoholic drink marketed internationally. A small process plant mixed the two main ingredients of the liquor, which was then put into bottles—of different sizes and variously labelled—in six production lines (see Figure 7–1). A seventh line handled a new product, operating at reduced capacity and for short production runs.

Until 1995 BOTPLANT had a traditional functional administrative structure with a centralized maintenance tradeforce reporting via trade supervisors to a maintenance manager. The management then decentralized the maintenance resources in order to create line-oriented operator–maintainer teams. In 1997 the management were concerned that plant availability and general plant condition were beginning to suffer. They asked me to undertake a fingerprint audit in order to identify the problems and to indicate their way forward. The audit was conducted over one day and involved interviewing five key personnel. Also, and prior to my visit, a questionnaire (see Appendix 2 for an example) was completed.

The Plant Maintenance Strategy and Organization

The administrative and resource structures at the time of the audit are shown in Figures 7–2 and 7–3. The 1995 changes—dividing the plant, as far as its management is concerned, into 'small manufacturing units' (centered around Lines 1 to 3, for example), and then into plant-oriented operator–maintainer teams for

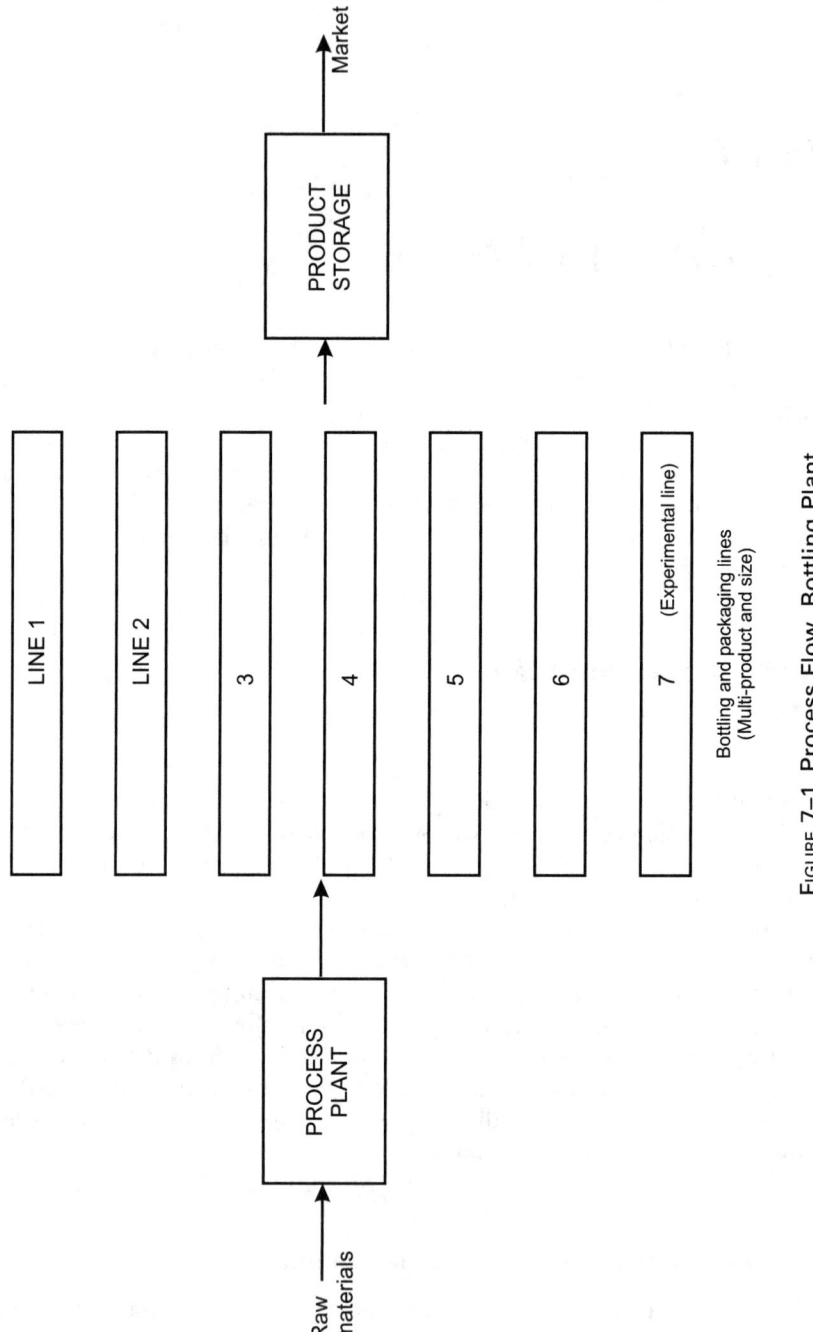

FIGURE 7–1 Process Flow, Bottling Plant

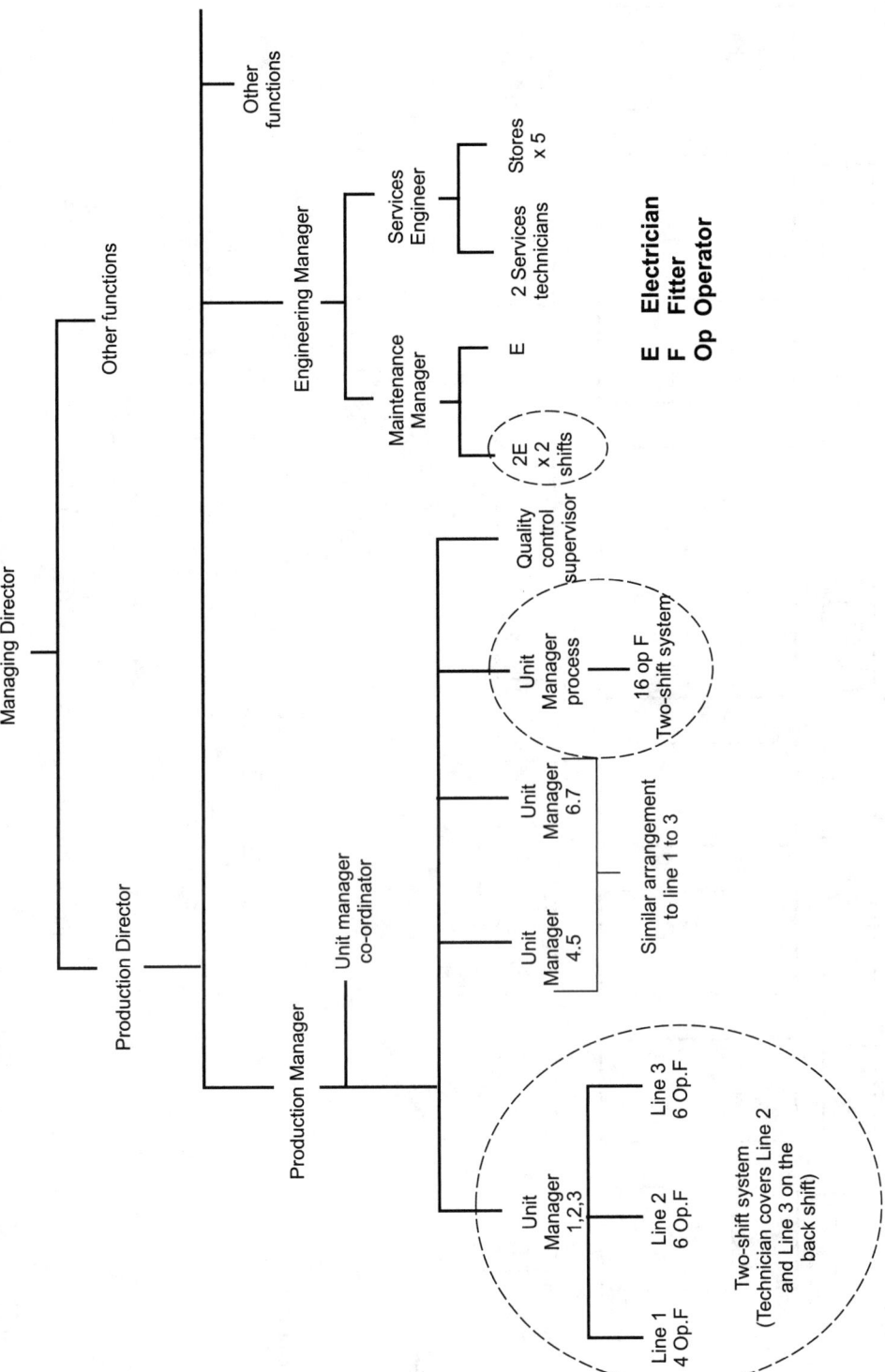

FIGURE 7-2 Administrative Structure, Bottling Plant

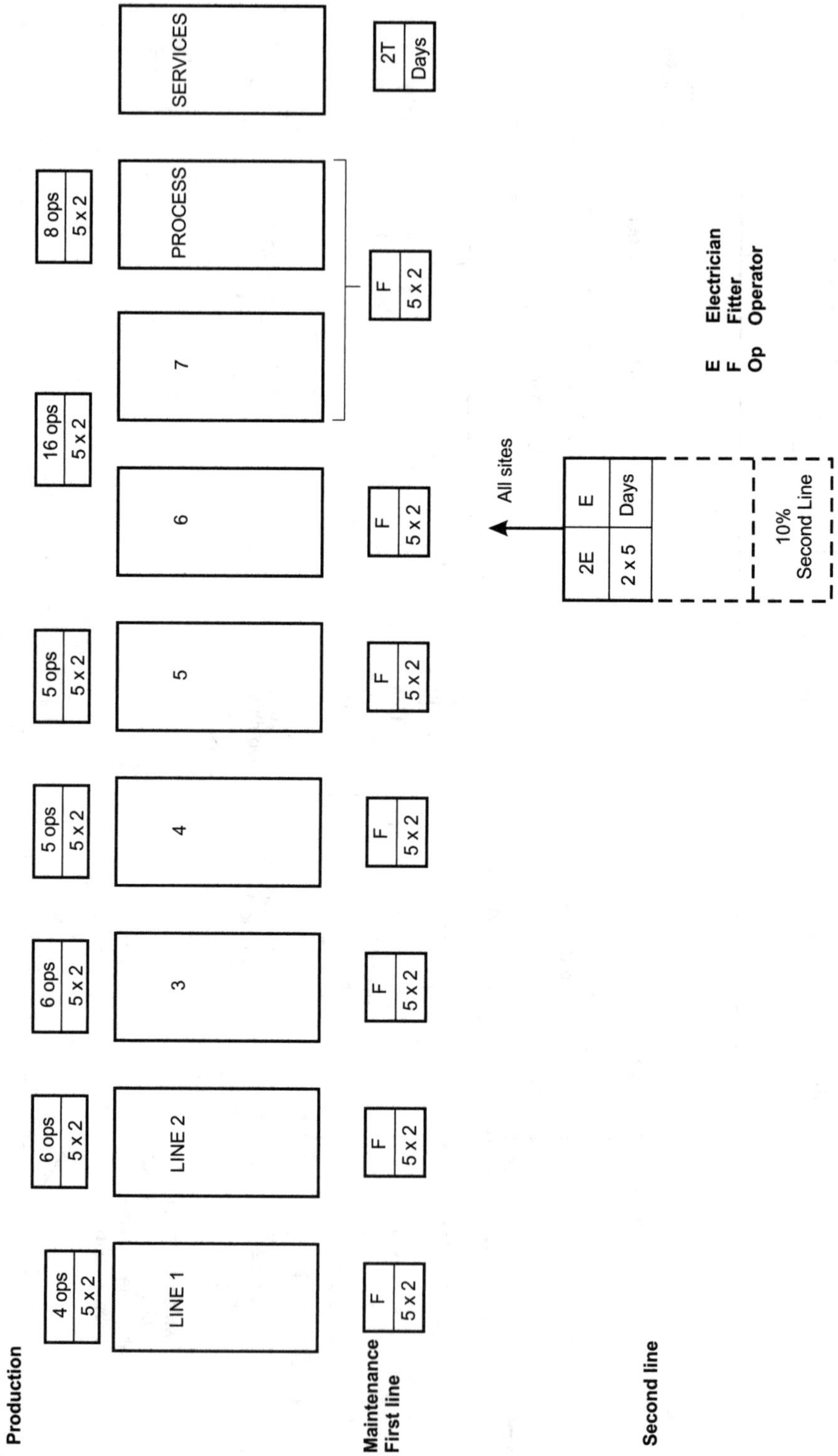

FIGURE 7-3 Resource Structure, Bottling Plant

each such unit—were in line with international trends. The maintenance staff was reduced to the Maintenance Manager (Mechanical) and the Electrical Engineer. The role of the services technicians (promoted tradesmen) was envisaged to include development of preventive maintenance schedules and routines, investigation of failure causes, planning and co-ordination of major jobs, giving technical advice to the line fitters, and collection and checking of plant history.

The tradesmen's role (see Figure 7–3) was to carry out the first-line maintenance (emergency work, changeovers and routine preventive tasks) for their own production line. The larger second-line jobs were undertaken by exploiting the potential for inter-line fitter flexibility while any necessary major overhauls were dealt with by a combination of internal labour and resources provided by the OEM.

The tradesmen, in conjunction with the technicians, were also expected to develop the equipment life plans for their own line, and I noted that these were based on lubrication routines and an operate-to failure-policy. The documentation system (life plans, equipment register, spares lists, descriptions of standard jobs, history) had not been developed. In general, the maintenance strategy was based on a reactive approach, and its costs were considered high (in comparison with that of other, similar, plants), a situation which appeared to have arisen because:

(i) there were no maintenance systems in place before the 1995 re-organization, and afterwards, the key role that the technicians could have played in developing such systems, and the matching strategy, was not exploited because, in the main, they were used primarily to supplement the fitting resource;

(ii) the line fitters regarded themselves as a fire-fighting force responding, from a central workshop, to calls for emergency work and changeovers; they did not even carry out simple line patrol inspections;

(iii) as is invariably the case, relying on inter-line flexibility to resource larger jobs was difficult, there being a resistance to moving a fitter out of one plant-oriented team to assist another team (As a result, second-line work was either under-resourced or neglected altogether.)

(iv) there was rigid inter-trade and operator-trade demarcation within the so-called teams, and the teams were not self-empowered;

(v) the unit managers had little engineering or maintenance knowledge and found their relationship with the fitters difficult.

(vi) an overtime culture existed throughout the maintenance department.

After just one day's visit I was left with the over-riding impression that the management had not taken maintenance seriously. There had been little point in setting up an organizational structure that met international best practice when the strategy, systems and control were poor.

Organizational Change—The Way Forward

Any changes to the organization to overcome its immediate problems had to bear in mind the following points:

* In the short term, the maintenance department needed to change if it was to provide the necessary technical resources for developing the essential documentation, strategy and systems. This could have been achieved via existing or additional personnel.
* The changes had to provide a resource for second-line corrective and preventive work. This in turn assumed that the plant would be released for such work, either because it would be done at weekends, or during production-agreed downshifts etc., or because production could be sustained via redundant plant.
* It had to be appreciated that the eventual aim would be to re-introduce plant manufacturing units and operator–maintainer line-oriented teams. Indeed, the ideal organization would have been one in which fitters (i.e., manufacturing technicians) were recruited into the operating teams, which would have released the existing first-line fitters (or a major proportion of them) for second-line work (I have always felt that changeover work was production work rather than maintenance (which was the perception at this plant). Furthermore, such a change had only to be introduced after a careful study, on each line, of the workload profiles of operators and fitters, e.g., How did they co-ordinate? What level of training was required? Any re-introduction of line-oriented teams needed to be accompanied by self-empowerment and the introduction of an annualised hours agreement to overcome the overtime culture.

Short Term Actions

The following actions were therefore suggested:

(a) The first-line fitters' responsibility for the maintenance of individual production lines should remain and it had to be ensured (if needed, by recruiting additional fitters) that there were enough of them to cover such work, i.e., it could be done without calling upon the assistance of the technicians then in place. The line-fitters needed to report directly to the Maintenance Manager, their role had to be clearly defined and should take in emergency maintenance, change-overs, line-inspection patrolling and the large preventive jobs. They had to understand that most of their time was to be spent on the production line. Additional training, to up-grade their skills in change-over work etc should be given as necessary, and they needed to be moved to different production-lines, from time to time, to broaden their knowledge and increase their flexibility.

(b) An alternative structure to that currently used is shown in Figure 7–4. This would retain the idea of the unit structure (the three lines) but would divide the maintenance resource into first-line shift-fitters and second-line day-fitters. Both groups would need to report directly to the Maintenance Manager, as in (a).

(c) The technicians should be released from fitting duties. Their main role would then be the development of maintenance life plans, documentation, standard job descriptions and lists of spares requirements. In addition, they

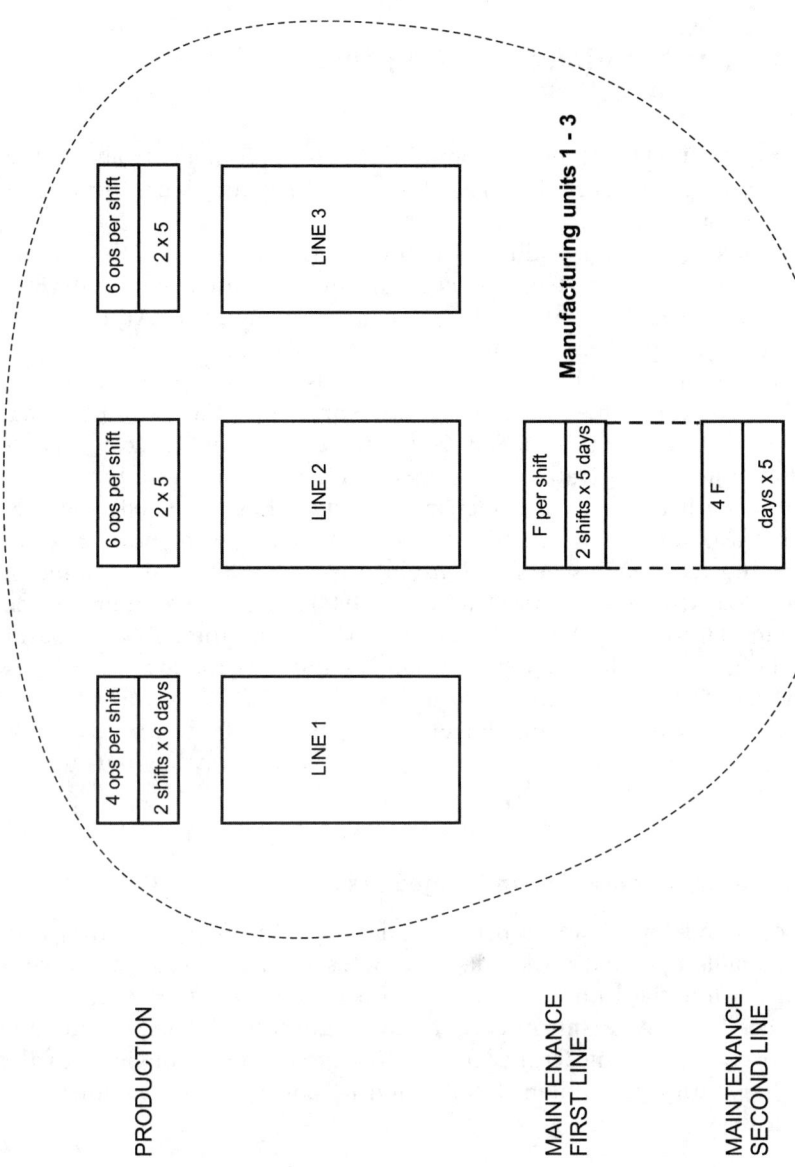

FIGURE 7–4 *Resource Structure Modification, Bottling Plant*

would have a role in the scheduling, planning and resourcing of the large jobs. The maintenance life plans should be developed in conjunction with the line fitters. In the short term, the technicians might need to be supplemented by contract technical or clerical resource.

Example (B): An Aluminium-Rolling Mill

Introduction

The company (ALROM Ltd) made aluminium products (ranging from plate to foil) for an international market. The plant layout is shown in Figure 7–5 and its process flow in Figure 7–6.

Some four years before this audit was carried out, and in order to improve throughput and quality of product, the company had updated the plant via a major capital investment in state-of-the-art control equipment. At the same time, some of the main production units were also replaced and others (e.g., the Hot Mill) retained and overhauled. There was also a heavy investment in improving the skills of the workforce and improving the organizational structure up to international benchmark levels (e.g., by introducing plant-oriented self-empowered operator–maintainer teams). I was told that, as a result, the company had expected to increase sales to a level of 38,000 tons per annum, some 6,000 tons of which was to be sold as Hot Mill product (Hot Bend) and the rest as products of the Finishing Area. However, at the time of the audit the Hot Mill output stood at only 30,000 tons per annum, which meant that considerable profit was being lost. The international benchmarks (see Table 7–1) indicated that the main reason for this was the low availability of the Hot Mill.

I was asked to carry out a two-day fingerprint audit in order to identify firstly the reasons for the low Hot Mill availability and secondly actions for its improvement.

Plant Operating Characteristics and Objectives

The plant operated for 49 weeks per year, having a three-week shutdown in December. The mills operated for six-days per week on a three-shift basis, with Sunday off-line, while the Finishing Area ran on a three-day, twelve hours per day, cycle (the Re-melt Plant operating continuously). As explained, the production objective and long term plan was to increase the throughput of the Hot Mill to 38,000 tons per annum. I could find no corresponding maintenance objective or strategy.

Life Plans and Preventive Schedules

Considerable effort had been put into the life plans for the main plant. The Hot Mill, for example, had a comprehensive list of lubrication, inspection, cleaning and service routines, including vibration monitoring and lubrication

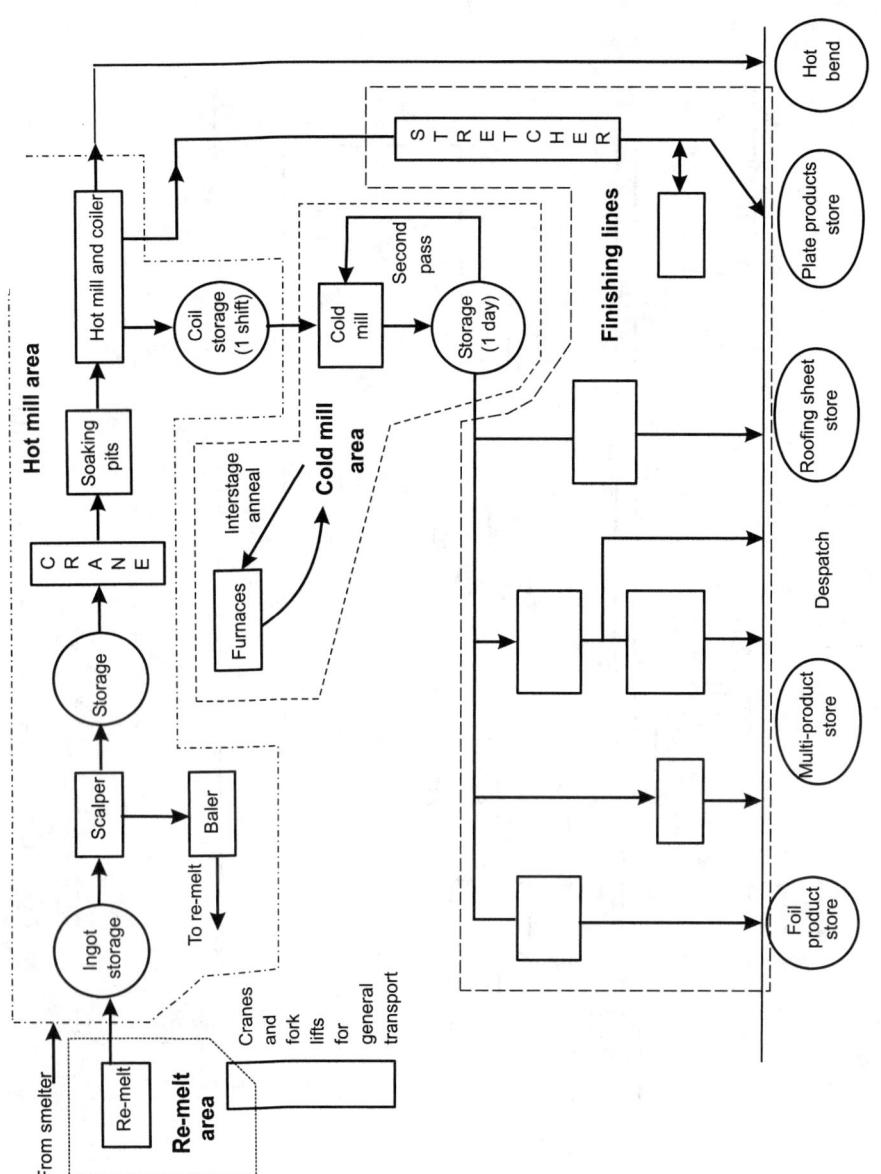

FIGURE 7–6 Process Flow, Rolling Mill

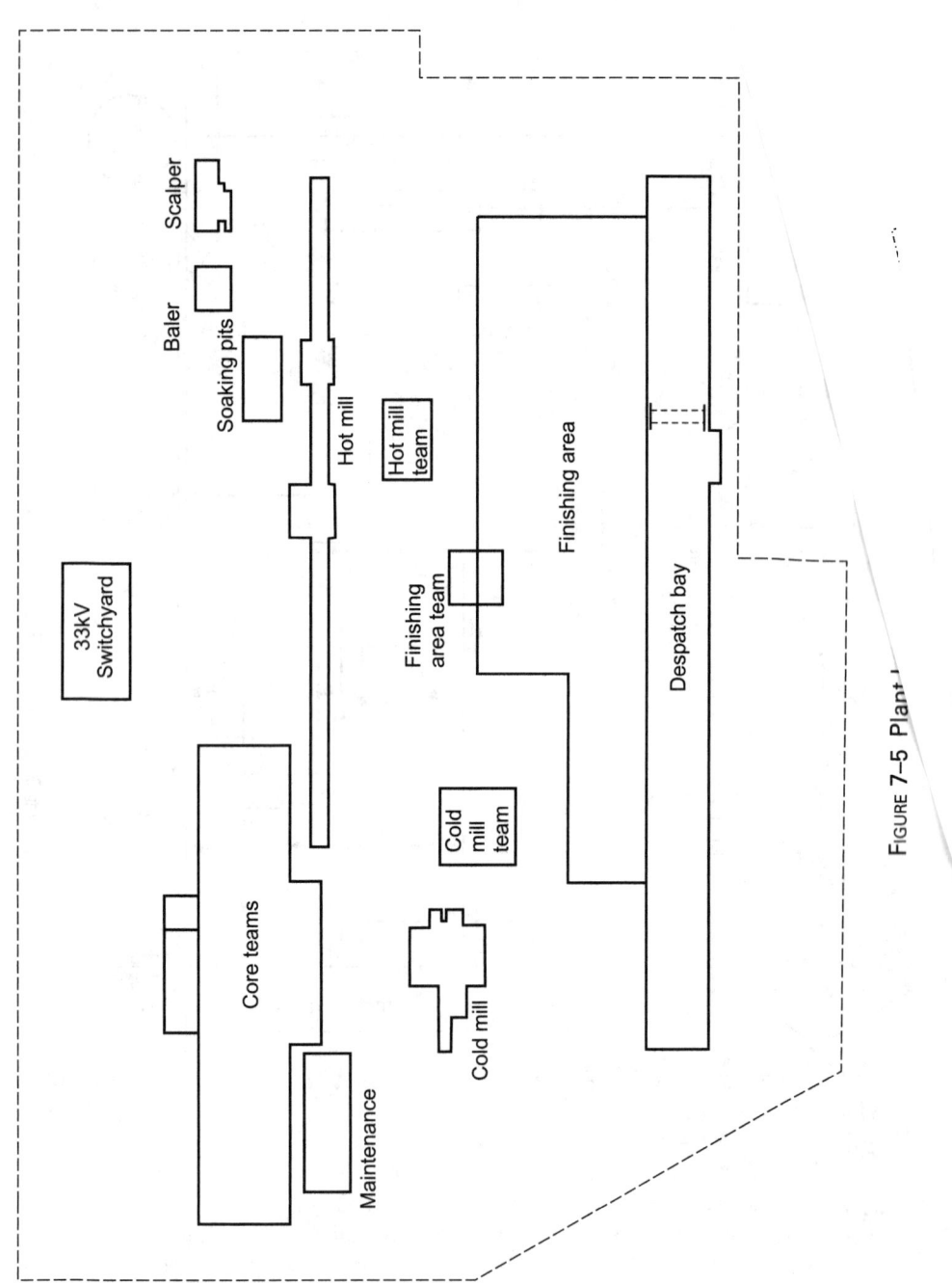

FIGURE 7-5 Plant

TABLE 7–1 International Comparison Maintenance Performance Indices for Rolling Mills

	AIROM Ltd	Plant X	Plant Y	Plant Z
Annual volume (tonnes)	30,176	104,223	50,812	44,567
Plant recovery (%)	65	65	64	63
Hot mill				
Uptime/Available time	47	82	79	66
Operation downtime	18	13	5	15
Maintenance downtime	18	1.0	1.8	9.1
Productivity, foil stock (ton/hr)	18	27	25	14
Cold mill				
Uptime/Available time	81	75	74	64
Operation downtime	7.5	18	12	17
Maintenance downtime	5.4	0.6	4.8	8.5
Productivity, foil stock (ton/hr)	10	7.3	9.0	4.6

oil analysis for motors and gearboxes. In the annual three-week window the Mill underwent a partial or full overhaul, depending on its condition. Most of the routines were carried out during a weekly Hot Mill downshift (Sundays were not used for maintenance). In order to smooth the weekly planned maintenance workload the Hot Mill and Cold Mill came down on different days and the Finishing Area maintenance was also scheduled to avoid these Mill downdays.

Observations

The life plan for the Hot Mill was both comprehensive and detailed and in spite of the high incidence of reactive work was mostly carried out. The Cold Mill was also well maintained. The Finishing Area life plans were, however, only 40% completed, but because of the spare capacity these were not considered important.

The following were typical comments by interviewees:

— 'The problem is not so much poor preventive maintenance but poor design. The modification of the Hot Mill finished up with some old equipment and some new equipment—they don't fit well together.'
— 'In the Hot Mill area we are snowed-under fighting fires—we have no time to look for improvement in life plans or to design-out problem areas.'
— 'What we would like to see is more engineering effort put into the Hot Mill area.'

I agreed. My over-riding impression was that the reliability problems were being caused by poor design. In such cases even the best preventive procedures will not improve reliability. What was required was major investigative engineering to establish the causes and prescribe solutions.

An Overview of the Organization

Before modernisation there had been a traditional functional organization, i.e., there were many single-trade maintenance teams reporting via supervisors to a centralised engineering manager (see Figure 7–7). A centralised tradegroup was responsible for the maintenance of the workshops, building fabric and services. In addition there were area tradegroups responsible for first and second line maintenance of the production plant.

Figures 7–8 and 7–9 show the resource structure and administrative structure after modification, Figure 7–10 being a schematic model of the Hot Mill work planning system. The essential characteristics of this updated organization are as follows:

* Manufacturing units were established (e.g., one based on the Hot Mill), each under its own manager and having its own Unit Engineer and Process Engineer; in the case of the Hot Mill there was also a Control Technician to ensure that the group held the correct mix of engineering skills (the mill engineer was a mechanical). Each shift team comprised six operators, an electrician and a fitter, were self empowered and undertook a 'star configuration' of duties (see Figure 7–11). The function of the shift tradesmen was to carry out first line maintenance. Each manufacturing unit had a degree of autonomy regarding its production and maintenance policy.
* The manufacturing units were supported by a centralised structure which included a limited engineering capability and two 'core' second-line maintenance teams. Because each plant area could be scheduled separately—for one day a week—for maintenance, the core teams, with the help of the local tradesmen, carried out all second line work.
* The operation of the work planning system was based on a multi-terminal maintenance documentation system (stand-alone software, see Figure 7–9). The system has a manual loop, i.e., work request to the Unit Engineer, he vetts and enters into the backlog. The downshift programme was established on a Wednesday meeting and is with the Core Team Planner on the Thursday before the downday (Monday).

Maintenance Systems

Spares management cost control and documentation were briefly examined. They seemed to be generally satisfactory, and as regards reporting of the top ten low reliability and high maintenance cost areas they were very good. The quality of history recording compared well with that of the top quartile of maintenance departments I have audited.

Because of the Hot Mill problem, I concentrated my efforts on plant reliability control (PRC) (which I have previously discussed in Chapter 1—see Figures 1–11 and 1–20). My comments on PRC at the Rolling Mill were as follows:

* Within the team procedures, a Level 1 system was in operation. In terms of concept and philosophy it was a good system and worked well for all the teams, with the exception of the Hot Mill team. This was in part due to the

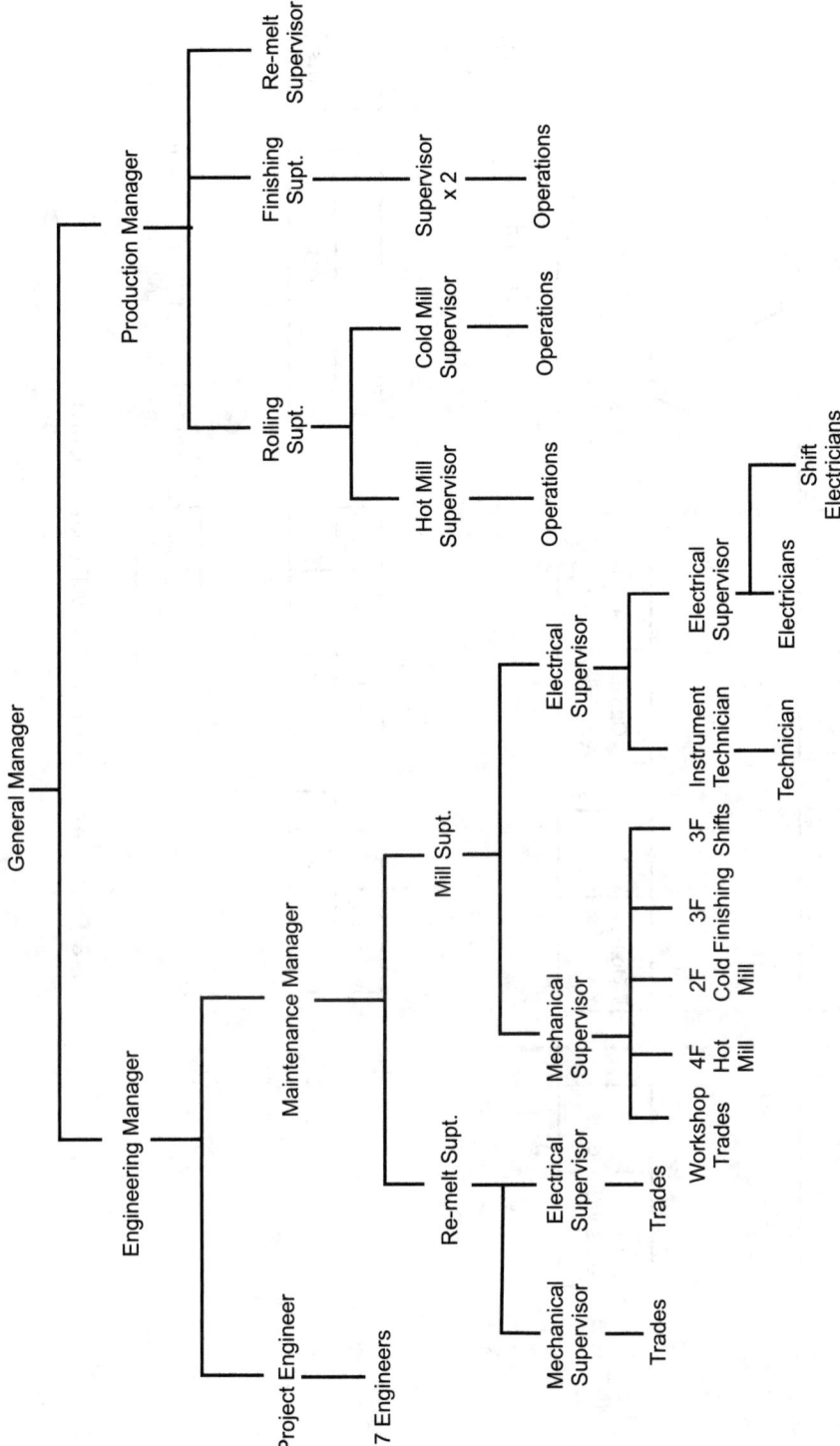

FIGURE 7–7 Rolling Mill Administration Before Plant Modernisation (Illustrative Only)

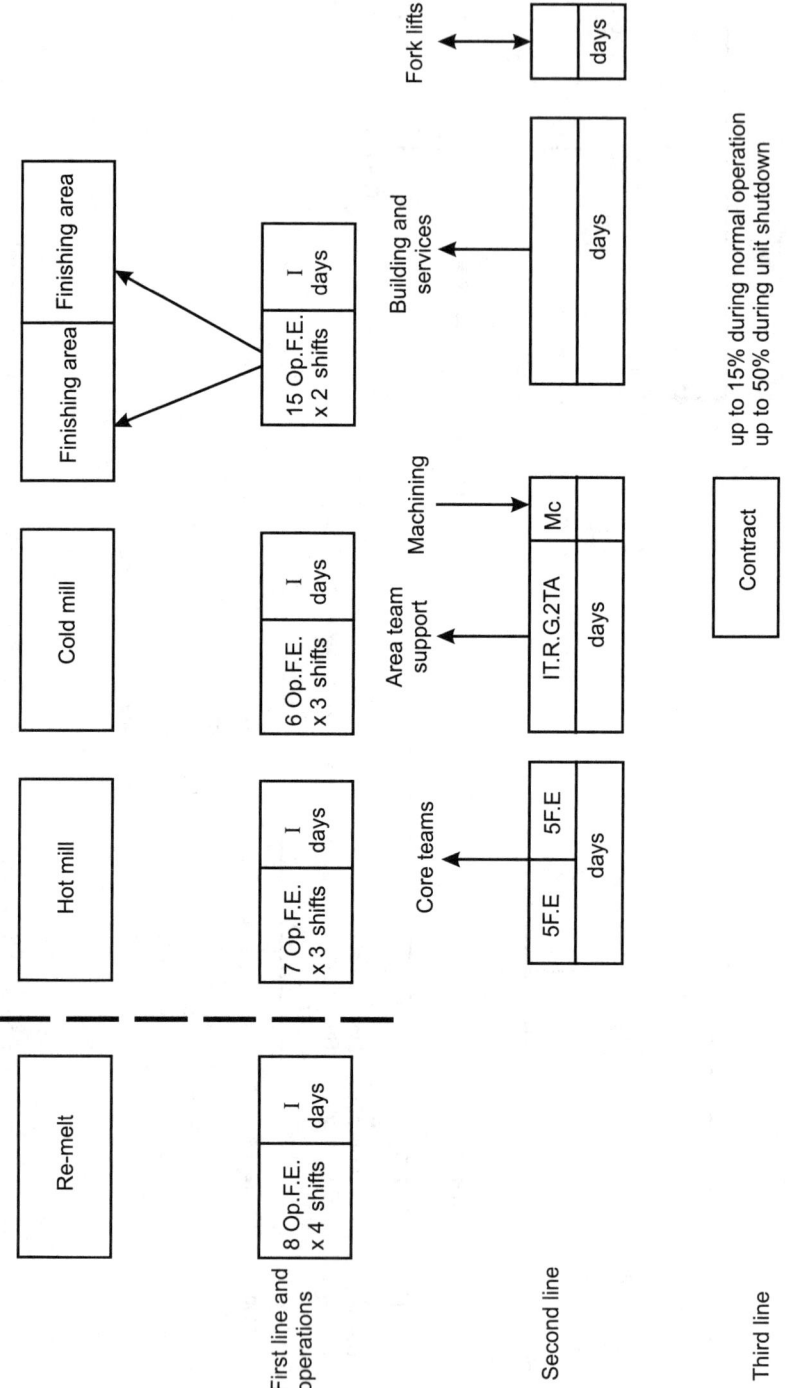

FIGURE 7-8 Resource Structure, Rolling Mill (Outline Only)

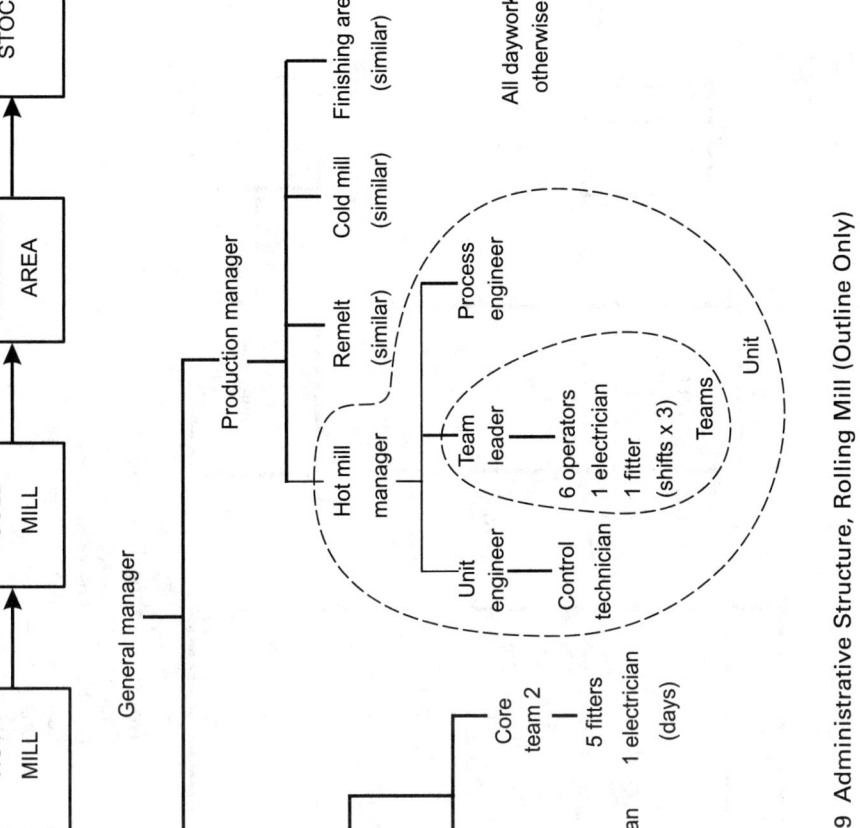

FIGURE 7–9 Administrative Structure, Rolling Mill (Outline Only)

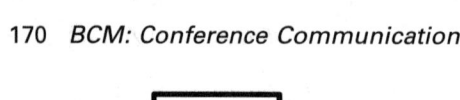

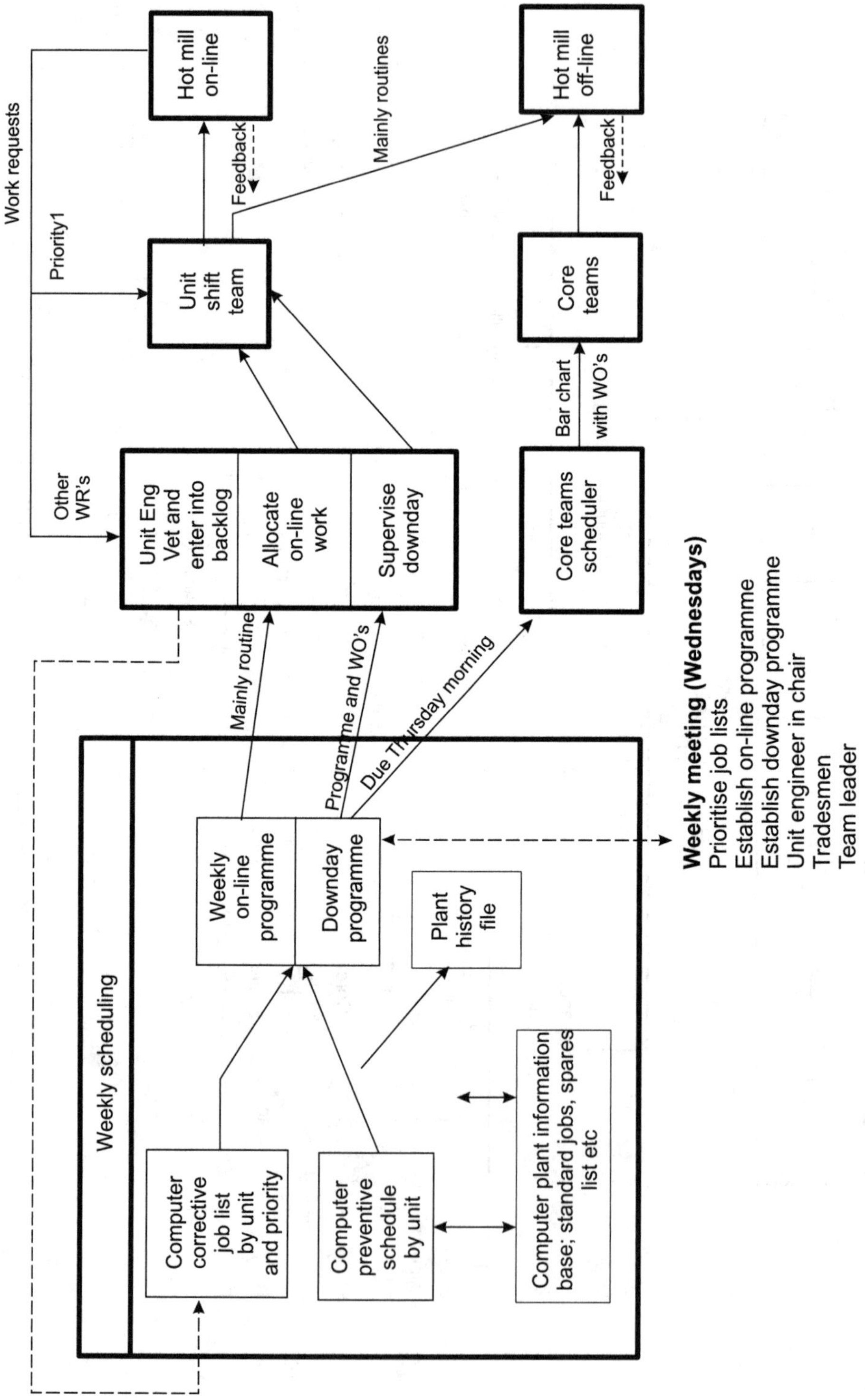

Hot mill on-line

Hot mill off-line

Work requests

Priority1

Feedback

Mainly routines

Feedback

Unit shift team

Core teams

Other WR's

Unit Eng Vet and enter into backlog

Allocate on-line work

Supervise downday

Core teams scheduler

Bar chart with WO's

Mainly routine

Programme and WO's

Due Thursday morning

Weekly scheduling

Weekly on-line programme

Downday programme

Plant history file

Computer corrective job list by unit and priority

Computer preventive schedule by unit

Computer plant information base; standard jobs, spares list etc

Weekly meeting (Wednesdays)
Prioritise job lists
Establish on-line programme
Establish downday programme
Unit engineer in chair
Tradesmen
Team leader

FIGURE 7–10 Planning System, Rolling Mill

FIGURE 7–11 Team Responsibilities (Core Maintenance), Rolling Mill

reactive nature of maintenance which was preventing the Unit Engineer/team from concentrating on designing out unreliability.

* The Level 2 and Level 3 systems were not operating in a satisfactory way, in particular in the Hot Mill area. This was caused by:
  — Lack of definition of the PRC system and of the roles within the system.
  — Lack of enthusiasm on the part of the project engineers to help with maintenance problems—they felt they should concentrate on projects.
  — Too few professional maintenance engineers in the centralised maintenance group.

Observations and Recommendations

The restructured organization (in particular the team concept) appeared to be working well, except at the Hot Mill, where the difficulties were exacerbated by the poor reliability of the electrical and control equipment, the Hot Mill Engineer coming from a mechanical background and therefore not having the expertise to solve such problems. The Control Technician was just out of an apprenticeship and did not have the necessary experience or knowledge of the process. In addition, the Mill Engineer was finding difficulty in obtaining assistance from the project group and from other Unit Engineers. (**NB Difficulties of this kind are not uncommon when an organization restructures into manufacturing units. It is inevitable that the engineering and technical resource will inevitably be spread thin, leaving a limited central support, if any.**) In such a situation it is not easy to operate the 'plant reliability control system' in the conventional way—the search for reliability hot spots and their eradication, becomes very limited.

The following actions were recommended:

* A group should be formed, from within the company, of engineers and technicians who would have the necessary expertise (in control, electrical and mechanical disciplines) in Hot Mill operation and maintenance. They should

be seconded, under the maintenance manager, in order to *purge* the Hot Mill of its reliability problems **(NB This periodic assembling of a company's engineering expertise is one of the best ways of controlling plant reliability in a de-centralised organization—it replaces the conventional second level system).**

* The Unit Engineers from each of the manufacturing units needed to improve their mutual sharing of knowledge.

* At least one additional professional maintenance engineer should be appointed under the Maintenance Manager.

CHAPTER 8

Case Study 1: Restructuring A Maintenance Organization

An audit can be a precursor to organizational change. A traditional and over-manned maintenance organization is mapped and modelled and proposals made to bring it up to international benchmark standards.

Introduction

Bauxal Ltd was, and is, one of the largest alumina refineries in the world. The basic structure and technology of the plant was, however, some twenty six years old. Over that time (1970–1996) the plant had been upgraded many times, increasing the 'nameplate capacity' but adding maintenance problems. The maintenance organization had also grown over this period and senior management felt that it was overmanned and in need of modernisation.

I was asked to map and model the existing organization and hence provide a vision of its way forward over the following five years. The audit methodology was used to gain an overview of the maintenance department with an emphasis on the modelling of its organization.

Plant Structure, Organization and Maintenance Strategy

The arrangement of the main process areas, maintenance workshops and stores is shown in Figure 8–1, which also indicates the location of the various maintenance tradegroups. The senior management structure is shown in Figure 8–2, which also indicates the main responsibilities of the refinery managers.

The basic operation, a sequence of processes applied to a recirculating fluid—caustic and bauxite (the main constituent of the fluid) being introduced at the head end (digestion) while impurities (sand, mud) and products (alumina) were extracted at various stages downstream—is shown in Figure 8–3. The 'raw material system' (conveyors, wharf loaders, stacker-reclaimers) brought in the raw materials (bauxite, coal, caustic, etc.) and took away the finished products (e.g., alumina) while the refinery itself—a large plant with a replacement value of more than a billion pounds and made up of a variety of equipment, including

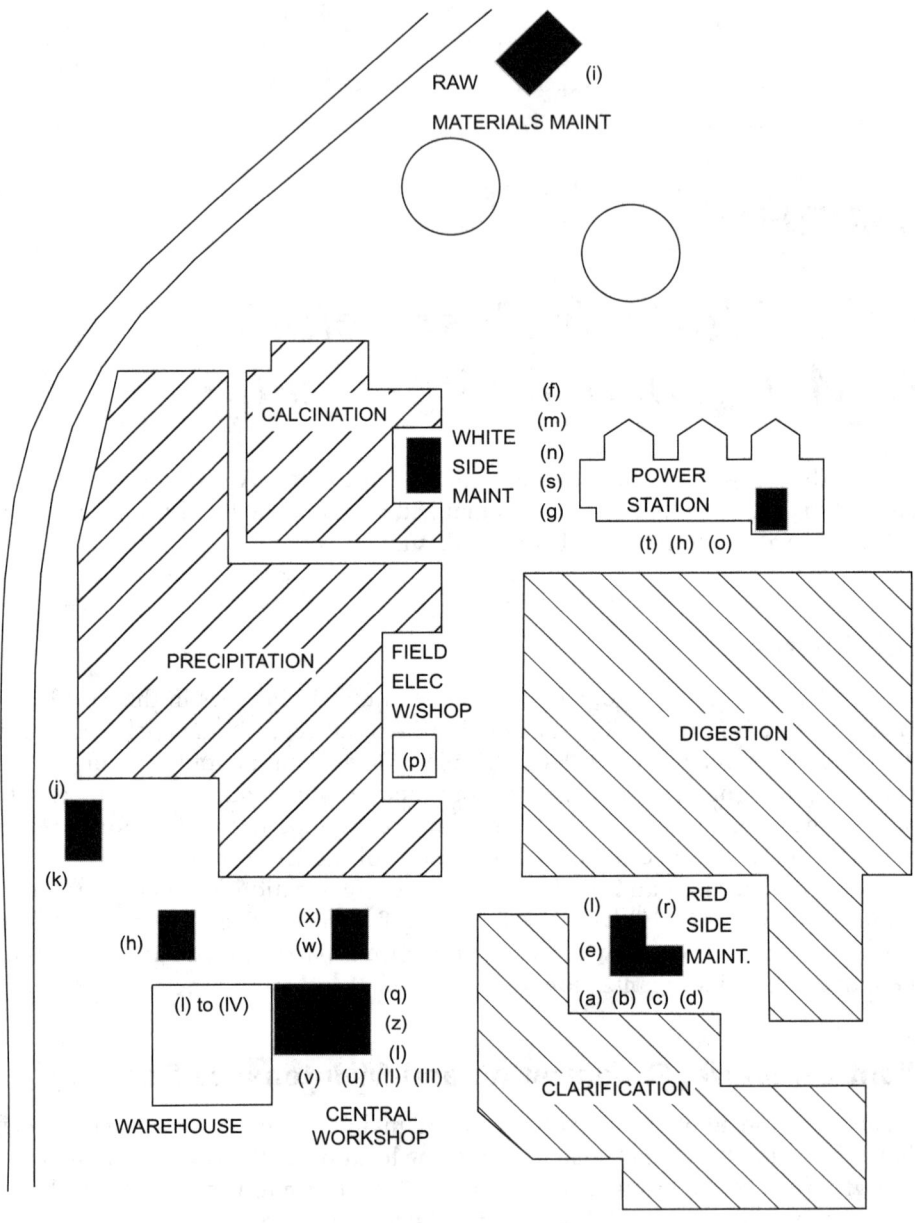

Letters indicate location of
trade groups eg. (i)= Raw materials
fitting group

FIGURE 8–1 Plant Layout

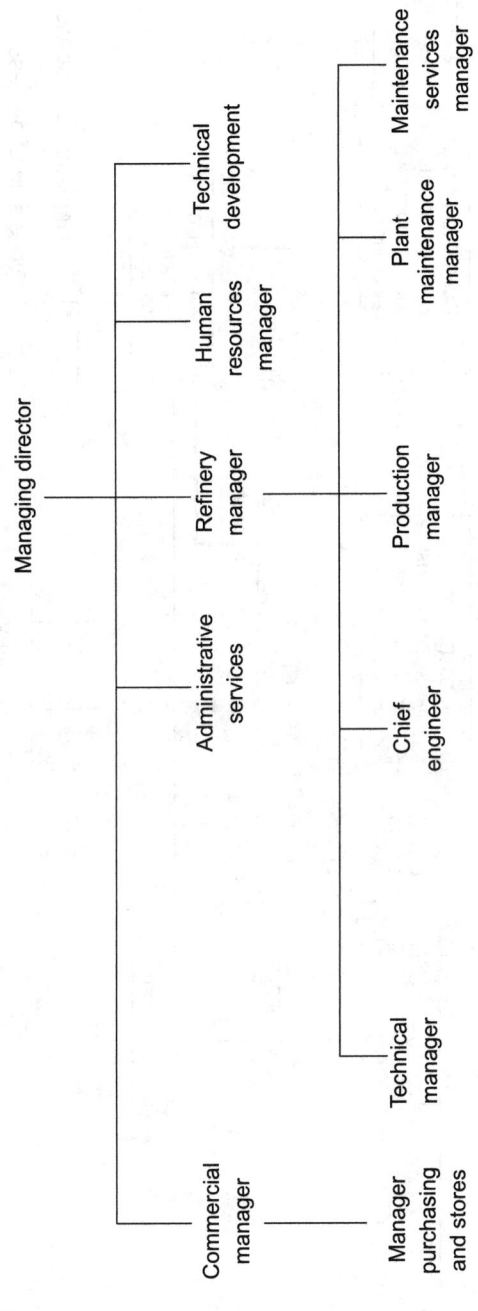

FIGURE 8–2 Senior Administration

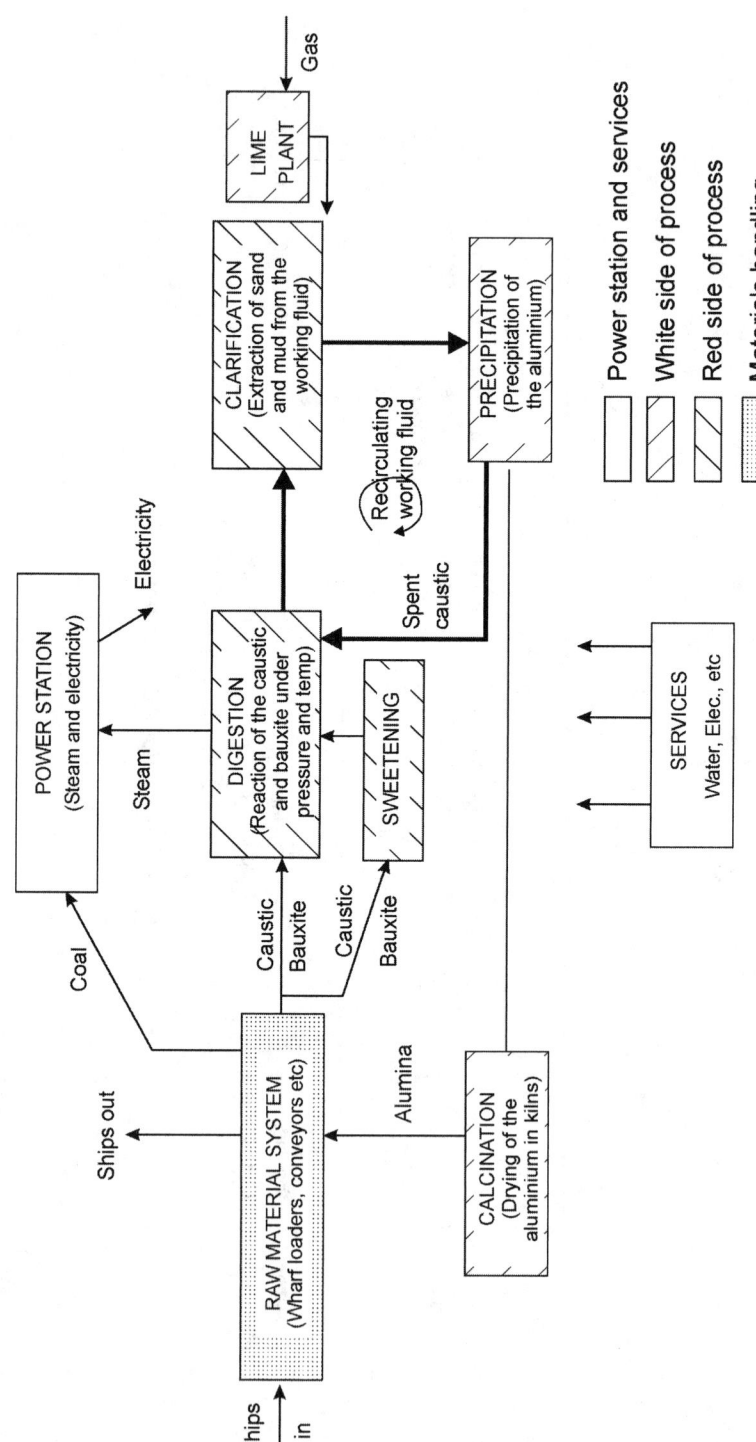

FIGURE 8-3 Alumina Refinery Process Flow

pressure vessels, large machines, settling tanks, kilns, mills and a power station—ran continuously, never coming off line at plant level.

A life plan for a bauxite mill (a typical unit) is shown in Table 8–1 and an extract from the maintenance schedule for the digestion plant is shown in Figure 8–4. The off-line work component of the life plans was scheduled by exploiting the extensive redundancy at plant stream, unit and item level. **It was noted, however, that the production department (the 'plant owners') were not adhering to the schedule and hence were causing a 'lumpy' third line work load which disrupted the planning process.**

TABLE 8–1 Summary of Life Plan for a Bauxite Grinding Mill

Operating policy
The system is made up of ten mills, nine of which are needed for full production. One mill is
    either on stand-by or under planned off-line maintenance. An hour-meter records on-line
    time and downtime.
Maintenance life plan

Frequency of procedure	Duration off-line	Procedure
Two-monthly (approx)	Zero	Bearings on IRD vibration route
Every 4–5 months	3 days	Intermediate ball/rod charges
		Plus necessary minor corrective work
Every 9 months (on grind quality)	14 days	Major service. Oil analysis
		Electric motor service
About every 25 years	6 weeks	Rebuild

Resource Structure

In order to map the resource structure, information on the size, composition (the trades that make up a team), shift roster and work function of each of the groups identified in Figure 8–1 was used to construct Table 8–2. Figure 8–5 maps the trade groups vertically by work function (i.e., first line, second line etc.) and horizontally by plant specialisation. The operator groups are shown above the plant equipment line. For example, Group (a) is made up of thirteen fitters, on days, carrying out second-line work in the grinding area of the digestion plant. Table 8–3, which ties up with the resource structure of Figure 8–5, shows a labour inventory of the refinery. The first-line work on shifts was carried out by groups (e), (d), (q2), (u2) and (h), the first-line work on days being carried out in part by the above groups with the overspill cascading back to the area second-line groups. The second-line work was undertaken by a combination of the area day groups, central project group, service group and contract labour.

A central workshop supported the whole site for fabrication, machining and reconditioning, while the central stores (see Figure 8–1) was supplemented by small area stores. Figure 8–6 shows a schematic model of the flow of rotables between the areas and the central workshop.

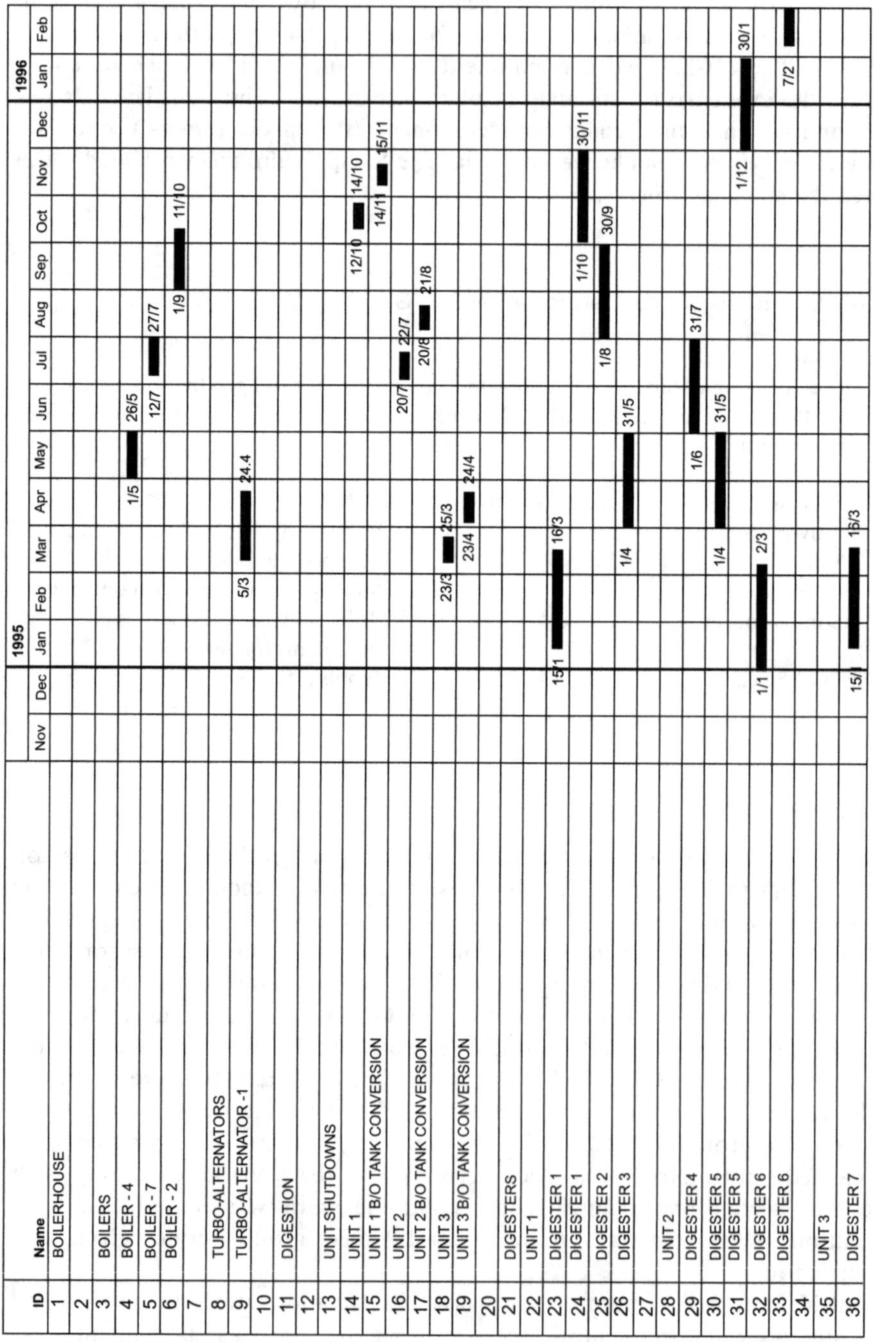

ID	Name	Start	End
1	BOILERHOUSE		
2			
3	BOILERS		
4	BOILER - 4	1/5	26/5
5	BOILER - 7	12/7	27/7
6	BOILER - 2	1/9	11/10
7			
8	TURBO-ALTERNATORS		
9	TURBO-ALTERNATOR -1	5/3	24.4
10			
11	DIGESTION		
12			
13	UNIT SHUTDOWNS		
14	UNIT 1	12/10	14/10
15	UNIT 1 B/O TANK CONVERSION	14/11	15/11
16	UNIT 2	20/7	22/7
17	UNIT 2 B/O TANK CONVERSION	20/8	21/8
18	UNIT 3	23/3	25/3
19	UNIT 3 B/O TANK CONVERSION	23/4	24/4
20			
21	DIGESTERS		
22	UNIT 1	15/1	16/3
23	DIGESTER 1	15/1	16/3
24	DIGESTER 1	1/10	30/11
25	DIGESTER 2	1/8	30/9
26	DIGESTER 3	1/4	31/5
27	UNIT 2	1/6	31/7
28			
29	DIGESTER 4	1/6	31/7
30	DIGESTER 5	1/4	31/5
31	DIGESTER 5	1/12	30/1
32	DIGESTER 6	1/1	2/3
33	DIGESTER 6		7/2
34			
35	UNIT 3	15/1	16/3
36	DIGESTER 7	15/1	16/3

FIGURE 8-4 Extract from Major Work Schedule

TABLE 8–2 Extract from Table of Work Groups, their Location, Size, Scheduling and Function

Tradegroup	Location	Trade Mix and Size	Shift Roster	Work Function
Raw materials mechanical (group i)	Wharf area workshop	24 fitters	6 fitters on a 4×7 shift roster	On Monday to Friday day shift, material handling equipment—second line work. On all other shifts plant wide first line work, other than where there is local cover
Raw materials electrical (group n)	Wharf area workshop	3 electricians	Days	Material handling equipment, first and second line work
Boiler house mechanical (group h)	Boiler house mechanical workshop	18 fitters	6 fitters on a 3×5 shift roster	First and second line cover for boiler house Monday to Friday

Observations

(i) The resource structure was made up of various small single tradegroups, each of which had its own specialised supervisor. Most of those interviewed (including the tradesmen) felt that these groups were under-utilised (see Table 8–4). A large amount of reactive maintenance was being undertaken and the groups were manned up to a level which would enable them to deal with the peak workload. This applied in particular to the project and services groups that had to respond to the fluctuating major workload—caused by the production department's non-adherence to the major work schedule (see Figure 8–4). These problems were compounded by a poor planning system (which was also audited but will not be discussed here).

(ii) Utilisation was also poor because of the perceived need to improve flexibility (between trades, between groups, between operation and maintenance, and in shift working). In the case of the area tradeforce ten percent of all its work was accomplished via overtime, and in the case of the services workshop twenty five percent. The average number of contract workers on the site was around seventy five, most of whom were employed on a day-work basis.

(iii) Although the core skills of the tradeforce were high, their plant-specific skills were not, and their morale was low. They felt neither a sense of plant ownership nor a sense of belonging to a plant team.

Maintenance Administrative Structure

The maintenance administrative structure is shown in Figures 8–7 (a) and (b) and an inventory of the staff, with some simple indices, in Table 8–5.

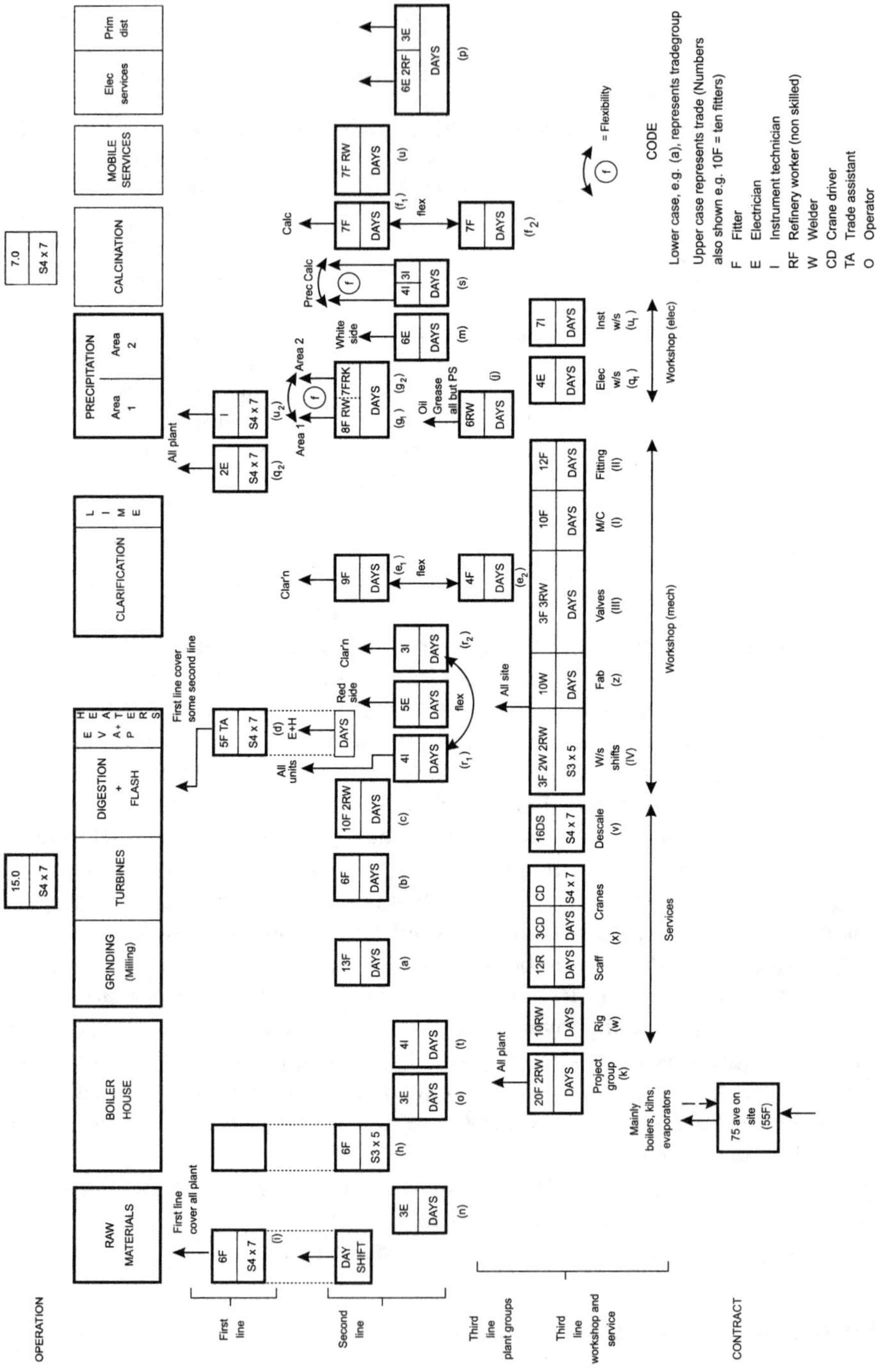

FIGURE 8–5 Resource Structure

TABLE 8–3 Tradeforce Inventory

Trades	
Fitters	194
Welders	16
Electricians	35
Inst. Tech.	29
Total	274
Non-trades	
Trades assistants	22
Lubrication	6
Crane drivers	7
Scaffolding	12
De-scale and others	74
Total	121
Total waged	395

Figure 8–7 should be analysed alongside the resource structure of Figure 8–5 and the plant layout of Figure 8–1, the tradegroup coding being common to each of the three diagrams. The main features of this traditional functional structure were as follows:

* The production area supervisors were considered to be the 'owners' of the plant in their area (e.g., in the precipitation area). Their responsibilities included ensuring that '...*all equipment (was) safe to operate (was) always capable of meeting required production goals, (was) maintained within planned costs, and (met) environmental standards.*' They reported to their respective production superintendents who in turn reported to the production manager. Thus the production department was responsible for all things operational and owned the equipment.
* The Maintenance Services Manager was responsible for plant-wide electrical and instrumentation maintenance and for all third line resources (other than the project group). The Plant Maintenance Manager was responsible for all the mechanical area groups, the project group and the planning group, *i.e., for the maintenance 'doers.'*
* The Project Engineer was responsible for the design and installation of new and modified equipment.
* The Commercial Manager was responsible for the management of spare parts, but not for the initial order quantity.

Observations

(i) The administrative structure was a classic example of a highly functionalised giant structure. The stated advantages of these is that they concentrate technical and professional expertise in lines of direct authority. They also

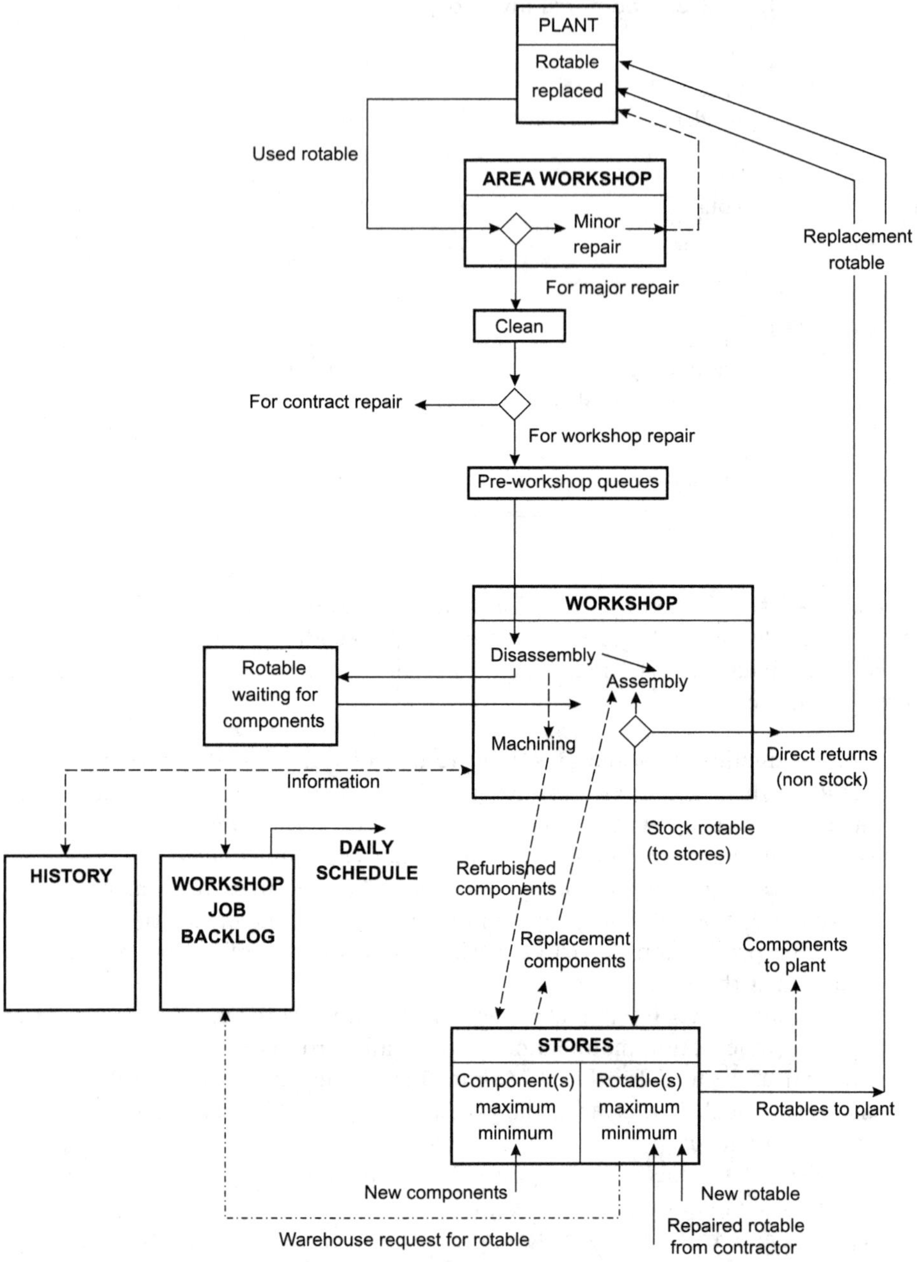

FIGURE 8–6 Movement of Rotables

have inherent weaknesses, however, which arise from the difficulty in achieving effective communication and co-operation across functional boundaries. This is especially the case for large structures with relatively long chains of command.

TABLE 8–4 Questionnaire (All Answers were Given as Ratings out of 10. Figures Shown are the Mean Scores)

Addressed to maintenance supervisors and tradeforce

	Digest (Mech)	Precip/Calc (Mech)	Central W/S (Mech)	Refinery	
				E	I
How do you rate the morale of the tradeforce?	5	5	5	7	7
How do you rate the productivity of the tradeforce?	5.5	5.8	5	8	9
How do you rate the plant specific knowledge and skills of the tradeforce?	6.2	5.3	6.5	8	8
How do you rate the plant condition?	7	5.7			
How do you rate the quality/supply of rotables?	5.3	–			

Addressed to production supervisors

	Mech	Elect	Inst
How do you rate the service you get from the following maintenance groups?	5.8	8	7.8

Addressed to superintendents, production supervisors and tradeforce

How well do you consider the maintenance supervisor performs the role?	4

Addressed to all supervisors and tradeforce

How do you rate the senior production management shop floor profile?	7
How do you rate the senior maintenance management shop floor profile?	3

(ii) A better way of understanding the administrative characteristics of a structure such as that shown in Figure 8–7 is to model the administration around one area of plant, the digestion area, say (see Figure 8–8). There, the maintenance and engineering personnel, while reporting functionally also had the common purpose of assisting the digestion plant 'owners' (Production) in ensuring that the process achieved its required levels of availability and performance. The structure was not operating effectively, some of the main problems being that:

* no attempt had been made to establish a 'digestion group' or formulate digestion area objectives;
* the division of plant responsibilities between Production and Maintenance was inappropriate (see Figure 8–9);

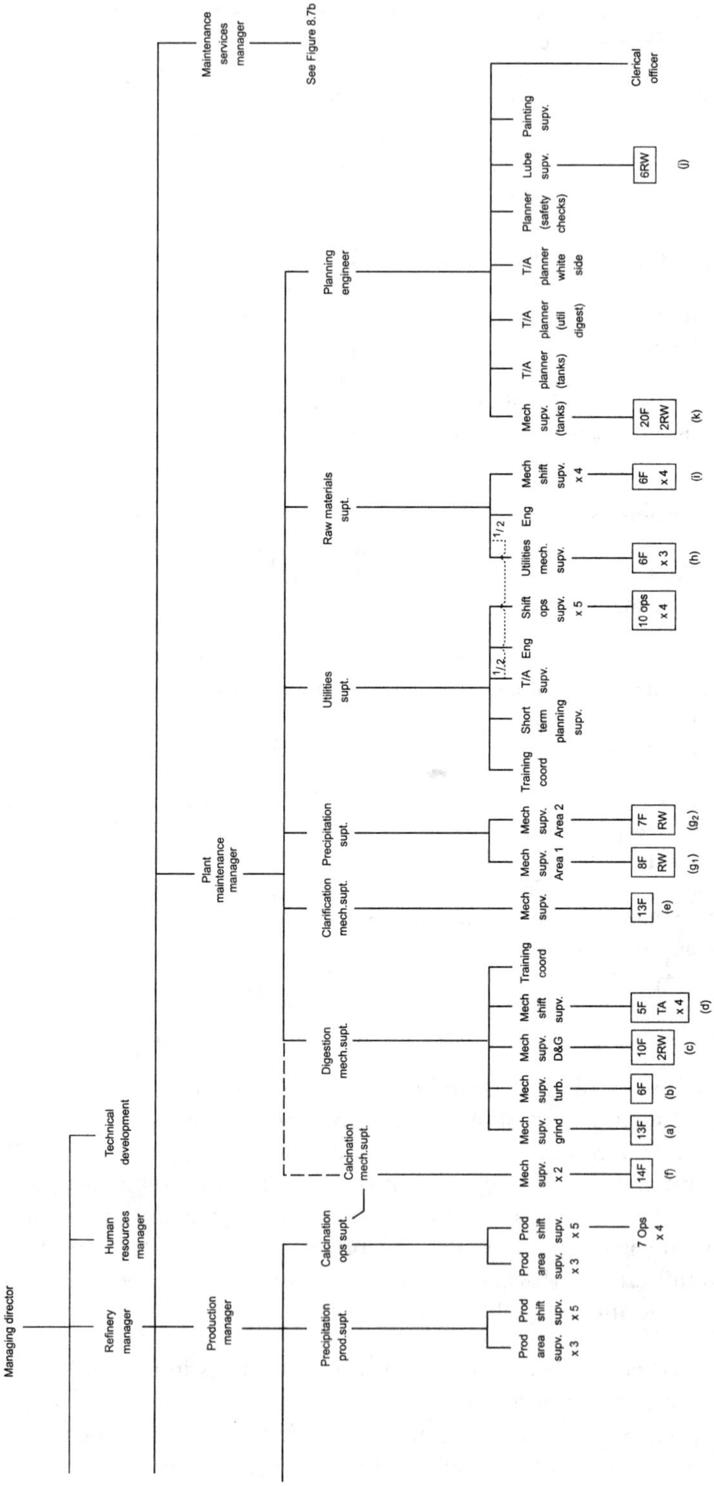

FIGURE 8–7 (a) Extracts from Maintenance Adminstrative Structure

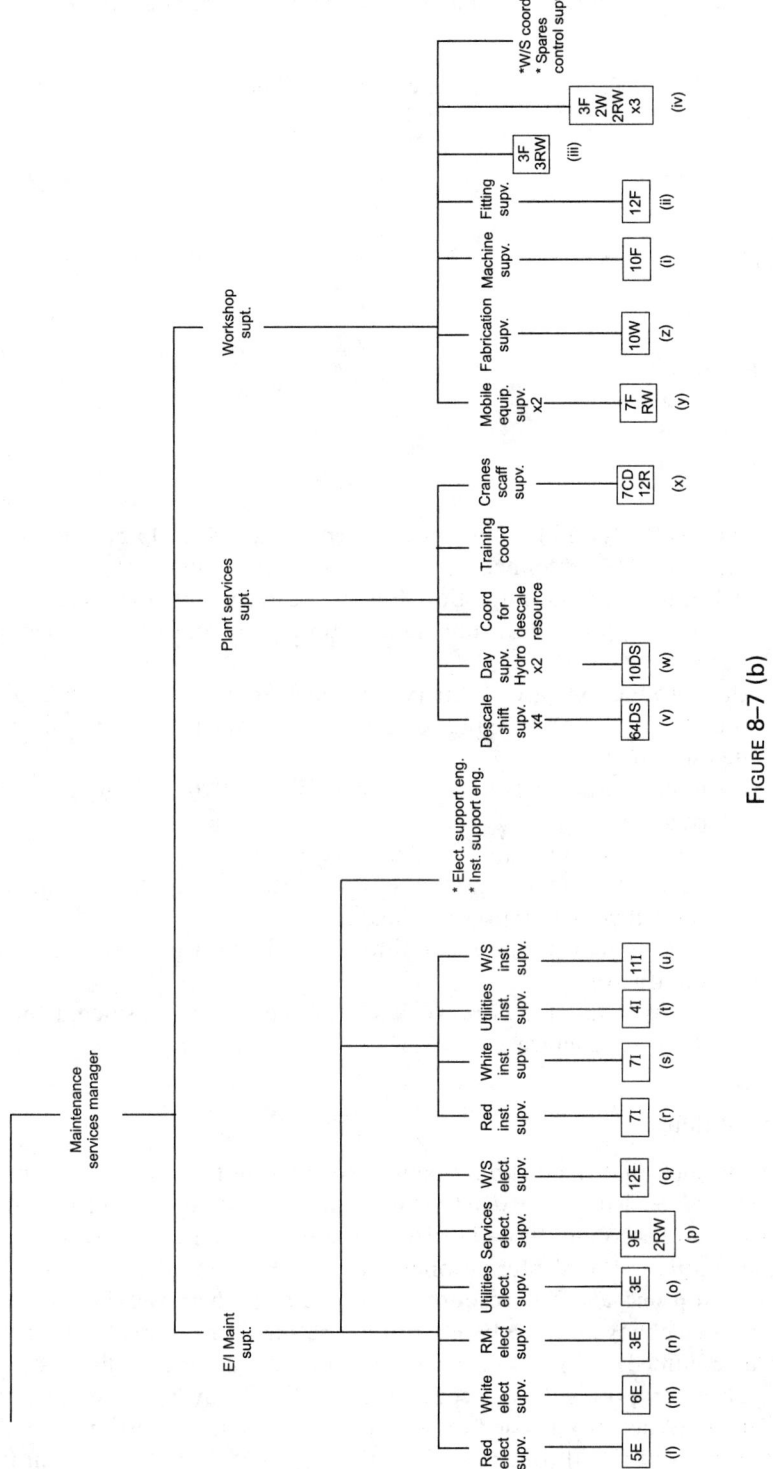

FIGURE 8–7 (b)

TABLE 8–5 Staff Inventory (for Salaried Maintenance Personnel, 1995)

Engineering managers			12
Engineers (including allowance for plant engineering support)			17
Supervisors	Direct	43	
	Planning	9	
	Training	4	
	Total		56
Clerical			4
Total staff			89

Simple indices	
Trade/non-trades +	8.0
Waged/salaried	4.4
Waged/direct supv	9.2
Waged/planning supv	4.4
Waged/total supv	7.1

* the electrical and instrument maintenance personnel and the mechanical maintenance personnel reported to different managers;
* delineation of the Digestion Engineer's responsibilities, between maintenance support on the one hand and project work on the other, had not been made clear;
* the production area supervisors lacked the necessary engineering qualifications and training to be effective plant owners and maintenance decision makers;
* by international benchmark standards (of 1996) the organization was overmanned, viz.:
  — there were too many levels of management;
  — other than in the power station, little attempt had been made to introduce self-empowered teams;
  — not enough of the reconditioning had been carried out by outside contractors;
  — more of the non-core work should have been considered for outside contract alliances.

Recommendations

It was decided that these should be implemented in two stages, covering firstly those changes needed in the *short* term (within a year) to correct the structural deficiencies, and secondly those needed in the *medium* term (two to five years) to bring the company up to international benchmark standards.

Short term proposals: The resource structure as it then was (i.e., as in Figure 8–5) was to be changed immediately to that outlined in Figure 8–10. The overall form was retained, in particular its dependence on decentralised second-line groups. These proposals were accompanied by the following observations:

(i) The first line work needed to be clearly defined and an estimate made of its pattern and size throughout the refinery. Using this information, it would

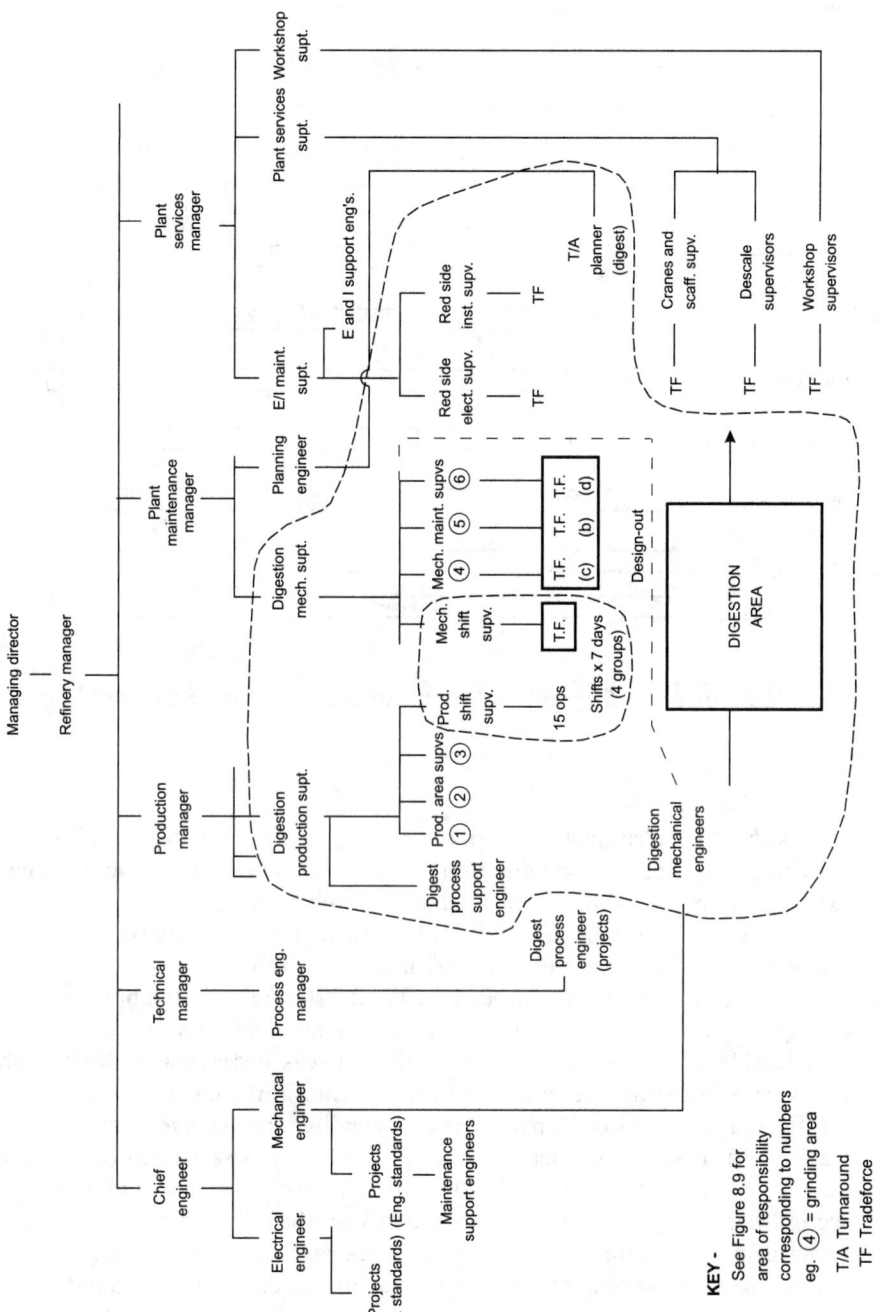

FIGURE 8–8 Model of Administration Based in Digestion Area

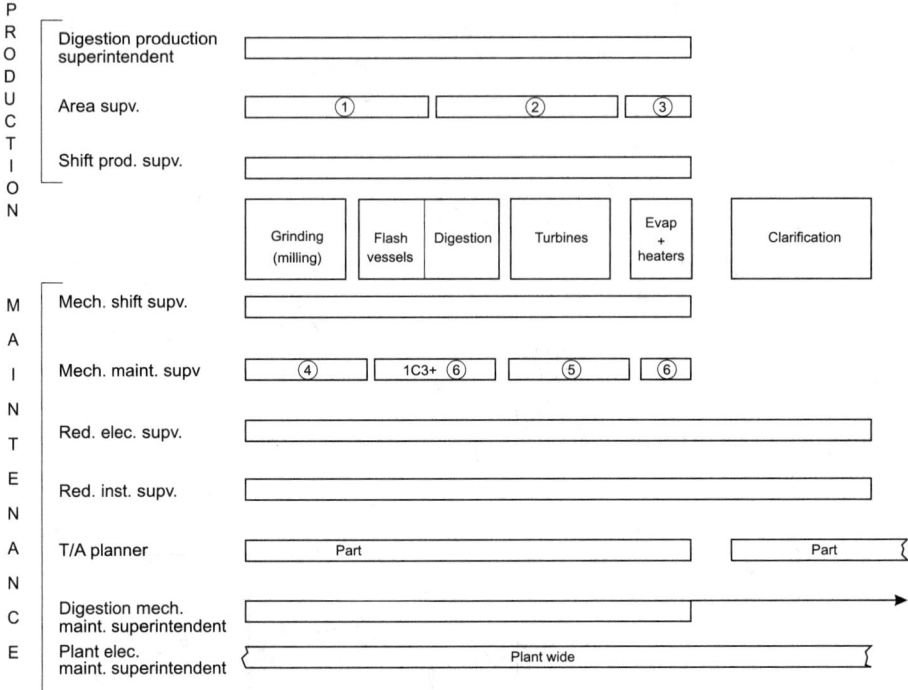

FIGURE 8–9 Comparison of Supervisors' Plant Responsibilities, Digestion Process

be possible to determine the size of a workshop-located, first-line, shift-crew (mechanical, electrical and instrumentation) to replace the several, then-existing, sources of shift cover. Such a first-line crew should also carry out first-line work during the day-shift, allowing (as far as possible) the second-line area crews to carry out the scheduled second-line work.

(ii) The second-line work also needed to be clearly defined. It appeared, for example, that a distinction could be made between the on-going schedulable work and the unit overhauls. It was necessary to distinguish the work (mechanical, electrical or instrumentation) that was best carried out by an area resource (for reasons of specialised knowledge, response and teamwork) from work, such as overhaul, that was best carried out by the centralised project group. It followed from this reasoning that the area second-line groups were then reducible in size, the manpower thus released being using as a supplement to the existing project group. This third-line group should be set at the minimum size, any peaks in its workload being cascaded to contract. Accompanied by better production scheduling, these changes would have meant that, initially, improvements in productivity would be gained by reducing the usage of the contract day-work labour, and not by reducing the company labour force.

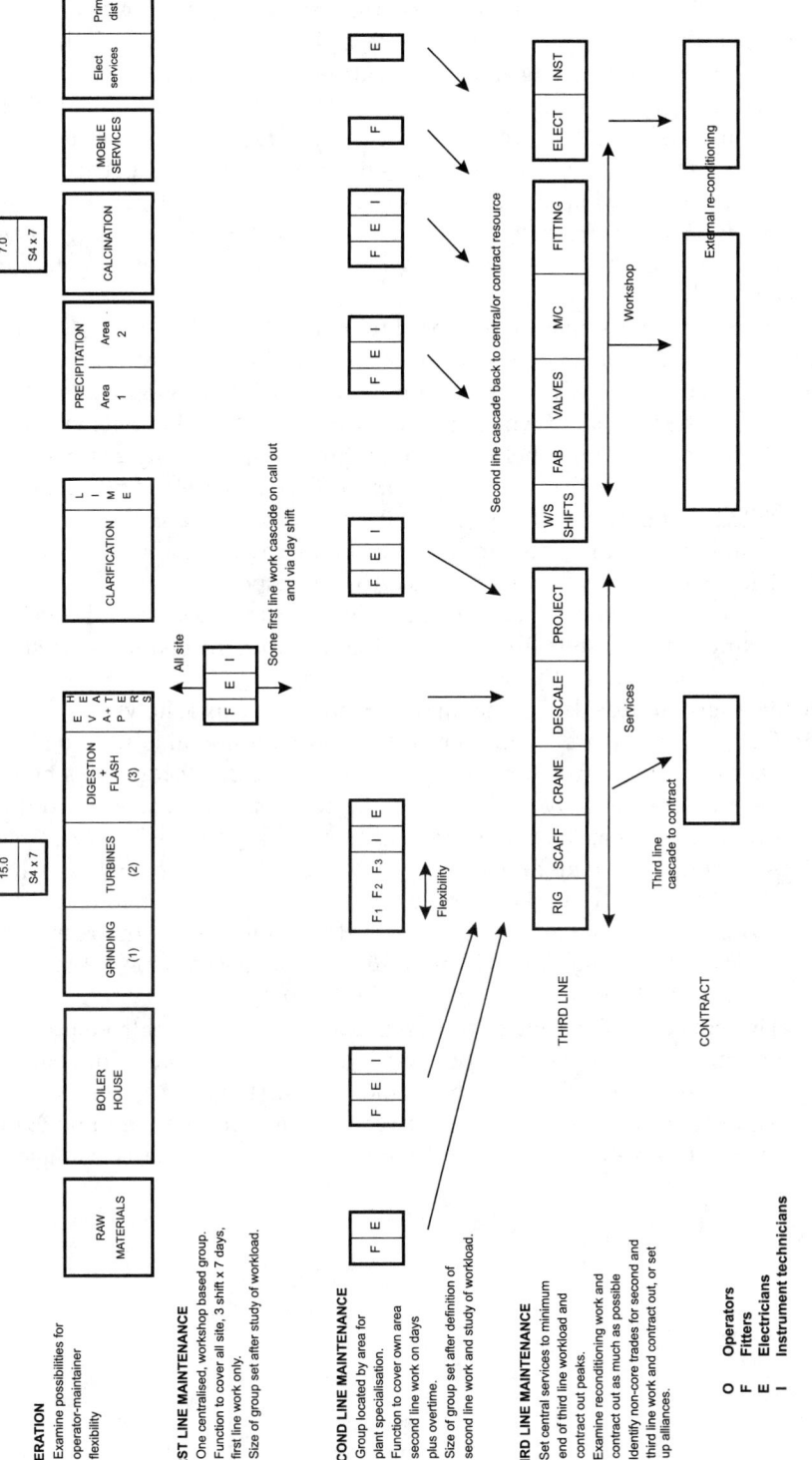

OPERATION
Examine possibilities for operator-maintainer flexibility

FIRST LINE MAINTENANCE
One centralised, workshop based group.
Function to cover all site, 3 shift x 7 days, first line work only.
Size of group set after study of workload.

SECOND LINE MAINTENANCE
Group located by area for plant specialisation.
Function to cover own area second line work on days plus overtime.
Size of group set after definition of second line work and study of workload.

THIRD LINE MAINTENANCE
* Set central services to minimum end of third line workload and contract out peaks.
* Examine reconditioning work and contract out as much as possible
* Identify non-core trades for second and third line work and contract out, or set up alliances.

O   Operators
F   Fitters
E   Electricians
I   Instrument technicians

FIGURE 8–10 An Approach to Improving the Resource Structure

(iii) The workload that was imposed on the central workshop was not analysed, neither as regards its size nor as regards the basis adopted for deciding whether reconditioning and fabrication should have been undertaken internally or externally. It was recommended that such an analysis should be done and as much work as possible contracted out. The impression, a purely subjective one, was gained that much of the work carried out within the workshops could have been handled by outside contract. *The main point here is that support activities of this kind should not be allowed to gain a momentum of their own* (*the company's business was alumina refining not engineering*).

The administrative structure proposed to match that of Figure 8–10 is shown in Figure 8–11. The main changes can be summarised as follows:

(i) The digestion area was one of a number of semi-autonomous manufacturing units each one of which had its own manager and maintenance section. Within a given unit there was to be 'plant responsibility matching' across the maintenance teams and the plant officers. The plant officers (formerly called production area supervisors) were to remain the plant 'owners' and would need training to improve their knowledge of maintenance and plant.

(ii) The Maintenance Manager was to be responsible for the third level (workshop) resources and the maintenance support section. In addition he would be responsible for setting and monitoring the maintenance standards within the manufacturing units.

Medium term proposals: The main suggestions were as follows:

(i) Over the two years leading up to the audit considerable training had been provided to the tradeforce to extend their core knowledge (this had been a government initiative). This should be used as necessary to improve flexibility among the trade-groups shown in Figure 8–10.

(ii) An exercise should be carried out to establish the extent to which the production shift workers could carry out first-line maintenance work. Would this be possible with improved training and/or the recruitment of tradesmen into the teams? Would this be more cost effective than the use of the existing first-line maintenance shift team?

(iii) The concept of a 'self-empowered team' should be introduced into the organization for both production and maintenance. Guidelines were discussed on how this was to be undertaken (Figure 4.8).

(iv) An alliance should be set up between a contract company and Bauxal to cover all third-line plant work, workshops and spare parts management.

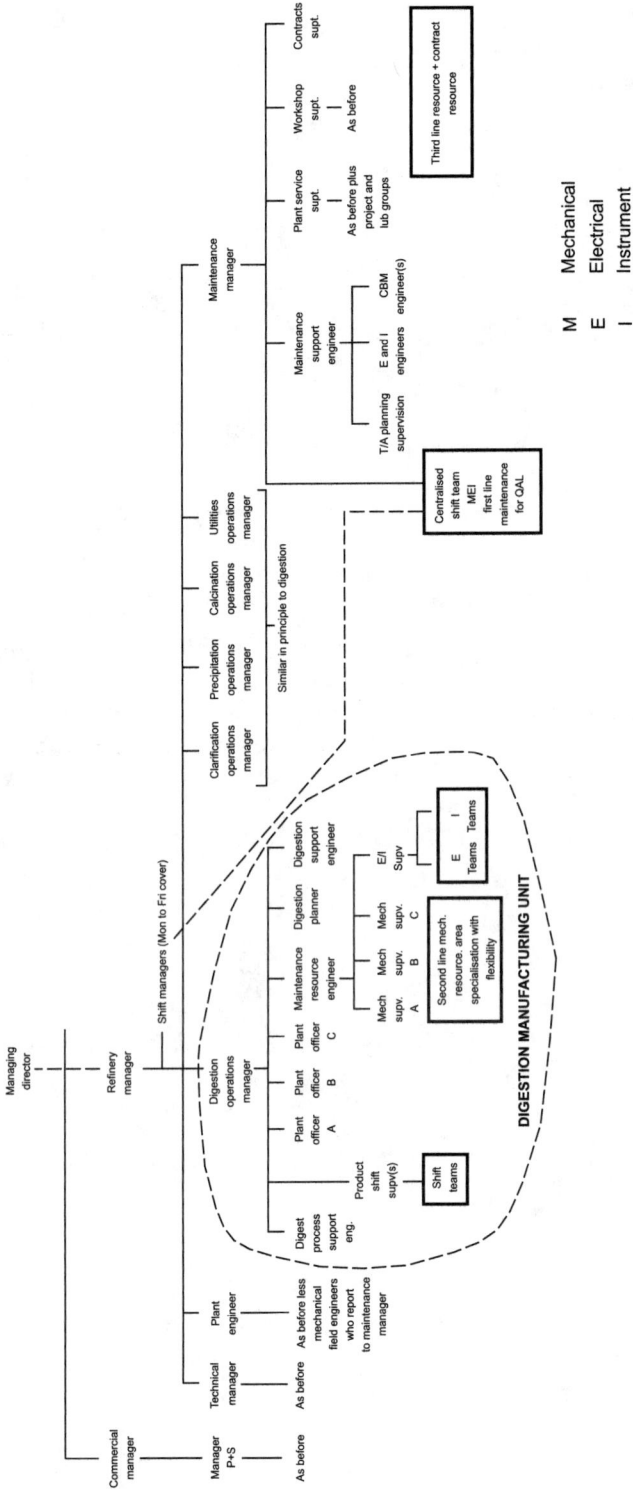

FIGURE 8–11 Proposed Administrative Structure Based on Manufacturing Units

CHAPTER 9

Case Study 2: Setting-up a Company–Contract Alliance

Here, the differences will be clarified between (a) the traditional use of con-tractors to undertake maintenance work and (b) outsourcing such a service via an alliance. A case study will show how a chemical company, pursuing trends in organizational change which occurred during the 1980s and 1990s, came to set up of a company–contract alliance to carry out maintenance work.

Introduction: Contracting, Outsourcing and Alliances

The employment of contract labour has been a commonplace feature of maintenance organization since the industrial revolution. The traditional use of contractors can be explained via reference to a resource structure such as that which was outlined in Figure 8–5. There, contractors were employed to:

- resource peaks in the demand for labour (mainly for the major overhaul, third line, work);
- undertake highly specialised, sophisticated, work (e.g., on gas turbines)— which is itself often peaky or intermittent in its impact on the workload;
- re-condition complex equipment (e.g., pumps, motors).

The advantages and disadvantages of the use of contract labour have been well documented [1] and are summarised in Table 9–1. It was traditional for a company to use a number of different contractors to provide these services. The usual method of payment tended to be based on some kind of measured daywork in the case of casual labour, and on fixed price contracts in the case of large overhauls or re-conditioning work.

I have encountered variations on this traditional approach. For example, a refinery I visited was using preferred contractors to carry out all maintenance other than first-line. The company still controlled the maintenance work and used

---

[1] A. Kelly, *Maintenance organization and systems,* Butterworth-Heinemann, 1997.

Table 9–1 Employing Contractors: the Benefits and Problems

Benefits
* Facilitates resourcing of peak demands.
* Facilitates reduction of overhaul duration.
* Stabilises the size of the internal workforce (at minimum levels for the maintenance problems).
* Enables internal tradeforce size to be controlled in the early stages of new plant operation.
* Allows internal tradeforce to be allocated to quality jobs.
* Contract organization may have specialist skills and resources.
* Helps to keep internal overtime under control.
* Helps to suppress costs of internal maintenance equipment.

Problems
* Contractors do not always have resources readily available.
* Contractors have no feeling of 'ownership' of the plant.
* Contractors need validating for skills and safety knowledge.
* Job definition needs to be more detailed and precise than for internal workers.
* Difficult to check productivity of a contractor.
* Problems can arise regarding the relationship between contract tradesmen and internal tradesmen.
* Union problems can arise (e.g., use of non-unionised contract labour).
* Contractor objectives are different from those of the company—they are not concerned with the long term aims of the plant.

measured daywork as the form of payment. Over the last few years, however, the new 'buzzwords' in maintenance management have been '*outsourcing*' and '*alliances*.'

Outsourcing has been defined as follows:

'*Outsourcing takes place when an organization transfers the ownership and control of a company function/process, e.g., maintenance management, to a contractor.*' [2]

The company tells the contractor what it wants and at what cost (laid down in a contract) and leaves him to decide how best to accomplish this. Generally speaking, those company functions that are outsourced are generally termed '*non-core*', i.e., they are not regarded as a part of the core competencies of the business.

Among the advantages of outsourcing are that it allows the company to:

– concentrate its business focus on its core operation;
– gain access to specialist contractors that bring in a high level of expertise and, through their size, bring economies of scale. This helps the company to control and reduce its operating costs.

---

[2] J. Johnson, *Outsourcing*, Butterworth-Heinemann, 1997.

However, it is not without its drawbacks, some of which are listed in Table 9–1 while others include the following:

- it is difficult to engender, among contractor personnel, a sense of equipment 'ownership'; at best they own a *job*. (The contractor would argue that this is counterbalanced by a contract which commits his personnel to achieving key performance indices on availability, cost etc. or losing the contract.)
- the company loses knowledge of the equipment and expertise in maintaining it. (And some of this may be relevant to the core competencies as well as being difficult to re-acquire in the future.)

A company–contractor alliance has been defined as:

'*...a transfer of the ownership and control of a company function (or part thereof) to a partnership made up of company and contractor personnel*'[3],

The partnership can take a number of forms. For example, the two alliance companies may report to the same board, one company—a water utility, say—*owning* and *operating* the assets while another company *maintains* the assets (and probably the assets of other companies). A more usual arrangement was modelled in Figure 5–16 and outlined in the accompanying text. The maintenance group was made up of personnel from the company and from the contractor, who reported via a steering group to the contract company. The main difficulty with alliances lies in setting up a partnership contract that achieves the objectives of both the company and the contractor. Whatever form the contract takes the essential ingredient of a successful alliance is to establish a culture of co-operation and mutual trust.

The key decision regarding an outsourcing alliance concerns the identification of core competencies.

Some electrical power utilities have decided that their core competencies should lie solely in the marketing and selling of electrical power; for the construction, operation and maintenance of their generating stations they have therefore arranged alliances with contract organizations. Likewise, universities, hotels, large public libraries and so on have identified maintenance as a non-core function and customarily now outsource it via similar alliances. Several airport authorities have set up alliances with contractors to operate and maintain their luggage handling equipment. Some offshore gas and oil extractors have arranged alliances with other companies to build and maintain their platforms.

The key characteristics of each one of these examples are: (a) that maintenance is regarded as a non-core function and (b) that the alliance partner brings considerable engineering and maintenance expertise—usually as a result of having designed, built, installed and commissioned the installation.

In the case of industrial companies (chemical processors, oil extractors, food processors, etc.) who have owned and operated their plant for many years the situation is very different. Firstly, deciding whether maintenance is core or not is more difficult, and secondly (and perhaps more importantly) the 'center of

---

[3] P. Bendor-Samual, Outsourcing Center, www.outsourcing-faq.com.

gravity' of asset-oriented engineering experience lies well towards such companies' engineers.

At the ammonia plant referred to in Chapter 5 (see Figure 5–16) it was decided that only the workshops, stores and third-line maintenance resources could be considered non-core. The area second-line resources and the professional maintenance engineers were retained as part of the core effort.

The case study* that follows traces the organizational changes undergone by a chemical company, Chemtow Ltd, during the 90s, changes which culminated in their setting up an alliance to carry out the maintenance function. The question they had to answer was '**How much of the maintenance function should be outsourced and how much retained in-house?'**

Background

Via several interlinked plants located on a single site (see Figure 9–1) Chemtow Ltd made a wide range of chemicals. In the early 90s the company had a traditional functional organization of the kind illustrated in Figures 9–2(a) and (b), i.e., all of the maintenance resources (centralised and plant-located) reported to the Maintenance and Engineering Department.

In 1995, the company re-organized itself into four autonomous business units (see Figure 9–3 which outlines the arrangement for one of them). Initially, the central maintenance group (CMG) was retained, to maintain the common site services (buildings, water, electricity, etc.) and to offer an 'internal contract' service to each of the business units. In addition, the CMG co-ordinated all the contract resources on site.

Audit of the Central Maintenance Group

In 1995, our consultancy group was retained to audit the site, in order to decide on the future size and composition of the CMG, where the resource structure was then as shown in Figure 9–4 and the administrative structure as shown in Figure 9–5.

Following the horizontal axis of Figure 9–4, the services (and trades within each service) provided by the CMG were identified, and listed as in Table 9–2. Also shown, across the top of that table (and stated more fully in Table 9–3), are the various criteria which were then applied in assessing whether each service was core or not. Finally, the last column of Table 9–2 shows (for each service and its assessment) the appropriate resourcing arrangements that were proposed—and which were drawn from the following list of possibilities:

(A) Keep the present service with CMG but up-rate to satisfy customers.
(B) Identify the core resources of the service and retain in CMG but disband the non-core resources.

---

*Carried out jointly by A. Kelly and H. S. Riddell.

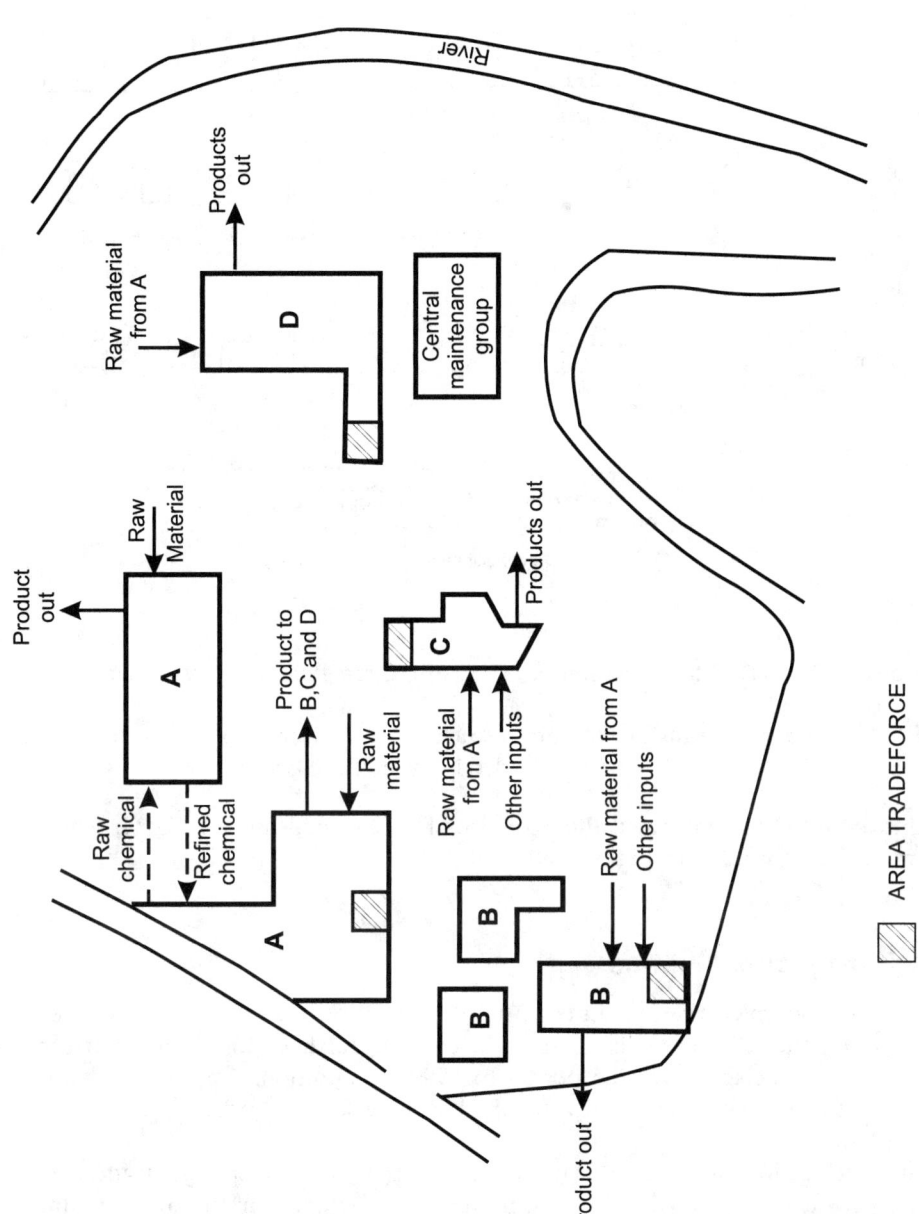

Figure 9–1 Chemtow, Site Layout

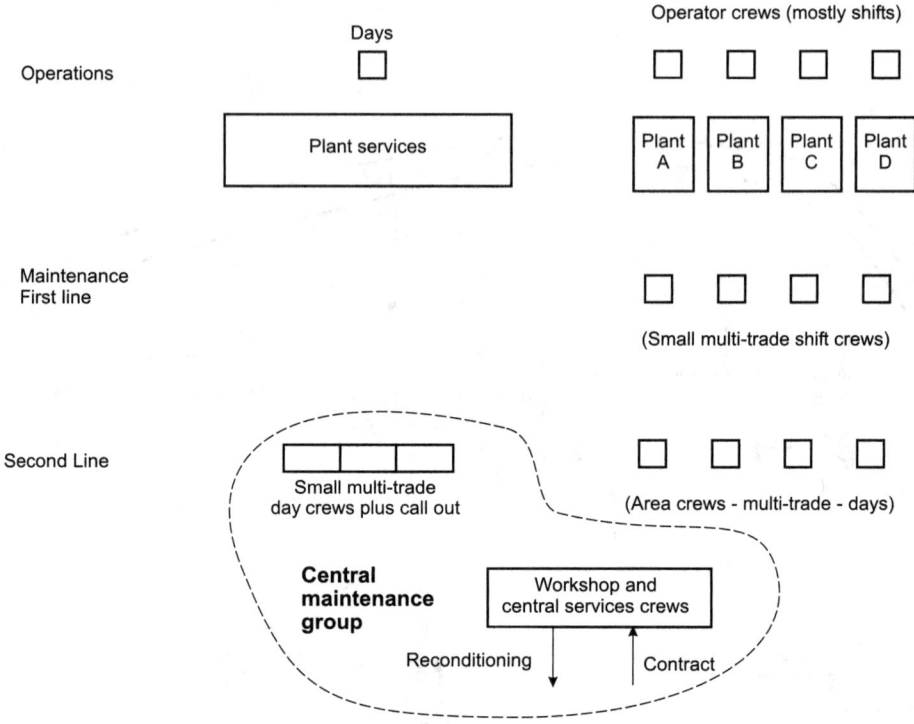

FIGURE 9–2 (a) Traditional Resource Structure, Circa 1990 (Illustration Only)

(C) As in **(B)**, but transfer the core resource to the primary business unit.
(D) Disband the complete service and rely on contractors.

This analysis then informed the proposals for re-organising the CMG, which are modelled in outline in Figures 9–6 and 9–7.

Setting up the Alliance

Chemtow accepted the recommendations of the 1995 audit and duly reduced the size of the CMG, which was reduced still further (to about fourteen tradesmen/technicians) over the period to 1999. In addition, the business units also moved their organization towards benchmark standards, as shown in Figure 9–8.

The production technicians (via training and recruitment of tradesmen within the team) operated as self-empowered teams and carried out first-line maintenance tasks. The maintenance technicians carried out the second line work, their numbers being set at a minimum level—supplemented as necessary for second-line and third-line work by the CMG or contract labour. Numerous contract companies were engaged, their very diverse contract arrangements being dependent on work type.

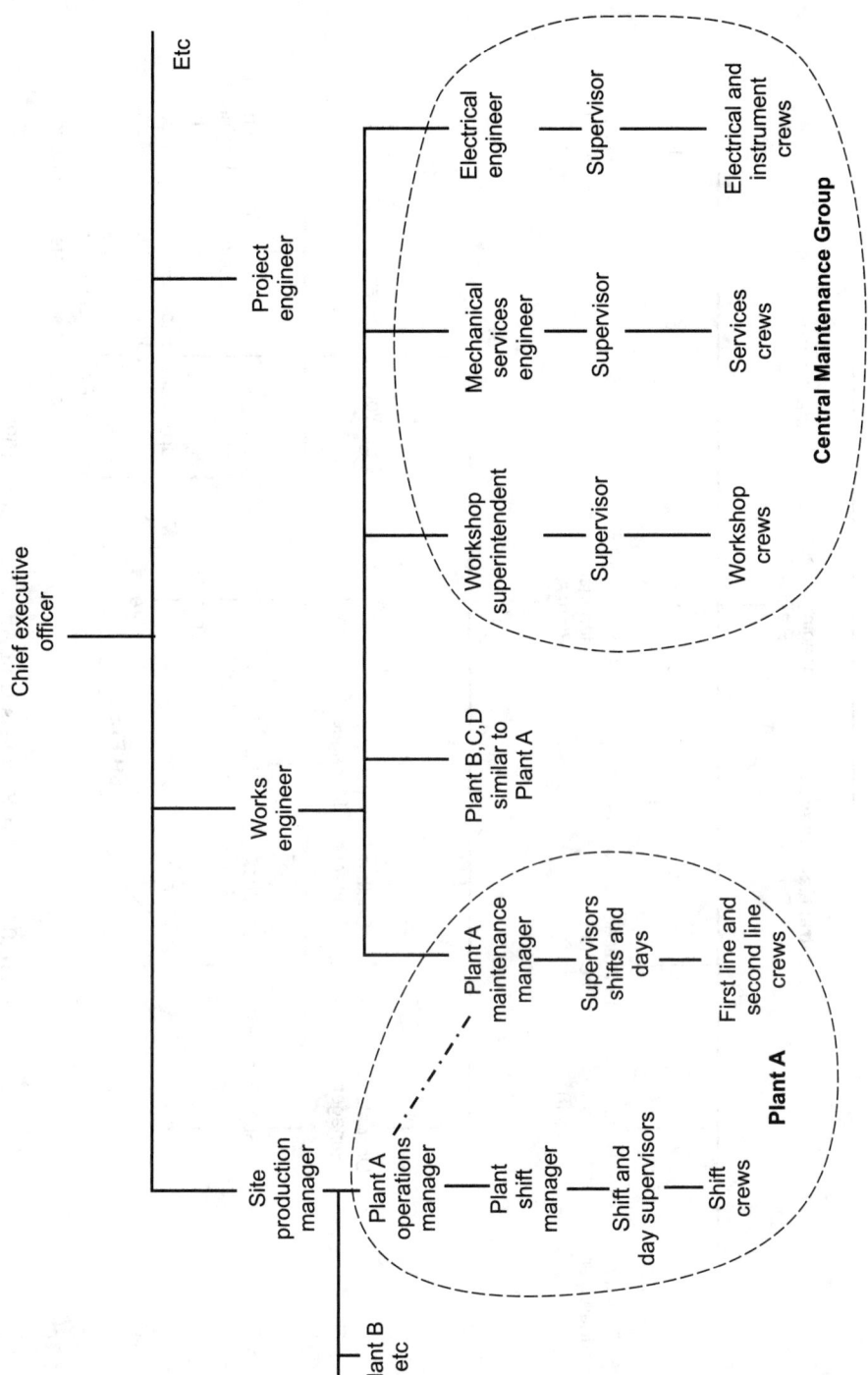

FIGURE 9–2 (b)   Traditional Administrative Structure, Circa 1990 (Illustration Only)

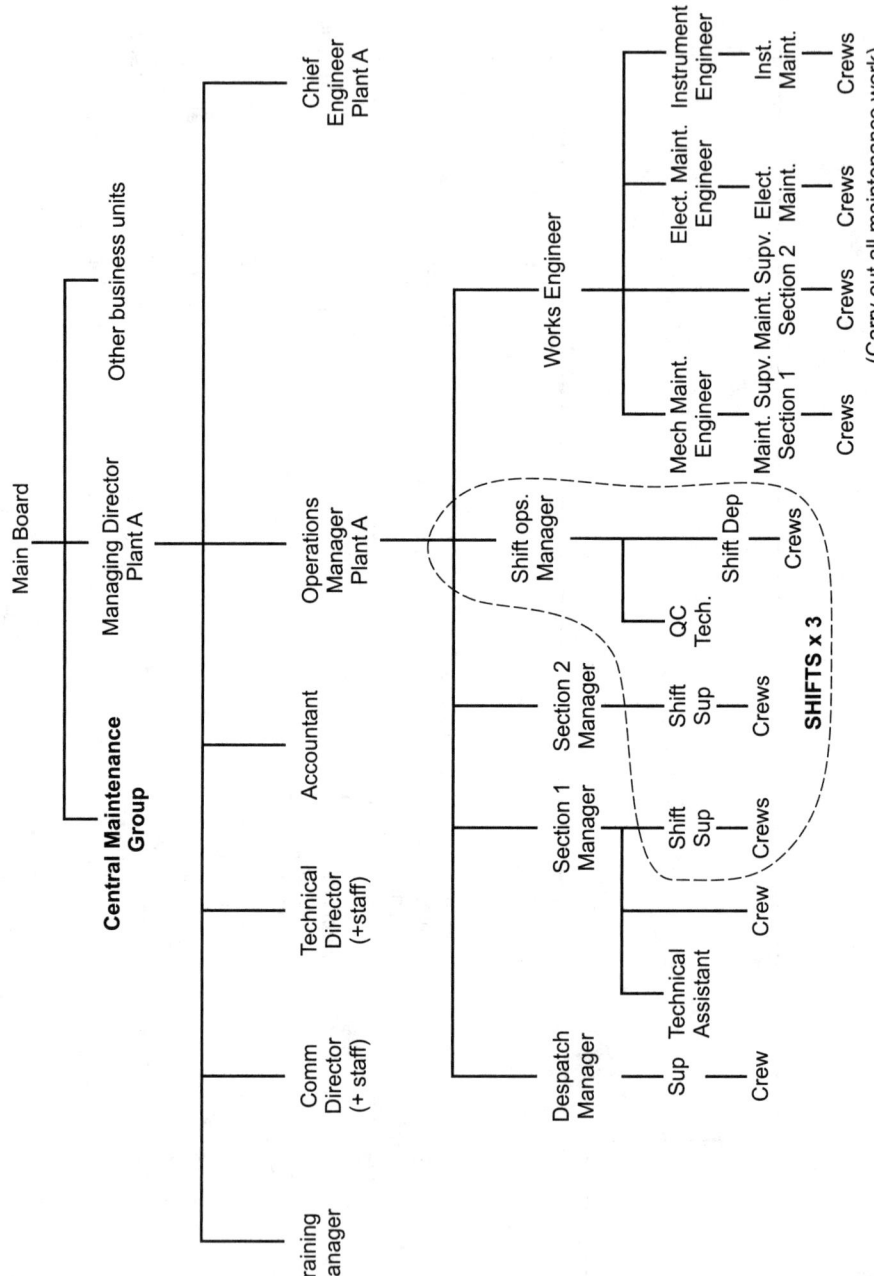

Figure 9.3 Plant A Business Unit Administration (1995)

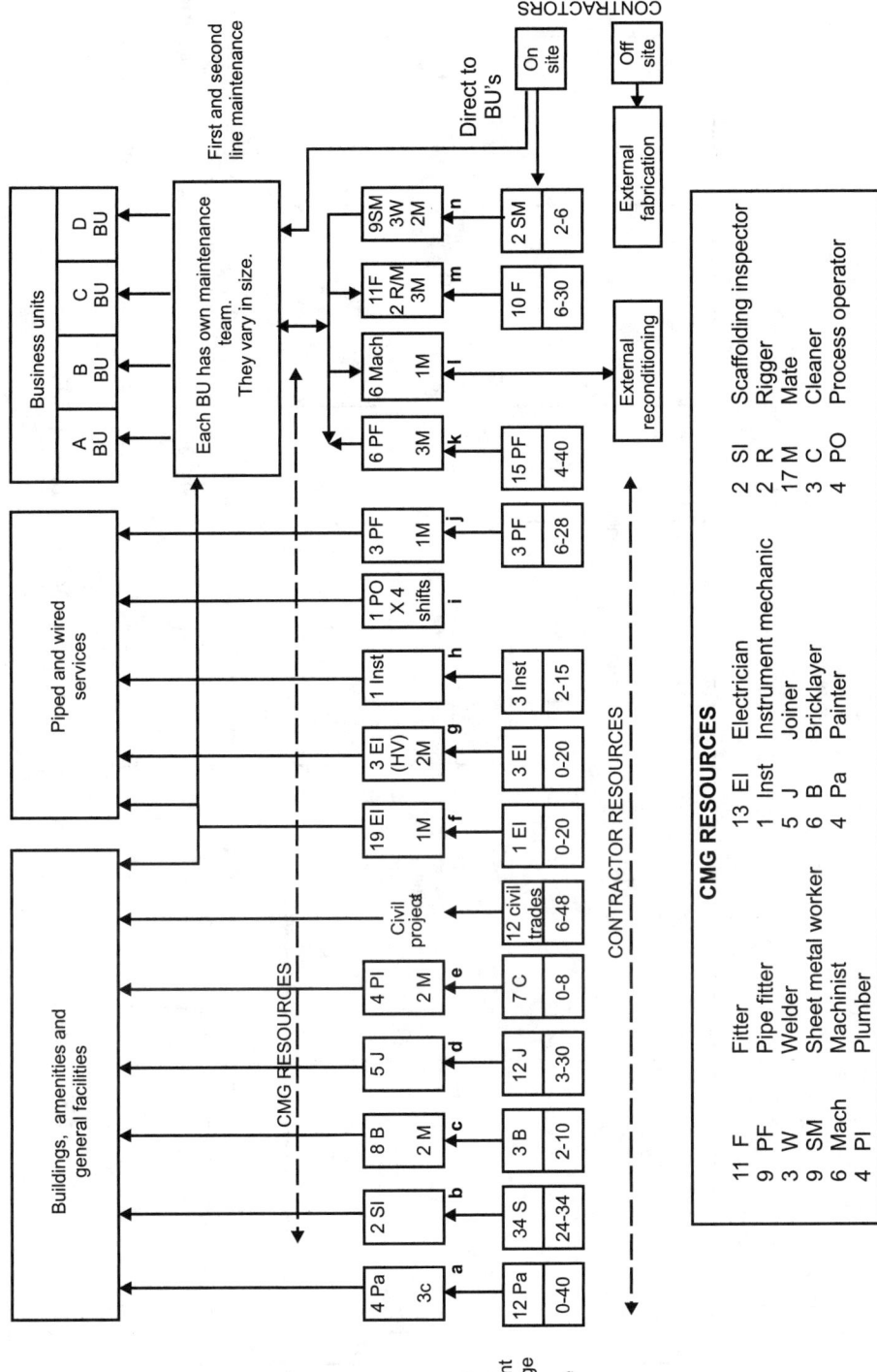

FIGURE 9–4 Central Maintenance Group Resource Structure (1995)

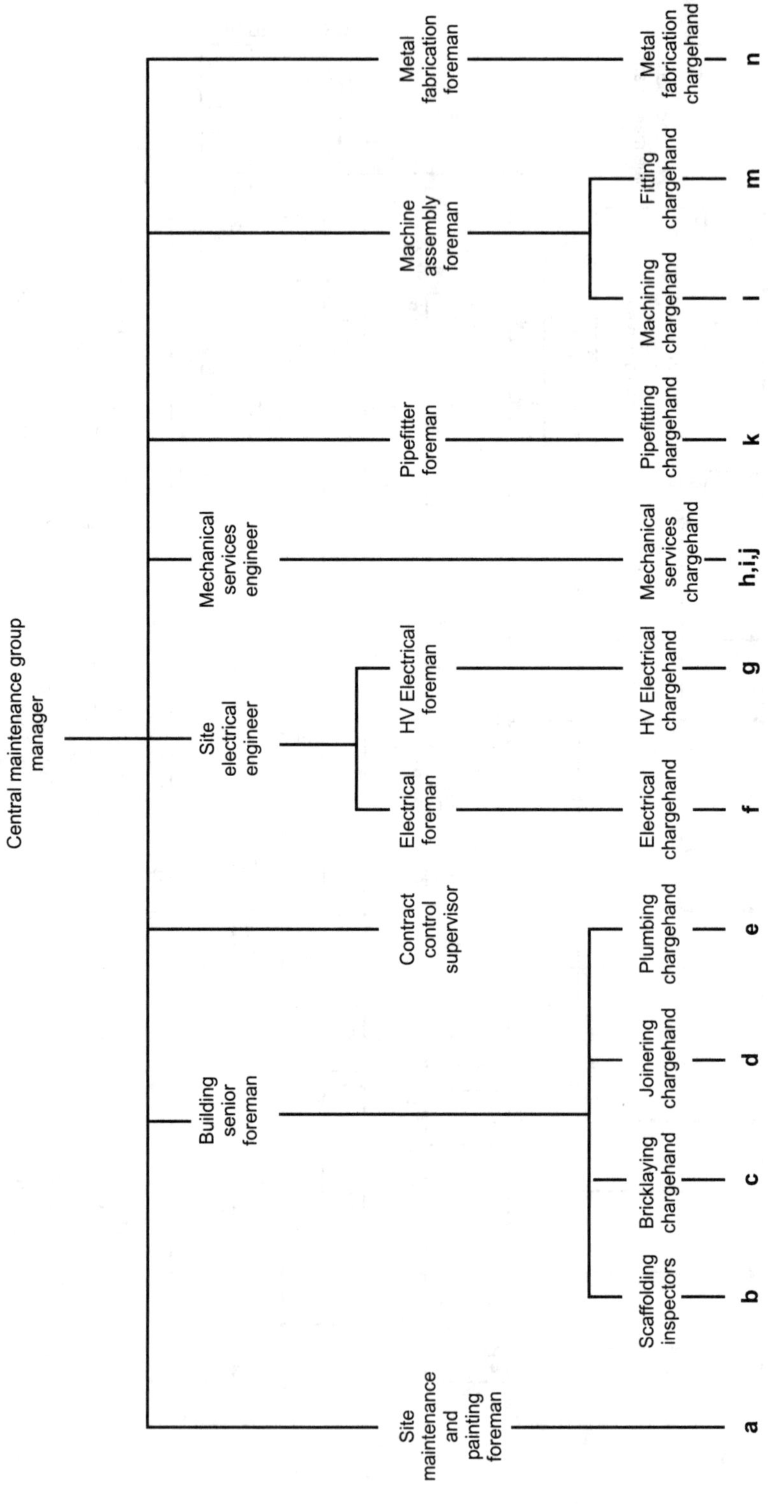

FIGURE 9-5 Central Maintenance Group Administration (1995)

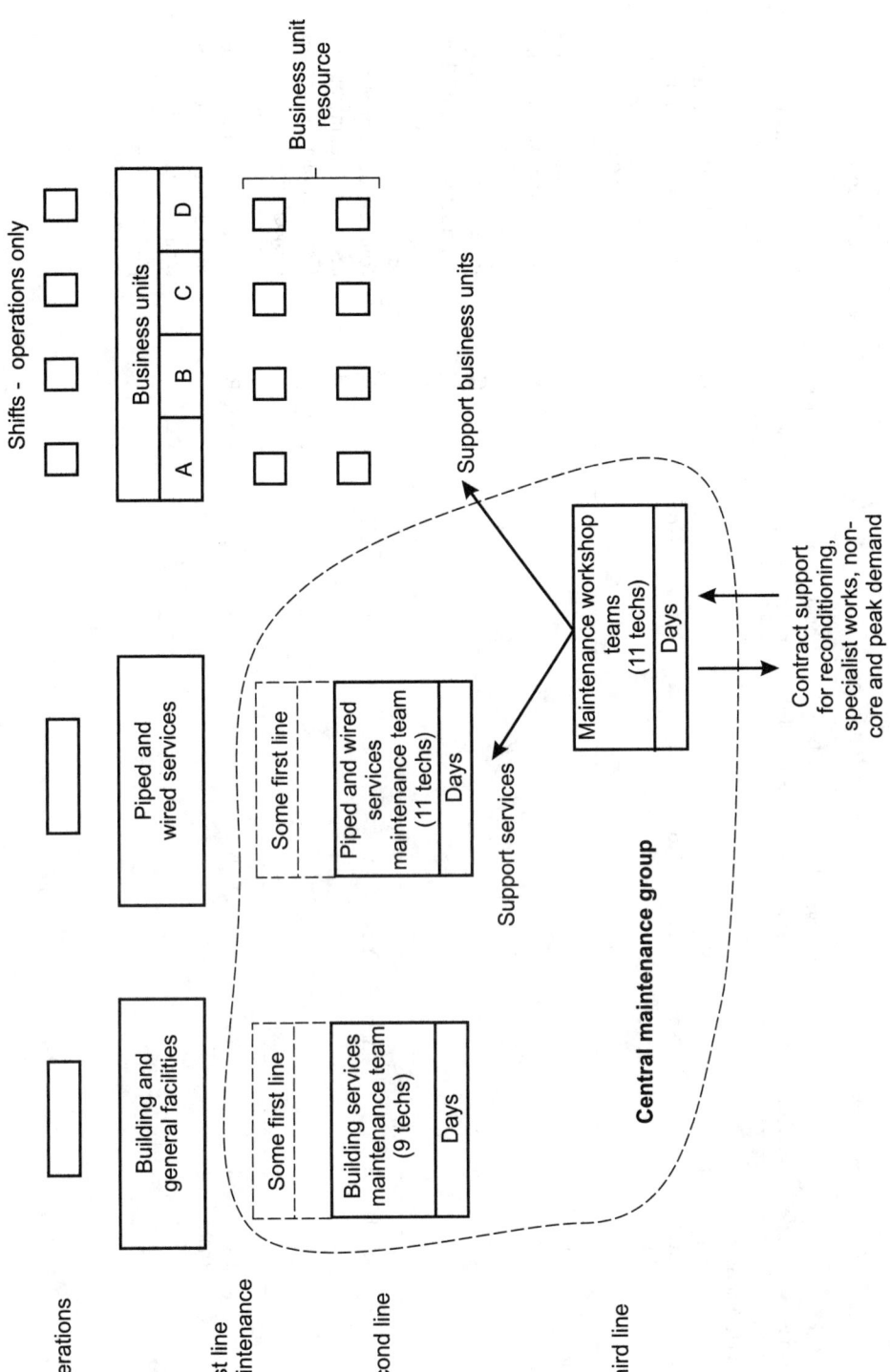

FIGURE 9–6 Proposed Resource Structure for CMG (1995)

TABLE 9–2 Decision Table Drawn Up to Aid Reorganization of the CMG (Contributed by H. S. Riddell)

CMG Resources			Criteria for Retention						Recommendation	
CMG Service	Trades	Numbers	Core Service	Emerg. Resp.	Special Skills	Many Small Jobs	Local Knowl.	User Contact	Alternative Resourcing Code	Comment
Site-Wide Services										
Factory general services	Build, EI, PF/PI	4 2 2	No	Yes	No	Yes	No	No	D or B	Consider all to contractors or retain minimum resources for 1st line maintenance.
Site piped services	PF/PI Build, F PO	5 5 1 4	Yes	Yes	No	Yes	Yes	Yes	B or C	Retain minimum resources for 1st line maintenance, but consider transfer to BU 1. Engage contractors for 2nd line and all project work.
HT Site wired services	HT EI	5	Yes	Yes	Yes	Yes	Yes	No	A	Retain minimum resources for all maintenance. Use contractors for all project jobs.
LT	EI Instr	4 1	Yes	Yes	No	Yes	Yes	No	B	Retain minimum resources for 1st line maintenance and use contractors for 2nd line and all project jobs.

Direct support to business units

	Unit		Service critical to the business units.	Provides a rapid skilled response to cover emergencies.	Provides a skill/knowledge which is not available from contractors.	Involves numerous short duration jobs scattered across the site.	Demands close interaction with operation.		
Capital work	PF/PI	5							
	SMW	4							
	F	8	No	No	No	No	No	D	Disengage.
	Mach	1							
	EI	2							
	Build	4							
Maintenance support	PF/PI	7	No	No	No	No	Yes	D	Disengage.
	F	7	No	No	No	No	Yes	D	Disengage.
	Mach	6	Yes	Yes	No	No	Yes	B	Retain minimum resources for reconditioning, critical repairs and specialised spares.
	SMW	10	Yes	Yes	No	No	Yes	B	
	Build.	9	No	No	Yes	No	Yes	D	Disengage.
	EI	3	No	No	No	No	Yes	D	Disengage.
Total ERG Resources		99							

TABLE 9–3 Criteria for Identifying a Mechanical Service as Core (Contributed by H. S. Riddell)

* Service critical to the business units.
* Provides a rapid skilled response to cover emergencies.
* Provides a skill/knowledge which is not available from contractors.
* Involves numerous short duration jobs scattered across the site.
* Demands close interaction with operation.

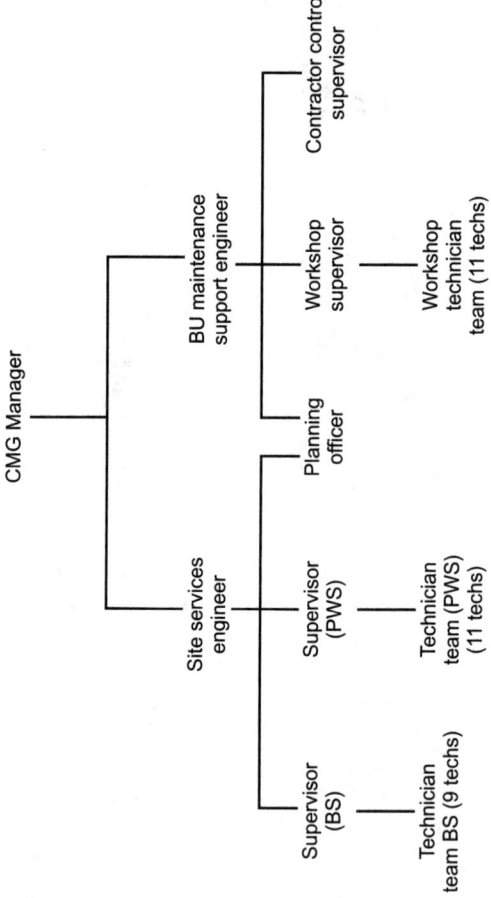

FIGURE 9-7 Proposed Administration for CMG (1995)

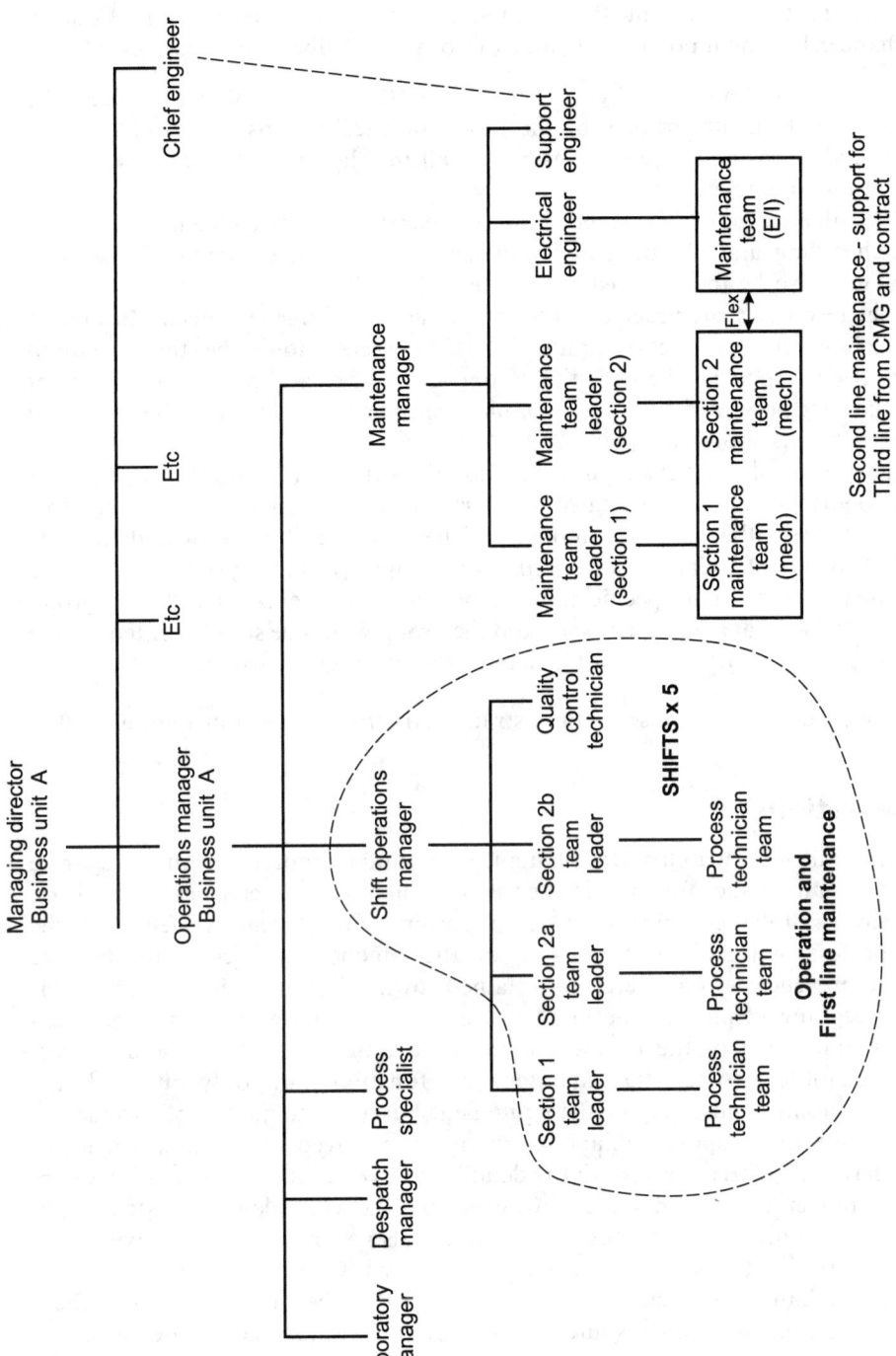

FIGURE 9–8 Typical Business Unit Administrative Structure at 1999 (Illustrative Only)

In 2000, we were again retained—to contribute to discussions aimed at deciding whether, and to what extent, the maintenance function should be carried out by an alliance. The main points that came out of these deliberations were as follows:

- An alliance should be set up to carry out all the maintenance work except the first-line tasks undertaken by the production technicians.
- The alliance should be responsible for all the shop floor workers associated with maintenance work.
- The alliance should be responsible for spare parts management.
- Scheduling and planning of maintenance work and planning of resources would also be the responsibility of the alliance.
- The resource structure had to contain some second-line technicians located in each of the production units. Their numbers should be the minimum necessary to meet the essential second-line workload and it was important that they possessed a high level of plant-specific skills. The proposed resource structure is shown in Figure 9–9.
- The 'ownership' of the equipment should reside in professional maintenance support groups, one in each business unit (and who would be Chemtow employees—the asset custodians). Their responsibilities would include improving life plans, establishing workscopes, designing-out maintenance and providing plant specific maintenance support. The size of each such group would be set at a minimum level and the group would be supplemented, where necessary, by specialist assistance from the contractor partner.

An outline of the proposed administrative structure is given in Figure 9–10.

Observations

(i) In multi-product chemical plants it is very much more difficult to separate the maintenance function into core and non-core competencies than it is in, say, a hotel complex or even a power plant. Chemtow felt that the professional and strategic side of the function was close to its core competencies and therefore retained ownership of this activity, their reasoning being that the plant process was specialised and in some areas unique, each of the business units using different processes and process technology. Also, the maintenance function not only affected the availability and safety of the equipment but also the quality of product.

(ii) While the proposed alliance structure was agreed in principle Chemtow have yet (2001) to establish the details and dynamics of the operation of the arrangement. We envisaged, however, that the work planning system might be as outlined in Figure 9–11, which also shows how the division of responsibility between the Chemtow Asset Care Engineers (the plant custodians who decide what maintenance is to be carried out, and when) and the alliance (the resource owner who decides how the maintenance is to be carried out and executes it) might be allocated. Some of the responsibilities would need to be jointly owned and communication would need to be good in both directions.

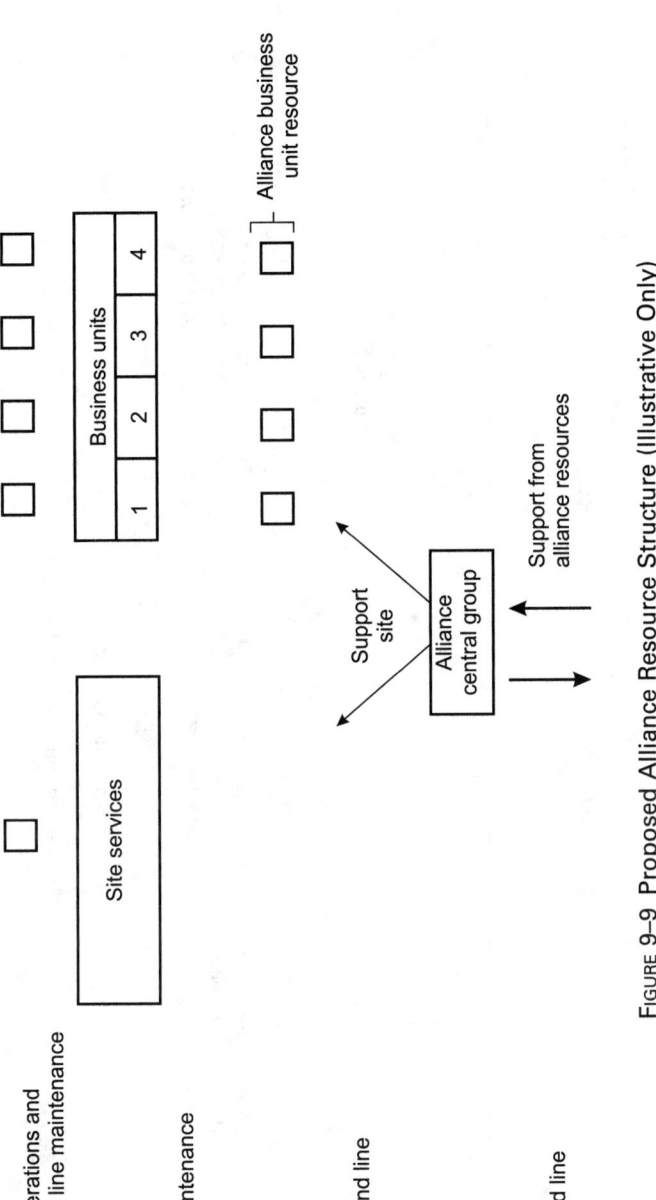

FIGURE 9–9 Proposed Alliance Resource Structure (Illustrative Only)

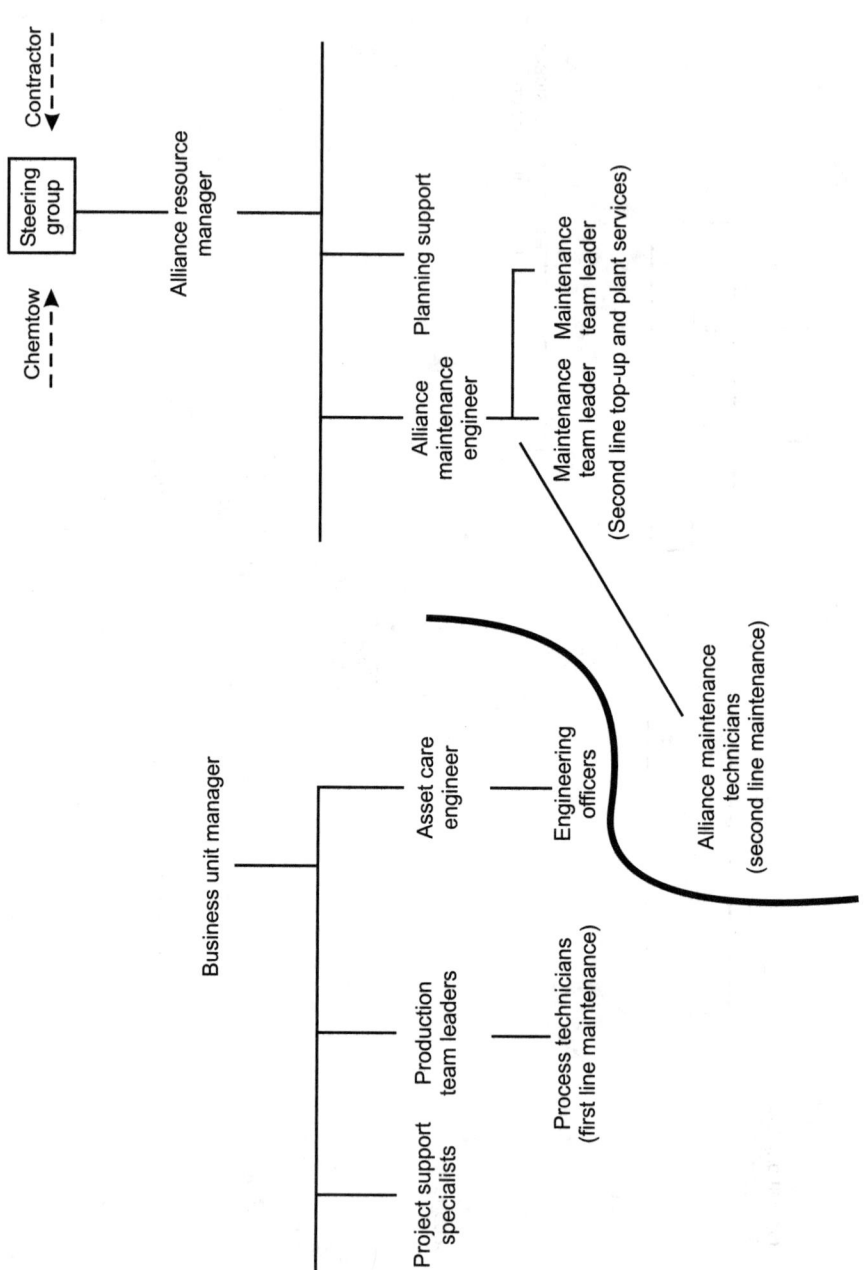

FIGURE 9–10 Proposed Alliance Administration

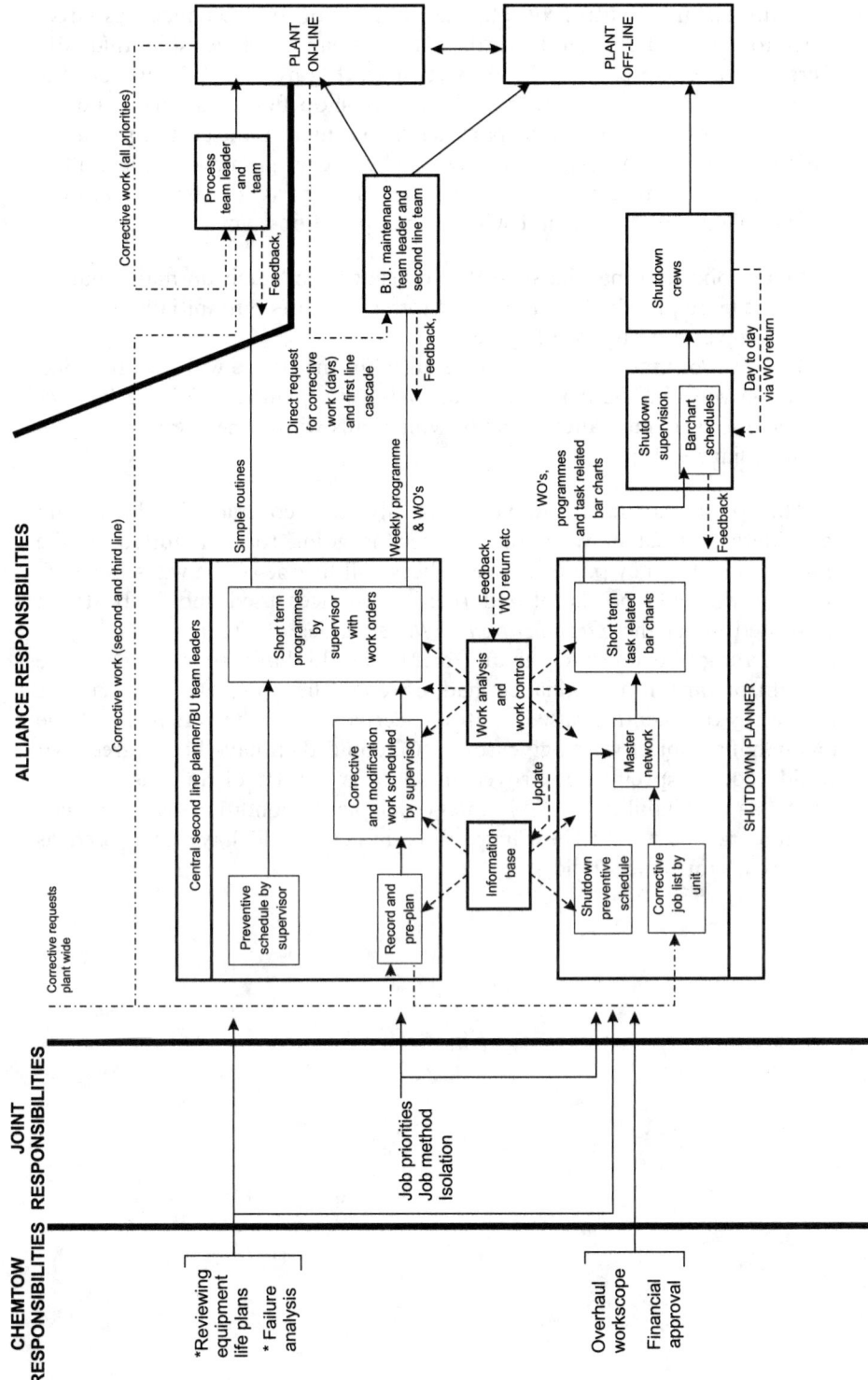

FIGURE 9–11 Division of Maintenance Responsibilities Between Chemtow and Alliance

(iii) In relinquishing control of all the shop floor maintenance resources Chemtow moved further towards a true alliance relationship than did Fertec (see Chapter 5 and, in particular, Figure 5–16) However, the alliance is limited to the responsibility for shop floor resources and, as such, the contract between the parties has to center on the cost of resources for a specified time to carry out a specified work programme. Some kind of conventional term-contract could be used as a basis for such a contract. Setting it up, however, is not without complications, viz.:

- Plant condition may be such that considerable 'catch up maintenance' might be required. Chemtow want to reduce costs but, initially, the cost may have to go up (see Figure 9–12)
- The level of maintenance work required in the future will be a function of the way the plant is operated, of the life plans and of the level of design-out maintenance, none of which falls within the responsibility of the alliance.

The point is that however carefully the contract is drawn up considerable trust between the partners is going to be required. If the measurement of key performance indices will be one of the ways in which the contract will be monitored then the indices used should be those indicated under the '*Organizational efficiency*' leg of Figure 4–11.

(iv) Formulating the contract arrangements would have been much more straightforward if the alliance had covered the complete maintenance function. An incentive-based contract, derived from the statement of the maintenance objective (as given on p. 6), could then have been agreed—it could require specified improvements, for example, of various outputs (such as availability, safety integrity, plant condition) at reduced maintenance cost, and the Figure 4–11 indices could have been used as the key performance indices.

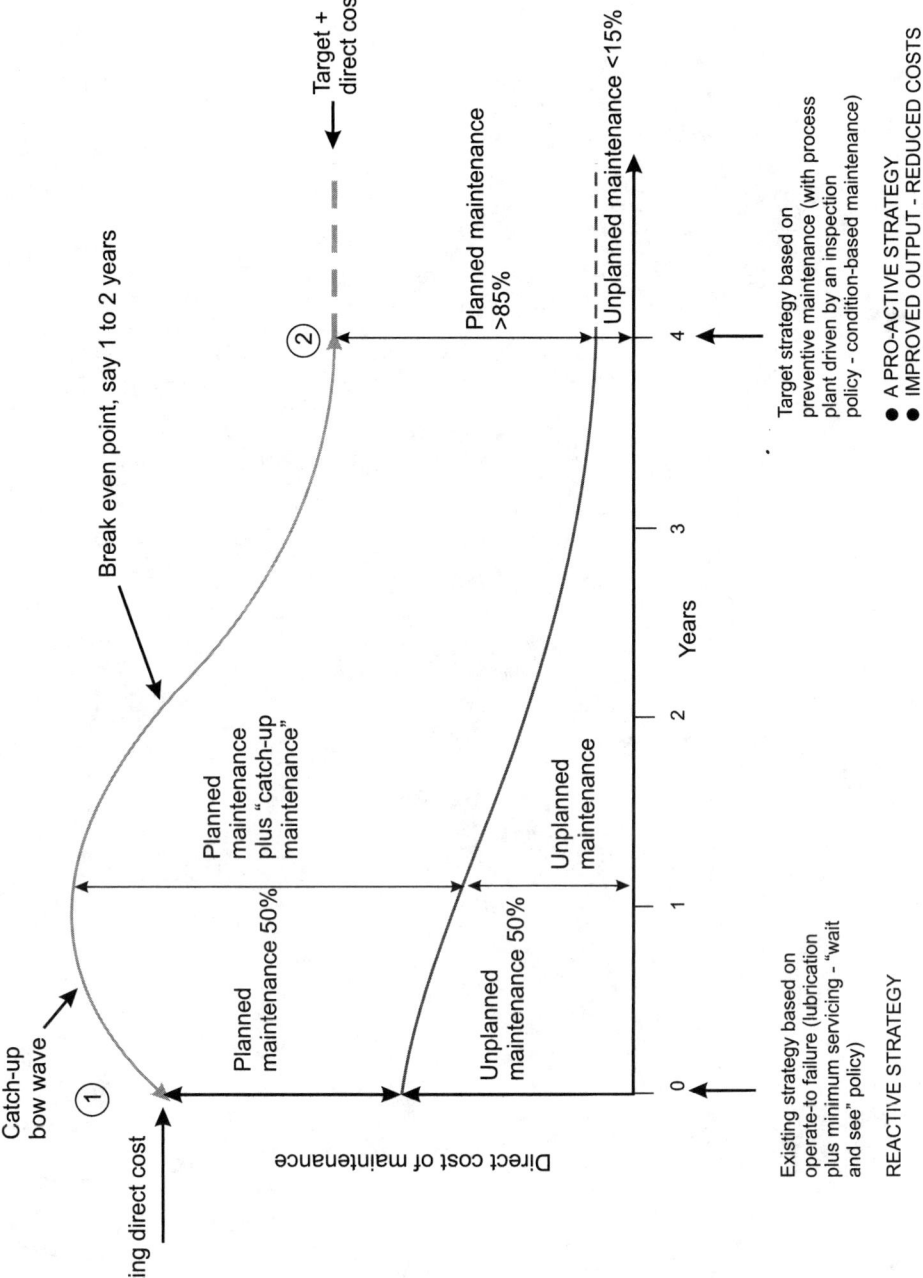

Catch-up
bow wave

① Existing direct cost

Break even point, say 1 to 2 years

② Target +
direct cost

Direct cost of maintenance

Planned
maintenance
plus "catch-up
maintenance"

Planned
maintenance 50%

Unplanned
maintenance

Unplanned
maintenance 50%

Planned maintenance
>85%

Unplanned maintenance <15%

0   1   2   3   4

Years

Existing strategy based on
operate-to failure (lubrication
plus minimum servicing - "wait
and see" policy)

REACTIVE STRATEGY

Target strategy based on
preventive maintenance (with process
plant driven by an inspection
policy - condition-based maintenance)

● A PRO-ACTIVE STRATEGY
● IMPROVED OUTPUT - REDUCED COSTS

FIGURE 9–12 A Catch-up Strategy

Part 3

Case Studies of the Application of the Auditing Procedure to a Variety of Industries

Have you heard of the wonderful one-hoss-shay, That was built in such a logical way. It ran a hundred years to the day –

Now in building of chaises, I tell you what, There is always somewhere a weakest spot, – In hub, tire, felloe, in spring or thill, In panel, or cross bar, or floor, or sill, –

The Deacon enquired of the village folk Where he could find the strongest oak, That couldn't be split nor bent nor broke –

That was for spokes and floor and sills; He sent for lancewood to make the thills; The cross bars were ash from the straightest trees, The panels of whitewood, that cuts like cheese, But lasts like iron for things like these; Step and prop – iron, bolt and screw, Spring, tire, axle, and linch pin too, Steel of the finest, bright and blue; –

That was the way he 'put her through' "There"! said the Deacon, "now she'll do."

First of November – (one hundred years to the day) – There are traces of age in the one-hoss-shay – A general flavour of mild decay But nothing local, as one may say. For the wheels were just as strong as the thills, And the floor was just as strong as the sills, And the panels just as strong as the floor, And the whippletree neither less nor more, And yet, as a whole, it is passed a doubt in another hour it will be worn out.

Extracted from 'The Deacon's Masterpiece' by Oliver Wendell Holmes.

CHAPTER 10

Case Study 3: Reviewing Maintenance Strategy

Given the overall aims (economic, environmental, safety) of an industrial operation, the most important decisions when formulating the maintenance strategy are likely to be those regarding the amount and type of preventive maintenance that should be undertaken. This case study will focus on some of the principles involved and will demonstrate the importance of the relationship between the maintenance strategy and the workload it generates (see the methodology diagram, Figure 1–3). There is no point in selecting a maintenance strategy that cannot be resourced!

Introduction

Smeltall Ltd ran one of the largest aluminium smelters in the world. The plant layout is shown in Figure 10–1 and the process flow outlined in Figure 10–2. The heart of the process involved the electrolytic reduction of alumina (aluminium oxide) in three series of large cells—the '*Potlines.*' A schematic of a cell (or '*pot*') is shown in Figure 10–3. In order to operate the cells (some 1080 in this case) a continuous supply of carbon anodes was required. These were manufactured in the '*Carbon plant*' and, after use, each spent anode was returned for renewal. The molten aluminium was collected from the cells for transport to the '*Casting and Finishing area.*'

The smelter organization was built around manufacturing units in the Carbon Plant, Potlines and Casting areas. Thus, the Carbon Plant had its own Maintenance Engineer and staff, and a resource group for the first and second line maintenance work. For major work the Carbon Plant employed the centralised service and/or contract labour.

The maintenance strategy had evolved over a considerable period of time without external review. In addition, there was concern that the existing strategy might require modification in order to cope with a recently completed expansion of the Potlines that had increased output by 30%. In particular, the Chief Engineer wanted advice about the future direction of maintenance strategy within the plant. I therefore reviewed the strategy for the complete smelter, but for

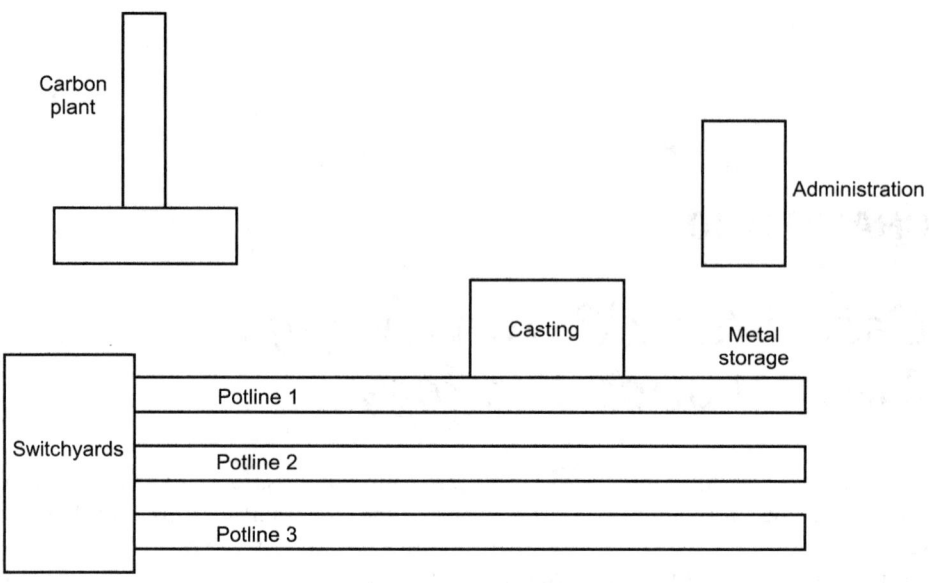

FIGURE 10–1 Smeltall Site Layout

the purposes of this case study I will concentrate on the strategy for the Carbon Plant only.

Carbon Plant, Overall Operation

The smelting operation as a whole was continuous and there were no windows of opportunity for maintenance at smelter-level (i.e., involving total operational shutdown). It is shown in Figure 10–3 that the Carbon Plant and Potlines, however, were de-coupled by a 24-hour storage of anodes.

Figure 10–4, which outlines the process flow within the Carbon Plant, shows that the latter could be considered as being made up of three separate, different, but inter-related sections or processes separated by inter-stage storage. The front end (or first process) involved the manufacture of the unbaked or '*green*' anode blocks – which were subsequently baked in the '*Ring Furnace*' (the second process) and then '*rodded*' (the third process). After this, the finished anodes went into the anode store and from there to the '*Potrooms*.'

The rate of production of anodes from the Carbon Plant was governed by the rate of production of the Ring Furnace, i.e., this last process was a 'bottle neck.' The average rate of production of green anodes from the green mix process exceeded (by far) the average rate of production from the Ring Furnace. The green anode stock was used to de-couple these processes and could hold two weeks of stock. Similarly, the rate of production of the rodding process exceeded the rate of supply from the Ring Furnace, and in this case the baked anode store served to decouple these processes. It was also important that the rate of cleaning

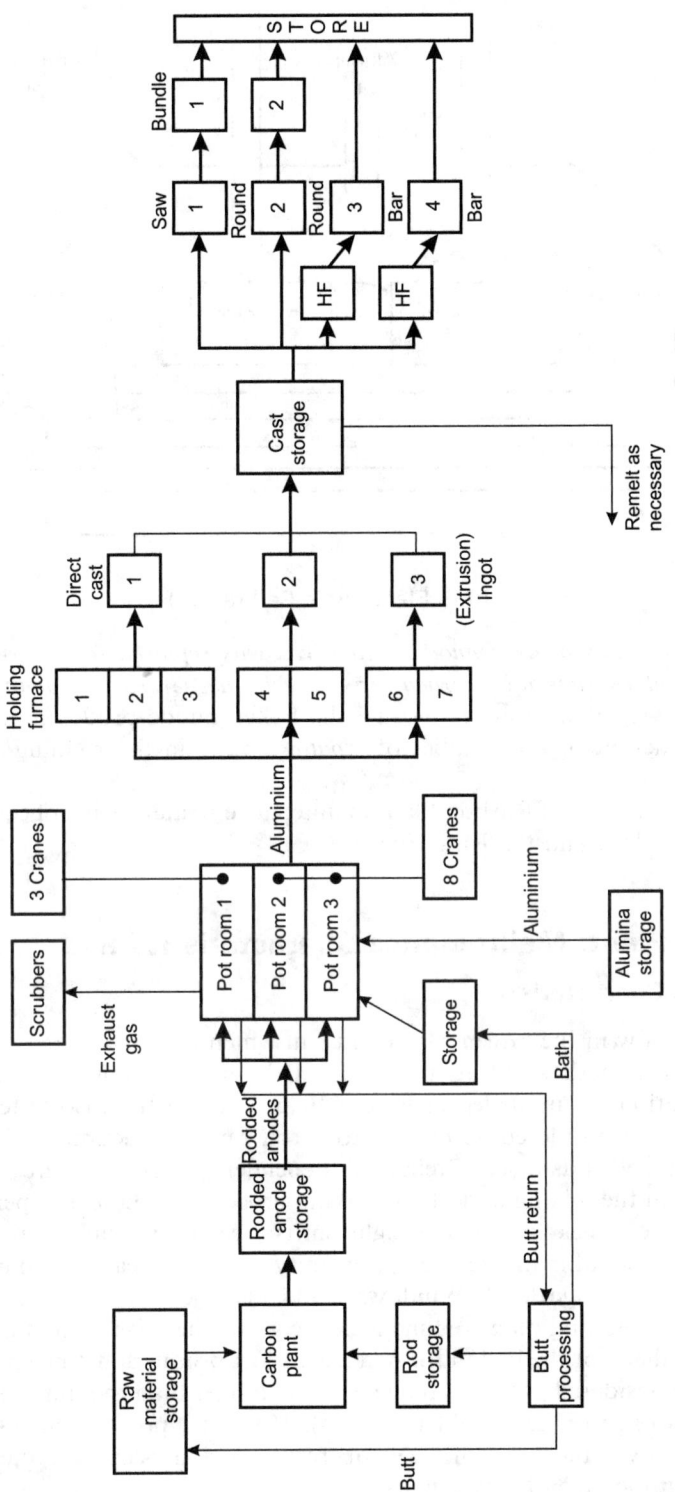

FIGURE 10–2 Smeltall, Main Process Flow

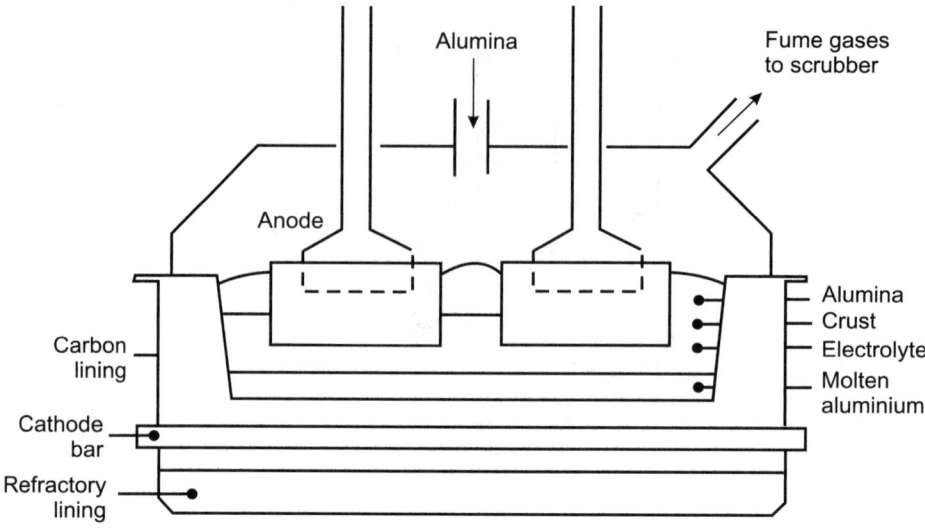

FIGURE 10–3 Electrolytic Cell (a Pot)

of '*butts*' *(the remains of used anodes—each rod was repaired for re-use and the remains of the block material returned for re-use in the 'Green Mix plant')* and of repairing rods was able to at least equal the baked anode production. This, in part, was a function of the number of '*floating*' butts in the rodding/smelting/cleaning cycle.

The following review of Carbon Plant maintenance strategy will concentrate on the Green Mix Plant and the Ring Furnace.

Green Mix Plant: Maintenance Characteristics and Strategy

Maintenance Characteristics

The process flow in the Green Mix Plant—in which four raw material process sub-systems, each with short term storage, fed into a weighing, mixing and blocking operation—is modelled in Figure 10–5. Each of the raw material sub-systems could be considered as critical to green mix production, which could therefore be modelled as a series reliability-dependency system. There was some spare capacity in the mixing and block making processes. The plant operated for thirteen shifts per week, which left eight shifts free for possible maintenance. Additional windows of maintenance opportunity could be created by building up the green anode storage level. Windows could also be created during normal production by exploiting plant redundancies (e.g., of the mixer units) and inter-stage storage (ahead of the ball mill). As regards lost production a green mix unit could only be considered critical if its repair took longer than the time covered by green anode storage (which could be weeks). However, production insisted on high reliability over the thirteen week operating period because failure had a major affect on the green block quality.

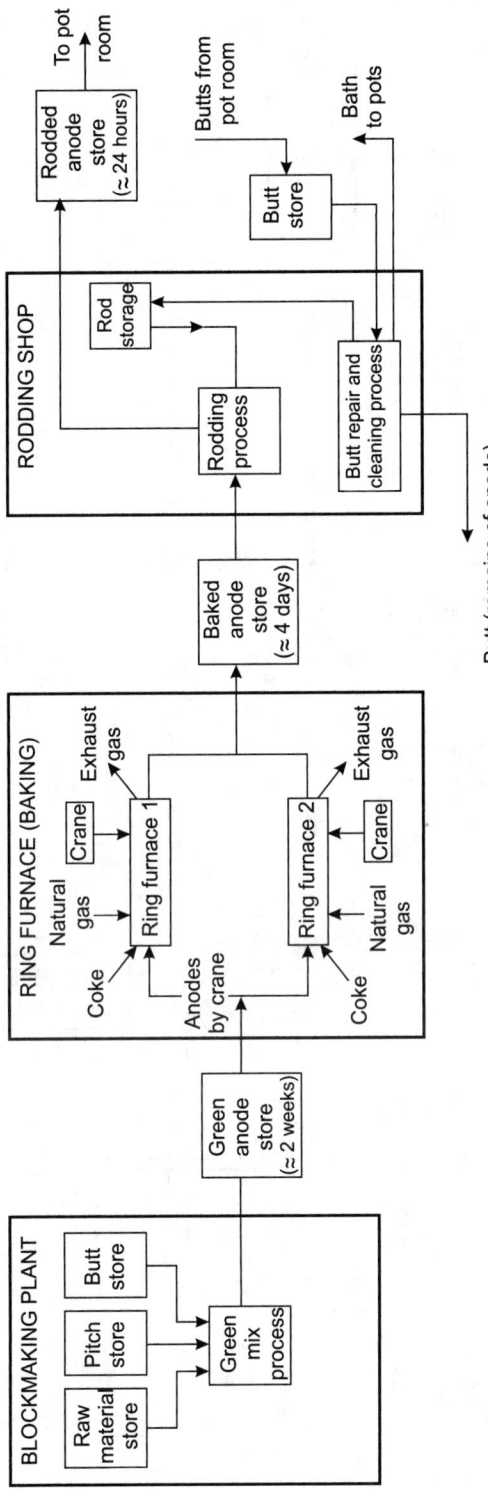

FIGURE 10–4 Carbon Plant Process Flow

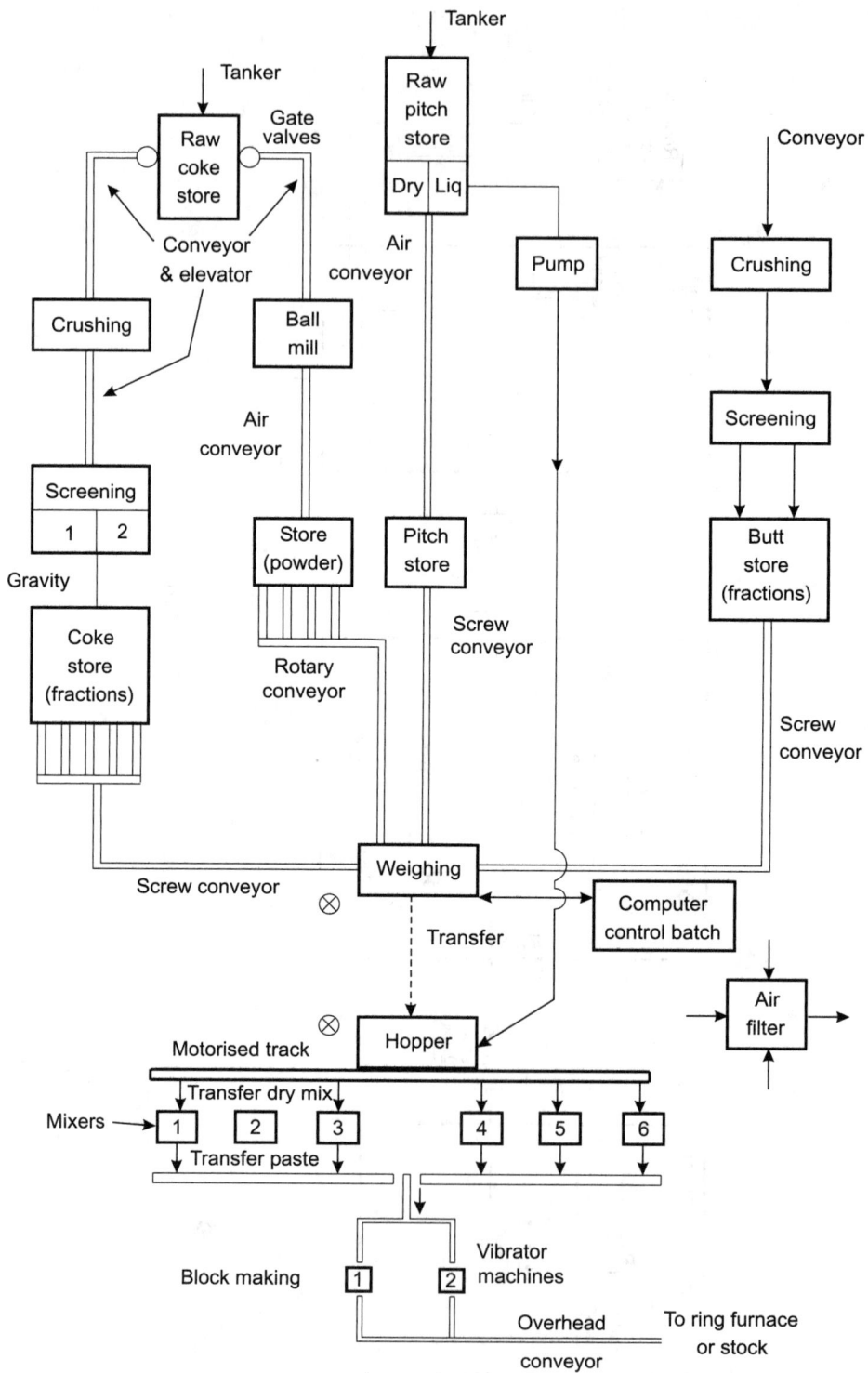

FIGURE 10–5 Green Mix Plant Process Flow

Maintenance Strategy

The equipment life plans were based on simple preventive service routines (inspection, lubrication and minor component replacement) for each unit of equipment. Table 10–1 shows the life plan for the Butt Breaker of Figure 10–5 and

TABLE 10–1 Outline of Life Plan for Butt Breaker

On-line work				
Weekly	Butt Breaker	On-line inspection	No. 81 inspection sheet	
				Specification no.
Off-line work				
Fortnightly	Guide	Inspect	Crusher jaw ram	3901 0101
Monthly	Guide	Check clearance	Crusher jaw ram	3901 0102
Monthly	Bolt	Check tension	Guides	2800 0101
Monthly	Stripping hand	Inspect & adjust	Stripping head	4000 0001
Two-yearly	Cylinder	Inspect & test	Main ram & aux. cyl.	3002 0202
Two-yearly	Lubricator	Replace	Stripping head	2301 0101
Two-yearly	Lubricator	Replace	Stripping head	2301 0101

TABLE 10–2 Example of a Preventive Maintenance Job Specification

Dept	Carbon plant	Frequency	Weekly		
Disp.	Mechanical	Revision no:	0	Date	18.4.84
Equipment	Butt Breaker-BA (PG103)				
Account no.	850-2120	Date Completed	0		

	Items	Tick Completed
1.	Observe full operation of butt breaker, check for signs of damage, excessive wear or unusual noises.	
2.	Check with operators for any problem.	
3.	Check hydraulic tank and pipework for leaks and security.	
4.	Check pumps and valve for leaks, signs of damage or deterioration and unusual or noisy operation.	
5.	Observe and record: (a) Tell-tale filter condition (b) Pressure switch settings— H1 H3 H4 H5 (c) Flow control valve settings (North to South) — Cap end — Rod end	
6.	Report any items requiring immediate attention to Supervisor.	

TABLE 10–3 Review of Condition Monitoring Techniques in Use at Smeltall

Technique	Application
Cooling water analysis and doping	Control of algae in water to compressor coolers.
Visual inspection	Inspection sheets completed daily/quarterly by tradesmen; wide range of equipment in use.
Thermometry	Potlines scrubbing fans bearings; automatically scanned—alarm when above set point.
Infra-red scanning	External contractor checks for potential hot points in switchgear every 12 months; initiated by preventive schedule.
Lube-oil monitoring	Oil sampled regularly from all hydraulic systems i.e., 5 litre oil capacity reservoir; laboratory debris analysis for alumina, iron and copper.
Vibration monitoring	Shock pulse monitoring of all critical bearings (identified by maintenance supervisors) on site, triggered by preventive schedule—uses local area tradesmen; results graphed and trended. An unsatisfactory trend will cause one of several consultants to be engaged by the maintenance supervisors to carry out frequency signal vibration measurements; consultants interpret signal chart as no one on site with appropriate special training.
Crack detection	Dye penetrant and magnetic flux used for all lifting eyes, crane hooks, and fork lift trucks triggered by preventive schedule. Request tests by contractors for any special situations.
Erosion monitoring	Ultrasonic thickness testing of bottom of bins and cones in Green Mix Plant; instruments available on site and used on an ad-hoc basis—about once a quarter.

an example of a job specification from this life plan is given in Table 10–2. These services were re-inforced for the critical units with condition monitoring (see Table 10–3). For ease of execution of the preventive jobs the plant was divided into 'routes', e.g., the butt route, within which all the equipment was inter-related in some way, e.g., by process and/or isolation etc. An example of a service route is shown in Table 10–4. Every week, the due services for each route would be carried out as 'route-services' which, for the plant as a whole, were scheduled over the year into a 'Green Mix preventive schedule' aimed at smoothing the workload (see Figure 10–6)

The *corrective* work resulting from preventive inspection, or requested by Production, was carried out by the local tradeforce supplemented as necessary by central services and contract labour.

TABLE 10–4 Preventive Services Listed by Plant Route

Ref no.	Freq.	Equipment	Service	Sub Assembly	MRC no.
1	W	Inspection	On-line	No. 81 Butt breaker	
PG 103		Butt breaker	Off-line		
2	F	Guide	Inspect	Crusher jaw ram	3901 0101
3	M	Guide	Check clearance	Crusher jaw ram	3901 0102
4	M	Bolt	Check tension	Guides	2800 0101
5	M	Stripping band	Inspect & adjust	Stripping head	4000 0001
6	2A	Cylinder	Inspect & test	Main ram & aux.cyl.	3002 0202
7	2A	Lubricator	Replace	Stripping head	2301 0101
8	2A	Lubricator	Replace	Stripping head	2301 0101
GA104		Pump		8A	
9	F	Tools	Inspect & add oil	Reservoir	2402 0004
10	Q	G/box fixed Ratio	Inspect & add oil	Drive	0501 0003
11	Q	Breather	Clean	Hydraulic reservoir	2901 0102
12	Q	Filter	Replace cartridge	Hydraulic unit	1704 0005
13	5A	Coupling	Inspect & align	Drive	0306 0008
14	5A	Reservoir	Take oil sample	Drive gearbox	7701 0001
15	A	Reservoir	Take oil sample	Hydraulic reservoir	7701 0001
16		G/box-fixed Ratio	Change oil	Drive	0501 0001
		Tank	Change oil after	Hydraulic unit	2402 0010
GA106					
16	5A	Coupling	Inspect and align	Drive	0306 0008

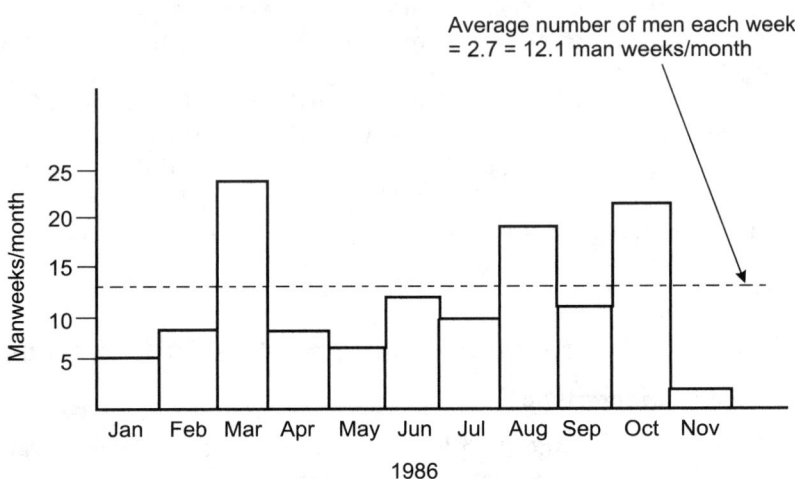

FIGURE 10–6 Profile of Green Mix Mechanical Maintenance Workload Arising from Requests to Central Service (Over and Above the Employment of the Dedicated Second-line Green Mix Resource)

Observations and Recommendations

The strategy was centered on condition-based maintenance. In general, the lead time resulting from the inspection procedures was long enough to allow the corrective maintenance to be carried out in the weekend window or, if necessary, by exploiting the interstage storage.

I felt that this strategy was much better than the alternatives—fixed-time maintenance or operate-to-failure—and I was impressed by The Carbon Plant engineer's justification of it, viz:

- There was little chance that a maintenance job (either planned or resulting from a failure) in the Carbon Plant would have incurred a loss of anode production.
- The inspection would identify *incipient* failures of the a Green Mix Plant and prevented their developing into *actual* failures—which would have had consequences for product quality.
- Over-maintenance, an inevitable consequence of fixed-time-maintenance (see the note below), was avoided.
- The resultant workload (see Figure 10–6) was relatively smooth (the equipment was very diverse, had already been overhauled, and anticipated running times to next major maintenance varied greatly, which, taken together, effectively randomised the future incidence of major jobs), and any unexpected peaks could have been be dealt with by contract labour.

[NB The Green Mix mixers at the plant's sister company were operated under a regime of fixed time maintenance, which came from knowing (from the plant records) that the average life of the critical parts of the mixer was two years and three months and that an overhaul took thirty shifts. The mixers were therefore overhauled at a rate of one every four months. This policy was considered more economic than operation-to-failure or condition-based maintenance (monitoring sigma arm wear and lining wear). It gave clear advantages as regards planning and spares provisioning and generated a high degree of confidence in the resulting reliability of mixer output. The disadvantage was over-maintenance. The key to the decision to adopt the policy, however, had been the predictability of the mixer life; although not entirely *eliminating* over-maintenance, overhauling at or about two years did *minimise* it.]

Ring Furnace: Maintenance Characteristics and Strategy

Maintenance Characteristics

The process flow within the Ring Furnace and its associated plant is shown in Figure 10–7. The rate of production from the furnaces was a function of the month-long firing and cooling cycle for a line of pits. The principal maintenance work on a pit was the repair of its brick lining (see Figure 10–8) and it appeared that about five days were available within the cycle for repairs, i.e., if a repair was completed within this time no pit unavailability was incurred.

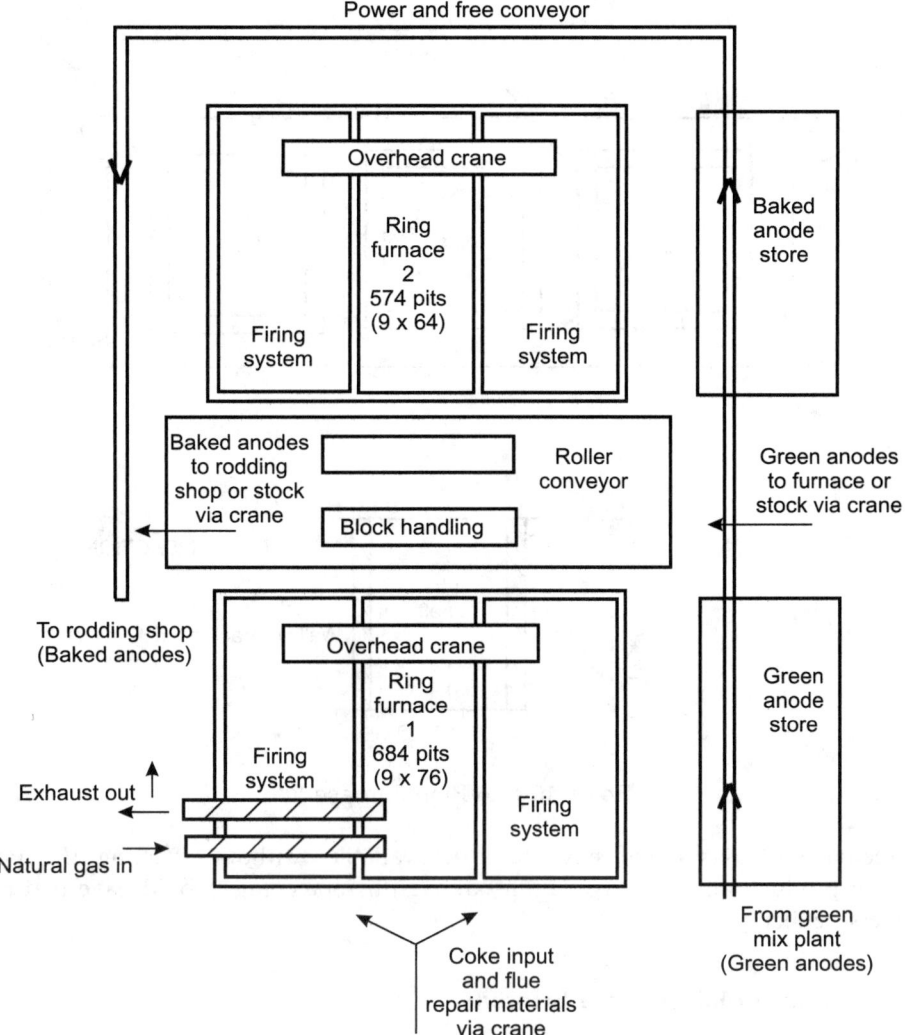

Power and free conveyor

FIGURE 10–7 Ring Furnace Process Flow

It appeared to me that the Ring Furnace was the plant which was most critical to the operation of the whole smelter. At the time of the audit the output of rodded anodes exceeded the Pot Room's demand by only a small percentage. Thus, if it were to have led to a reduction of Ring Furnace output, the failure of any unit within the Ring Furnace process would have had a critical effect on the total performance of the smelter. Units identified as having that level of criticality were the power and free output conveyor, the roller conveyor and the cranes. In general, these could be maintained in the windows of opportunity arising out of the production operating pattern and/or unit duplication. The pits themselves could also be considered as critical. A small

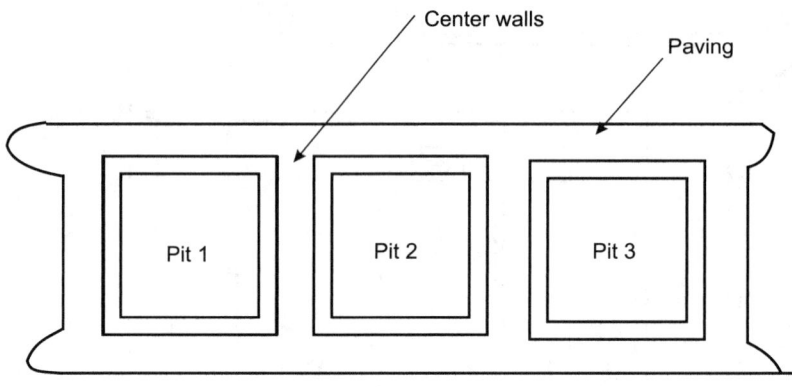

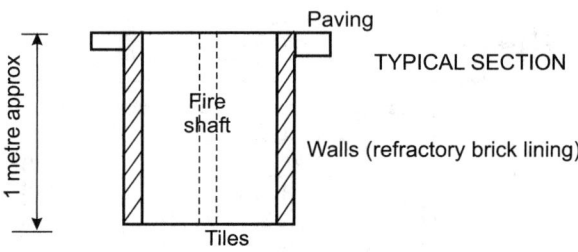

FIGURE 10–8 A Ring Furnace Pit

percentage of pits could have been unavailable, without affecting the Pot Room production, but unavailability above this percentage would have had an adverse effect.

Ring Furnace Maintenance Strategy

Before the commissioning of Pot Rooms 2 and 3, which had been the core of a just previous expansion, the Ring Furnace had had excess capacity. The maintenance strategy had been to inspect pits after unloading and then to repair as necessary. Unusable pits would go into a backlog until repaired. There had been enough spare capacity to maintain Pot Room 1 production. I did not ask (and neither was I told) whether, under this regime, sections of the furnace had been taken out for repair on a fixed-time basis. Experience from this operation had shown that the average pit life was about fifty firing cycles (i.e., approximately four years) and our own analysis at the time of the audit also revealed that the distribution of times-to-pit-repair exhibited the classic form for units failing by wear-out (see Figure 10–9).

After Pot Rooms 2 and 3 were commissioned the maintenance strategy appears to have remained unchanged. I estimated the proportion of pit life remaining at the time of the audit and this is shown in Figure 10–10. Approximately 70% of the

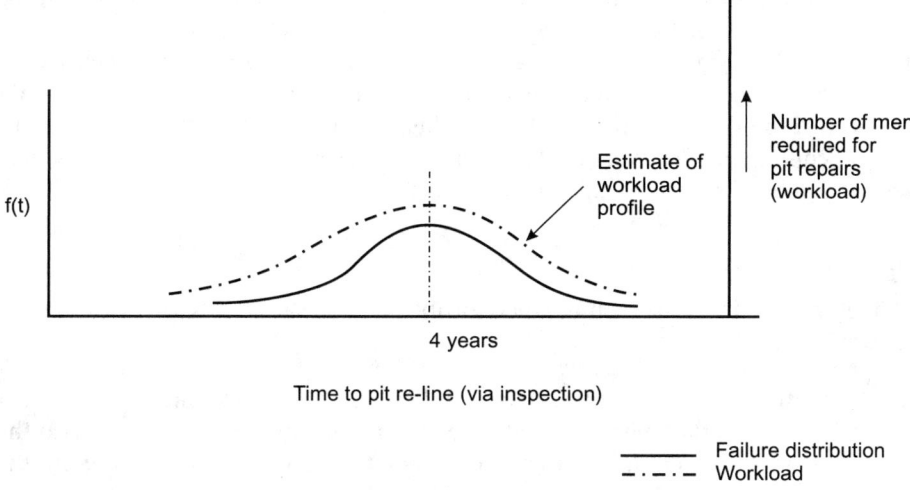

FIGURE 10–9 Distribution of Ring Furnace Pit Failures

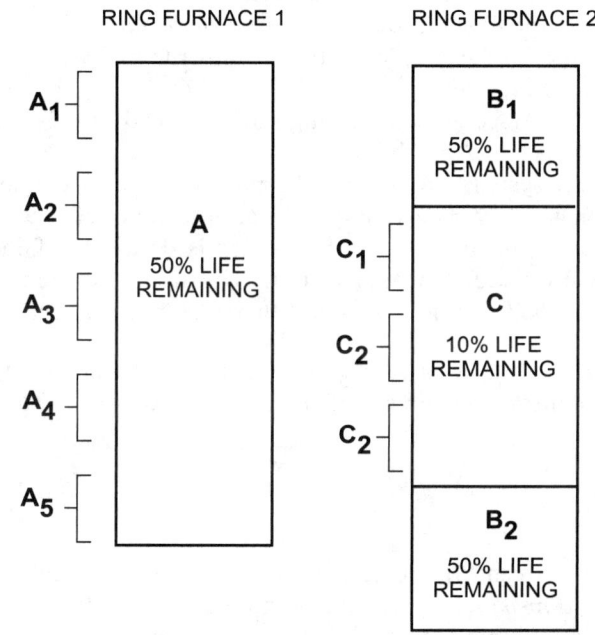

FIGURE 10–10 Condition of Ring Furnace Pits

pits (A + B1 + B2) had about a half of their life left and the remaining 30% about a tenth. Thus it was likely that the pit repair work load would have built up to a major peak two years later, assuming that pits would be left to go to their full life (see Figure 10–9). Such a strategy would have maximised pit life but would have only been acceptable if the production rate from the furnace had continued to be sufficient to meet Pot Room needs. This would only have been the case if the pit repair rate, during the five-day maintenance windows, could have been set to match the increasing work load. Any estimate of the rate of such repair would have needed to take into consideration the higher failure rates of the 'center walls' and the consequent likely need to work on adjacent pits. *Given the available internal resources such work appeared not to have been possible.*

Observations and Recommendations

To eliminate the pit maintenance problems two alternative schemes were proposed:

(a) Retention of the condition-based policy and the employment of contract labour (if available) to cope with the then imminent work peak, and also the peak which would have arisen two years later (and possibly carrying out the repair over a three shift roster). The subsequent work peaks would be lower, would have a wider spread and would therefore be easier to resource. This policy would maximise pit life.

(b) Repairing sections of the furnace at fixed intervals of time, *even though this would mean pulling the pits out of operation prematurely and forfeiting part of their useful life.* For example, at the time of the audit sections B1 and B2 required immediate attention (probably necessitating the employment of contract labour); sections C1 through to C3 would then be dealt with, and then sections A1 to A5. The faster the repair rate (a function of the gang size and shift system) the longer the pits could be left before premature repair. Such a policy needed only to be adopted once because thereafter the failure rate of the pits would be randomised, the pit failure rate (and therefore the workload) would be fairly constant, and the repair gang size could be matched to this and would therefore be well-utilised.

It was recommended that these alternative actions should be investigated (as regards available contract resources and material) and costed and a decision taken without delay.

Summary

In the case of the Green Mix Plant a fixed-time policy was a viable alternative to the existing condition-based approach, because sufficient data was available to show that most of the equipment failed due to some form of time-dependent mechanism (e.g., wear). Thus, either of these policies could be considered as *effective* for controlling plant reliability. However, the condition-based approach was the more *cost*-effective, allowing as it did a longer operating period before repair (i.e., it avoided over-maintenance). In addition, the resulting workload (see Figure 10-6) was easily resourced. At first glance it would appear that the existing condition-based policy was also the most appropriate for the Ring Furnace pits. In this case, however, the workload (see Figure 10–9) could not be easily resourced.

Chapter 11

Case Studies 4 and 5: Maintaining a Fleet

Two case studies will demonstrate how the business-centered maintenance approach can assist the reviewing of maintenance strategy for the particular case of an equipment fleet. The first of the studies will also show how a mining operation, using such a fleet, can be modelled as a process flow.

Case Study 4: a Mining Vehicle Fleet

MAXCOAL Ltd, a coal extraction business, ran two underground mines and an adjacent open-cast mine, as outlined in Figure 11–1. Emphasised in the diagram is the open-cast operation, which started with the stripping and removal of the overburden (the soil and rock above the coal seam) using drilling, explosives and a dragline. Coal from the exposed seam (which was some metres thick) was then extracted and loaded into trucks for haulage to the preparation plant, where it was firstly crushed and then washed and graded before finally being conveyed to a nearby rail head for transportation. There were a number of points of interstage storage and also a final product storage, which gave operational flexibility to each individual process and also to the activity as a whole.

The main feature was that the process depended to a large extent on the performance of small fleets of diesel-powered equipment. For example, five front-end loaders for the mining operations and eight large dump trucks for the haulage. (Other mobile equipment included dozers, scrapers, graders, drills, etc.) It is this equipment—rather than the fixed or semi-fixed units such as coal washing plant, draglines, etc.—that caused the maintenance problems and is the subject of this study.

Modelling Fleet Operation: Status Diagrams

Each of the fleets could be represented by a status diagram as in Figure 11–2 (e.g., a loader could be in any one of the states A to E). The availability of a single item could be measured conventionally, i.e.,

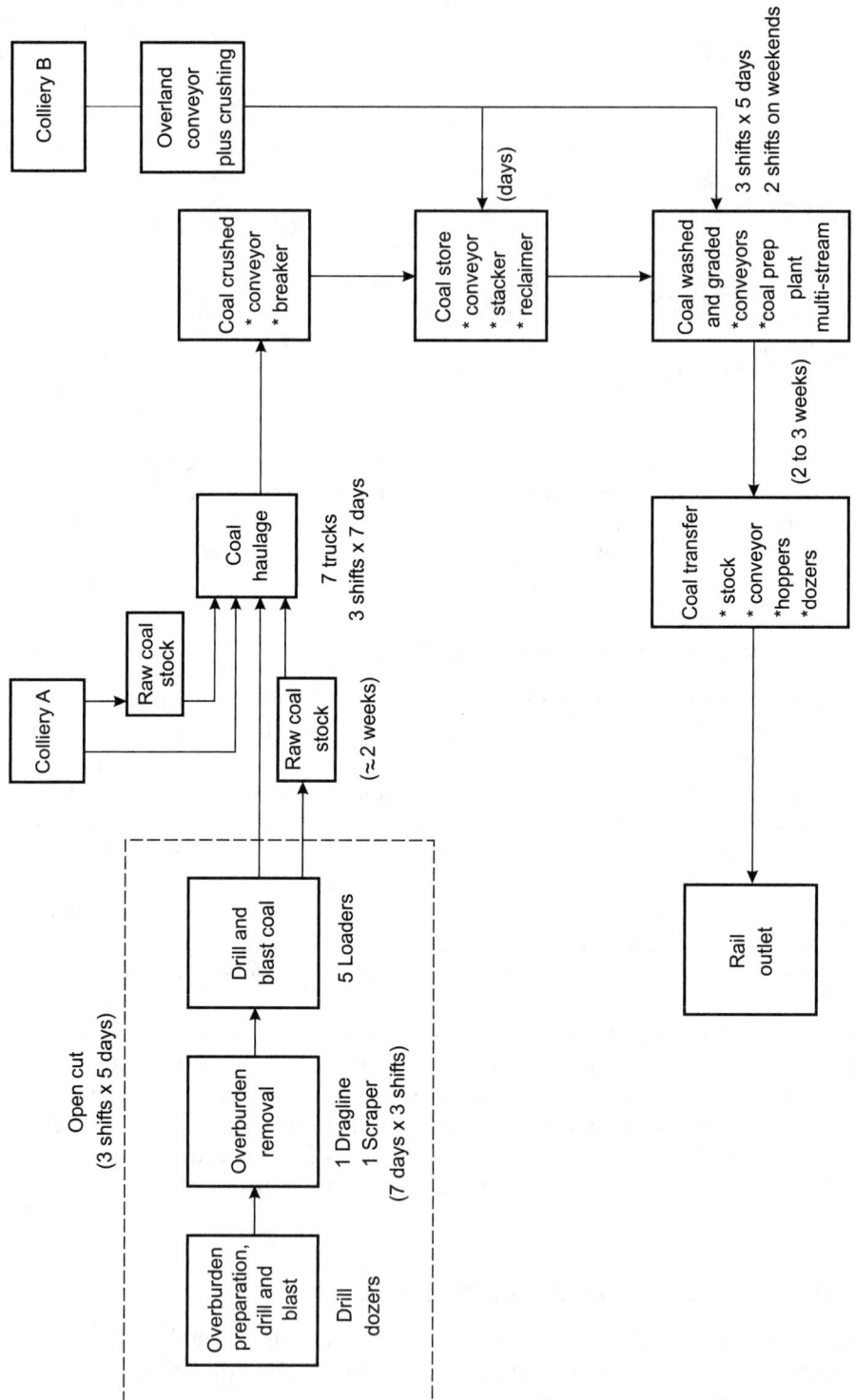

FIGURE 11–1 Coalcom Open-cast Process Flow

$$\text{Availability} = \frac{\text{Time up}}{\text{Time up} + \text{Time down}}$$

$$= \frac{\text{Time in A} + \text{Time in B}}{\text{Time in A} + \text{Time in B} + \text{Time in C, D and E}}$$

Such a measure was useful because it provided an index of effectiveness of the maintenance effort for that unit. It also provided a comparison with the manufacturer's specified availability (which is usually defined in a similar way). For the loaders, the manufacturer had quoted an availability of 85% if the equipment was operated correctly and maintained according to his recommended life plan. The important index for the small fleet of loaders, however, was the proportion of the fleet that was required, by Production, to be in operation at all times during production shifts—an index known as the *Fleet Demand Ratio (FDR)*.

A minimum of three loaders had been specified, and to satisfy this—and to carry out maintenance in states C, D, and E—the company carried a fleet of five. Thus, the FDR was three out of five, or sixty percent.

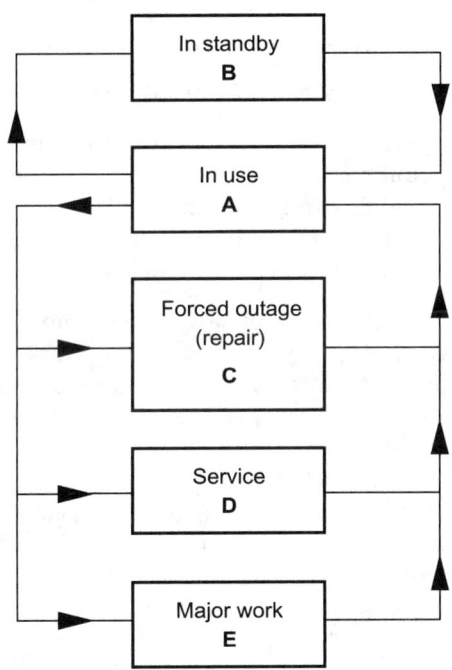

Haulers - 21 shift operation.   Operations require minimum of 5 out of 8
Loaders - 21 shift operation.   Operations require minimum of 3 out of 5

FIGURE 11–2 Status Diagram For Fleet

It appeared, from the manufacturer's availability figure, that the company had played safe. However, the decision to carry five loaders rather than four was based on the following influencing factors:

- The operation was production limited and a high downtime cost would be incurred if the number of loaders operational were to fall to two.
- Production wanted cover when a loader would be undergoing major overhaul (which was every two years) or major repair after failure.

The specification and measurement of availability ratios could have been usefully supplemented by some monitoring of the level of in-service failures. The best way of doing this would have been to keep a simple count as a function of shift, day, unit number, unit type etc. (It could be argued that unavailability costs did not occur in the same way as with fixed plants; they had been 'bought off' in the capital cost of the extra fleet capacity.)

Observations

An interesting point was that the maintenance supervisors felt that their objective should be:

'to ensure Production a minimum of three loaders at all times, at minimum maintenance cost.'

The maintenance manager, however, felt that it should be:

'to achieve a loader minimum availability of 85%, at minimum maintenance cost.'

His view, which I sympathised with, was that such an availability would also meet the production requirement.

The availability or reliability of mobile mining equipment is normally less than that predicted by its manufacturer, and its maintenance costs often considerably higher. There are several commonly occurring reasons for this, viz:

- **(a)** The equipment selected may not have been the most appropriate for its duty.
- **(b)** For many reasons (e.g., pooled use) its operators may have little sense of ownership. This leads to much maloperation, especially when coupled, as it often is, with severe operating conditions and bonus payment arrangements.
- **(c)** For several reasons—including (a), (b) and poor maintenance organiza- tion—the preventive programme is often neglected, equipment condition deteriorates and more corrective work is needed. This in turn results in even less preventive work being done—and so on until the maintenance of the whole fleet becomes purely reactive.

All of this was evident at MAXCOAL. Clearly, the long-term solution was to upgrade the fleet with new, wholly appropriate, equipment. For the shorter term I recommended that:

- the sense of ownership be increased by assigning operators (who would carry out simple pre-shift inspections and other minor maintenance) to equipment and improving their training in both operation and maintenance, this to include improving their understanding of the links between symptoms and the failures;

- a condition audit of the existing equipment be carried out and a corrective maintenance programme implemented to bring the equipment up to an acceptable state, reviewing and modifying, as necessary, the equipment life plans;
- the maintenance organization be changed—a preventive and overhaul group and a corrective group being created, and it being ensured that the work planning system and its priorities reflected the importance of the preventive programme.

Case Study 5: a Local Passenger Transport Fleet

Fleet Operating Characteristics

This study will reinforce the principles and concepts, introduced in the previous study, of fleet maintenance. The transport authority concerned operated from twenty or so depots located in different parts of a large conurbation, each providing transport in its own area and also the necessary parking and maintenance facilities. The depots were divided into three groups and in each one the major maintenance work (i.e., overhauls) and reconditioning were carried out at a central works. The system for a single depot and works is outlined in Figure 11–3.

The buses employed were mostly of the double-decked, front entrance, rear-engine type. The various models are enumerated in Table 11–1, which also shows the peak demand. The existence of a surplus of vehicles—i.e., above the level of this peak demand—provided a small stand-by pool on which essential maintenance could be carried out. In the analysis of the previous case study it was assumed that the production demand for fleet units was constant (i.e., it was always for a minimum of three). In most fleet operations, however, it fluctuates with time and the bus fleet in this case was no exception (see Figure 11–4, which indicates numerous 'production-related' windows of opportunity for maintenance). Because of the difficulty and expense of night-time and weekend working the most convenient of these windows occurred midweek—from 9.00 am to 4.00 pm—and facilitated the routine inspections and servicing, and other minor maintenance.

Although time for maintenance was available *outside* these midweek windows, the number of buses being 16% in excess of the peak demand, it was clearly advantageous to try to make maximise use of the opportunity they provided, because this would reduce the need for excess buses and hence the capital cost of the fleet.

The Maintenance Strategy at The Time of The Study

The maintenance *life plan* for a bus was based on a policy of '*inspect, service and repair as necessary*,' the basic service being carried out at three-weekly

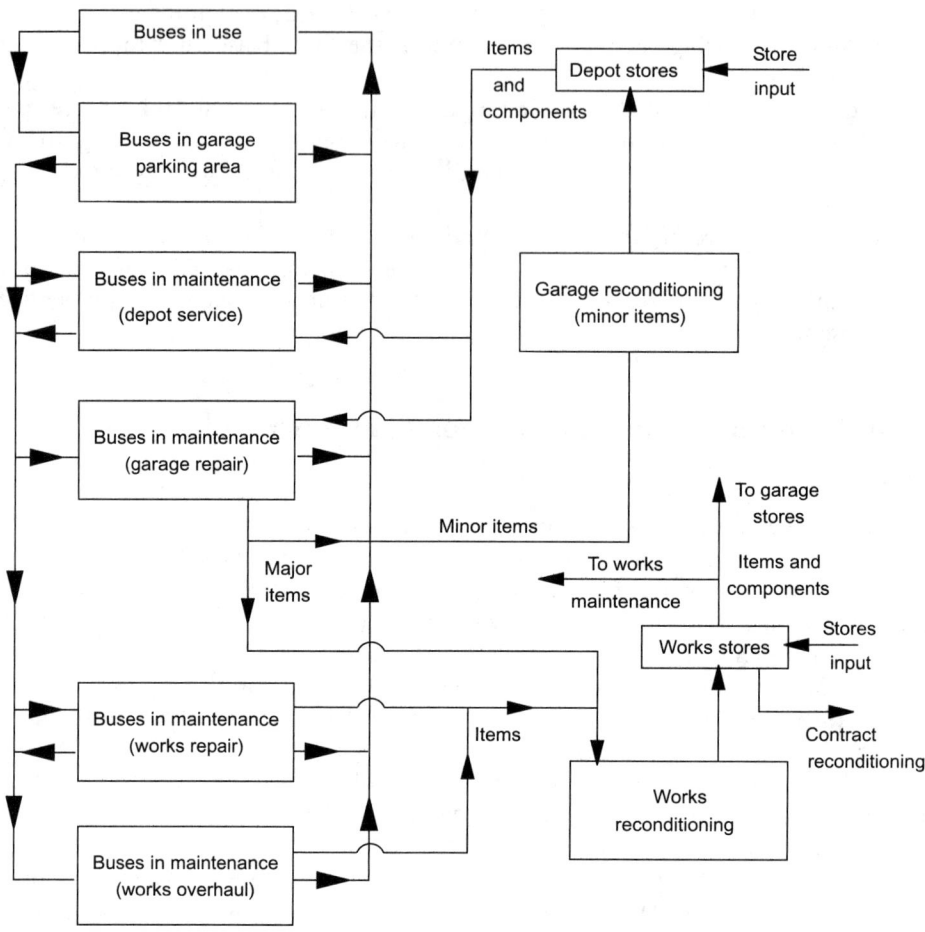

FIGURE 11–3 Status Diagram for a Large Fleet of Buses and their Maintenance System

TABLE 11–1 Fleet Inventory and Maximum Demand

Bus Type	Bus Make	Number in Fleet	Maximum Demand
Single deck	A	6	4
Double deck	B1	1	
	B2	14	
	B3	16	
	B4	13	
	B5	40	
	C1	23	
	C2	86	
	D	10	
		203	177
	Total all buses	209	181

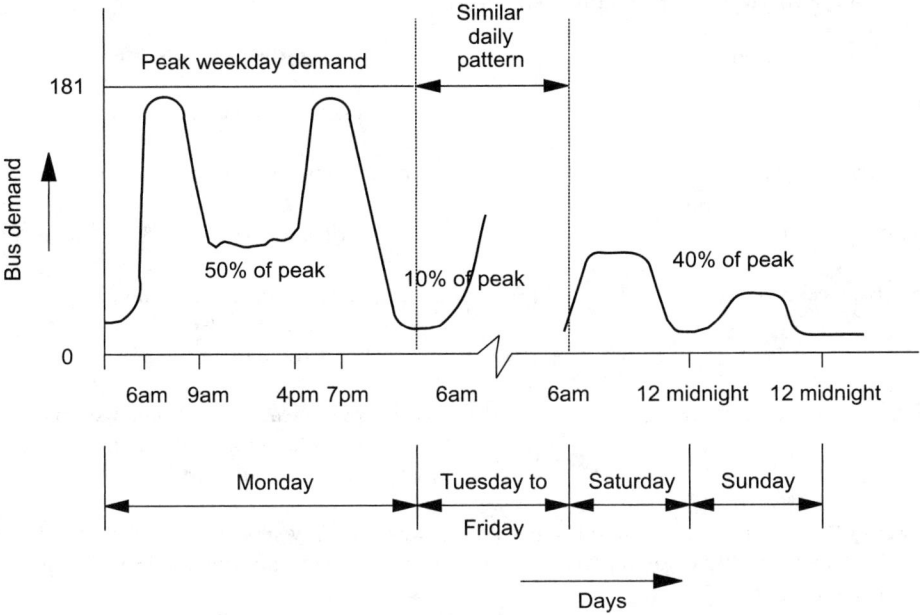

FIGURE 11-4 Pattern of Demand for Buses

intervals (3000 miles). Additional work was added to this basic service at 6000 miles, 12000 miles etc., and at the end of the year the bus was prepared for its statutory annual test. Overhauls were carried out at intervals of approximately three years. The *preventive schedule* of services and minor repairs was carried out in the mid-week windows (see Figure 11–4). The scheduling of the major work relied on the excess buses in the fleet.

This strategy had evolved over a period of time and was in need of review because it was felt that:

(i) the Fleet Demand Ratio (FDR, see previous case study) was too low;

(ii) the incidence of in-service failures (and unscheduled corrective work) was too high;

(iii) the existing inspection procedures were too subjective and often not carried out.

Maintenance Strategy Review

The existing life plans for each bus type—which had evolved via custom, practice and manufacturers' recommendations (and were felt, by the supervisors and tradeforce, to involve a degree of over-maintenance, especially as regards routine servicing)—were reviewed. The main thrust of this exercise was to extend the basic service period from three to six weeks (see Tables 11–2(a)

TABLE 11-2(a) Revised Bus Life Plan - Minor Work

Work and Frequency	Outline Description
Daily checks	Tyre pressure, engine oil, cleaning etc.
Weekly safety checks	Steering gear and lubrication etc.
Six-weekly service	Basic service, see Table 11-3
Twelve-weekly service	Basic, plus engine oil change and oil analysis check. Also valve clearances and fuel cylinders.
Eighteen-weekly service	Basic, plus gearbox oil change and oil analysis. Gearbox calibration and bearing adjustment on front axle.
Twenty-four-weekly service (continued to 48 weeks in multiples of six weeks, then repeated.)	Twelve-weekly service plus checking of fuel system, king pin bushes, gearbox, piston seals.

and 11-2(b)) and to move towards thorough and comprehensive inspection procedures (see, for example, the basic six-weekly checks listed in Tables 11-3(a) and 11-3(b)). Only minor changes were felt to be necessary to the preventive schedule.

The *services and minor repairs* were carried out in the respective depots in the mid-week windows. The basic six-weekly service was scheduled by dividing the year into eight six-weekly periods, leaving two weeks for holiday and two weeks for statutory work preparation. Because the total number of buses was 209, this

TABLE 11-2(b) Revised Bus Life Plan—Major Work

Frequency	Inspection and Corrective Maintenance	Inspection Time	Duration (weeks)
Three-yearly	Complete bus inspection and repairs at works. Thorough inspection/replacement/repair of all items and/or components. On completion bus to undergo a 'Freedom from Defects' test.	Four to five hours	Ten
Six, nine and twelve-yearly	Same as three-yearly	Same	Ten
Fifteen-yearly (Economic life of bus)	Fixed by management on a criterion based on a combination of economic obsolescence, and condition factors.		

TABLE 11–3(a) Revised Basic Six-weekly Servicing, Inspection

Check all engine mounts and tighten
Check and torque cylinder head nuts
Check operation of fuel injection pump
Drain and refill cam box
Check lubrication system for oil leaks
Check and adjust radiator fan belt tension
Check exhaust manifolds for leaks and torque nuts to 25lbf.ft.
Check front axle ball joints for free play
Check and tighten clutch fluid coupling drain plug
Check engine-clutch fluid coupling-gearbox alignment
Check gearbox-angle drive alignment
Check propeller shaft joints and splines for wear
Check propeller shaft needle roller bearing for wear-lift up
Check propeller shaft and check amount of free play
Check propeller shaft circumferential movement
Check propeller shaft for noise and vibration
Check electro-pneumatic unit for leaks using shock pulse meter (SPM)
Drain away water from electro-pneumatic unit (drain plug)
Check brake and transmission system and items for air leaks using SPM
Check brake liners for wear and damage
Check brake liner-drum clearance using feeler gauge
Check and lubricate automatic slack adjusters
Check starter motor commutator and brushes
Operational test of all electrical items in alarm and warning system, lighting
    system, trafficator system, start and stop system, and auxiliary items
Check security and rubber buffer of suspension springs
Check shock absorber-fluid level, link rubbers, leaks
Check torsion bar stabiliser for security, damage and distortion
Check body panels for damage and loose riveting
Check chassis frame for damage and security of attachment
Check to ensure all autolube chassis lubrication bearing points are not clogged
Check alcohol evaporation unit strainer (winter only)

TABLE 11–3(b) Revised Basic Six-weekly Servicing and Lubrication

Grease water pump bearing
Grease fan shaft joint and splines, and fan center bearing
Grease power steering ram ends
Grease propeller shaft splines and joints
Lubricate footbrake pedal linkage
Top up shock absorber level
Check, clean or replace heater and demister filters

required seven buses to be serviced per day. The estimated time for each service is shown in Table 11–4(a), and the daily loading—which does not take into consideration the resulting corrective work—in Table 11–4(b). In the majority of cases the servicing, and any corrective maintenance, could be completed

TABLE 11–4(a) Maintenance Service Type

Service period (weeks)	6	12	18	24	30	36	42	48
Estimated time (hrs)	1/2	11/2	11/2	3	1/2	11/2	1/2	4
Maintenance class	A	B	B	C	A	B	A	D

TABLE 11–4(b) Daily Workload for Red Group

Maintenance Period (weeks)	Maintenance Class	Red Group — 35 Buses				
		Day 1	Day 2	Day 3	Day 4	Day 5
6	A	—	—	—	—	—
12	B	—	—	—	—	—
18	B	—	—	—		—
24	C	—	—		—	—
30	A		—	—	—	—
36	B	—		—	—	—
42	A	—	—	—	—	
48	D	—	—	—	—	—
Buses per day		7	7	7	7	7
Hrs per day		12.5	11.5	10	11.5	12.5

within the window; where this would not be possible the bus would not be available to meet the peak demand and this would count against the Peak Demand Ratio (PDR). In addition, this planned workload could be augmented by the unscheduled corrective work resulting from in-service failure, which could be minor or could demand several days' effort.

The *overhauls and major repairs* were scheduled to be carried out in the central maintenance workshops. As shown in Table 11–2(b), the timing of major work was governed by the statutory requirement for the annual Freedom From Defects (FFD) test and by the requirement for a three-yearly overhaul. Thus the buses could be scheduled for overhaul and FFD test, at the central workshops, on a three-yearly basis. Taking into consideration the time (ten weeks) needed to carry out an overhaul, about fifteen buses would be in the works for overhaul at any one time. As before, this would count against the PDR.

Observations

Would the new plan reduce the combined costs of unavailability and of resources used? The daily, weekly and six-weekly scheduled preventive work would be carried out in the windows and would therefore not affect the PDR— and would not involve an increase in the workload. Changes in the major preventive work would be small and they also would have little effect, therefore, on the PDR or on the resources used. The most important point was whether the revised inspection and servicing procedures would lead to fewer in-service failures and less unscheduled corrective work. The level of such work that would result from the new plan was difficult to estimate. The more thorough consideration of the maintenance procedures for each item, the resulting increase in the number of items covered, and the greater objectivity of inspection procedures would result in a reduction of corrective work. Even a small reduction would result in fewer buses being in repair, a higher PDR and a smaller workload.

Three additional recommendations were made, viz:

- The three-yearly overhaul period should be extended, initially to four years and, after experience with this period, to five.
- The time required for an overhaul (ten weeks, sometimes more) was excessive; the procedures involved should be reviewed with a view to its progressive reduction.
- The economic life of the buses should be extended to at least twenty years.

These last recommendations were not accepted. At the time, the bus company was publicly owned and controlled. It has since been privatised and these and many other changes (not all positive) have been implemented.

CHAPTER 12

Case Studies 6–9: Maintenance in the Generation, Transmission and Distribution of Electricity

The principles and concepts of Business Centered Maintenance can also be beneficially applied to the very diverse equipment and processes employed at each stage in the operation of the electricity industry.

Introduction

Figure 12–1 is a schematic of a generation and supply system typical of the southern hemisphere. Demand for electricity varies throughout the year as shown in Figure 12–2. The demand also varies, of course, throughout the week (it decreases at the weekend) and throughout each 24 hours (it is lower at night). Several generating units (GUs), of various sizes, feed the distribution grid. The most efficient of these units, usually the larger ones, meet the base load (non-varying) demand, the less efficient ones being brought on intermittently to meet peaks in the demand. Not uncommonly, gas turbine or hydro units are employed to meet demand peaks of *short* duration (a practice sometimes referred to as *peak lopping*).

Case Study 6: A Gas-Fired Station

A review of the maintenance strategy for a gas-fired power plant highlighted the importance of the linkage between that strategy and production policy.

The Station and its Operating Characteristics

The station concerned had an installed capacity of 600 MW(e), made up of five 120 MW(e) generating sets, each of which comprised a gas-fired boiler and a steam-driven turbine. Until a year before the maintenance review the station had been part of the base load supply. It had then moved down in the merit table and at the time was being used on a two-shift operating basis, i.e., it tended to be used each day from 6 am to 8 pm but was not required at night, when the demand fell.

243

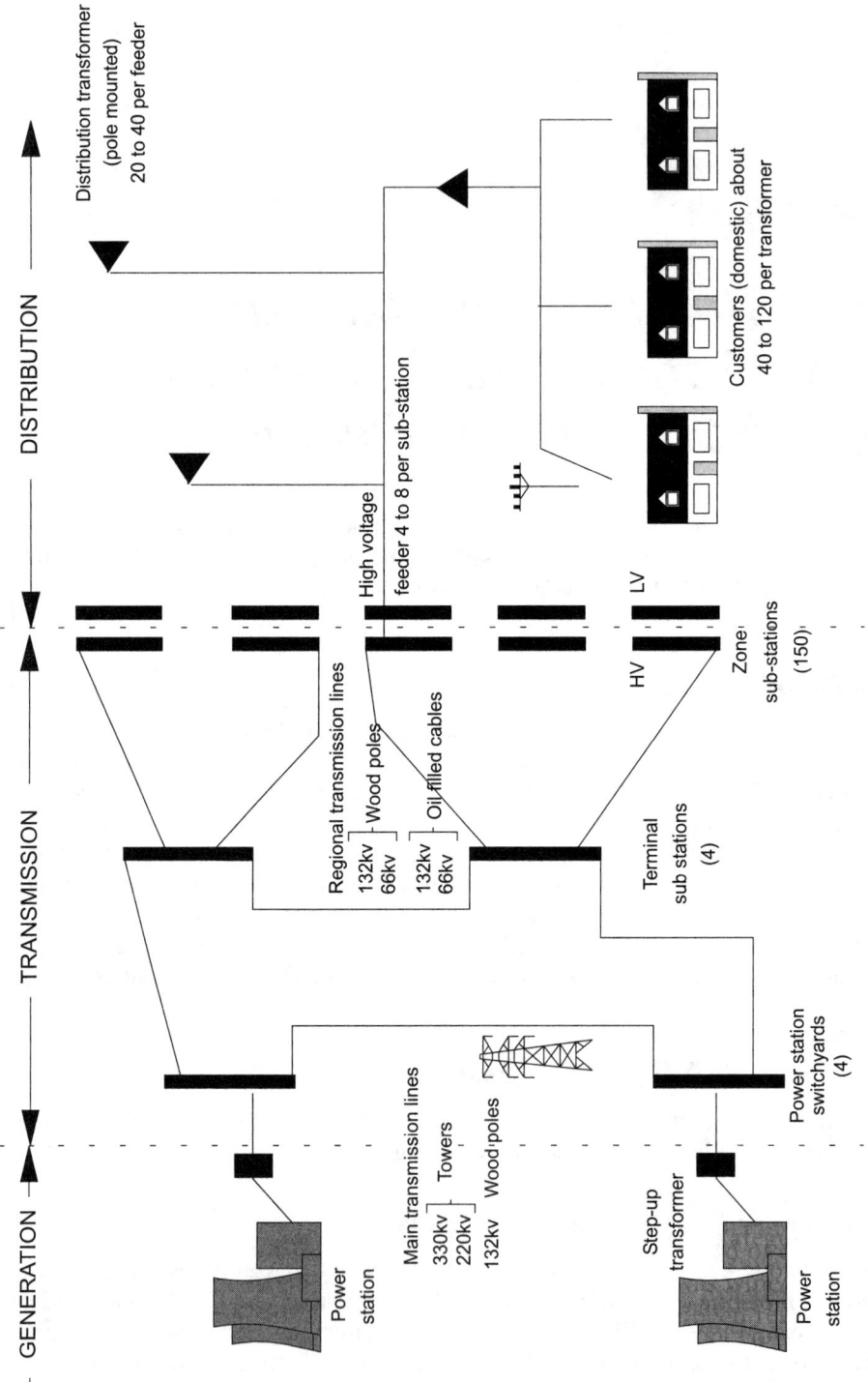

FIGURE 12-1 Schematic of Electricity Supply System

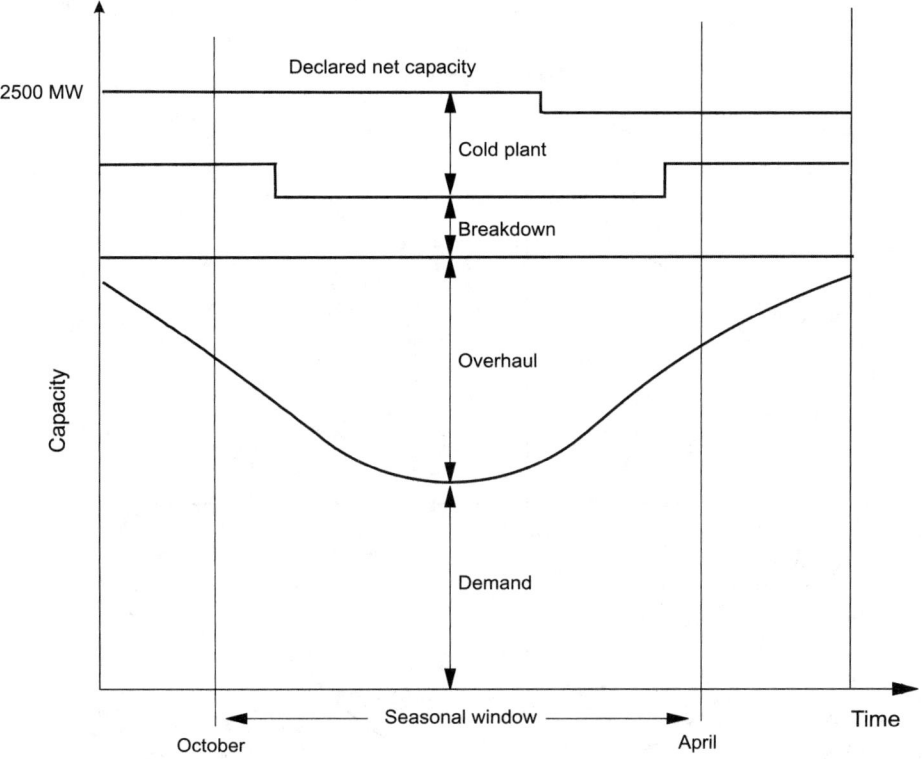

FIGURE 12-2 Annual Variation in Demand (Southern Hemisphere)

Relatively little off-line work could be carried out at night because of shortage of time for cooling and isolation, and also because the station was expected to provide a 'spinning reserve.' However, production-related windows of opportunity for maintenance, on one or more of the GUs, occurred on a more random basis and could be up to two weeks in duration. Such windows occurred—mainly during the annual low demand period—on average, about three times per year per GU. The planning lead time for these randomly occurring windows was relatively short (about one week, at most).

The Maintenance Strategy in Use When the Station Provided Base Load

The major-outage life-plan for a GU when the station was operating to provide base load is shown in Figure 12–3. This programme was the main element of a GU's life plan, relatively little work other than lubrication and simple inspection being undertaken outside the major shutdowns. The *major shutdown schedule* took account of the pattern of grid demand and also of the availability of internal and contract labour. For the station as a whole there was a ten-year plan, a maximum of two units being overhauled in any one year. This generated a work load of the kind illustrated in Figure 12–4.

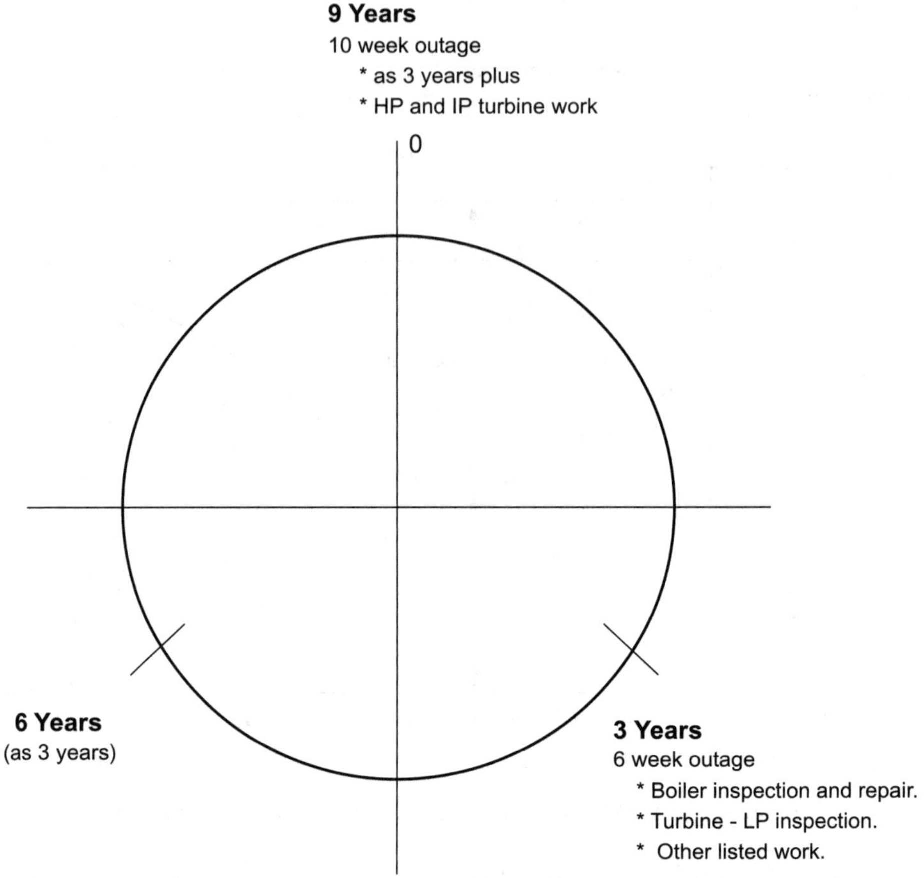

9 Years
10 week outage
    * as 3 years plus
    * HP and IP turbine work

0

6 Years
(as 3 years)

3 Years
6 week outage
    * Boiler inspection and repair.
    * Turbine - LP inspection.
    * Other listed work.

FIGURE 12–3 Outline of the Major Outage Life Plan for a Generating Unit

Review of Maintenance Strategy for Two-Shift Operation

The work content of a major shutdown was examined and, as far as possible, reduced by taking the following actions:

(i) jobs were identified which might possibly be scheduled into the randomly occurring windows of opportunity;

(ii) jobs which could be carried out in windows provided by the presence of redundant or spare plant—e.g., work on duplicate pumps—were identified and rescheduled;

(iii) on review, many jobs that were previously done at fixed intervals became condition-based; in other cases it was decided to do them only after failure.

The review resulted in an improvement of availability, mainly due to the reduction of the duration of scheduled outages (the maintenance transferred

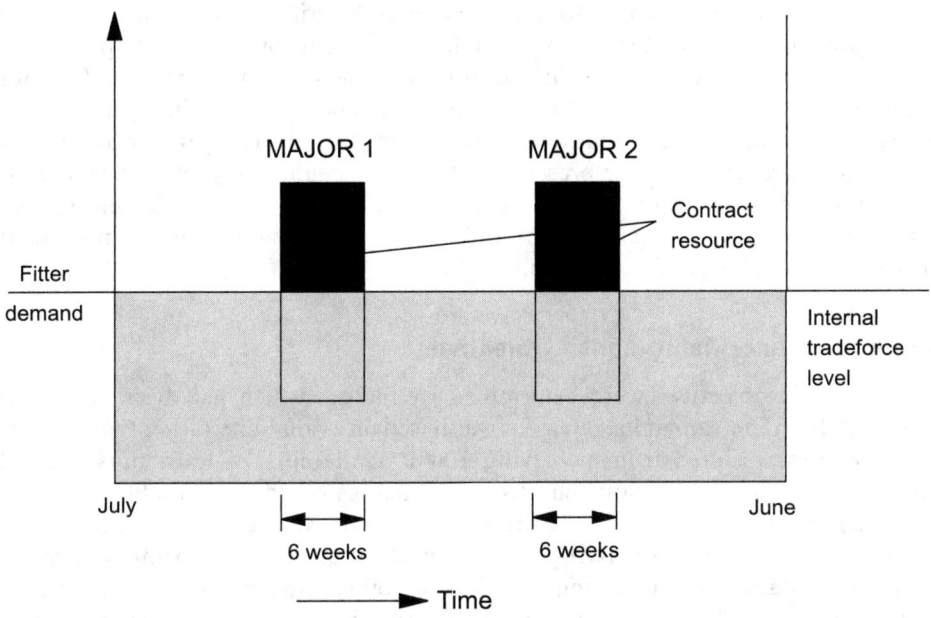

FIGURE 12–4 Workload Pattern and its Resourcing

into the randomly occurring windows not then having any direct impact on availability) but also because the revised maintenance policy was more effective. *In order to implement this revised strategy and, in particular, to facilitate the necessary opportunity-scheduling, improved work planning systems (based, among other things, on better computer software), were needed.*

Case Study 7: An Oil-Fired Station

This study illustrates the linkage between production objectives and maintenance objectives and shows how pursuit of the latter can drive changes in the life plan and maintenance organization.

The Station and its Operating Characteristics

An installed capacity of 360 MW(e) was attained via five 60 MW(e) sets, using oil-fired boilers and steam-driven turbines, and a 60 MW(e) gas turbine. The steam-driven units were some thirty years old and the gas turbine 22 years old. By the time of the study the station was privately owned, having been run down— with a view to decommissioning—under its previous state ownership. The management had a contract to supply electricity until the year 2000 using the steam-driven units, and until 2010 using the gas turbine. This depended on many uncertain factors, among which were whether the local grid would be connected to other grids, what the future demand for electricity might be, what environmental legislation might be enacted, and so forth.

The station provided a peak lopping service to the grid. For this, the gas turbine could provide an immediate response while the steam turbines could respond with as little as four hours' notice. The contract for the steam turbines was for four units out of the five—i.e., 240 MW(e)—to be available at any time. Thus, these units could be considered separately from the gas turbine as regards most aspects of maintenance strategy. The presence of the extra steam unit provided numerous windows for scheduling off-line maintenance work without losing system availability. Taking the gas turbine off-line for maintenance always meant, at any time, a total loss of *its* availability.

Production and Maintenance Objectives

Production objectives were determined by factors which had been set under contract. For the steam units, payment was based on availability rather than supply. Full payment resulted from achieving 100% availability of four units (i.e., of 240 MW(e) capacity); various checks and penalties could then modify this. The availability actually achieved at the time of the study was about 98%. For the gas turbine, payment was based partly on availability (e.g., 50% of maximum payment could be obtained by achieving 100% availability) and partly on operational reliability (e.g., 50% of maximum payment could be obtained by achieving 100% successful response to all the demanded starts). At the time of the study the gas turbine availability was over 80%, its operational reliability of the order of 90%.

Environmental and personnel safety standards were not discussed so it was assumed that they were satisfactory. A plant-condition audit was not carried out but it was known that the equipment was old and that, during the previous ten years, it had been allowed to deteriorate. An important question was '*What was the expected remaining life of each steam unit, given its age and condition?*' The answer to this would have a major influence on the maintenance life plan for that unit.

The management were aware of the above considerations and their inter-relationship. They had identified the maintenance objective as being:

'*to maintain or improve the (existing) output performance of the generators while reducing the resource cost via improvements in maintenance organizational efficiency.*'

Maintenance Strategy Before Privatisation

Steam units
The life plans for these could be summarised as follows:

- A major outage of twelve weeks duration every six years, to carry out statutory inspections, boiler, turbine and ancillary equipment overhaul.
- A major outage of three weeks duration every 26 months. The frequency of the shutdown had been that of the statutory inspection of the boiler but other necessary work had also been carried out.

- An annual outage of 10 days duration, to undertake boiler and turbine inspection and ancillary plant maintenance.
- On-line lubrication and simple inspection routines.

The station maintenance schedule had been aimed at spreading the outages as evenly as possible over the six-year cycle, in order to smooth the station workload. Essentially this meant that, on average, there had been 25 weeks of outage work per year. The station's internal maintenance labour had been manned up to a level which met this shutdown workload. Little use had been made of any contract resource.

Gas turbine
The life plan had been built around a major outage, every four years, of six weeks duration and an annual outage of two weeks duration. Because of its specialised nature and the high cost of spares holding, this work had been contracted out to specialists, except for the first line work which had been covered by internal labour. This policy remained the same after privatisation.

Maintenance Strategy after Privatisation

After privatisation, considerable effort was devoted to changing the life plans and station outage schedule in order to maintain the steam unit availabilities and reliabilities at reduced maintenance cost. This was achieved via the following actions:

(i) Discontinuing, after 1995, the six-yearly outage because the steam unit lives would have come to an end by the year 2000. The remaining two twelve-week outages were scheduled for the summers of 1994 and 1995 (the last of these being a precautionary outage).
(ii) Discontinuing the traditional annual outage and incorporating its work into the 26 monthly statutory outage. This extended the duration of that outage to four weeks. These outages were scheduled for the summer months at a rate of three in one year, two in the next year, and so on.
(iii) Reviewing all the shutdown work to identify the jobs that could be undertaken outside the main shutdowns by taking advantage of plant redundancy. This work was incorporated in preventive maintenance programme (a 'window' schedule) for ancillary equipment and was scheduled to smooth the workload between outages.

The resulting changes in workload and resourcing are shown in Figure 12–5. Peaks were resourced via a combination of (mostly) contract labour and overtime. The main benefit was a reduction of 40% in the internal maintenance tradeforce and of an overall 30% in labour costs. In other words, the change of strategy facilitated an improvement in organizational efficiency without a loss of maintenance effectiveness

The management of the station also embarked on measures to reduce labour costs by improving flexibility, i.e., by reducing the non-trade workforce,

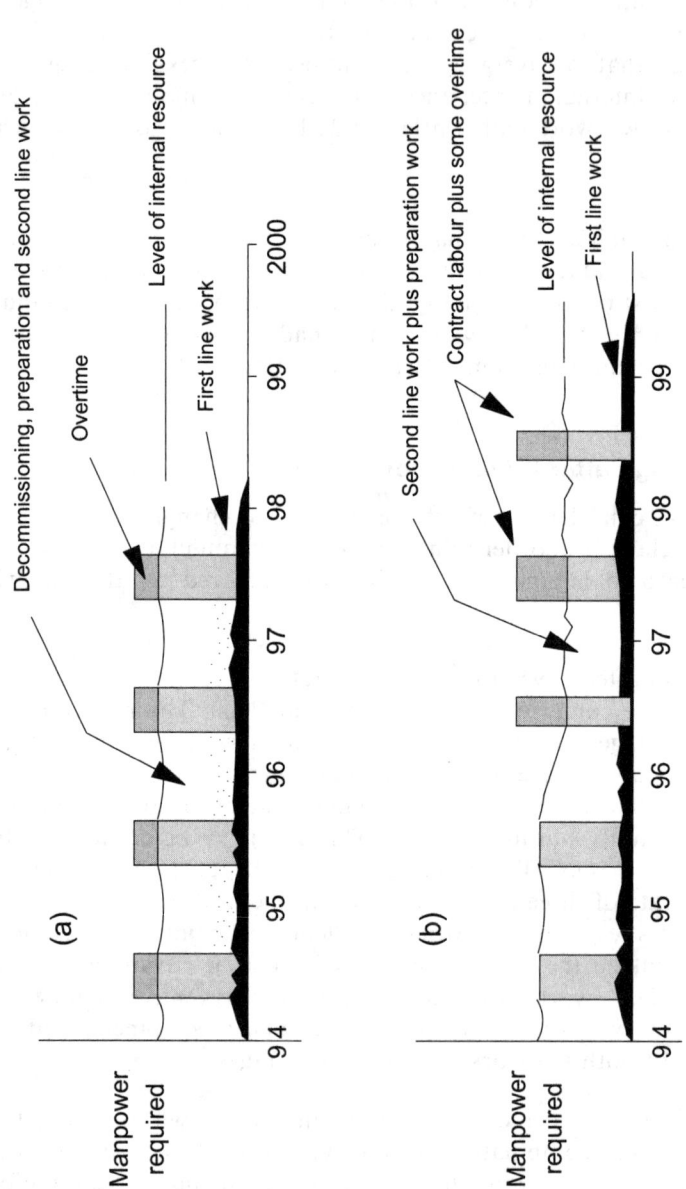

FIGURE 12–5 Workload and Resourcing, (a) Before and (b) After Strategy Change

improving inter-trade and operator–maintainer flexibility. This would lead to the same workload being undertaken by less labour and at lower labour cost.

Case Study 8: A Transmission System

Here, the Business Centered Maintenance approach was applied to non-process plant in order to map the maintenance strategy.

Equipment Operating Characteristics

The transmission grid was outlined in Figure 12–1. Its function was to transmit power from the generating stations to the zone sub-stations and then to the local distribution systems. In order to transmit the power efficiently the station transformer stepped up the voltage to 330 kV; the power then going via the main switchyards to the grid.

The grid itself comprised main sub-stations, zone sub-stations, main transmission lines carried on steel towers, and regional transmission lines carried on wooden poles and in oil filled underground cables (see Figure 12–1); these were the *primary* assets. In addition there were the following *secondary* assets:

Grid control system, including the host computer at the control center and the transducers etc. at the generating station and sub-stations. This was mostly solid-state electronic equipment.
Communication systems, including the grid protection communication system and the microwave systems which passed information from the transducers to the host computer.
Protection systems, made up mainly of solid-state electronic equipment that protected the power stations, sub-stations etc.

The *maintenance objective* for the transmission grid could be expressed as for process plant, i.e., '*to achieve the agreed system operating requirements*, with agreed and defined plant condition and safety requirements, *at minimum resource cost.*'

The system operating requirements were set as 'transmission practice standards.' Supply reliability, and safety were monitored via various quantitative indicators, and targets were set based upon these indicators. These requirements could then be translated into user requirements at main asset (e.g., sub-station) level and used to develop maintenance life plans.

Maintenance Strategy Mapping

As a part of the strategy review an equipment criticality ranking—similar to the procedure for process plant (see Table 5–2)—was developed. For example, consider the outline, in Figure 12–6, of a part of the transmission grid. The thick line indicates a main transmission line that could be regarded as critical, in the sense that if it failed it would restrict the flow of electricity from the generating stations. If this transmission line were to be required for off-line

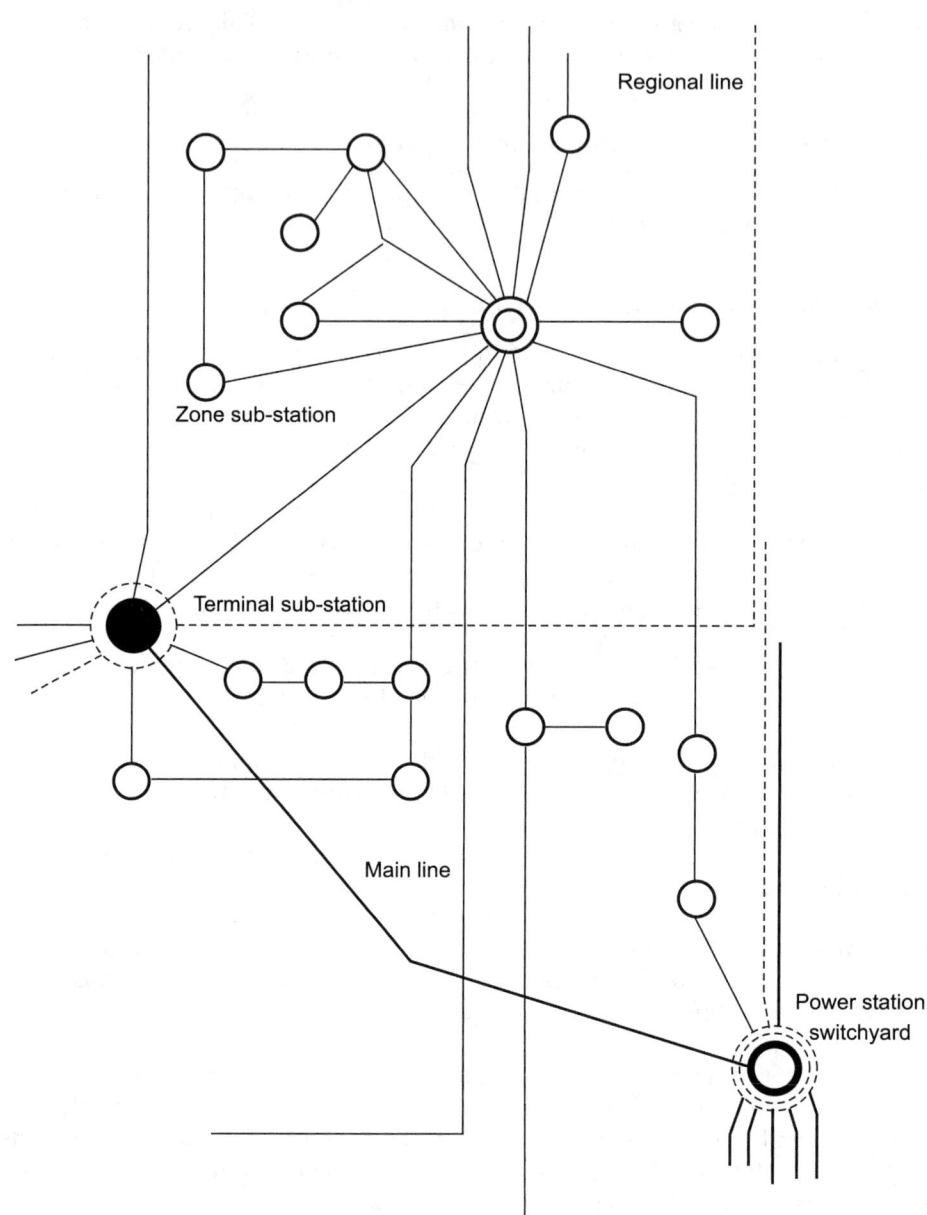

Regional line

Zone sub-station

Terminal sub-station

Main line

Power station switchyard

FIGURE 12–6 Part of the Transmission Grid

work it would have to be taken off when one of the GUs was on outage maintenance (or perhaps when two of them were). This particular transmission system was audited and one of the main resulting observations was that more attention would have to be given to identifying and ranking those lines, switchgear and failure modes which were critical to system reliability or safety.

Such a *criticality ranking* was probably understood but, as far as could be seen, had not been documented as a part of the transmission system maintenance strategy.

The maintenance life plan for the *primary assets* had been developed in the conventional way. The plan for a typical sub-station, for example, was as outlined below:

Tasks	Frequency
Inspection and lubrication routines	Monthly
A-grade service (a combination of inspection, proof testing, minor adjustments and replacement of simple items)	Three-yearly
B-grade service (broadly similar to A-grade)	Six yearly
Overhaul	Based on the results of the services

In general, the life plans for the *secondary assets* were different from the above because these assets were mostly solid state electronic equipment. The plans were therefore based on routine cleaning and calibration, some proof testing and some planned corrective work.

Formulation of the schedule for the *main lines* was an activity driven by the outage requirements for the GUs. The structure of this schedule then drove the outage schedule for the switchyards, main terminals and sub-stations and hence influenced the schedule for the secondary assets. Although all this seems quite straightforward it should be appreciated that the various responsibilities—for the GUs, main lines, regional lines, switchgear and secondary assets—were disseminated among different parts of a large organization. Thus, the effective co-ordination of effort required communication systems that had to be excellent.

Case Study 9: A Distribution System

This will complete discussion of the generation and supply system of Figure 12–1. It is instructive because it will show that even if an otherwise satisfactory maintenance strategy is being followed, preventive work is in danger of being neglected if objectives and work priorities have not been clearly laid down beforehand.

The distribution system boundary was at the zone sub-station of Figure 12–1. Even in this example's relatively small (2500 MW) grid the magnitude of the distribution assets was considerable, viz. 150 sub-stations and thousands of wooden poles each one carrying some appropriate equipment (a distribution transformer, for example).

Although both corporate and maintenance objectives had been specified for the generation and supply systems they had not been interpreted into objectives for the distribution system. Simple life plans—broadly similar to those for the transmission sub-stations (i.e., based on inspection-oriented services)—had been formulated for each of the sub-stations. In general, there were life plans for the pole-mounted equipment, based on simple inspection when the wooden pole

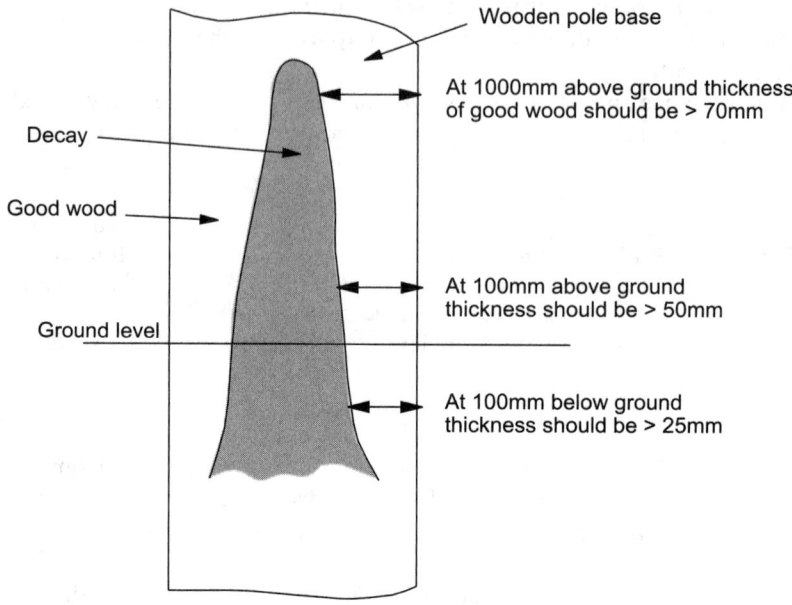

Four yearly inspection, based on the following

*   If below-ground criterion is met then chemically treat base only.

*   If below-ground criterion is not met but upper criteria are met then reinforce the base with steel stakes and chemically treat.

*   If lower and upper criteria are not met then replace pole.

FIGURE 12–7 Pole Maintenance Policy

structure was being maintained (which, because of the age of the poles—as much as thirty years—and the prevalence of adverse ground conditions, was itself the main source of work). The maintenance policy for the pole structure was as indicated in Figure 12–7. An additional maintenance task in some areas was tree clearing around the lines.

Audit of the distribution system maintenance revealed a backlog of work on the poles, and on the equipment mounted on them, which was many years long. The condition of these assets was clearly deteriorating and causing senior management concern, both for safety and for security of supply. The basic cause of this problem can be deduced from Figure 12–8, which shows the maintenance workload for a typical distribution area. The tradeforce had to carry out not only the maintenance of the existing network but also its expansion to new homes and industries—which generated new income and therefore took priority. The absence of asset condition and safety standards led to continued deferral of maintenance. At best it was carried out only when expansion work eased off.

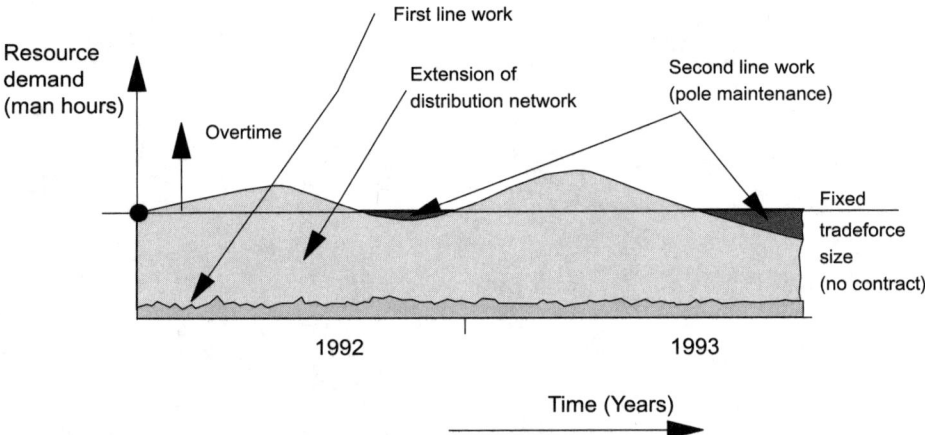

FIGURE 12–8 Long Term Workload for Line Tradeforce

The following recommendations resulted from the audit:

- Distribution maintenance objectives should be set and translated down to main asset level. Safety and longevity standards should be specified.
- Either a separate 'maintenance group' should be formed or work priorities changed so as to ensure that maintenance is carried out at the required time.

APPENDIX 1

*Audit Aide-Memoir**

(NB The quoted Tables A1–1—A1–6 are given at the end of this appendix)

1.0 Understand the Characteristics of Plant Operation

1.1 Establish Nature of Process

1. Construct a site layout diagram (include an indication of the main plant areas, the store(s) and tool store(s) locations and the workshops, with a simple coding to identify the location of the tradegroups). See Figure 5–1 as an example.
2. Establish size of site.
   Capital cost of plant?
   Age of plant?
   Age of process technology?
   Is it multi-product?
3. Construct a process flow diagram partitioned at unit (e.g., mixer or compressor) level. See Figures 5–2 and 5–5 as an example.
   This may be hierarchical.
   Indicate flow direction, capacities, all storage points and capacities.
   Indicate stand-by units and/or excess capacity.
   Identify bottle-necks.
4. Identify total number of employees, and of *maintenance* employees.

1.2 Understand Operating Policy and External Influences

1. Understand the operating policy for the plant.
   Identify operating pattern (e.g., continuous, 5×3 shifts, etc.)
   Understand the relationship between the plant and its market (is it steady or dynamic).
   How is this affected by final stage storage?
2. Understand the operating policy for the plant units taking into consideration the level of redundancy (e.g., where there are three units, how are they

---
*Developed in conjunction with Dr H. S. Riddell.

operated if (a) all three are required, or (b) only two out of three are required, etc.?) Identify and record operating procedures for the main units.

3. Understand how other production factors affect the plant operating pattern. For example:
   - Catalyst changes.
   - Raw material supply.
   - Availability of services.
   - Cleaning.
   - Manpower availability or policies.

4. Determine the effect of other external factors on operating policy (e.g., statutory safety regulations).

5. Estimate the 'lost production' cost of a plant failure. Is this constant or variable (over 24 hours or seasonally)?

1.3 Understand Plant Unit Criticality

Identify two important units for each plant audited. Use an importance-deciding criterion based on consequences of failure (lost production, safety, quality) and failure probability (previous history etc).

1.4 Identify Scheduling Characteristics

1. Identify the plant maintenance windows (their pattern of occurrence and duration) resulting from production scheduling, cleaning, catalyst changes, excess capacity etc. Establish whether the windows occur predictably (e.g., at weekends, during statutory inspections etc) or more randomly due to external factors such as market demand.

2. Identify those areas of plant (streams, groups of units, or individual units) that can be maintained via inter-stage storage or redundancy.

1.5 Acquire Plant Performance Information

1. Acquire overall availability figures for the plant and, if possible, international comparisons.

2. Acquire other plant performance indices (depending on the nature of the plant these could be: plant outages per period, main shutdown duration and frequency, energy efficiency, etc.).

3. Acquire accident history.

4. Identify – Operation labour cost per ton produced.
   Maintenance labour cost per ton produced.
   Contract labour cost per ton produced.
   Raw material cost per ton of product produced.

5. Acquire information as per items 1 to 4 above on the important units of plant as identified in 1.3.

1.6 Clarify Company Maintenance Terminology

Clarify and agree the specialist maintenance terminology used within the company. Give particular attention to local non-standard or ambiguous usages.

2.0 Understand Business, Production and Maintenance Objectives

2.1 Identify Business Objectives

- Identify mission and vision statements.
- Identify manufacturing plan and objectives.
- Identify manager's personal objectives (including those for maintenance).
- Identify whether management by objectives (MBO) is being used.

2.2 Identify Maintenance Objectives (See Figure 1–5)

- Identify the maintenance department's objectives. Are they stated in general terms or quantified?
- Are the maintenance objectives split into those for plant (regarding availability, equipment condition, etc.) and those for people?
- Have the plant maintenance objectives been interpreted at unit level (for critical equipment, at least)?
- Is safety represented in the maintenance objectives?
- Is product quality represented in the maintenance objectives?
- Identify the organizational efficiency objectives (labour performance, utilisation, flexibility, etc.)
- Are there first-line management and tradeforce objectives, if so, identify them.
- Has MBO been used to bring objectives down to unit level and first line management level? (see Figure 5–4)
- Where there are no written objectives identify the management/tradeforce perception of the department/section/personal objectives.

3.0 Review Maintenance Life Plans (Process Plant)

3.1 Select Plant Units for Each Main Plant Audited

1. Identify, via 1.3, at least two critical units to represent the equipment in use (e.g., pressure vessels, large compressors, duplicate pumps).
2. Draw a schematic of the units and identify on the diagram the rotables (see Figure 5–6). For each unit carry out Steps 3.2 to 3.5.

3.2 Identify the Operating Procedures

1. Identify the unit operating procedures and establish if they are documented. Is the unit running time recorded in any way?

3.3 Identify the Maintenance Life Plans (See Table 5–1 and Table 5–3)

1. Record the lubrication routines and identify who carries them out.
2. Identify the service work content and frequency of execution. Establish whether the service is written up as a job procedure. This should be carried out for mechanical, electrical and instruments equipment associated with the unit.
3. Identify all inspections (other than those carried out during the service), including vibration, lube oil and thermography tests etc (see Table 5–4).

Establish who carries them out and how the results are recorded and analysed.

4. Identify and record the corrective maintenance policies, including those for the solid state electronic equipment associated with the unit. Note whether there are any standard corrective job procedures.
5. Record any in-situ maintenance techniques that are used.
6. Identify the maintenance policy for the major work on the units (or systems), e.g., is the timing of the major work based on a major shutdown (fixed-time) but the content of the overhaul based on inspection (i.e., is condition based), or is major work carried out after failure.
7. If the unit under analysis is duplicated (e.g., is a stand-by or a redundant unit) identify the operating procedure and maintenance policy for the group of such units.

3.4 Identify Spare Parts and Rotables

1. Identify the spares list for each unit.
2. Identify the rotables for each unit and the present stores status.
3. Establish whether there have been problems with the supply of parts and rotables.
4. Establish whether a spares criticality analysis has been undertaken, in particular for the slow-moving expensive parts.

3.5 Review Arrangements for Monitoring Life Plans

1. Identify the procedures that are in place for periodically reviewing life plans.

4.0 Review Maintenance Life Plans (Electrical and Instrumentation)

4.1 Select Plant Units and Systems

1. Identify at least two critical units or systems in use (e.g., electrical motors; programmable logic controllers, control valves etc)
2. Establish the way in which each type of equipment is maintained. Include the following:
   - the operating procedures,
   - preventive routines and their documentation,
   - inspections (including proof-testing),
   - cleaning routines,
   - corrective maintenance guidelines (including level of replacement in the case of solid state equipment).
3. Review spare parts and rotables:
   - Identify the spares list for each unit.
   - Identify the rotables for each unit.
   - Establish whether there have been problems with parts supply.
   - Establish whether a spares criticality analysis has been undertaken.
4. Identify the procedures that are in place for reviewing the life plans.

5.0 Review Condition-Based Maintenance (CBM)

5.1 Clarify General Issues

1. Identify the personnel responsible for the CBM programmes, their responsibilities and the reporting structure. Establish if the NDT personnel are separate from the CBM personnel.
2. Establish the linkage between the CBM programmes and the life plans.
3. From the list of Table A1–1 identify the CBM techniques employed. Each should then be investigated to establish where it is used, who uses it and how.
4. Ask all those interviewed and who are responsible for plant performance '*How effective do they believe the condition monitoring and NDT programme is?*' Ask the question by technique used. Ask for possible examples. Ask '*Are there any problems and what are they?*'

5.2 Review Vibration Monitoring: Continuous On-Line Systems

1. Determine the make of systems in use.
2. Identify how many units are monitored, at how many points, and what is being measured.
3. Check on how the data is recorded and how it is used.
4. Check on limitations of the system. Does it cover high frequency problems?
5. Determine how alarm conditions are set. Check on how alarm conditions are dealt with—is there a procedure?
6. Ask how often the monitoring points and alarm conditions are reviewed.
7. Check how often the transducers are calibrated and the wiring checked.
8. Review operating personnel and experience.

5.3 Review Vibration Monitoring: Periodic On-Line Systems

1. Determine the make of systems in use.
2. Identify how many units are monitored, at how many points, and what is being measured.
3. Check on how the data is recorded and how it is used. Check on the monitoring period; how was it determined?
4. Check on data recording, storage and usage.
5. Determine how alarm conditions are set. Check on how alarm conditions are dealt with—is there a procedure?
6. Check limitations of system. Does it cover high frequencies, etc.?
7. Review operating personnel and experience.
8. Check procedures for reviewing alarm levels and monitoring points.

5.4. Review Vibration Monitoring: Portable Systems

1. Determine the make of systems in use and the number of units on which they are used.
2. Determine what they are used for, how they are used and who uses them.
3. Determine whether they are contract-operated.
4. Examine any associated software for scheduling and data processing.
5. Determine the extent to which vibration diagnostics are undertaken. By internal or by contract labour?

6. Determine how good the monitoring records are
7. Assess the level of relevant training given to in-house users.

5.5 Review Oil Analysis

1. Determine type of monitoring systems used.
2. Establish number of units monitored and average number of compartments per unit.
3. Establish who is responsible for the analysis—consultants, in-house personnel or a combination? Who does the actual sampling on-site?
4. Ask for an example of a sampling frequency and ask how it is arrived at.
5. Establish the training given to the personnel involved in oil sampling.
6. Establish whether tests (if any) are carried out on site.
7. Establish the tests carried out off-site and the method of assessment of the results. Check what records of off-site tests are held on-site. Check systems of data transfer and storage.
8. Establish the alarm conditions and the way in which they are handled.
9. Enquire how the arrangements are reviewed?

5.6 Review Thermography

1. Determine type of system in use.
2. Determine which units are monitored and why.
3. Establish who does it—consultants or in-house personnel.
4. If carried out in-house check on the training given to users.
5. Ask for an example of the monitoring frequency and how it is determined.
6. Ascertain the data recording, storage and analysis arrangements
7. Enquire regarding the alarm levels and how they are set.
8. Enquire how the arrangements are reviewed.

5.7 Review Performance Monitoring

1. Determine number of units monitored.
2. Establish the parameters monitored and the maintenance conditions thus predicted
3. Establish who does the monitoring and the training they have they received.
4. Establish alarm levels, procedures, data recording and the frequency of checks.
5. Enquire how the arrangements are reviewed.

5.8 Review Non-Destructive Testing (NDT)

1. Ascertain types of testing system in use.
2. Determine number of units tested.
3. For each testing system in use, establish whether it is operated by consultants, by in-house personnel or by some combination.
4. If undertaken in-house, establish the extent of relevant personnel training.
5. For on-load testing, establish frequency with which an alarm condition (discovery of a crack etc.) is triggered (and the subsequent procedure).

6. Establish the procedure for off-load testing and the procedures after discovery of an unacceptable condition (e.g., arrangements for repair, root cause analysis etc)
7. Investigate NDT history recording (including availability of computerised analysis).
8. Investigate the use of NDT records for predicting the shutdown workscope.
9. Enquire how the arrangements are reviewed.

6.0 Review Corrective Maintenance and Plant Condition

6.1 Review Corrective Maintenance Policy

1. Establish the extent to which a planned operate-to-failure policy (i.e., let it fail and repair it before plant output or safety is compromised) exists .
   For such cases consider whether this is the best policy and how well it is conducted. Are spares available? Are corrective guidelines and job procedures available? Investigate this area for solid state, electrical and mechanical equipment
2. Establish the extent to which in-situ corrective engineering techniques are used (see Table A1−2)
3. Identify whether standard job procedures are being used for corrective jobs carried out on the plant. Are these covered by the maintenance documentation system? Is their quality good?

6.2 Review Logical Fault Finding (LFF)

1. Establish what techniques of LFF are in use in the maintenance department, and covering mechanical, electrical, instrumentation and control equipment.
2. Establish the extent of training, including equipment specific training, in this area.
3. Ask a sample of those interviewed how effective the maintenance department is in finding faults after failure.

6.3 Review Reconditioning Policy

1. Create a schematic (showing decision points) of the flow of parts/rotables after plant repair. Include indication of role of area workshops, main workshops, stores and contract reconditioning (see Figure 5−9 as an example).
2. Establish how good the workshop job procedures are. Are they documented with test points? How good are the manufacturers' manuals? Are they readily available?
3. Establish the ratio of external to internal reconditioning.
4. Determine the selection procedure for external contractors.
5. Establish the percentage of re-work for external and internal reconditioning.

6.4 Review Plant Condition and Housekeeping

1. Visit each plant audited (including those units identified in 3.1) to establish the following:
   - The general housekeeping in the plant and control rooms. This includes spillage, old parts left behind, condition of building etc.
   - The superficial condition of equipment, its appearance, paintwork, any fluid leakage and obvious signs of wear etc.

   During the visit talk with the tour guide about equipment criticality, age, condition and any problems. *Note*: *It is essential to go on an **inside** tour even of the most dirty and hazardous of plants—obviously with proper protection and safety induction.*

2. Visit each of the plant workshops and the main workshop to establish the following:
   - The general housekeeping, and the condition of the equipment
   - Whether there are local spare parts and tool stores—official or otherwise.
   - The activity of the tradeforce.

3. Visit the main stores to establish the following:
   - General housekeeping.
   - Stores layout and clarity of labelling in bin locations.
   - Labelling of rotables.

7.0 Review the Preventive Maintenance Schedule

7.1 Establish the Lubrication Routines for Each Plant Audited

1. How were the lubrication points, oil types and frequency selected?
2. Are the routines carried out internally or by contract? If internally, by whom — tradesmen, operators or some combination?
3. Establish whether any reliability problems due to poor lubrication have been encountered.

7.2 Establish the On-Line Inspection Routines (This Should Link with Section 5.0)

1. Establish degree of operator monitoring (including performance monitoring).
2. Establish extent of inspection (look, listen, feel and smell) by tradeforce.
3. Determine whether the routines are properly documented.
4. Ask all those interviewed how effective they feel these routines are.
5. Estimate what percentage of the routines is actually being carried out.

7.3 Establish the Schedule for Minor Off-Line Work (Mechanical, Electrical and Instrumentation)

1. Obtain, if possible, a print-out of the schedule of minor off-line work (services, minor preventive. jobs etc.)
2. Establish how such work is scheduled. Is it by exploiting windows occurring during nights, weekends, scheduled down-days, production stoppages, or by exploiting plant redundancies etc.?

3. Establish what percentage of the work that is thus scheduled is, in fact, carried out. If this percentage is low, establish why.

7.4 Establish the Schedule for Major Off-Line Work (Mechanical, Electrical, Instrumentation)

1. Establish how the major maintenance work is scheduled. For example, the schedule might be based on:
   - The occurrence of statutory shutdowns (every three years, say),
   - The shortest unit running time, determined via CBM,
   - Opportunities arising due to production stoppage or lack of demand for product,
   - The exploitation of plant redundancies.

   Obtain an outline example of the schedule.
2. Establish the main shutdown durations and frequencies.
3. Establish the procedure for building the shutdown workscope.
4. Ask all those interviewed how well the major work is being carried out.
5. Examine the history and case study material of previous shutdowns — how good is it?

8.0 Establish the Maintenance Workload

Needs to be carried out after the resource structure has been modelled. Workload categories are shown in Table 1–3.

8.1 Establish the Profile of the Major (Third Line) Workload

1. Use the Section 7.4 information, in conjunction with an estimate of the manpower requirements of the major work, to model the major workload profile (i.e., manpower required vs time—see Figure 5–17).
   The profile should be drawn for the main trades with an indication of the percentage of manpower contributed by contract workers.
2. Establish the percentage of the work that is (a) preventive and (b) corrective.
3. Establish the percentage of corrective work that occurs, unscheduled, after the shutdown has started.
4. Ask a relevant sample of the interviewees to comment on the utilisation and performance of the shutdown manpower. If there are problems ask for an explanation.

8.2 Establish the Profile of the First and Second Line Workload

1. For each plant audited use the information from Section 7.1 to 7.3 and the resource structure information (see Section 9) to estimate, for each trade, the second line workload profile (see Figure 5–17). If possible, show within the main model the profile for first line and preventive work.
2. Ask a relevant sample of the interviewees to comment on the utilisation and performance of the manpower. If there are problems ask for an explanation.

9.0 Establish the Maintenance Resource Structure

The resource structure model represents the location, size and work function of the non-managerial, shop floor, personnel, and of the spares and tools.

Establish, from the Section 1 and Section 7 information, the various states of the plant and how they affect the required structure of resources. In the case of the FPP of Chapter 1, for example, a structure (see Figures 1–14 and 1–15) is needed for the on-going (fifty weeks per year) state that needs to be revised for the major shutdown (e.g., necessitates an influx of contractors).

9.1 Draw an Initial Model of the On-Going Resource Structure (See Figure 5–8 as an Example)

1. Complete a table similar to Table A1–3 for the following personnel:
   - Each of the tradegroups and operator groups identified in the plant layout model of Figure 5–1.
   - All contract labour (identified by trade and indicated as contract labour by a '*suffix-c*').
2. Establish an inventory of the operators, tradeforce and average contractor force and validate it against the above table.
3. Model the on-going resource structure: essentially a matrix, the horizontal axis indicating the main plant areas and the vertical axis the operator groups (above the plant axis) and tradegroups (below the plant axis), the tradegroups being distinguished by work function (first line, second line etc). See Figure 5–8 for an example.
   Where contract labour is used indicate whether resident or temporary. With less complex structures super-impose the parts and tool stores on the same structure model—otherwise draw up separate models.
4. If the plant is either partially or completely shut down at set periods (annually, say, or three- yearly) for major maintenance, model the 'shutdown resource structure' in a similar way (see Section 11.3— Turnaround Planning).

9.2 Ascertain the Extent of Work Flexibility

- Establish the following:
- The extent of operator–maintainer flexibility in plant-oriented teams or other forms. Where it exists determine how well it is working.
- The extent of inter-trade flexibility. Where and why is it used? How well is it being used and where are the deficiencies?
- The extent of inter-plant flexibility. Where is it being used and where could it be used? Identify any consequent problems.

9.3 Ascertain the Extent to Which Supra-Normal Labour Resources are Used

1. On average, and for each trade, what percentage of work is done on overtime and how does this vary:
   - over the week?
   - over the year?
   - between groups?

Who decides what overtime shall be worked and on what basis?

2. What is the level of call-outs?
   Who decides? For what type of jobs?
3. What maintenance shift system is used?
   For which trades? Who supervises them?
   Is it rigid or flexible (e.g., can extend to night working when needed)?
4. What use is made of contractors:
   - for daily, general, maintenance work?
   - for specialised on-site maintenance?
   - for shutdown or turnaround work?
   - for modifications and installations?

9.4 Understand Interaction Between Maintenance Tradesmen and Production Operators (See Also Section 9.2)

1. Do operators carry out any maintenance tasks? List and obtain detailed examples.
2. Do maintenance tradesmen operate production plant? List and obtain detailed examples.
3. Do maintenance tradesmen operate service plant (e.g., water treatment units, power units, air compressors)? List.
4. How close to each other are tradesmen and operators located? Do they work the same shifts?
5. Other than on the job, do they meet formally or informally, i.e., through:
   - joint production/productivity meetings?
   - quality circles?
   - daily or weekly plant performance reviews?
   - canteen, sports teams, social events?
   - joint training?

9.5 Assess Labour Skills Available (See Also Section 9.2)

1. What range of skills exists in each trade? Include both basic-trade and plant-specific skills.
2. What arrangements or plans exist for increasing, changing or broadening the tradesmen's skills?
3. How, when and by whom are personnel' skills reviewed?
4. How available are skilled tradesmen in the region?
5. How quickly are current skills likely to become obsolescent?
6. Is there any apprentice, new-starter, new-technology or updating training?
7. Carry out a skills audit – see Table A1–4 for an example of a plant-specific training audit. Select at least four units of plant (including the critical units selected under Section 3.1).

9.6 Establish the Human Factors Profile Within the Workforce

1. As a minimum, enquire into the sense of ownership, goodwill, motivation, morale, culture of relationships, and horizontal and vertical polarisation within the workforce (see Table 3–2 for a sample questionnaire).

9.7 Understand the Sizing of Tradegroups

1. How has the size of each group been determined—or has it just evolved?
2. When is the size reviewed and by whom?
3. What determines the number of non-tradesmen in the maintenance department? Establish how this has changed over the last few years.

9.8 Assess Utilisation of Performance Indicators

1. Establish whether any performance indicators are in use or could be calculated. For example:
   - Tradegroup utilisation
   - Tradeforce performance (would need some form of standard data)
   - Inter-trade flexibility index
   - Absenteeism
   - Overtime index
   - Tradeforce percentage turnover
   - Ratio of non-tradesmen to tradesmen
   - Ratio of production operators to maintainers
   - Per period, ratio of contractor hours to internal labour hours

9.9 Draw a Final Model of the Resource Structures

1. Using the information from Section 9.2 to 9.8 modify the initial model of the resource structure as necessary. On completion, use a narrative to explain its operation and essential characteristics. List the problems that have surfaced about the existing structure and your initial thoughts on improvements.

10.0 Model the Maintenance Adminstrative Structure

Draw up the so called '*organization chart*'. This section is concerned with the management structure from first level upwards. Nevertheless, the shop floor is shown on the diagram and coded to link with the plant layout and resource structure.

10.1 Model the Existing Administrative Structure

1. Obtain, or develop, a chart of the senior management structure (see Figure 5–3 as an example).
   Identify the most junior manager who is responsible for the entire maintenance activities (i.e., the '*manager in charge of maintenance*').
   Identify those managers who link with maintenance (e.g., in charge of production, purchasing, engineering).
   Identify, for interview, key roles in maintenance, production and other functions. Locate unusual spans of management.
2. Obtain, or develop, charts for lower levels of management and supervision (see Figure 5–11) mapping the positions of:
   - all maintenance personnel,
   - all production personnel,

- relevant purchasing or stores personnel,
- relevant engineering personnel.

3. Establish the type(s) of organization in use within the maintenance and production administrative structures. These could be:
   - line,
   - functional,
   - matrix (project),
   - product,
   - process,
   - geographical.

   Identify the levels of diversity and the impact of diversity on maintenance function. Obtain detailed inventory of maintenance staff at each level.

4. Identify whether any type of alliance has been set up with a contract organization. If so, show its position (linkage) on the administrative diagram.

   Establish how the alliance was set up and what functions and roles it is expected to perform.

   Ascertain the nature of the contract that covers the relationship between the company and the contractor.

10.2 Establish the Geographical Location of Relevant Administrative Staff

Identify them on the plant layout diagram.

10.3 Establish Degree of Decentralisation of Authority

1. Identify those management functions that are de-centralised and those that are not.
2. Check for benefits and disadvantages.

10.4 Establish Co-ordinating Mechanisms

1. Identify where a degree of departmentalisation indicates need for integration and co-ordination.
2. Identify normal regular relationships within the maintenance structure and between maintenance, production and others:
   - at middle management level,
   - at maintenance engineer level,
   - at supervisor level,
   - at planner level
3. Identify what co-ordinating mechanisms are used and relate to need for co-ordination above.

10.5 Identify Work Roles

1. Establish the senior maintenance manager's work role (see Table A1–5) and the work roles of several of his maintenance engineers (see Table A1–6)
2. Establish the chief engineer's and project engineer's work roles.
3. Establish the production or plant manager's work role.

4. Via information from these Steps 1 to 3 identify how the responsibilities for procuring, operating and maintaining and the plant have been divided — who owns the plant?

10.6 Map the Structure of the First Level of Management and its Relationship to the Resource Structure

1. Identify whether plant oriented operator-maintenance teams are used for first line maintenance. Establish the degree of self-empowerment in use. Is the lower order structure based on the traditional arrangement of *'supervisor, leading hands, and trade groups,'* or on *'facilitators, planners, advisors and team leaders'*

2. If the traditional structure is in use study the supervisor's work role and the planners work role. Also examine the inter-relationships within the structure and the relationships with production.

3. If self-empowered teams are in use (including operator-maintainer teams) study the way team objectives are set, the team leader is selected and the other duties are allocated. Establish the way the teams were set up and the training they received. Study the payment system, including overtime payment. Establish how the teams carry out their on-going planning function. Are there planners? Identify as far as possible how well the teams operate and list the problems.

10.7 Examine the Interface Between Operations and Maintenance

1. Do any production managers have the responsibility for directing and controlling any maintenance resources? If so, obtain 'job description' or further details of the scope of this responsibility, i.e.:
  - Identify links with the maintenance management.
  - Obtain views about this responsibility from production and maintenance staff.

2. Establish the degree and the method of co-operation and co-ordination at the following levels:
  - Long term planning of plant replacements and operating strategy.
  - Annual planning of plant or unit overhauls and shutdowns.
  - Weekly production planning.
  - Daily production priority setting and maintenance resource allocation..

3. Identify any joint production-maintenance performance reviews.

4. Ask maintenance about their successes, and their problems with production.

5. Ask production about their successes, and their problems with maintenance.

6. Establish whether any future developments to promote a closer linkage are anticipated?

10.8 Examine Interface Between Engineering Design, Development and Projects and Maintenance

1. What is the primary engineering activity outside the maintenance functions (design, development, project, construction?).

2. At what level do the two functions share the same manager?
3. Is the engineering function centered on-site or off-site?
4. Are capital asset management techniques and policies in operation (e.g., maintenance data feedback, joint problem solving, life cycle costing and trade-offs?).

10.9 Understand Shutdown Administration Arrangements (Links with Section 9.1.4)

1. What changes are made to the normal administrative structure to accommodate major shutdowns?
2. Establish whether a shutdown manager is seconded for the duration of the shutdown.
3. Map the typical shutdown administration. Is an executive committee appointed? Is there a planning and preparation team and how long before the shutdown is it appointed?

10.10 Identify the Human Factors (Links with Section 9.6, 10.7 and 10.8)

1. Establish the individual and group human factors impacting on the administrative structure.
   Use simple questionnaires to assist interviewing. The questionnaires should cover goodwill, morale, motivation, culture, polarisation.
   Also ask questions of the managers about the human factors influencing their first-level supervision and tradeforce.
   As far as possible, use some kind of rating scale to assess the strength of opinion (see Table 2–2)

10.11 Identify Performance Indicators

1. Establish whether any performance indicators are in use or could be calculated. For example:
   - Spans of management at senior management and supervisor level.
   - Levels of management.
   - Ratios of staff to shop floor.
   - Levels of absenteeism.
   - Ratios of first level management to shop floor.
   - Ratio of professional engineers to maintenance tradeforce.

11.0 Review Work Planning and Work Control

To be carried out after modelling the resource and administrative structure.

11.1 Review the Systems

1. From the resource structure determine the levels of planning (see, for example, Figure 5–8), e.g., shift (first-line), weekend (second line), workshop (third line) and shutdown (third line). Establish the linkages between the planning levels, in particular between the short-term systems (first and second line) and the shutdown systems.

2. Where possible, create a simple model to show the flow and storage of jobs within and between the different levels of planning. This will provide an appreciation of the overall operation of the planning systems (not shown for the FPP).

3. Identify the personnel concerned with planning in the administrative structure (see Figure 5–11).

4. Establish whether the planning system is computerised and identify the electronic interfaces between the system and stores/costing/shutdown planning. Is a network planning system in use and how does it link to the work order system?

5. Decide on the part(s) of the plant to be referred to in the detailed modelling of the work planning systems. Use the following guidelines:
   - Study shutdown planning separately from the short term systems.
   - Study the planning system for the workshops in conjunction with the rotable flow diagram (see Section 6.3.1).
   - Study short term planning by selecting one area tradegroup where it has been done well and one where it has been done poorly.

11.2 Model Short Term Work Planning and Work Control

1. Create a schematic of the short term planning system for the selected area tradegroup (see Figure 5–18 as an example). The form of the resource structure will have already determined the nature of their workload, i.e., whether they undertake first and second line work or whether the first line work is carried out by a separate group (operators or shift trades etc.).

   The model should show the flow of work coming into the tradeforce, how it is stored, the priority system, who plans it etc. An explanation is required of the levels of planning, time estimation, the use of job catalogues and the handling of multi-trade jobs..

   If a computer system is used, determine who uses it and how well it is used. Identify the meetings associated with planning, their function, composition and how well attended.

2. Map and understand the permit-to-work and isolation procedures. Establish how permit-to-work procedure links to work planning and scheduling.

3. Create a schematic of the short-term work control system. This should indicate the job storage system and information on future manpower levels, taking into consideration holidays and sickness.

4. Identify performance indicators. Establish if any are in use or could be calculated. For example:
   - Ratio of unplanned to planned work.
   - Percentage of planned work deferred each week.
   - Total outstanding workload in man-days.
   - Outstanding workload by priority in man-days.
   - Percentage of preventive routines completed per period.
   - Re-work as a percentage of all work.

5. Assess effectiveness of work planning and control.

Use the above models during interviews with those directly or indirectly concerned with planning to:
- Verify the accuracy of the models.
- Identify system problems.
- Ask for possible solutions to the identified problems.
- Discuss possible improvements to the system.

11.3 Review Shutdown Scheduling and Planning (Should Link with Sections 9.1.4 and 10.9)

The amount of effort put into this section will depend on the nature of the plant. For those that have complete shutdowns every few years shutdown procedure should be audited as a separate exercise (see Figure 5–19)

1. Identify the linkages with the on-going planning system.
2. Establish how the shutdown workscope is assembled.
   Include validation, freezing, pre-shutdown work and task specifications.
3. Establish the planning lead time.
4. Identify the planning procedures, both for internally executed work and for contractor packages. How are long-delivery items dealt with?
5. Establish how the shutdown schedule is assembled and what software (if any) is used. Discuss optimisation of the schedule and cost estimates. Discuss the safety and quality plan.
6. Draw up a schematic model of the shutdown planning system during the execution phase. Show linkages with the short-term planning system, workshop planning and contractors.
7. Refer to the model during interviews to discuss how the planning system operates, how extra work is defined and costed, how progress is monitored.
8. Refer to the model during interview to identify system problems and possible solutions.
9. Identify appropriate performance indicators, e.g.:
   - Percentage of planned work actually completed.
   - Actual cost as a percentage of budget.
   - Ratio of actual time out to planned duration, etc.

12.0 Review Maintenance Control

Where possible, use the plant units identified during Section 3.1 as the costing examples

12.1 Review Budgeting

1. Establish the budgeting process, including:
   - Frequency of budgeting.
   - Down to what level of management?
   - What resources are included?
   - Is the budget an estimate against last year's expenditure and next year's proposed activity?

- Is it a zero-budgeting exercise?
- Is it based on achieving agreed output factors (OEE, availability etc.).

12.2 Review Cost Control

1. Draw up a schematic of the inputs and outputs of the costing system (see Figure 1–19 for an example).
2. Identify the cost codes in use and establish whether they allow costs to be allocated at unit level of plant (or below).
3. Establish how rotables are costed.
4. Establish whether the financial system (the ledger) is electronically linked to the maintenance work order system.
5. Establish how major overhauls are costed.
6. Identify the main outputs from system, i.e., costs allocated against plant, unit, tradegroup, work type, resource or job.
7. Are the costs compared against budget estimates?
8. Are the costs linked in any way to output factors, e.g., to availability?
9. Are there any standard cost performance indicators, for example (and per period)
   - (Total maintenance cost)/(Total value of product)?
   - (Cost of spares used)/(Cost of labour)?

12.3 Review Plant Reliability Control (Maintenance Effectiveness)

1. Draw up a model of plant reliability control (see Figures 1–11 and 1–20 as examples).
2. Investigate the Level 1 system in more detail. Is there a pro-active effort to identify potential equipment faults? Is there a reactive system to determine the cause of the fault or potential fault and prescribe a solution? If possible, obtain examples.
3. Investigate the Level 2 system. How are hot spots identified? What linkages are there with the Level 1 system? How is the investigation of hot spots carried out—by permanent designated staff or by a seconded group (a purge arrangement)? If possible, obtain examples of the successful use of a Level 2 system.
4. Investigate the Level 3 system. Show how it links with the Level 2 system, the engineering section and the OEM. Does this work on a regular basis or only via the specification of new plant — or not at all? Does the OEM ever contact the company about equipment improvements?

12.4 Identify Indicators of Maintenance Organizational Efficiency (In Part, Covered in Sections 9.8, 10.11, 11.2 and 11.3)

1. Other possible measures include:
   - Job delay ratio.
   - Job delay profiling.
   - Training cost per tradesman.
   - Number of trades employed.

13.0 Review Spare Parts Supply and Storage

Restricted mainly to the linkage between maintenance and stores.

13.1 Review Stores Organizational Structure (Linked to Sections 9, 10 and 6.3)

1. Model the structure of stores resources (using the plant layout diagram to identify the number of stores, their location and function).
2. Ascertain the stores administrative structure—detailed from senior manager level down to storekeeper level. Show the linkage, if any, with the main administrative structure and the maintenance structure.

13.2 Assess the Stores Service

1. Establish whether the stores is open or closed and how it is manned outside weekday shifts.
2. Establish how easy it is to use the stores catalogue to identify spare parts and to requisition them from stores.
3. Establish how easy it is to find the stores location of a part.
4. Ask the tradeforce how good is the service they get from stores and where are the problems.
5. Establish the level of stock-outs and the main reasons for their occurrence

13.3 Review Inventory Policy

1. Establish the categorisation of parts for inventory purposes.
2. Identify any strategic policies for high-cost insurance parts.
3. How is the inventory policy established for slow-moving parts?
4. Identify the checks and balances for the re-ordering of high-cost parts.
5. Establish the extent to which consignment stock is used.
6. Have there been efforts to rationalise and modularise?
7. Establish who takes the decisions on the initial stock holding for new equipment. How is this carried out? Determine the procedure.
8. Who is responsible for setting the inventory policy and how is it reviewed—for slow movers, in particular?
9. Identify any software used to aid the setting of inventory policy, e.g., the nature of any EOQ calculations within standard stores packages. Does the stores software automatically review usage rates?

13.4 Review Stores Systems

1. Establish the procedure for reception of parts. Are they checked against specification? Are rotables included in this procedure?
2. Are the parts correctly identified? Do rotables have clear labelling?
3. Check the procedures for maintenance of parts in stock.

13.5 Identify Performance Indicators

1. Obtain an approximate value of the total parts in stock. What is the ratio of this to the plant replacement value?

2. Obtain an approximate value for the slow-moving items in stock and assess this as a percentage of the total value of the stock.

3. Assess the value of the annual turnover as a percentage of the total value of stock held.

4. Assess the stores administration costs as a percentage of the total value of stock held.

5. Evaluate the number of stock-outs per period.

14.0 Review Maintenance Documentation

Where possible, use the plant units identified in Section 3.1 as the vehicles for examples of documentation.

14.1 General

1. Establish whether the documentation system is computerised or paper-based.

2. If computerised, establish if there are any hardware problems affecting access or speed of response.

   Establish the name of the package, length of time in use.

   Does the system cover the maintenance department alone or is it electronically linked to other software; identify the links (financial, project management, stores purchasing, invoicing, human relations, document imaging etc.). Establish whether the links are interfaced or whether the package is integrated.

3. Identify all other software used within the maintenance department. Are there databases used in connection with shutdown maintenance that are not linked to the main system? Is there a separate E/I system? etc.

4. Identify the documentation functions that are not computerised, e.g., major shutdown history, case studies, library of manuals etc.

5. Develop a functional documentation model (see Figure 1–21).

6. Discuss the ease of use of the system with its users. What problems do they have? How good has their training been? How effective do they think the system is? How could the system be improved? Also try to get a feel of the human factors influencing data collection, e.g., attitude to using the computer, to data collection etc.

14.2 Review Plant Inventory

1. Establish whether the whole plant is covered. Understand and document the plant coding system.

14.3 Review the Plant Information Base

1. Establish the coverage and quality of the functions listed below. In each case check on their use and if they are being kept up to date. In the case of the manuals and drawings, check on the updating procedure for reviews and modifications (either from inside the company or via the OEM).

   Job catalogue and application parts list.

- Operating procedures.
- Life plans.
- Technical information.
- Manuals index (and library and condition of manuals if not computerised).
- Drawings index (and library if not computerised).
- Spare parts list per unit of equipment, and tracking procedures.
- History held per unit of equipment. How easy is it to interrogate? What information does it hold?

14.4 Review Preventive Maintenance Scheduling (Ties Up with Section 7.0)

1. Is the schedule based on calendar time, running hours, output, or some combination? How flexible is the schedule?
2. Can the schedule handle major shutdown work, if necessary? If yes, establish how well this is done.

14.5 Review Condition-Based-Maintenance Software (Ties Up with Section 5.0)

1. Establish the scheduling procedures and history that are used for the CBM techniques listed in Section 5.0. Does the main documentation software carry out this function or is it a separate but linked system? Or does each monitoring technique have stand-alone documentation?
2. Check the history for each monitoring technique in use. Is it comprehensive? Is it complete? Is it of a satisfactory quality?

14.6 Understand the Work Order System (Ties Up with Section 11.0)

1. Draw up a schematic tracing the flow, storage and the functions carried out by a work order, work request document (hard copy or electronic).
2. Establish how the preventive maintenance schedule and the condition monitoring system link into the work order system.
3. Understand the 'different states' in which a job can be, e.g., raised, waiting for parts etc. Understand the different ways in which jobs can be filed, e.g., against tradegroup, unit of plant, major shutdown etc.
4. Understand how the planner and/or team leader schedule work by the shift, day, week, (or by longer periods). Establish the flexibility of the procedure, e.g., can a schedule be changed rapidly to facilitate opportunity work?
5. Establish how the work order system is used during major shutdowns, in particular for cost collection and control.
6. Understand the network planning software and the software (if additional) used for major shutdown cost control.

14.7 Review Control Documentation

1. Check on the reports that are generated automatically and those that are available on request, e.g., cost information, organizational efficiency indices, 'Top-Tens' regarding low reliability, high maintenance cost etc.
2. Check on the ease of interrogating the information base.

TABLE A1–1 Summary of the Main Condition Monitoring Techniques

Type	Method	On-Line or Off-Line	Comments
1. Visual	Human eye	On	Covers a wide range of ad hoc methods. Surface inspection only.
2. Temperature	Optical probes	Off	Can be used for internal inspection of aero engines, steam turbines, chemical vessels, etc.
	Optical probes with television	Off	
	Temperature crayons and tapes.	On	Mainly surface temperature over a wide range of temperatures.
	Thermometers	On	Use of infra-red to monitor surface temperature of equipment surfaces. Covers a wide range of temperatures but limited area.
	Thermocouples		
	Infra-red meter		
	Infra-red scanner	On	As above but can cover much wider surface area. Can provide surface temperature picture and can be calibrated to give quantitative measure.
3. Lubricant monitoring	Magnetic plugs, filters	On	Analysis of debris picked up by plugs of filter in an oil washed system. Mainly large debris picked up, 100—1000 microns.
	Ferrography monitoring		Instrument to separate ferrous debris by size to enable microscopic examination. Non-ferrous debris also separated. Direct reading instrument also available. Wide range of debris size analysed, 3-100 microns.
	Spectroscopy		Spectrographic analysis of oil samples to determine elements present. Analysis for small debris size 0—10 microns. Contract service usually available.
4. Vibration	Total signal	On	Monitors vibration signal from rotating or reciprocating machine as an averaged number. Problems on one frequency can be masked by overall signal.

	Technique	On/Off	Description
	Frequency analysis	On	Records vibrations signal over wide frequency range (signature) and monitors. Can establish out of balance or roller element bearing problems.
	Shock pulse monitoring S pulse energy and kurtosis meter	On	All three techniques use high frequency signals for roller element bearing monitoring. Considerable experience built up in the use of SPM methods. SPM can also be used for leak detection.
5. Crack	Dye penetrant	On and off	Detects cracks bearing surface.
	Magnetic flux	On and off	Detects cracks at/near surface of ferrous materials.
	Electric resistance	On and off	Detects cracks at surface and can be used to estimate depth of crack
	Eddy current	On and off	Detects cracks near to surface. Also useful for inclusion and hardness, etc.
	Ultrasonic	On and off	Detects cracks anywhere in component. Directional sensitivity, therefore general searches lengthy. Use to back up other techniques.
	Radiography	Off	Detects cracks anywhere in component. Section and source (steel). Access to both sides of component necessary. Radiation hazard.
6. Corrosion monitoring	Weight loss coupons	Off	Coupons weighed when plant off-line.
	Corrosometer	On	Electrical element and potentiometer. Detects less than 1 mm corrosion loss.
	Polarisation resistance	On	Only indicates corrosion. No accuracy with estimate of rate.
	Pulse indicator holes	On	Indicates that present amount of corrosion has occurred.

TABLE A1–2 Summary of the Main In-Situ Repair Techniques

1. Inerting of flammable materials storages.
2. On-site machining.
3. Welding up and re-machining of items.
4. Flatness checking with monochromatic light.
5. Alignment checking/inspection with lasers.
6. Laser cutting/welding/cleaning.
7. Laser gas absorption (leak detection).
8. Repair of problem joints by correct gasket selection.
9. Leak sealing under pressure.
10. Pipe lining.
11. Pipe freezing.
12. Tube plugging.
13. Explosive repair techniques.
14. Hardfacing.
15. Brush planting.
16. Hot tapping.
17. Cold tapping.
18. On-line valve replacement.
19. Bolt tensioning.
20. Thread inserts.
21. Metal stitching.
22. Repair of floating tank roofs.
23. Repair of glass-lined vessels.
24. Cold forming materials.
25. Adhesives.
26. Concrete additives.
27. Grouting.
28. Jointable transmission belts.
29. Repair of electric cables with shrink insulation.
30. Special techniques.

TABLE A1–3 Extract from Table of Work Groups, their Location, Size, Scheduling and Function

Tradegroup	Location	Trade Mix and Size	Shift Roster	Work Function
Raw material processing (RMP) (a)	Mechanical shift workshop	8 fitters	4 Shifts covering 5 days plus days on every other weekend (Thus 2 fitters on weekday shifts)	Monday to Friday first line work in RMP. Every other weekend second line work plant wide

TABLE A1–4 Extract from the Check Sheet for the Mechanical Plant Specific Skills Audit

Plant area—Raw Materials Processing	Name _____
Equipment—Weiler Grinder	Position _____
Have you received any formal training on the operation and maintenance of this unit?	Yes ☐ No ☐
Who provided this training?	Original Equip Man. ☐ Training Dept ☐ Other ☐
How much time was involved?	Hours ☐

Check on the tradesman's knowledge of the following areas	In each check if:
Understanding of the start-up and shutdown procedures	Fully competent (FC) ☐
Understanding of the operational characteristics of the Grinder	Some experience (SE) ☐ Need training (NT)
His logical fault finding capabilities for the grinder	☐
Understanding of the routine maintenance and inspection procedure (Go through procedure with him checking his knowledge of the procedure and tolerances and checks)	☐
Understanding of the dis-assembly and re-assemebly of the feedscrew including checks and spacings	☐

TABLE A1–5 Auditing the Role of the Manager in Charge of Maintenance

1. Obtain copy of any written job description.
2. Personal objectives and targets: have these been discussed and agreed with job holder? How do they link with maintenance objectives?
3. Which of the following tasks is he responsible for? (Identify the key responsibilities)
   (a) Translation of the business objectives and plans into appropriate maintenance objectives and developing a maintenance strategy for all key physical assets on-site.
   (b) Organization of staff and management of all maintenance resources in accordance with the firm's current production, financial, personnel and other objectives and policies.
   (c) Ensuring appropriate co-ordination of maintenance and production short and medium term plans.
   (d) Ensuring the long-term availability, life and performance of the physical assets to meet business plans.
   (e) Monitoring, controlling and improving the overall performance of the maintenance function.
   (f) Ensuring co-operation of maintenance personnel with all interface functions
   (g) Identification and planning of the optimum long term (e.g., 10 year) development of the maintenance function.
   (h) Contributing as part of the senior management team to the pursuit of the firm's business plans, and to its policies for capital investment and replacement.
   (i) Developing his/her immediate sub-ordinates and encourage their promotion.
   (j) Any other responsibilities (please list).

(cont on p. 282)

4. Establish his level of authority. Is it commensurate with responsibility?
5. Establish his span of management and factors relating to wide/narrow spans, viz.:
   1. Similarity of function—the more similar the functions performed by the work group, the larger the span.
   2. Proximity—the closer a work group is located physically, the larger the span.
   3. Complexity of functions—the simpler and more repetitive the work functions performed by subordinates, the larger the span.
   4. Degree of direct supervision required—the less required, the larger the span.
   5. Degree of supervisory co-ordination required—the less required, the larger the span.
   6. Planning required of the manager—the less required, the larger the span.
   7. Organizational assistance available to the supervisor—the more assistance the supervisor receives in functions such as training, recruiting, and quality inspection, the larger the span.
6. What authority does the manager delegate to subordinates?
7. Which senior managers does the manager for maintenance respond to?
8. If more than one, examine proportion, frequency, conflicts, etc.
9. What does the manager actually control and how? What feedback is available? How does the manager check achievement against the above targets?
10. What is the frequency and method of communicating to subordinates and visa versa?
11. What proportion of time is spent on maintenance matters? Split between technical, administration, personnel.

TABLE A1–6 Auditing the Role of the Maintenance Engineer

---

1. Obtain copy of any written job description.
2. Establish personal objectives and targets—have these been discussed and agreed with job holder?
   How do they link with maintenance objective or his manager's objectives?
3. What are the engineer's responsibilities:
   (a) in technical matters?
   (b) in management/personnel matters?
   (c) in administrative matters?
   (d) in any other areas?
   Which of the above are the key responsibilities?
4. What authority has been delegated to the engineer in these key areas? Is it commensurate with the responsibility?
5. Is there any conflict between technical responsibilities and management/personnel responsibilities?
6. Establish the span of management and factors relating to wide/narrow spans.
7. What authority is delegated to subordinates?
8. Which senior managers does the maintenance engineer report to?
9. If more than one, examine proportion, frequency, conflicts, etc.
10. What does the maintenance engineer actually control and how? What feedback is available?
    How does he check achievement against the above targets?
11. What is the frequency and method of communicating to subordinates, and vice-versa?
12. What proportion of time is spent on maintenance matters? Establish the split between technical, administration, personnel.

APPENDIX 2

Information Requested prior to the Site Visit

(This is an illustrative extract only; it is not the full list. Figures and Tables are given at the end)

Please Provide the Following

1. A simple map of your plant showing the location of the maintenance trade groups. Also show the location of the stores and sub-stores (see Figure A2–1 for an example. The letters indicate the different trade groups, e.g., 'h' indicates the power station mechanical group). Also provide an outline process flow diagram (see Figure A2–2 for an example).

2. The location, composition, shift roster and function of each group—using a list of the type shown in Table A2–1.

3. An outline of the structure of your administration, from Chief Executive downwards, using a diagram of the kind shown in Figure A2–3. This is only needed in detail for the plant areas covered by the audit. However, it would be useful to receive an outline of the structure of your *senior* management for the whole company. Also note how the trade group identification letters have been used to link the diagrams. *This structural outline is needed as soon as possible because it enables us to decide who we want to interview.*

4. A complete inventory of the shop floor personnel and the management, as in Tables A2–2(a) and (b).

5. A sample of the job descriptions (if any have been drawn up) for each level of management (down to supervisor level).

6. **(a)** An estimate of the average weekly level of overtime, and of its variability over the year, worked by the trade groups listed in Table A2–2(a).

   (b) An estimate of the average weekly level of contract labour employed (main trades only) and of its variability over the year?

7. A nomination, for *each* of the main areas of your plant covered by the audit, of two important units (a compressor and a reaction unit, say) and the following information about them:
   - Schedule of lubrication.
   - Schedule of inspections, both simple and sophisticated (e.g., vibration monitoring).

283

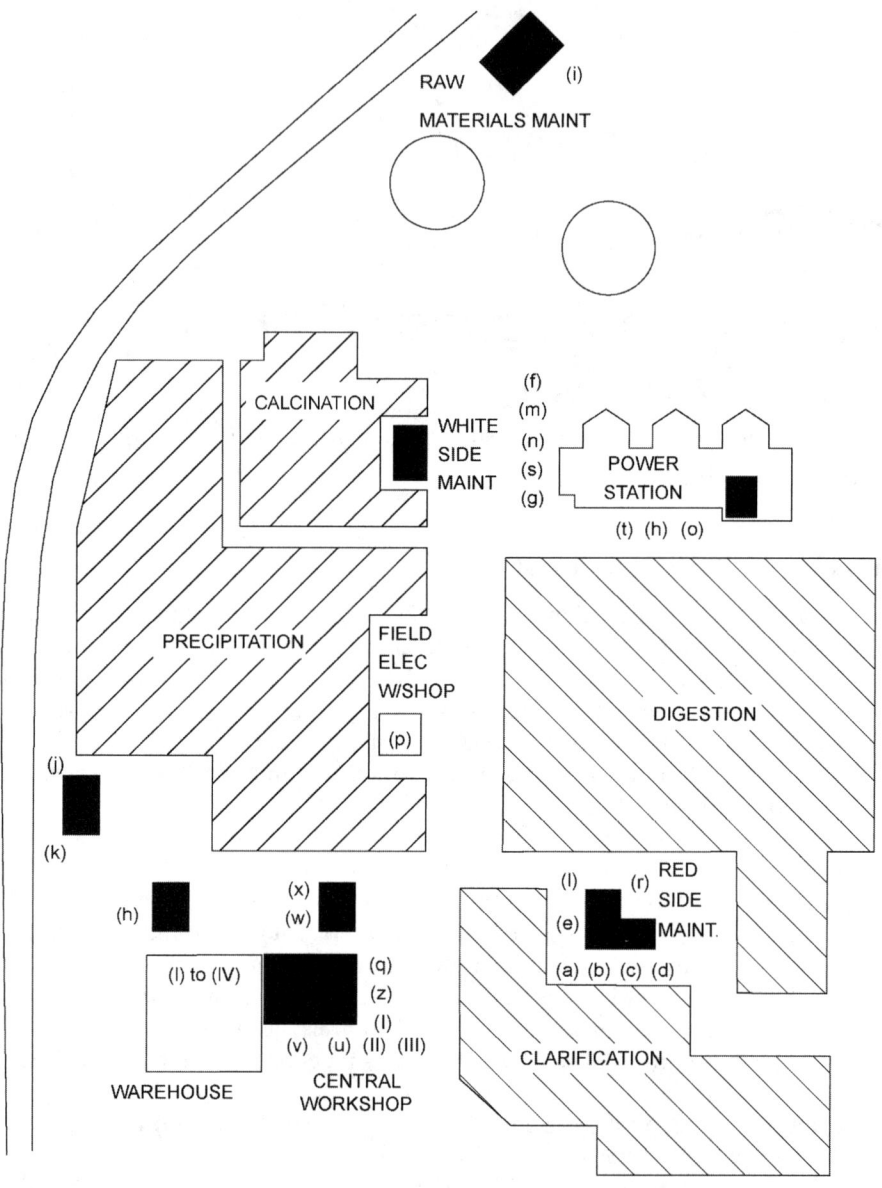

Letters indicate location of trade groups eg. (i)= Raw materials fitting group (see Figure 4.3)

FIGURE A2–1 Plant Layout

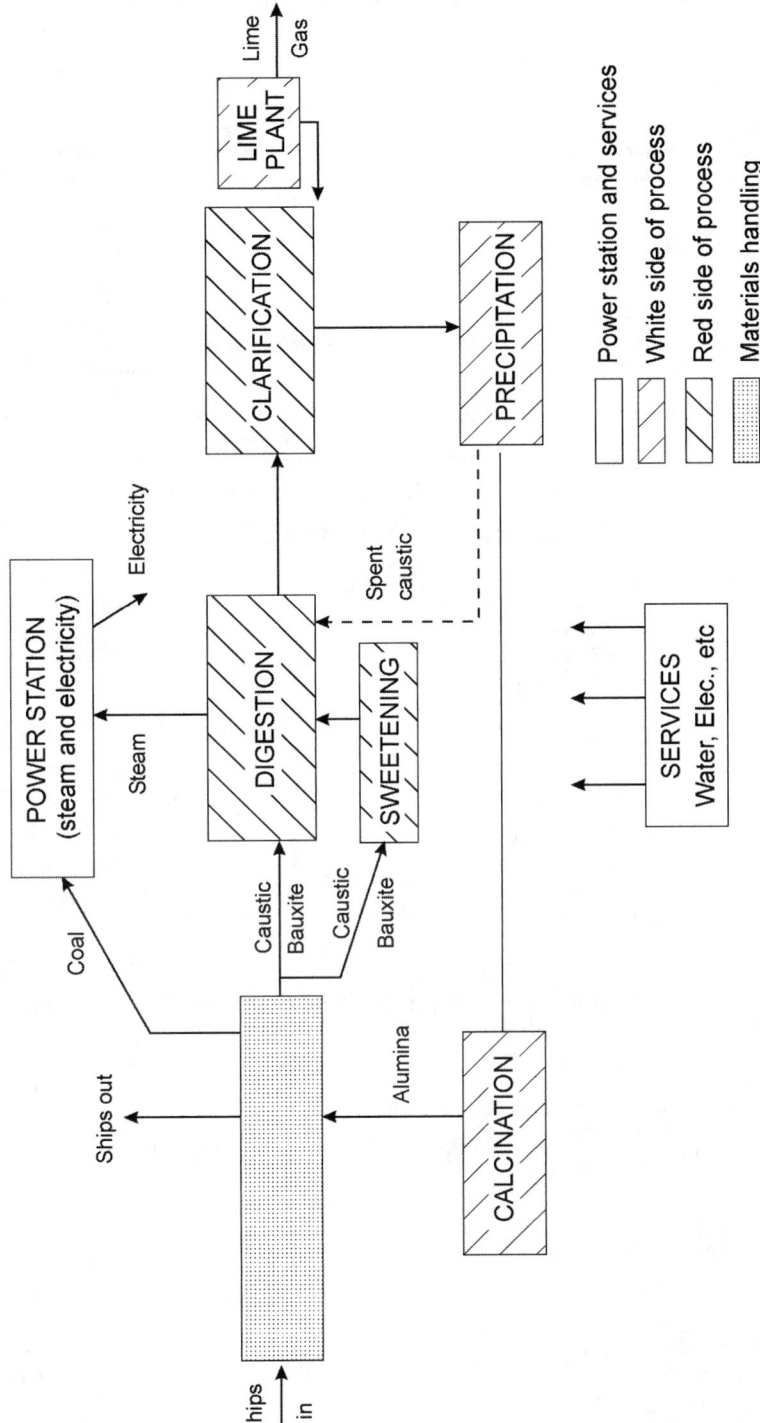

FIGURE A2-2 Alumina Refinery Process Flow Diagram

TABLE A2–1 Extract from Table of Work Groups, Their Location, Size, Scheduling and Function

Tradegroup	Location	Trade Mix and Size	Shift Roster	Work Function
Raw materials mechanical (group i)	Wharf area workshop	24 fitters	6 fitters on a 4 × 7 shift roster	On Monday to Friday day shift, material handling equipment—second line work. On all other shifts plant wide first line work, other than where there is local cover.
Raw materials electrical (group n)	Wharf area workshop	3 electricians	Days	Material handling equipment, first and second line work.
Boiler house mechanical (group h)	Boiler house mechanical workshop	18 fitters	6 fitters on a 3 × 5 shift roster	First and second line cover for boiler house Monday to Friday.

TABLE A2–2a Tradeforce Inventory

Trades	
Fitters	194
Welders	16
Electricians	35
Inst. Tech.	29
Total	274
Non-trades (RW)	
Trades assistants	22
Lubrication	6
Crane drivers	7
Scaffolding	12
De-scale and others	74
Total	121
Total waged	395

TABLE A2–2b Staff Inventory (for Salaried Maintenance Personnel, 1995)

Engineering managers			12
Engineers (including allowance for plant engineering support)			17
Supervisors	Direct	43	
	Planning	9	
	Training	4	
	Total		56
Clerical			4
Total staff			89
Simple indices			
Trade/non-trades +			8.0
Waged/salaried			4.4
Waged/direct supv			9.2
Waged/planning supv			4.4
Waged/total supv			7.1

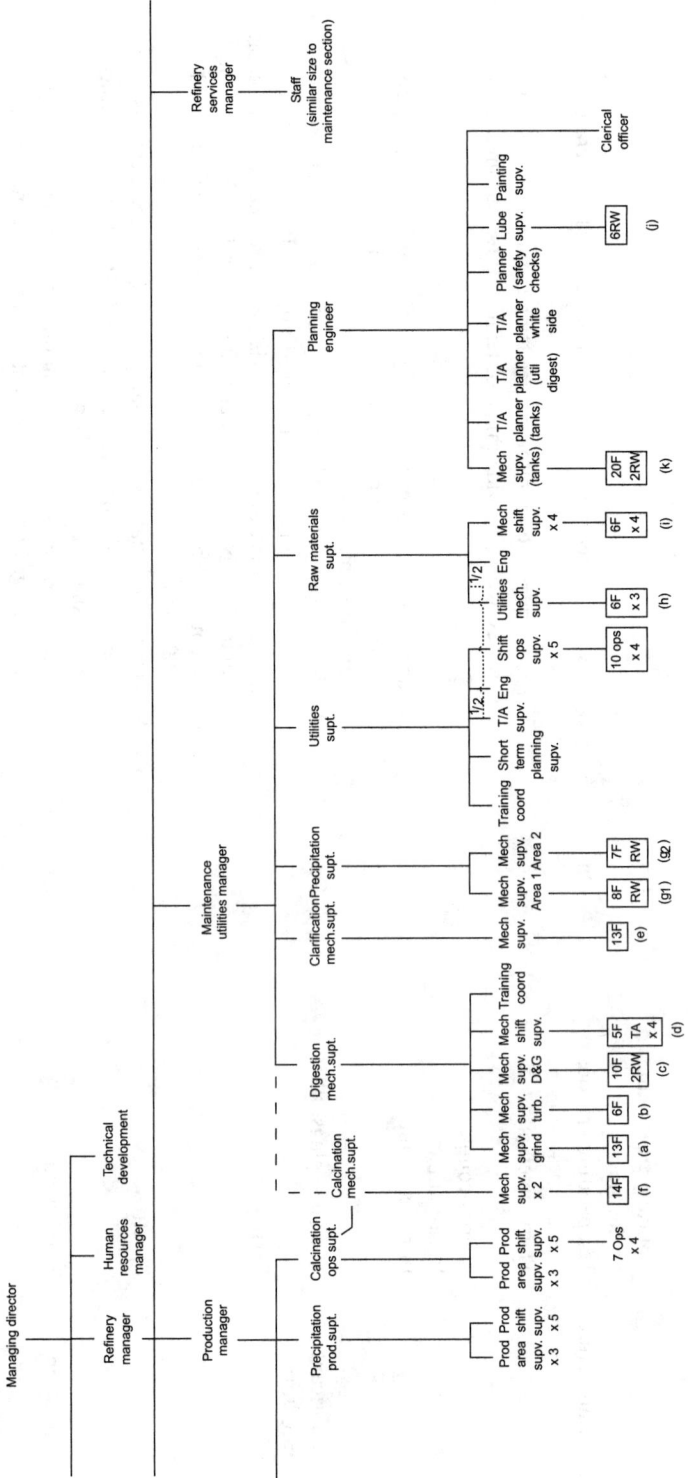

FIGURE A2–3 Alumina Refinery Administrative Structure (Extract Only)

TABLE A2–3 Summary of the main Condition Monitoring Techniques (see reference on Page 290)

Type	Method	On-Line or Off-Line	Comments
1. Visual	Human eye	On	Covers a wide range of ad hoc methods. Surface inspection only.
	Optical probes	Off	Can be used for internal inspection of aero engines, steam turbines, chemical vessels, etc.
	Optical probes with television	Off	
2. Temperature	Temperature crayons and tapes.	On	Mainly surface temperature over a wide range of temperatures.
	Thermometers	On	Use of infra-red to monitor surface temperature of equipment surfaces. Covers a wide range of temperatures but limited area.
	Thermocouples Infra-red meter		
	Infra-red scanner	On	As above but can cover much wider surface area. Can provide surface temperature picture and can be calibrated to give quantitative measure.
3. Lubricant monitoring	Magnetic plugs, filters	On	Analysis of debris picked up by plugs of filter in an oil washed system. Mainly large debris picked up, 100–1000 microns.
	Ferrography		Instrument to separate ferrous debris by size to enable microscopic examination. Non-ferrous debris also separated. Direct reading instrument also available. Wide range of debris size analysed, 3–100 microns.
	Spectroscopy		Spectrographic analysis of oil samples to determine elements present. Analysis for small debris size 0–10 microns. Contract service usually available.
4. Vibration	Total signal	On	Monitors vibration signal from rotating or reciprocating machine as an averaged number. Problems on one frequency can be masked by overall signal.

(Continued)

TABLE A2-3 (*Continued*)

Type	Method	On-Line or Off-Line	Comments
	Frequency analysis	On	Records vibrations signal over wide frequency range (signature) and monitors. Can establish out of balance or roller element bearing problems.
	Shock pulse monitoring S pulse energy and kurtosis meter	On	All three techniques use high frequency signals for roller element bearing monitoring. Considerable experience built up in the use of SPM methods. SPM can also be used for leak detection.
5. Crack	Dye penetrant	On and off	Detects cracks bearing surface.
	Magnetic flux	On and off	Detects cracks at/near surface of ferrous materials.
	Electric resistance	On and off	Detects cracks at surface and can be used to estimate depth of crack
	Eddy current	On and off	Detects cracks near to surface. Also useful for inclusion and hardness, etc.
	Ultrasonic	On and off	Detects cracks anywhere in component. Directional sensitivity, therefore general searches lengthy. Use to back up other techniques.
	Radiography	Off	Detects cracks anywhere in component. Section and source (steel). Access to both sides of component necessary. Radiation hazard.
6. Corrosion monitoring	Weight loss coupons	Off	Coupons weighed when plant off-line.
	Corrosometer	On	Electrical element and potentiometer. Detects less than 1 mm corrosion loss.
	Polarisation resistance	On	Only indicates corrosion. No accuracy with estimate of rate.
	Pulse indicator holes	On	Indicates that present amount of corrosion has occurred.

- List of services.
- Schedule of major maintenance (How often does the unit come off for major work? Is the frequency governed by inspection needs or is it time or usage based? List the main work carried out).
- Relevant spares held in stores.
- Any written specifications—regarding method, spares list etc.—for standard jobs.
- An extract from the history record.
- The downtime record (if any) over the last year.
- The cost record (if any) over the last year.

8. A list (see Table A2–3) of the condition monitoring techniques in use at your company.

9. For one of the main plant areas, the following information, which we need in order to arrive at an understanding of your maintenance work planning system(s):

   (a) A list of formal and informal meetings regarding maintenance work planning. What is the function of each one? Who is present? Who is in the chair? What are the outputs?

   (b) An outline of your job priority procedure.

   (c) Whether you estimate job times.

   (d) Whether you pre-plan before a job request goes into the work file?

   (e) Examples of: a work order/request (if hard copy); a shift report; a work programme.

   (f) Whether you keep a work backlog. If you do, an example, and whether it can be listed by unit, priority or supervisor. Provide an example

   (g) Examples of any other work control or planning control indices, e.g., the percentage of the work planned for this period which was actually completed.

10. The following information regarding your costing system:

    (a) An example of your cost codes.

    (b) Whether the system is able to evaluate the maintenance costs—down to unit (e.g., compressor) level, say—over a specified period (one month, one quarter, one year).

    (c) Whether you record the downtime (or any other measure of reliability) of the main units or sections of plant. If so, an example.

11. **(a)** A list of the units of plant that incur high maintenance costs.

    (b) A list of the units of plant that cause reliability problems.

12. Any other indices or data that you monitor, e.g., labour productivity, overtime, absenteeism etc.

13. The output from each of your plants in tons/year/month. The total cost of maintenance per annum and its division into the total cost of (a) labour and (b) material.

14. As clear a picture as possible of the maintenance workload pattern for each of the main trade groups in each of the main plant areas. Ideally, the data should be taken from your records, but if these are not available please provide your 'best estimates' (although we understand that this may be difficult).

The Auditors Responsibilities will be Divided as Follows:

AK—Plant operation, life plans and PM schedule, on-going work planning systems.

HSR—Objectives, work load, organization.

TL—Shutdown planning.

DH—Condition based maintenance.

Please indicate the key personnel that each of the above auditors should interview in their respective areas. It would also be helpful to establish the availability of these people as soon as possible.

APPENDIX 3

Maintenance Terminology

Definitions are given below of some of the more important terms used in this book. They are broadly in line with those given in the British Standards publication BS 3811:1984, but some have been significantly amended or extended by the author. The list does not include definitions already given clearly in the main text.

Maintenance	The combination of all technical and associated administrative actions intended to retain an item in, or restore it to, a state in which it can perform its required function.
Preventive maintenance	The maintenance carried out at pre-determined intervals, or corresponding to prescribed criteria, and intended to reduce the probability of failure or the performance degradation of an item. Preventive maintenance is planned and scheduled (or carried out on opportunity).
Condition-based maintenance	The preventive maintenance initiated as a result of knowledge of the condition of an item derived from periodic, routine or continuous monitoring.
Condition monitoring	This periodic, routine, or continuous measurement and interpretation of data to indicate the condition of an item.
Corrective maintenance	The maintenance carried out after a failure has occurred and intended to restore an item to a state in which it can perform its required function. Corrective maintenance can be planned and scheduled.
Emergency maintenance	The corrective maintenance which it is necessary to put in hand immediately to avoid serious consequences. Thus, emergency maintenance cannot be scheduled. In some cases, however, it can be planned for by ensuring that decision guidelines have been prepared and that necessary resources will be available.
Unit life plan	The programme of preventive maintenance work to be carried out on a unit of plant unit over its entire life.

Preventive maintenance schedule	A schedule of preventive maintenance work for the whole of a plant (or plant section). The schedule is a listing of jobs, with trades, against plant units and dates.
Maintenance window	The opportunity to carry out off-line maintenance on a plant without incurring production loss. Windows can arise at plant, unit or item level.
On-line maintenance	Maintenance which can be carried out while the plant or unit is in use (also called *running maintenance*).
Off-line maintenance	Maintenance which can only be carried out when the plant or unit is not in use.

Review Questions

Chapter 1

Review question 1–1

"The resource structure should be designed to match the workload in the most efficient way". Discuss possible ways to make the matching of the resources to the workload more efficient.

Review question 1–2

The resource structure has been drawn on two separate diagrams. Redraw the resource structure as a single diagram. Discuss the advantages of the resource structure drawn this way.

Review question 1–3

The work planning model of Figure 1–17 has been drawn using information from the resource structure and the administrative structure. In order to get a better understanding of the operation of the work planning model, carry out the following exercises:

(a) Sketch on Figure 1–16 the first line and the second line of work flow from origination (say an operator) to completion. In the case of an emergency job, the completion will be by a shift tradesman and in the case of a second line job- by the weekend tradegroup (not shown on Figure 1–16).

(b) Repeat the above exercise using the resource structure (instead of the administrative structure) you drew for Review question 1–2.

Review question 1–4

Explain the relationship between the maintenance objective, maintenance key performance indices (KPIs) and inter-firm comparison indices.

Review question 1–5

Go through the audit of the FPP and make a list of the main elements you would include in an audit procedure. Select one of the elements and list the information (models, indices, and other data) you would require to adequately describe its operation and its potential problems. When you have completed this task, compare your list with the audit aide memoir of Appendix 1.

Review question 1–6

The sales department of the FPP wanted to increase output and the production department agreed to do this. Explain the effect this had on the following:

Unit life plans.
Preventive schedule.
Maintenance workload.
Maintenance organization.
Work planning

Review question 1–7

Use your answer to Review question 1–6 to help you explain to your Managing Director the concept of the 'strategic maintenance management thought process'.

Chapter 2
Review question 2–1

Define 'human factors' in maintenance.

Review question 2–2

List the main 'individual' and 'group' human factors that can affect the performance of maintenance work.

Review question 2–3

Explain how the trend toward outsourcing maintenance work and the setting up of company-contractor alliances to carry out maintenance work has affected human factors within organizations.

Review question 2–4

Construct a 'human factors' questionnaire to help you to audit the maintenance tradesmen of your own company.

Review question 2–5

To answer this review question you will need to refer to the fingerprint audit of the aluminum rolling mill and in particular Figure 7–9. The company had recently moved from a functional organization to an organization based on small manufacturing units. Identify the possible negative and positive human factor changes that could (or did) occur as a result of this reorganization,

Chapter 3
Review question 1–3

You have been asked by your Managing Director to write out a specification for a full maintenance audit of your company. List the main points you would include in the specification.

Review question 3–2

You are a senior consultant in a maintenance management partnership. You have been commissioned to carry out a full audit of Fertec A- see Chapter 5. The site is located two hours away by air. Make a list of the essential preliminary information you would like collected and sent to you before the on-site data collection begins. Assume you have not seen this particular plant but you are familiar with agro-chemical plants.

Review question 3–3

Refer to Figure 3–3 and explain why it is necessary to build the resource structure and the administrative structure before building the work planning model.

Review question 3–4

Table 3.4 is the interview/data collection schedule that was used for day two and day three of the Fertec audit (see chapter 5). Use this schedule in conjunction with the aide-memoir and the administrative diagrams of Chapter 5 to set up an interview schedule for day four.

Review question 3–5

You are a Senior Consultant carrying out on-site interviewing as part of a full audit of Fertec A- see Chapter 5. Tomorrow, you are scheduled to interview the Ammonia Mechanical Engineer (see Figure 5–11) about the maintenance life plans and maintenance strategy he has set up for the Ammonia Plant (see Figures 5–2 and 5–5). The interview is scheduled to last for 90 minutes, after which he goes on holiday. Make a list of the main questions you intend to ask him in order of importance. You already have an understanding of the way the whole complex operates from the Manufacturing Manager.

Chapter 4

Review question 4–1

Assemble a list of the essential information you consider necessary to benchmark the maintenance practices of your own company against a similar company regarded to have the 'best of the best' maintenance practices.

Review question 4–2

Refer to the case study of self directed work teams discussed in this chapter. Fertec A clearly had problems while Cario was operating well. It could be argued that Fertec B was always going to find it more difficult to operate teams successfully than Cario. What was the 'key difference' between these companies that might justify this statement? Do you consider this 'key difference' flawed the benchmarking exercise?

Review question 4–3

(a) Define the following terms:
Maintenance objective.
Key performance indices.
Inter-firm comparison indices.
Benchmarks.
(b) Outline the relationships between the terms listed in (a).

Chapter 5

Review question 5–1

List some of the key information that you need to collect to understand the overall operation and management of the plant (the first stage of the audit is to try to get a top-down feel for the operation of the plant).

Review question 5–2

How do the three fundamental questions that the audit had to answer relate to Figure 1–5?

Review question 5–3
Carry out an internet search to see if you can find out more about 'management by objectives'- in particular maintenance management by objectives.

Review question 5–4
By using Figure 5–4 and Figure 5–11 propose some typical KPIs that you would expect to see being used at the Plant Manger level, the Mechanical Engineer level and at the Maintenance Team level.

Review question 5–5
(a) Write down a brief description of the maintenance strategy for the Ammonia Plant. Identify the key factors that influence the selection of this strategy.
(b) Write down a brief description of the maintenance life plan for a pressure vessel.
(c) List the personnel you would schedule into an interview program to obtain information about the Ammonia Plant strategy and pressure vessel life plans.

Review question 5–6
With reference to Figure 5–7 (four year operating pattern) define 'opportunity scheduling' and what it might help Fertec improve plant availability.

Review question 5–7
Assume you have gathered sufficient information to draw the resource structure shown in Figure 5–8. Now list the main information you need to collect to provide a comprehensive picture of the characteristics of the tradeforce. Refer to Figure 5–11 to indicate who you would want to interview to provide you with this information.

Review question 5–8
The resource structure of Figure 5–10 has been proposed to overcome the problems of the original resource structure of Figure 5–8. How do you think these changes to the resource structure will affect the administrative structure (you might like to refer to the methodology model shown in Figure 1–3)?

Review question 5–9
Discuss the main advantages of the revised resource structure Figure 5–10 over the original structure Figure 5–8.

Review question 5–10
(a) With reference to Figure 5–11, Figure 5–13 and Figure 5–14, explain what you understand by matrix structures. How are the responsibilities for the engineering and maintenance of the Ammonia Plant allocated?
(b) In order to get a full explanation of electrical maintenance within the Ammonia Plant, who would you interview?

Review question 5–11

The workload profile show in Figure 5–17 was a simple estimate (by agreement with Fertec not a great deal of effort was put into this part of the audit) as it would have been time consuming and increased the audit cost. Assume you have been commissioned as part of an audit to establish an accurate workload profile. Explain what difficulties you might encounter.

Review question 5–12

The workload profile indicated that the first and the second line work was costing almost twice as much as the third line work (carried out in the shutdowns). Explain how you would go about reducing the level and cost of the first and the second line work.

Review question 5–13

Draw a work planning model for the proposed resource structure of Figure 5–10 and the proposed administrative structure of Figure 5–16. Use the work planning model of Figure 5–18 as a template, i.e. your model should be drawn in the same style as Figure 5–18.

Review question 5–14

The audit of the Stores was limited to 'establishing how good the stores system was in giving the maintenance department the service it needed'. Bearing this statement in mind, make out a list of who you would interview to provide you with this information.

Review question 5–15

The actual audit report included an executive summary. Read through the audit and list the main points and diagrams you would include in the executive summary.

Chapter 6

Review question 6–1

The COALCOM audit was regarded as a 'snapshot' taking only five man days of onsite data collection time. Read through the audit and indicate the elements of the methodology that have been covered in depth and the elements that have been covered to provide an overview.

Review question 6–2

In spite of being 'production limited' COALCOM used two mid-week downshifts rather than the weekends to carry out the second line maintenance. Why did they do this? Do you think this policy is acceptable?

Review question 6–3

The snapshot audit proposed the administrative structure shown in Figure 6–9. Particular emphasis was placed on making the Equipment Supervisors responsible and setting up a kind of matrix structure, namely:

Under normal operation the shift trades report to the Shift Supervisor and the day trades to the respective workshop supervisors. During down days all trades report to the respective equipment supervisor, e.g. the Longwall Supervisor.

The re-audit showed that this approach had not been adopted. Examine Figure 6–12 and explain what structure was being used and why it was not working well. Do you consider Figure 6–13 clarified sufficiently the way I expected the administration to work?

Review question 6–4

Many of the key recommendations of the snapshot audit had not been adopted e.g. the recommendation incorporated in Figure 6–10. Discuss what you consider were the main reason(s) for this.

Chapter 7
Review question 7–1

The BOTPLANT audit was regarded as a 'fingerprint audit' taking one man day of onsite data collection time. Read through the audit and indicate how the audit methodology has been streamlined.

Review question 7–2

(a) Outline the 'maintenance advantages' BOTPLANT hoped to achieve by using the organization modeled in Figure 7–2 and Figure 7–3.

(b) Explain why BOTPLANT did not achieve these hoped for advantages.

(c) What advice would you give to a company embarking on the kind of organizational change carried out by BOTPLANT?

Review question 7–3

ALROM carried out the same kind of organizational change as BOTPLANT but they had a good maintenance system in place before the change. Nevertheless, they still had serious maintenance/reliability problems in the Hotmill area due in part to a poor plant reliability control (PRC) system. A lot of companies decentralizing into manufacturing units have problems with PRC.

(a) Describe what you consider to be the key reasons for these problems

(b) Outline what you consider to be the best way of overcoming these problems.

Note: In order to answer this question you may have to refer back to Figure 1–11 and Figure 1–20 to understand the idea of PRC.

Chapter 8
Review question 8–1

The resource structure is about matching the resources to the workload in the most efficient way. With reference to Figure 8–5, identify the main ways in which the matching was improved in the proposed structure of Figure 8–10.

Review question 8–2

With reference to Figure 8–10, explain the concept of the 'cascade resource structure' and its advantages over Figure 8–5.

Review question 8–3

Explain how the 'plant responsibility model' of figure 8–9 can help in understanding the operation of the administration.

Review question 8–4

Explain how the administrative structure model of Figure 8–8 can assist the auditor in understanding the operation of the administration.

Review question 8–5

With reference to the proposed redesigned administrative structure of Figure 8–11, identify the main changes:

(a) at senior management level

within each manufacturing unit

(b) Comment on whether these organizational changes will require a radical redesign of the work planning system.

Review question 8–6

The operation of an Alumina Refinery means there are no refinery level maintenance windows. The plant has been designed to enable 'major lines/units' to be taken off-line for maintenance without serious disruption to production. Hence, the maintenance strategy is based on the fixed-time-maintenance schedule shown in Figure 8–4. The schedule has been set up to smooth the maintenance workload over the year.

A comment was made in the strategy section of the audit that 'the production department was not adhering to the schedule'. Comment on the effect this might have on the resource structure and on the work planning system.

Chapter 9

Review question 9–1

(a) Identify the key characteristics that help to make a success of alliances between an industrial company and a contract maintenance company for carrying out the day to day maintenance work of the industrial company.

(b) Would you consider forming a company-contractor alliance to carry out the maintenance work of the Alumina Refinery of chapter 8? Give the reasons for your answer.

Review question 9–2

Chemtow, over a period of 15 years, followed the USA and UK maintenance organizational trends. List these trends in chronological order.

Review question 9–3

(a) Wither reference to Figure 9–9 and Figure 9–10, describe the way in which the responsibilities for maintenance work have been divided between Chemtow and its alliance partner.

(b) Explain how this division of responsibilities for maintenance work affects the nature of the contract between Chemtow and its alliance partner.

Chapter 10

Review question 10–1

Explain the reason why condition-based-maintenance was the preferred strategy for the Greenmix plant while fixed-time maintenance appeared to be the preferred strategy for the Ring Furnace.

Chapter 11

Review question 11–1

With reference to Figure 11–1, comment on which part of the operation is most likely to be 'production critical'.

Review question 11–2

With reference to figure 11–2, define availability for the bus fleet.

Review question 11–3

About the time the author audited this UK city bus fleet, he also had the opportunity to discuss the way in which a USA city maintained their bus fleet. (The size of the fleet was comparable.)

One of the key differences was that the USA transport authority had only one make of bus and far fewer types of major components (engines, gearboxes, etc). Discuss the 'maintenance advantages' of this policy.

Chapter 12

Review question 12–1

With reference to Case Study 6, discuss the concept of the strategic thought process –see Figure 1–26.

Model Answers to the Review Questions

Chapter 1

Review question 1–1

Reduce the number of trades on shift to match the true first line workload. Employ a separate group of trades working 2×12 hr weekend shifts plus overtime as necessary (this may not be politically possible but it illustrates the idea of matching resources to the workload).

Review question 1–2

The model should be redrawn with the weekend 'planned maintenance group' below the second line day group. The way the shift group 'rotates' into the weekend group should be indicated on the model. Drawn in this way it is much easier to visualize the operation of the resource structure and the work planning system.

Review question 1–3

Self evident.

Review question 1–4

Maintenance objectives come first (both at plant level and if necessary at unit-level- see Figure 1.5). From these objectives, KPIs can be established, e.g. availability, tradeforce utilization, etc. These can be monitored to establish if they are getting better or worse. This provides a means of controlling the maintenance performance of a company. Inter-firm comparison indices can be derived from KPIs to compare the performance across companies.

Review question 1–5

See the aide-memoir of Appendix 1.

Review question 1–6

The effect of the change in the operation pattern is explained in Table 1–4 and in the text from page 28 to 31.

Review question 1–7

Explained under the section entitled, "The Strategic Thought Process". Although the audit is important in mapping the structure, life plans, organization structure etc. it is also important to use the strategic thought process to visualize and understand the overall operation of the production-maintenance system.

Chapter Two

Review question 2–1

Characteristics which define the way in which an individual or group behaves or acts in an industrial setting can be called human factors. Those that influence the way the maintenance department operates are termed 'maintenance management human factors'.

Review question 2–2

Individual characteristics: ownership, goodwill, motivation. Group characteristics: culture, esprit de corps, polarization.

Review question 2–3

Discussed in the section entitled, "The effect of outsourcing on alliances". The most important influence has been to decrease the tradesmen's sense of equipment ownership. It can also create polarization between the operators/tradesmen employed by the company and the alliance tradesmen.

Review question 2–4

Use Table 2–2 as a template but identify those human factors you believe are important in your own company.

Review question 2–5

Possible human factor changes:

Improved equipment ownership via the first line maintainers, the operators and the teams.

Improved esprit de corps within the manufacturing unit.

Reduced production-maintenance polarization within the manufacturing units.

Possible negative human factor changes:

Increased parochialism within the manufacturing unit.

Increased polarization between the manufacturing units and the centralized groups.

Chapter 3

Review question 3–1

Refer to section entitled (A) Audit Specification.

The main points must include:

The audit objective, i.e. what do you want to achieve from carrying out the audit? This must be clearly stated.

The audit scope- perhaps better described as 'breadth". Do you want all the plant(s) covered or the 'problem plants'?

The depth- you need to give an indication of the detail you require the audit to cover, for example, do you just want a model of the resource structure or, in addition, an in depth review of skills, flexibility, human factors and so on.

Review Question 3–2

Using Appendix 2 as a template, I would tailor this questionnaire to suit the audit specification. Bear in mind that some of the information is needed to help you to set up the audit data collection schedule, e.g. see Question 2 of Appendix 2. You need sufficient information from this questionnaire to help you to complete a fingerprint audit by the end of the first day on site, i.e. plant layout diagram, outline process flow models, an understanding of the maintenance strategy, a preliminary resource structure, an outline administrative structure and a simple work planning model.

Review Question 3–3
The work planning model is built around the resource structure and the administrative structure. Thus, the resource structure and administrative structure are required first. This is also the reason for completing the fingerprint audit on Day 1. Refer to the Fertec audit of chapter 5 to understand the dependence of the work planning model (See Figure 5–18) on the resource structure (See Figure 5–8)

Review question 3–4
I accept this is difficult to set up without a more detailed knowledge of the plant and the personnel. However, you can see from Table 3–4 and Figure 3–3 (also the aide- memoir) that the next stage of the audit is to collect further information about the life plans and preventive schedule (AK) and (HSR) moves onto the administrative structure. The main purpose of this review question is to make you think about the data you need, the order in which it is best collected and who and when to interview. The nest step (see Review question 3–5) is to prepare yourself for the interview.

Review question 3–5
You should take your guideline for the interview from the aide-memoir. Remember, you should already know the way the Ammonia plant is operated which gives you a good indication of the existing strategy. Using Figure 5–5 ask the Ammonia Plant Engineer to identify at least two typical key units of plant and then go through 3–1 to 3–5. Talk in outline about the condition monitoring techniques in use; see section 5 before concentrating on section 7 and in particular 7–4. Ask the Engineer who he considers you should talk to in order to get additional information about the life plans and other information with which he cannot help you.

Chapter 4
Review question 4–1
Such a list should include the numeric benchmarks and also the non-numeric benchmarks, e.g. a resource structure model.

The **numeric benchmarks** are best thought of with reference to Figure 4–11. The key indices are clearly those of maintenance productivity, maintenance effectiveness and organizational efficiency.

The aide-memoir has a number of indices at the end of each main section (See 10–17)

The essential **non-numeric benchmarks** would include:
A workload mapping.
The plant operating pattern

The resource structure
The administrative structure

Review question 4–2

The essential difference between the two companies was that Fertec set up teams on a 'brown field site' with considerable industrial relations history. Cario was a green field site.

This key difference limited the possible benefits of the benchmarking exercise. However, Fertec was still able to learn much from the exercise e.g. the need to clearly define the responsibilities and relationship of the team with other members of the Ammonia Plant administrative structure.

Review question 4–3

A **maintenance objective** is a statement about the aims and goals of the maintenance department.

It is possible (see Figure 1–5) to translate such a statement into a numeric form to provide indices that reflect the objective in terms of plant output and the efficient use of maintenance resources. The higher level indices are sometimes called '**key maintenance performance indices**'. Such indices can be monitored to guide the effort of the maintenance department.

Inter-firm-comparison-indices can be derived from maintenance performance indices (see Figure 4–11) and can be used to compare maintenance performance across companies.

Numeric **benchmarks** and inter-firm comparison indices are different names for the same thing.

Chapter 5

Review question 5–1

The outline process flow diagram (Figure 5–2) and an understanding of its operation.

Identification of the critical plant, i.e. the Ammonia Plant.

An estimate of the cost of plant unavailability and the cost of energy.

The operating period of the Ammonia Plant (and complete plant complex) and the shutdown duration.

An outline of the company administrative structure.

Review question 5–2

The three questions relate directly to Figure 1–5. The question 'how good are the maintenance life plans and preventive schedule'; relates to the effectiveness question. The remaining questions relate to organizational efficiency.

Review question 5–3

'Management by objectives' has been around a long time. Many papers were published in the 1970s on 'management by maintenance objectives'.

Review question 5–4

Manager level- mainly manufacturing KPIs but would certainly include plant availability, downtime (with causes), mean-time-between- plant failure, time-between-shutdown, and shutdown duration.

Engineer level- the above plus key unit availabilities and mean-time-between-failures.

Team level- shorter term performance indices such as utilization, overtime index, rework, and response time.

Review question 5–5

(a) The main thrust of the maintenance strategy for the Ammonia Plant was based on fixed-time maintenance after four years of operation. The duration of the outage was four weeks and the workscope was made up of a mix of fixed-time-replacement and condition-based-maintenance. During the operating period, the extensive condition monitoring of key units was carried out and also maintenance services and routines on ancillary equipment.

The influencing factors are listed on page 103.

(b) The life plan for a typical pressure vessel (a unit that had to operate for four years) was based on condition-based-maintenance. Some monitoring was carried out on-line and some (non-destructive testing procedures) during the shutdown. The maintenance work carried out during the shutdown was based on the on-line monitoring, inspection history from previous shutdowns and the inspection data from the current shutdown.

(c) The Ammonia Mechanical Engineer (Figure 5–11) the Pressure Vessels Engineer and perhaps the Pressure Systems Engineer (Figure 5–13).

Review question 5–6

Figure 5–7 (A four year operating pattern) indicates that there are numerous unscheduled shutdowns (sometimes called 'forced outages') occurring between the scheduled four yearly outages. These forced outages can occur for maintenance reasons e.g., failure or for non-maintenance reasons (raw material shortage). 'Opportunity scheduling' is a term used to indicate a maintenance strategy based in part on scheduling outstanding maintenance work into the forced outage periods. The objective of this approach is to reduce the amount of work needed to be carried out during the scheduled shutdowns and hence reduce the shutdown period.

Review question 5–7

This information can be obtained from the aide-memoir. The main information is work flexibility, shift rosters, contract usage, skills, human factors, and performance indicators.

With reference to Figure 5–11, I would interview the following personnel: Plant Manager, Planner, Maintenance Team Facilitator, Process Team Facilitator, and at least one tradesman and one operator. This would provide me with the information about the Ammonia Plant resource structure. I would have to interview a similar group of people for each of the other plant areas. When interviewing each of these people, information about the recourse structure is only part of the interview content. It is also important to decide the evening before the interview the agenda for each interviewee.

Review question 5–8

Any substantial changes in the resource structure will have an effect on the administrative structure (see Figure 1–3). Some of the main changes (see Figure 5–16) are as follows:

The Nitrogen Area Team is common to Ammonia and Urea and creates the need for a Nitrogen Plant Manager.

The Nitrogen Area Team reports via a scheduler directly to the Plant Manager. The Planner plans each 2nd line job for their own areas (with priorities) but the scheduler establishes (via planning meetings) the weekly schedule for the Area Team.

Review question 5–9

The main advantages are:

The creation of a first line plant dedicated shift resource should allow the second line Nitrogen Team to carry out greater than 90% of their scheduled program.

The Nitrogen Team is of sufficient size to tackle the larger jobs and to cover absenteeism due to sickness, training requirement and so on.

Review question 5–10

(a) With reference to Figure 5–11, the structure implies that the responsibility for plant operation and maintenance resides with the Ammonia Plant Manager. He has delegated the responsibility for mechanical engineering and maintenance to the Ammonia Mechanical Engineer. These are line responsibilities. However, this is somewhat confusing because the maintenance teams do not report to the Mechanical Engineer- he can only advise. (Note- this has been changed in figure 5–15 because the existing relationship between the teams and the Mechanical Engineer/Planner/Support Officer had not been clarified and was causing problems).

Figure 5–13 and Figure 5–14 shows that the centralized (over Fertec A and Fertec B) Reliability Group also had responsibilities for the maintenance of the Fertec A Ammonia Plant. These responsibilities concerned the development of life plans, reliability control and plant history. With any matrix structure of this kind, it is essential that the duties and responsibilities are correctly assigned and clearly understood by all concerned.

(b) The electricians within the Ammonia Plant and E/I reliability group engineers.

Review question 5–11

The main difficulties are likely to be:

The terminology used by companies varies and is mostly different from that used in these notes and will have to be interpreted.

In many companies workload data will not be available making the estimate more of a 'guesstimate'.

Review question 5–12

Many of the routines and services had not been reviewed for many years. In the authors opinion a review of this work using up to date maintenance techniques would reduce this workload appreciably. In addition the proposed resource structure would improve the ability to plan and schedule the second line preventative workload.

Review question 5–13

This revised work planning model has already been discussed in recommendations to the existing work planning systems. The model is best drawn around the revised resource structure (see Figure 5–10) and the revised administrative structure (see Figure 5–16). The model would appear similar to Figure 5–18 with the following modifications:

The first line day teams would handle all the priority 1 jobs arising during the day and spill-over from shifts.

The area planners in the Ammonia Plant would plan and prioritize all jobs originating in Ammonia and feed them to the Nitrogen Area Team Facilitator for scheduling. The Facilitator and the Planner would work as a team.

Review question 5–14

With reference to figure 5–11, the following would be interviewed to establish their opinions on 'stores level of service': Maintenance Planner; Maintenance Facilitator; and a maintenance tradesman. With reference to Figure 5–12, the following people would be interviewed to understand the operation and characteristics of stores management: Site Service Manager; Stores Superintendent; Stores Staff; and Maintenance Systems Superintendent.

Review question 5–15

See table 3–5

Chapter 6

Review question 6–1

The elements covered in depth were the resource structure and the administrative structure. The maintenance life plans/schedule were also well covered. All the other elements were covered superficially to get a feel for the overall maintenance strategy.

Review question 6–2

Two main reasons were given. First, the longwall 'coal shearer' would not last 15 shifts without maintenance and second, the management did not want to pay overtime rates at the weekend.

The auditor felt that the shearer could be made to run 15 shifts with proper care and/or improved design-out effort. The 'overtime reason' did not make sense when compared with the lost profit.

Review question 6–3

Instead of adopting the matrix arrangement outlined in Figure 6–9, the Maintenance Superintendent had allowed all the underground resource to report (at all times) to the Shift Supervisor. The equipment supervisors, e.g. the Longwall Supervisor, had become planners and did not spend much time underground even on the Longwall down days. The Shift Supervisor owned the resources and 'called the shots'.

Figure 6–13 tries to clarify how the reporting should work. The Shift Maintenance Supervisor was responsible for all maintenance shift trades other than when they were involved in the down days. The day shift tradegroup ((g) of Figure 6–11) would report to the Electrical and Mechanical Coordinators other than when they were involved in down days. During down days, the down day tradegroup would report to the Equipment Supervisor, e.g. during the Longwall downday, the downday tradegroup would report to the Longwell Supervisor.

Review question 6–4

Two of the most important audit recommendations were:

Operating the Longwall for 15 shifts per week and carrying out the maintenance on weekends.

A move towards operator-maintenance flexibility and self directed work teams (see Figure 6–10).

Both of these recommendations were not acted upon because of potential industrial relations problems.

Chapter 7

Review question 7–1

The fingerprint audit has concentrated on mapping and describing in outline the following elements: the process flow diagram and plant operation, an understanding of the current maintenance strategy and a sample of unit life plans and the maintenance organization (administrative resource structures). The operation and interaction of these elements are investigated at high level (see Figure 1–26) to understand the strategic thought process, and thereby identify problem areas.

Review question 7–2

(a) The BOTPLANT management changed a functional organization into an organization based on manufacturing units- they hoped the change would generate the following improvements:

A sense of plant ownership from the operators and tradeforce for their own lines.

Better teamworking.

The tradesmen should increase their 'plant specialized knowledge'.

Faster response for emergency work.

All of the above should mean better plant availability.

(b) When the reorganization took place, the maintenance systems were non-existent. Such systems should have been in place before the organizational change was made. There were also 'industrial relations' problems that needed sorting out.

(c) Ensure that excellent maintenance systems are in place before organizational change takes place and that there is sufficient centralized personnel to maintain these systems.

Review question 7–3

(a) The key reason was that as a result of decentralization, the professional engineers (and technicians) were distributed thinly across the organization into the various manufacturing units. They were under considerable pressure on day-to-day issues and found it difficult to carry out PRC within their manufacturing units. In addition, they became professionally isolated.

(b) By using the so-called 'purge procedure' of PRC. Periodically, a group of engineers are seconded from their respective manufacturing units to form a 'company-wide PRC team'. The team concentrates on the problem area of plant for a short period to "purge out the reliability problems".

Chapter 8
Review question 8–1

The resource structure was modified into a cascade where at each level (first line) the tradeforce size is adjusted to below the peak of the workload and the work peak allowed to cascade to the next level or to contract. The second line structure remained decentralized. But again the tradeforce size adjusted to a cascade for the workshop trades and/or contract (see also review question 8–2).

Improved inter-trade flexibility.

Reduction in the size of the workshop by carrying out more contract reconditioning.

Review question 8–2

A typical maintenance workload is made up of three main types of work, namely first line, second line and third line (the workload characteristics are explained in Table 1–3). All three types of work vary in size with time. The frequency of the first line peaks much smaller (shifts) than the second line (days/weeks). The frequency of the second line peaks much smaller than the third line (weeks/months/years). Thus the resource structure is designed with trade groups at each of the three levels sized below the level of peak workload. The excess work can then flow from first line to second line to third line to contract. This arrangement should improve the tradeforce utilization.

Review question 8–3

The main purpose of the 'plant responsibility model' is to check how well the responsibilities for plant operation and maintenance match across the physical assets. With reference to Figure 8–9:

At shift supervisor level, there is a match across operations and mechanical maintenance for the Digestion Plant.

At day supervisor level, there is a complete mismatch between operations, mechanical maintenance, and electrical maintenance for the Digestion Plant.

At superintendent level there is a match across operations and mechanical maintenance for the Digestion Plant.

As far as possible, it is advantageous to have plant responsibilities matching.

Review question 8–4

The Digestion Area is typical of the other five areas making up the Refinery. Thus, a model to represent how this area is administered will provide an insight to the operation of the complete structure. With reference to Figure 8–8 those personnel within the outer dotted line are directly involved in the operation and maintenance of the Digestion Area. Those personnel outside of the outer dotted line provide a centralized service to the Digestion Area and the five other areas.

Review question 8–5

(a) The functional structure has been changed into a structure built around six manufacturing units, each with its own Operations Manager.

There is now one Maintenance Manager to replace the Plant Maintenance Manager and the Maintenance Services Manager.

Each manufacturing unit is autonomous in terms of operator and maintenance. Thus, the support engineers, planners, maintenance and production supervisors and tradeforce report to the Operations Manager.

The 'responsibility for equipment' has been matched across the production supervisors (Plant Officers) and the Maintenance Supervisors.

(b) The maintenance planning system was superficially audited (although it was not discussed in this case study) and did require some improvement. The existing planning system had been designed around the existing resource structure (Figure 8–5). This resource structure has been streamlined (see Figure 8–10), but not structurally changed. Thus, the planning system did not require radical redesign.

Chapter 9

Review question 9–1

(a) The key characteristics in successful alliance arrangements are that the maintenance is regarded as non-core, and the alliance partner has considerable engineering and maintenance expertise, relevant to the physical assets being maintained- often as a result of having designed and installed them.

(b) Yes, but in a limited way- perhaps similar to the Chemtow Alliance. The main reasons for this comment are as follows:

It is unlikely that any contractor would have a better engineering/technical knowledge of the Refinery Plant than the existing refinery professional engineers.

First line maintenance would be regarded as core.

Review question 9–2

Early 1900s- Functional Organization

1995 Business Units

1995 Downsizing

1995–1999 Self-directed, plant-orientated, operator-maintenance teams and self directed maintenance teams.

1999–2000 Company-contractor alliance.

Review question 9–3

(a) Chemtow have retained responsibility for first line maintenance through their operator-maintenance teams. More importantly they have retained the custodianship of physical assets via their professional engineering and maintenance staff.

The alliance has been made responsible for carrying out the second and third line maintenance work. This includes planning of the work and stores management.

(b) This division of responsibilities means that the contract can only involve the 'cost of carrying out the maintenance work', i.e. the alliance being expected to reduce the cost of the carrying out the maintenance over a period of five years.

It is not possible to incorporate 'improvements in availability' into the contract because the alliance does not have control over the decisions that directly effect availability, e.g. life plans, shutdown workscope and so on.

Chapter 10
Review question 10–1

A condition-based policy has inherent advantages over a 'fixed-time' maintenance policy because it avoids overmaintenance. The policy is effective in the Greenmix Plant because the inspection techniques used give sufficient lead time to plan and schedule the maintenance work at weekends. A key point is that the workload resulting from this policy is relatively smooth and can be carried out mainly by the Greenmix Plant maintenance tradeforce.

If either operate-to-failure and repair, or condition-based-maintenance is used as the policy for the maintenance of the brickwork of the Ring Furnace pits the resulting workload would be difficult (impossible) to resource. This is because most of the pits started life at the same time and have a 'wear out' failure pattern with a mean life of about four years. In order to smooth this workload (to make it manageable), the furnace was divided into 10 sections and each scheduled separately on a fixed-time regime.

Chapter 11
Review question 11–1

To establish the critical processes/equipment a lot more information would need to be provided. For example it may be that Colliery B is the most important process and the overland conveyor could well be critical. However, looking at Figure 11–1 it would appear the coal haulage fleet is production critical in that it is only part of the operation working 21 shifts. There is also limited interstage storage after this part of the operation. However, the Fleet Demand Ration in this case is generous at 63% and contract trucks could be brought in the event of serious problems.

Review question 11–2

This is best explained by labeling each 'state' from A= Buses-in-use to F= Buses-in-works-overhaul.

Thus:

$$\text{Availability} = \frac{A + B + C}{A + B + C + D + E + F}$$

Buses-in-service (C) is regarded as available because the services are carried out in the mid-day window.

Review question 11–3

The advantages include:

Smaller stores inventory.

Easier training for 'plant-specific knowledge'.

Higher FDR.

Better plant history.

Less maintenance documentation.

Chapter 12

Review question 12–1

With reference to Figure 12–1 and Figure 1–26, the production requirements had changed. The station had been downgraded from a base-load station and was not being used at night. In addition, maintenance windows now occurred between October and April, which could be used for a limited level of maintenance work that was normally carried out during the main shutdown. Thus, the maintenance schedule (and perhaps the life plan) had changed and this would have an impact on the maintenance organization.

Index